Tremble Chin

Back cover photo of Mr. Dunn by Ruby Hodgman.

Cover design by ThomasMax (Lee Clevenger & R. Preston Ward)

ISBN-13: 978-0-9822189-3-8
ISBN-10: 0-9822189-1-1

First Printing, August 2009

Published by:

ThomasMax Publishing
P.O. Box 250054
Atlanta, GA 30325
www.thomasmax.com

Tremble Chin

By Paul B. Dunn

ThomasMax

Your Publisher
For The 21st Century

Also by Paul B. Dunn from ThomasMax Publishing

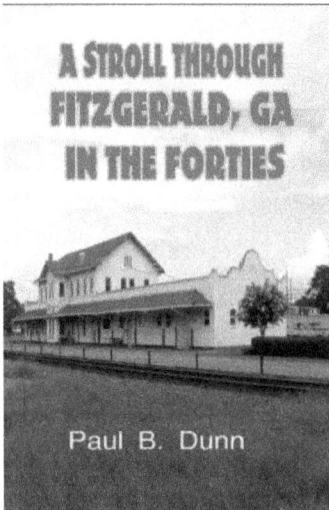

A Stroll Through Fitzgerald, GA, in the Forties, $ 14.95

Take a mythical stroll through the streets of Fitzgerald in this historic yarn as the author recalls his youth in the Colony City of Fitzgerald. Includes photographs and introduction by Sherri Butler of the *Fitzgerald Herald-Leader.* Paul B. Dunn's first published book was released in 2005.

Lightning Slinger of Andersonville, $ 14.95

After the Civil War, railroads were built to link the Atlantic and Pacific Coasts of the reunited nation. South of the Mason-Dixon line, work gangs were either Negro or Irish. The O'Dunn family was employed for three generations as Trackmen that built or maintained the railroad. Teddie O'Dunn was a telegrapher-depot agent, or "lightning slinger." He learned telegraphy at the knee of a kindly woman agent-operator at the Central of Georgia Railroad Depot. Sixty miles southeast of Andersonville was a Colony City, Fitzgerald. Teddie went to Fitzgerald to work as a lightning slinger on the railroad connecting the new town to Atlanta and Florida. His family admonished him to have no association with Yankee girls that paraded the sidewalks of Fitzgerald. But Teddie was lightning struck, so to speak, by a small bundle of charm, the granddaughter of a Calvary man in General Sherman's army. Their trials, tribulations and heartaches through their years fill this book.

This book is dedicated to the memory of my mother, "Tremble Chin"

Table of Contents

Chapter I

Passengers Aboard a Midnight Train

All aboard!" the conductor of this mixed passenger train shouted as it jerked to a start. A mixed train meant it actually was a freight train, with a couple of creaking, wooden passenger coaches that had been in service, surely, on the train that served as an office for Abraham Lincoln when he signed the surrender papers to end the Civil War thirty years ago. The little eight-wheel, wood-burning engine gave two ear-splitting blasts of its brass whistle as the white steam which escaped the throat of the whistle shot skyward. The bell atop the boiler swung to and fro, sometimes tumbling completely over, one side of the bell calling out "ding," the other side answering "dong." The petcocks under the cylinder on each side of the engine hissed and blew scalding water and steam into the gallberry and palmetto thickets growing beneath the towering long-leaf pines that seemed to march endlessly into the flat woods. The fireman somehow fed oak and split pine wood into the inferno that roared away in the long narrow coffin shaped firebox, generating the all-powerful steam. The steam coaxed the long heavy-laden cars, which had just as soon stayed at this woebegone wood rack and water tank deep in South Georgia, that someone had named "Big Wheel."

The engineer leaned out the cab window, glanced at his watch, and saw the conductor's highball signal from the rear coach. He answered him with two long whistle blasts, letting the last one tarry a bit to change the note into a rather melodic sound, which really served to alert the herd of spotted, long horn, "cracker" or woods cattle that roamed freely with their new calves. This stock loved to come up around the water tank on cold nights and bed down on the bank that the railroad ran on, as the woods often were flooded. They also liked to lick the ashes that the engine left in piles between the rails when the fireman cleaned fire. Reluctantly they stood up, stretched, hooked their calves awake with their horns, and scattered into the gloomy pine forests.

The engine had the name "*Suwannee*" painted on the huge head lamp that cast a fairly bright, yellowish beam down the track. On its tender, or tank, which hauled the water and wood to quench its thirst and stoke its never dying fire, the big yellow letters spelled out "Georgia and Florida RR." This train runs every night, but tonight is the night when our story's characters are aboard. They may hold your interest much more firmly than the greasy little engine struggling south to virgin land and a fresh start for tired old grizzled men, limping old women, crying babies, and sleeping children. Most of the passengers tonight are from the northern states — Michigan, Iowa, Illinois, Pennsylvania, perhaps even Ohio. January nights can be cold, even in

Georgia, but not as cold as in the northern states. The big potbellied stove warmed the creaking old coach as it floated down the rails which took our northern family ever nearer to the plot of land which was to become the long anticipated home of Chasity and Shepard Barrick and their growing family, who had never put down permanent roots. This last decade of the nineteenth century was a period of massive immigration to the newly developing USA, which had many frontiers and opportunities galore awaiting the downtrodden and weary people of the Old World. The Civil War, with all its horrors and upheaval, had healed somewhat, and America was on the move again.

Our players on this stage, which is more likely to become a three-ring circus, are truly destiny's children. I have introduced the father and mother to you. There are many more players to pass across the stage that comes nearer with each clickety-clack on the railroad track, which has been laid through the gently rolling hills carpeted with wiregrass and shaded by the towering pines that moan and groan with every breeze that sweeps in from either the broad Atlantic to the east or the brooding storm cradle called the Gulf of Mexico to the west. Fate, that fickle lady, this very night on this swaying lamp lit vintage railroad coach, is dealing a hand of brand-new cards, which will lie in tatters in wrinkled, time-worn hands in days to come. May we, the audience, become better acquainted, and you will recognize the names of Chasity and Shepard, now called Chase and Shep.

Fate will have trouble with this young man with piercing blue eyes, a shaggy topknot of greasy hair and a handlebar mustache, baggy blue serge trousers that must have missed the last washing, and the top to his union suit. He must have lost his shirt in a card game. This is no problem, because he has the outfit anchored by a stout pair of leather suspenders that had been yellow, but are now badly stained by good, honest sweat. A bright red bandana is tied loosely around his leathery neck. His feet are well shod in a pair of battered, hobnailed brogans. In his mouth is a crooked stemmed brier root pipe that is smoldering away and removed from his thin-lipped mouth, beneath his brushy mustache, only to spit across the coach aisle to the shining spittoons or to pack with twist tobacco, which he cuts off the hank and carries in his spacious pants pocket.

The pipe is not removed from his mouth when he speaks, emitting a strange brogue, a mixture of North Michigan, Yankee flavored Australian dialect that needs polishing, but he doesn't care. He drags each word until we wonder if he will ever get it out. He is riding in the smoker section of the coach where the stove and toilet are located. Only men occupy the mohair seats in this end of the coach. Any decent, well bred woman would probably be offended not only by the smoke but also by the language and ribald stories that break the monotony of the much delayed train trip. Across the aisle, sound asleep or drunk, is Shep Barrick's father-in-law, whom I will introduce to you after you have become better acquainted with his only daughter and constant companion, Chase Barrick, Shep's beloved wife.

Poke up the fire, will you, boys? It looks like it's going to be a long, cold night. It must be the locomotive engineer's first trip by the way he is jerking and jolting this train.

He must have gotten his running papers on a log railroad. Oh well! Gather around, all you fellow travelers. Looks like we all have a long, jolting night ahead of us. The *Suwannee*'s powerful engine is going to do all the hard work, if that stout young fireman can keep the fire going and the engineer can keep his eye upon the road and his hand upon the throttle instead of the whistle cord, which activates that deep-throated, steamboat whistle he so loves to blow. But it only wastes the hard-earned steam that the woodchopper and the young fireman have worked so hard to generate.

This is a long story. If you get bored, slide your hat down over your eyes, prop your feet up, and take a nap. I can talk above your snoring, maybe. Tonight we may well be in the company of several of destiny's children. The train just gave a bone shattering jerk, and the coupling slack ran out on the string of box and flat cars that are rumbling along, ahead of us. The jolt almost caused Shep's pipe to fall from his mouth as he sleeps. Let me tell you of his younger years, if I may.

The year was 1882; the place was the northern peninsula of Michigan, more than a thousand miles north of this pine forest. Stretching to the prairie lands of mid-America, to the Arctic tundra lands of northern Canada, the virgin forest on the shores of the Great Lakes is just waiting for sharp axes and saws, wielded by strong young backs of mostly immigrant youth and mustered-out Yankee soldiers. One of the latter was a middle-aged veteran who had served a long enlistment as a saddlemaker, attached to a Michigan cavalry unit that accompanied General Sherman's Army when they cut a swath of devastation, looting and burning everything they came to, from Alabama, Georgia's west border, to the seaport of Savannah.

This saddlemaker never fired a shot or burned a farmer's home. He probably helped his unit by repairing their saddles or building harnesses, and he was good with horses and mules. He probably minded the string of horses and mules the soldiers confiscated along the route and butchered the hogs and milk cows that produced the food that tasted so good around the campfires at night. Those boys were hungry and tired after a hard day in a hard leather saddle. Here he comes now, to this logging camp in the North Woods. He is named Daniel Cooper and has a slender dark-haired daughter by his side. They have a tent pitched near a kitchen wagon. Dan, as the boys call him, is stirring up last night's fire and starting to prepare a hearty breakfast for the hearty lads. Some are sharpening their tools to an even sharper condition. They call themselves lumberjacks. One of these jacks seems to want to hang around the cook site, which could hardly be called a kitchen. He is quick to help the young woman split firewood and handle heavy pots and pans.

Let's keep an eye on this dandy and the serious young daughter of the old vet, Dan Cooper. The North Woods have stood here since the ice age, and the white pine, hemlock, ash, and cedar trees stand tall, but the ring of axes, the shouts of teamsters, and the high pitched shriek of steam-driven sawmills sing a death song to these majestic trees that were so long in maturing. They are needed to rebuild a war-torn nation and build an empire reaching to the Pacific Ocean. They are, in a small way, shaping the lives of the actors in our story of love, hate, and happiness for many generations far south of here. There are few sounds as dramatic as a hundred foot pine tree when it cracks and with a swish of needles slowly begins to lean in to gravity's unceasing pull, picking up speed in its plunge to solid ground. The popping of limbs, then the thunderous crash of tons of living trees die before your eyes as the dust settles. The lumberjacks attack the fallen giant with axes, double-bitted axes. These axes, if you have never seen one, are not used in wood piles. Those are chop axes with only one sharp edge. The top is flat and can be used as a maul to drive a wedge to split firewood or rails for fences. These double-bitted axes the lads are using have blades on each end of the tool. They save time in the forest because both cutting edges can be sharpened while the workers are on break, and the axe has a sharp bitt after it is sharpened.

Sharpness is the name of the logging business, but logging is not the only business where sharpness is vital. Romance is the other, and I will be a horn-toed biddy if the lad with the thick brogue wasn't present at the cook shed more and more. He himself looked pretty sharp. He shaved and trimmed his mustache often, wore his checked shirt even on warm mornings, smiled a lot, and I believe I saw a twinkle in his piercing blue eyes that sat back in an angular face. He might have been called handsome. His face might not have been as great as his muscular body, honed to great condition by a lifetime of outdoor work and play. He took on a special glow when the young cook, the cavalry veteran's daughter, flung the tent flap aside and stretched to welcome the rising sun and fill her young lungs with the fresh breeze that rose from Thunder Bay on the Great Lakes, still called Gittchey Goomy by the Indians. I don't see Old Nocomis, daughter of the moon, coming from her wigwam, only a slight girl with a strong face, ready to face the world and whatever fate, or maybe I should say, destiny, might offer. She had no fear for the paths unknown, or she wouldn't have been here at this logging camp in the great North Woods. Now, mind you, she was aware of the strange young man who shone like a new penny, especially when she was around, but she would have been the last to admit that he had made quite an impression on her. After all, she was the only female in the rough camp. All the lumberjacks smiled and tipped their broad-brimmed hats still dusted with yesterday's sawdust. But this lad! She half-hoped he would just pass on by, but she hated herself for hoping he would be there each morning, splitting that ever important firewood since her father had more pressing business to attend to.

Have you begun to wonder if this trio could possibly be the weary travelers that were on the rattley old train about as far south of the North Woods as a body could go, without catching a China Clipper? Yes, it's them, all right, twelve years later. Times had not been too good in northern Michigan. The North Woods were beginning to be depleted. The lumberjacks, on down from the legendary Paul Bunion and his blue ox Babe, had accomplished what the fierce north winds couldn't, winds that roared down from the Arctic Circle, turning Lake Superior and Thunder Bay into a tempest of huge waves crashing ashore and freezing the lakes over solid. The Indians' fires failed to accomplish what this army of axe-swinging hardies did, laying low the towering giant trees, which now were timbers in Chicago's towering skyscrapers.

Dan Cooper, the Civil War veteran, had seen devastation and hardship in his swing through the south thirty-one years ago. His daughter Chase, now married, had two big boys helping her with the chores. They were strong lads, much like their father. Yes, you guessed it. The proud papa was Shepard Barrick. The lads' names were Bob and Daniel.

Now is as good a time as any to relate the adventuresome past of this high stepper, Shep Barrick. All we knew was what he told us around the stove at the camp, which served as home for these itinerant men and boys, who spent long days felling and loading logs. He had been born in New South Wales, Australia, to an Australian mother of good Irish stock and a Yankee adventurer who had washed ashore from a wrecked four-mast schooner out of New Bedford, Connecticut. He never said whether it was a trader or a whaler. This washed-ashore seaman made his way from Kangaroo Island to the port city of Adelaide, a boom town situated at the mouth of the Murry River, one of the very few waterways that was navigable for any distance from the Indian Ocean, on the bottom side of the mysterious island-continent of Australia.

The sailor was named Frederick Barrick, or so he said. He was not a timid man, nor did he suffer from an inferiority complex. His strength was prodigious, but his murder of the Queen's English could hardly go unnoticed. His Yankee brogue earned him the name of "Yankee Fred." Some local people around the bars that lined the riverfront at Adelaide wagered a drink that he was a pirate who had eluded the British admiralty, who were trying to rid the costal isles of Yankee freebooters, as they were known hereabouts.

His long curly, almost kinky blond hair was held in a pigtail by a bone clasp, and his scarred face with its red beard only strengthened the speculation about his former occupation. He had some gold money in the deep pockets, Spanish doubloons that were rare in this far corner of the watery world. The bar girls had never seen any coins like these, but they passed the tooth test when the girls bit them to see if the metal was soft enough to be dented by their snaggled teeth. Not only his money, but his rough manner and his rugged features also passed these ladies-of-the-night's inspection. He ate a huge bowl of mutton stew and a mug of steaming hot East India tea. Yankee Fred held the bar flies' and whore girls' undivided attention as he spun his wild yarns of worldwide adventures. He never failed to leave a few of his coins on the table. He wasn't a rag picker. No, Fred was a man of some means.

Lady Fortune had smiled on this area of South Australia and Kangaroo Island, where Fred had washed ashore. It was odd he had no shipmates, but who would question a fine man like Yankee Fred? Even the young wenches, who flitted from man to man, fought in the dusty streets for his rough favors, which helped him forget his awful hardship as a shipwrecked seaman from a far away Yankee land. Poor lad! You know, we have only his son's recollections of his father, so form your own opinion, but even I, myself, am beginning to like, if not admire, Yankee Fred. Now, mind you, old Fred knew a lot about boats. His Spanish gold coins closed his negotiations for a stout riverboat, which lay at the foot of the water street docks. This boat was what is known as a pole boat. These boats were propelled by men with strong backs and weak minds, and Fred had both a strong back and a strong mind. He brought quite a bit of knowledge of steam propulsion from the rivers of America. He looked around and located a blacksmith who was talented at boiler making and pipe fitting.

Fred also had quite a talent for guzzling a great deal of rum.

On a bright sunny day, Yankee Fred and a motley crew fired up the boiler amidships, and the river steamer, newly christened the *"Victoria,"* eased up the muddy Murry River. Captain Yankee Fred was at the wheel, high above the lower deck in the pilot or wheelhouse. Please, please, bear with me, and I hope not to bore you with a detailed description of this player. He will one day reappear but not in person, for his offspring's destiny is being molded many years to come in far away Georgia, USA. Let me finish, if I may. Lord, Lord, that man is certainly destiny's child. As those wooden paddles churn the muddy river water, ideas churn in the mind of this man, who now wants the locals to call him "Captain Fred," and he is just cussed enough to get what he wants, one way or another. His rock hard fist has, on several occasions, left men spitting blood and teeth. Some observers say he has a horse shoe in his fist.

He loves to go in the ring to demonstrate his bare knuckle boxing, no gloves, mind you. When the chips are down and things look bad, ole Fred's face will twitch, and he seems to have a little problem keeping his chin still, but, look out, fellows! That is when he is at his best, and don't you forget it. Some even say he is fixin' to make the very earth tremble.

Don't forget! Lady Luck, along with several other ladies, had taken a shine to Captain Fred, and as the years passed, he prospered upon the river, out in the vast desert interior of Australia. Gold had been discovered, and the easy found riches lured many men and the camp followers who lived off these prospectors for gold. More often than not, these camp followers were scalawags who prospered off the mistakes and excesses of the men who labored in the gold fields.

I hope I have convinced you poor dejected travelers here tonight on this lurching, drafty coach, deep in the pine woods of South Georgia that our stalwart character would not pass up an easy gold nugget, or a well turned female ankle. Strong drink seemed no problem for Captain Fred. You will agree that somehow the word "captain" carries more prestige than the word "Yankee." After all, our man was a seafaring man. He strikes quite a figure, pacing the deck of the steamer *Victoria* in his navy blue suit with the brass buttons. His trim little cap with the shiny black visor set atop that thatch of curly blond hair, makes you wonder if the cap is too small or the Captain's head is too large. Maybe he will have it shorn, like the flock of Merino sheep the drovers are herding aboard the *Victoria*, amid the red dust of this thirsty land, and the shouts and curses of the lads, along with the frantic barking of the herd dogs. Some days his cargo is camels, imported from Arabia, well adapted to the hardships of the burning Australian Outback. They split the air with an ear-splitting shriek or merely spit on you. Other days, he has a load of wine bottles, for the winemakers at the foot of the snowy mountains, where enough rain falls year around to grow grapes and other crops.

The Darling River meets and joins the Murry River, mixing its clear water, ever flowing from the snow capped coastal mountains. This influx is the life blood, or rather water, that makes navigation possible to the baked interio, where gold has been discovered. Water might be more valuable than gold, but after all you can't put water in your pocket. You can't buy picks and shovels with it, or the Chinese sing song girls, imported here to keep the successful miners contented by practicing the arts of oriental sexual satisfaction. They had much rather have a little gold dust, but there is no telling what they could do for a gold nugget shining in the kerosene oil lamp light. Old Captain Fred had probably transported both these girls with their slanting eyes and childlike well educated bodies and the smelly oil for lamps. It could be whale oil. Who cares, just so it dimly lights the bars and brothels that line the dusty streets of Broken Hill, a mining town that sprang up to welcome the fortune seekers.

Sail on, Fred, count your gold while the waves generated by your steamboat and its churning paddles lap the mud banks. All this commotion, not to mention the black smoke, has awakened the salt water crocodiles that were asleep in the mud, causing them to slide into the current. Count on, old

Captain, while Lady Luck is beside you. She can become a little fickle, you know. Back to those old crocodiles, they just lie there and sleep. They have plenty of time. Some of them are a hundred years old. They open their gaping mouths to let the birds pick their teeth. They just wait for some critter, man or beast, to make a mistake. Then they tremble a little and strike like lightning. There must have been lots of mistakes made over the years because some of those old crocs are twenty feet long and weigh half a ton. Take heed, old Captain, don't get greedy. Sail on, good buddy! Or you may find yourself on their menu, maybe the main course.

The hiss and exhaust of the steam engine, which was manufactured in Liverpool, England, as many other things were, tirelessly plodded up the surging current. The long eucalyptus wood poles reached to the rear of the vessel to crank the eccentric gear that steadily turned the tall paddle wheel mounted on the stern of the *Victoria*. The passenger list contained no royalty, but each of the groups would readily shout out, "God save the Queen!" The desolated river bank was populated by stark naked black aborigines. They needed no clothes in the unbearable heat. They had an uncanny knowledge of the land, its creatures, snakes, parrots, great turkey-like birds called cassowaries that can't fly, the cockatoo bird, laughing Jackass birds that sound like fools laughing uncontrollably; all sizes of kangaroos, hopping among the patches of high grass; koalas in the eucalyptus trees; and a multitude of other species. No place on earth even resembles this landscape that one season is a vast desert, and a month or year later, a lake about knee deep, if it isn't a mirage. The people who are pouring in here are not much different from the landscape. They too are, to say the least, not like any other species of mankind. Beggars, thieves, knaves, debtors, defrocked ministers, unemployed actors, gamblers, and a few women who keep company with the above mentioned guests who are deck passengers.

There might even be a pirate at the helm of the *Victoria* with a price on his head. Who knows? Or in fact, who cares? I do wish the old, toothless hag that calls herself the cook could come up with something to eat besides mutton stew and hardtack bread. The natives love to eat spiders and grubs, with a huge water snake for dessert. Excuse me, as dinner is now being served on the foredeck of the trembling old scow. "Land ho!" is shouted by the lookout as we chug around a swift bend in the Murry River. A pier looms ahead on the starboard side of the steamer. I hope some fortune seekers will debark here and catch a camel for Alice Springs, located about in the center of the Outback.

Old Captain leaned against his whistle cord, blowing a prolonged blast. Unknown to him, he was striking a figure who would soon come to resemble the most famous river pilot plying the mighty Mississippi River, in a far away civilized America, by the name of Mark Twain. When Captain Barrick shouted to his mate to "cut power," the old tub hesitated and drifted with the current to the dock. The deck hand cast a line to a wharf hand who pulled the slack from the line and quickly looped it over a piling, causing the stern to swing around to hit the wharf with a "thud" that nearly knocks the passengers down. The stern line was secured and the gangplank lowered to the pier. The mail bag was thrown to the waiting arms of the post rider, who scurried away. One more landing was complete.

Captain "Yankee Fred" Barrick is aging. In fact, each day he is finding more gray in his tousled head of hair and his stained mustache than was there the day before.. Yes he, even in his idle moments, is thinking of – can you believe it – settling down, if he can find a decent woman. He even longs to hear the patter of little feet, and to have a decent meal set on the table three times a day. Some day, some day – but a little voice deep in his strong heart says, "Some day is here tomorrow, or the boat you miss may not be the weary old *Victoria*. The boiler is leaking! That drunken old blacksmith who hammered it out years ago, must have been having a bout with old demon rum the day he set the line of rivets, which are now hissing jets of white steam and dripping scalding water into the bilge."

Ole Captain just shrugged and spit tobacco juice in the river that was the same color brown as most everything in Australia. Even the deadly little snake that loves to sleep in the bed with you is known as the "common brown." If he bites you, the undertaker will be the one who bathes your dusty butt.

Oh well, the price of gold just went up. Blow the whistle Captain, aren't you one of destiny's children? Time and fortune wait for no one. How can you lose? Lady Luck has a way of smiling on you, but she isn't much of a cook. You aren't much of one to complain, so sop that mutton stew with those moldy biscuits that your smiling toothless cook is handing you, old sport.

If I were a portrait painter with a fine studio, I would try to capture the image of the next player to appear on this stage. You have your choice. If you are the painter you say you are, please place the look of an angel on the face of the young woman with the flaming red hair that falls in perfect waves upon her shoulders. A look of confidence in her blue eyes, a generous crop of freckles on her cheeks; yes, my friends, a lassie straight from the old sod of far away Galway. Behind those twinkling eyes that my painter can't see is an indomitable spirit that even this dreary land has failed to diminish. Probably the only mistake she will ever make is about to occur.

Decent, God fearing women are not abundant in the countryside around the junction of the Murry River and the Darling River. Trading houses and the usual assortment of dens of iniquity abound along the river front. However, behind this festering scene is a fairly normal village, much like you would expect to see in the British Isles. After all, the settlers are from those cultivated islands, and the immigrants have brought their skills of agriculture, stock breeding, and masonry here. Our darling lass grew up here and truly brought with her a bit of the old sod from thousands of miles away.

Now mind you well, her travels may not be over! The next act is beginning and the curtain is rising. Our new player with the flaming waves of red hair is named Bridgett O'Leary. On the way to the market with a basket of hen eggs, a mold of cow butter, and a green four leaf clover pinned in her tresses for good luck. She sits side saddle on a Welsh pony, as any lady must do, that is, if she is a lady, and this one truly is. She now is squarely in the mystic power of the now wilting clover leaf. Most everything wilts in this Australian midday sun, but things can always get hotter, and it isn't always the sun that sets in the west that will give you some relief. Oh well, what will be, will be. The Irish, or was it the Italian, I can't be sure, but one of their bards wrote, "What will be, will be, the future is not ours to see. Will I be wealthy, will I be wise? The future is not ours to see. What will be, will be."

At this point, let me make it clear that I, the storyteller, know what the future will be. This is the past I am telling you about tonight in 1895, on this midnight local that makes this journey all night, every night. Who, may I ask, is that striding up the cobblestone village street? It's none other than our own Yankee Captain Fredrick Barrick, no less, followed by a yapping pack of neighborhood dogs, which can tell by one sniff that he is a rogue of a river rat. Those brass buttons and salty cap set on his brow don't fool them. They won't allow him to walk on the neat sidewalk. Anyway, he is out of his element in this God-fearing section of Twin River. He is a sailor and sailors are not famous for walking. He has what is known as sea-legs, and some say they are hollow to hold a good supply of rum. Oh, well, you can't believe all you hear. May your winds and tides be fair, and to your back, old salt, set sail and check your stars well, because unknown to you, you are setting sail on the stormy sea of matrimony, a sea for which you have no maps.

Bon voyage, old skipper. You can run the Jolly Roger flag down now. Here comes Bridgett O'Leary with the steady clop-clop of her pony's unshod hooves up on the cobblestones that were once the ballast weights in some tall sailing ship. Our good captain is now out of his element. He went only to trade for a few items of fresh provisions for his bare galley aboard the steamer *Victoria*, moored at the junction of the Muddy River and the crystal clear waters of the Darling, which only yesterday was a snow and ice mantel on the lofty peaks of the Snowy Mountains. Let's wonder if the same blazing sun that melted the frozen masses can now melt the heart of the pure Bridgett O'Leary.

Let's, if we may, make a fair comparison this fair day of the two rivers. One is clouded with much silt and mud; the other clear and pure, as the driven snows of the moisture laden winds of the blue Pacific when they rise on the slopes of the Blue Coastal Mountains to condense and evaporate their sea moisture into rain and higher up, snow. It is a good mixture, as the parched interior is dependent on these waters that are the very life blood of the interior. The meeting of the jaded, worldly Captain and the fair lass, so well bred and pure, are a fair comparison to the mixing waters of the surging rivers below this tranquil street in the village above. If those street dogs would only be quiet. They are causing Bridgett's pony to shy around and dance a little jig, and I don't mean an Irish jig. Her eggs in their basket and the four leaf clover in her hair, could be, shall we say, upset. Hang on, Bridgett. Those eggs may not be all of your possessions that, may we say, be upset. Hang on, gal, you probably know more about ponies than you do about men. Maybe your cold air will evaporate some of the salt out of our beloved captain. Who knows? I do. Just listen on, mates. The wheel of fortune has been spinning for quite some while, but believe me, it has just sped up. In the south of Ireland, where the grass grows green, clovers usually have only three leaves to the stem, but legend has it that if on occasion your luck is good, you will come upon, rarely, one with four leaves.

Bridgett is aware of the mystic power of the fourth leaf, which can greatly attract the attention of that fairy hard luck that the Irish place so much power in, commonly known as the Luck of the Irish. Bridgett, me lass, you will need all the luck that the lady has in her poke. Now, mind you, the captain, although he is not Irish, has been lucky. He should have been hanged on the yardarm of Her Majesty's man-of-war for his crimes upon the high sea, and cast into the deep blue waters of the Indian Ocean, there to dwell in the chambers of Davy Jones' locker. But old Davy owed Lady Luck a debt, and he paid her off with the worthless carcass of this Yankee, who washed ashore on Kangaroo Island. She did, in fact, fill his pockets with Spanish gold before the tempest scattered the prosecutors and the plaintiff to the four winds, and his fair head took no sunshine into the depths.

Now he stands squarely in the cobblestone street, face to face with the fair, if not a bit fiery, red-haired Bridgett O'Leary, sitting in her side saddle on her nervous Welsh pony. She was every inch of her well built body a lady, which was rare in this neck of the woods. Oh, I was about to forget another well established custom that the leprechauns taught me. It is a sly little trick that a lass keeps under her sleeve until she is ready to tell the world that she is available and has a fair dowry and is waiting to be selected by some laddie to be her life long companion. If the saints, Patrick in this case, and stars aligned properly, she places a four leaf clover in her well brushed tresses.

Turn your head a mite, me buxom lady, so, by chance the Yankee chap can see the bit of green in that wavy sea of red hair that spills to your heaving bosom, so like the waves that wash on to the white sandy beaches of Kangaroo Island, where our weary captain rested his tousled head. For a spell, their eyes met, and nothing was said. The street dogs hushed their barking and slunk into the alley. The pony stood still, breathing hard from his flared nostrils. The lady raised her riding crop to shoo the flies and spoke, "Do you not recognize a lady when you see one in this street, or have you just arrived here, among decent God fearing people? Be off with you, I can see the devil's gleam in your lying eyes. 'Tis probably true you have kissed the Blarney stone. Be off with ye!"

Chapter II

On the River

I wish I knew more about true love, my friends, but I must have been absent from the school of life, course one, called "Romance." In fact, all of us marchers in this parade of life only follow our own instincts. Maybe I should say Lady Luck is at the helm on the ship of love as it sets sail on the stormy sea of matrimony. Yankee Captain Barrick was a dropout from the school of love, no doubt. All he ever loved was his own rusty butt, a chest of gold coins, and maybe some flirty wench who hoped to raise the lid of his sea chest to see how many gold coins he had thereabout, as she raised her skirts above her shapely knees, not to mention her chest, which contained a heart of stone, pure hard granite! It has been said that only fools and dead men don't change their minds, and our captain was neither. Truly he was a treasure chest himself that had never been opened. Perhaps our sparkling young Bridgett had the gold key, invisible as it might have been, swinging on a strong chain right between her snow white breasts that no man had plundered and a strong heart which beat just a little faster at the sight of this Yankee, who somehow had braved the many pitfalls between New South Wales and the state of Connecticut, America, that fair new land of opportunity.

As the pony clopped away down the street, Frederick had a feeling deep down in the depths of his heart. He had never had this feeling before, and it rather frightened him. Aw, come on Captain, don't let a slip of a girl unnerve you. You, the one who could shrug off any pleasure of the flesh that didn't bear you a profit, buy your provisions, set your cap a little squarer on your bonny head, and return to your true love, the Victoria and her motley crew. That night, as he lay in his bunk aboard his creaky vessel, he rolled and pitched about. Go to sleep, old fellow. That woman, the one on the Welsh pony, with the wavy red hair and the calm, sure countenance on her fair face, will not cease to haunt him. He never cared for strong drink, so toss on. The dawn will surely come, and the duties of the day will clear your mind, maybe.

A railroad was under construction to connect the great port city of Sydney with the sleepy town of Port Pine, which gave access to the Indian Ocean by way of the mining town of Broken Hill. For the present, our captain had a brisk trade hauling cross ties and rails, not to mention construction workers and their varied supplies to the point on the Darling River where the proposed railroad would cross it, on a high, spidery trestle, or bridge. Being the soldier of fortune that our dear captain was, he lined his pockets with the new windfall of both the gold rush and the surge of immigrants who soon populated this livable area of the otherwise brutal Outback, which stretched endlessly to the setting sun in the west. Maybe he should be thinking of building a new and larger river steamer to replace the aging Victoria that had served him so well. A small voice told him that river traffic, which was limited by high and low water, would be soon replaced by the rumble and screeching wheels of the railway cars or wagons as the Aussies called them. They could travel through dust storms or floods. Speed was the thing that always intrigued the young generation. A train would cover in a day a distance which the Victoria and her like craft required a week to navigate, and a fortune could be made or lost in a week in a mining camp.

So chug on old *Victoria*, the captain may change course before too long. He has seen gentlemen with their ladies and children riding in their fine carriages, a driver sitting on a high seat with a lad to help the lady from the leather seat, a footman, mind you, as the gentleman lit a long black cigar and guided the apple of his eye into a fine café or pub. Frederick Barrick could afford such a life, and it looked pretty good to him at this point. He was tired of scalawags, barmaids, and big shooters whose powder had gotten wet. He might even stroll up the bank to the trading house for a spot of tea around 4:00 p.m., and tip his hat, or excuse me, his cap, to some decent, educated lady who knew the needs of a weary waterman upon whom fortune had smiled. He longed to hear the unshod hooves of a Welsh pony with its clipped mane standing erect and its generous tail bunched up in a bun to keep it from lashing milady, the lady with the flaming hair which lay in waves upon her white shoulders and also that four leaf clover, if she could find one about the paddock that her doting father kept groomed to perfection.

But she didn't show up today, which rather riled Fred as he was accustomed to things going his way. Among his crew aboard the *Victoria* was a lad of dusky complexion, a half-breed aborigine or native Australian and half pure Irish, if such a creature exists hereabouts. Now, mind you, his black mother had raised him to read the clouds, to navigate by the stars, and to survive the dry times by digging roots and frogs that bury themselves in dry rivers or billabong beds, to await the rains which some day would turn the desert into a vast lake. He had a ready smile and an indomitable will of his Irish father, who was hanged at a water tank for stealing a lamb away from an ewe because he needed a bit of lamb chop for his dinner.

The lad was on a walkabout along the Murry River bank with his naked mother and her mob. She approached the captain to trade a huge turtle she had captured for a pouch of tobacco. The lad was fascinated with the old steamer. He clung to the captain's pants leg and wouldn't let go. The group of natives had a pow wow and soon one of the elders, after drawing signs of stars and moons in the sand with a stick, leaped into the air and began a chant. He cast his boomerang into the air and studied its flight as it gracefully sailed by the captain's head and stuck in the ground at his feet. The group danced and sang their chant even louder now. As the mother led the sturdy lad, his blue eyes were shining and his tawny skin glowed a strange shade of red, or maybe the red dust of the Outback had stained him that shade. I want you to know, although not a word of English was spoken, the group had decided the boy was now Fred's property. A gallon of rum sealed the deal. No tears were shed. The signs and the stars had spoken to the people who lived for ages by them and never disobeyed these omens. Our captain noted his new possession, noting the boy's strong arms and feet, tough as leather, and blond hair that matted itself to his skull, and thought, "Why not?" He now owned a turtle for the stew pot that the toothless cook was dressing and a strong lad who was already studying the machinery which propelled the craft effortlessly against the brown current of the Murry River, about the only stream that didn't go dry, thanks to its tributary, the Darling River, fed by the melting snow of the Coastal Blue Mountains.

Rest well, my trio of weary migrants on the train which is rumbling south and carrying you to your new home. I will continue spinning the yarn that is to weave the fabric of your parents, long, long ago, in a distant land. Captain Yankee Fred was truly destiny's child. Many unseen forces had thus foreshaped our character's life. First, fate had dealt him a hand of wild cards. Lady Luck had ridden with him, and the Irish leprechauns had eyed him over. Now, another fairy took a turn with his old carcass, might it be that mischievous little chap, who goes by the name of Cupid, a plump, little fellow wearing only a diaper and a long ribbon or sash, with bold letters spelling only one word, "Love." His chubby hand is clutching a recurve bow upon which is mounted a razor sharp arrow, always ready to make flight to some unsuspecting person's heart. He has unerring aim, and if by chance he misses, he has a quiver full of sharp arrows which he just loves to shoot. You might even hear him laugh when his missile hits its mark.

No one is immune to Cupid's efforts. Even hoot owls think each other are beautiful if by chance one of the little rascal's arrows finds its mark. Our captain has suffered a direct hit by the laughing little imp. He may stagger on for a while. It might even untie his purse strings, much as his heart strings which are now a disaster. May we watch him carefully as he capers about, wondering why he has the thoughts he does, even his appetite is affected. Some days he just isn't hungry, other times he craves chocolate candy. At night, he has strange dreams and feels very lonesome in the midnight hours. Yes, my attentive audience, all the symptoms of true love. That sharp arrow which flew so true to its mark was dipped in a love potion, a most powerful drug. Cupid saw that four leaf clover pinned in Bridgett O'Leary's red tresses, which tumbled to her shapely shoulders, and he winked at her, causing her full red lips to tremble just a mite as a lilting laugh rippled out. Is it Cupid's wand the one dipped in pure stardust forming a halo around her bonny face that will surely bring her under his spell?

Come on, old story teller, come on back to reality. That creaking old riverboat was loaded with railroad cross ties and the ship needed a new master. The half-breed lad who was now the captain's ward had shown much interest and pure out skill as a deck hand and mechanic aboard the *Victoria*. He could look at the stretch of water ahead and read the ripples in order to know the depth. He could read the sunsets and sunrises to predict the weather a week ahead. He could find food where there was none. To say the least, old Fred had come to depend on him. He bought him some clothes, even a seaman's cap which sat at a jaunty angle on his smoky wooly head. He had a smile for everyone. Quite a lad he was, the best of two totally different worlds. Let's keep an eye cocked on this lad. You do understand, Australia is a land of shocking contrast. So let's ride it like we find it.

Each sunrise brought strange new creatures which exist nowhere else on this fair earth! Selecting a new name for the lad, who is fast becoming a capable man, is at hand. The native group called him "Guma," but the captain decided to name him Sinbad, as he was a born sailor, although he was born in a vast desert. A surname, though not a great necessity, would be nice when he becomes a man. Being a fair-minded man, the captain decided a Christian name would be appropriate, as it was apparent that he leaned heavily towards his Irish blood. Thus Sinbad Barrick became his formal name. Let him pass a spell on the *Victoria* and the riverbanks she may be moored to. More recently she was moored to Swanpool, a settlement near the town of Broken Hill, not too far a distance from the station, as a ranch is known hereabout, of Limon O'Leary, our dear Bridgett's doting father.

Now, old Limon knew a lot about horses as he had been a drover since he was but a lad. A never-ending supply of wild horses roamed the slopes and gorges of the Snowy Mountains. These horses were brought to Australia by the early British settlers and thrived on the wild native grass, which was most nutritious and was able to squeeze the last bit of moisture from a thirsty landscape. The horses were the result of a survival of the fittest situation. This was true of the men who wangled them, who were known as "ringers." The wild horse was a "brumby." The men, who had no roots and slept beneath the stars or in some station bunkhouse, were known as swagmen. They sheared sheep, mended fences, led carefree lives and added a little color to an otherwise drab hard land. They had rather be called stockmen, a rather dignified term usually reserved for more mature, more successful souls. So remember these terms when we get back to Georgia and the weary travelers asleep on the train!

If I may bring your attention back seven thousand miles from the prairie of New South Wales, you must listen closely, my friends. An event is about to happen that will shape the lives of three generations of people yet unborn. Bear with me, be ye swagmen or squatters, ringers, subjects of the Queen, or just Georgia crackers. The old *Victoria*, battered as she may be, belched black smoke from her funnels, her whistle sputtering away as the stoker was carrying too much water in the hissing boiler. She was coming about at the mouth of a dry billabong along the Darling River, a shrinking water hole beside a giant Coolabah tree, which cast welcome shade from the brilliant South Wales sun. A shade for a group of drovers to camp by and fill their water bags with the crystal, cool water of the Darling River.

The campfire roared with each man's Billy kettle boiling away for making tea. Their tucker-bags were hanging from the limbs of a dead eucalyptus tree, or rather a gum. Beside the fire on a spit was a jumbuck (lamb) roasting away for dinner, no doubt. The ringers lounged about. One strummed a battered old banjo to the tune of Waltzing Matilda — "Who'll come a-waltzing Matilda with me?" They were just as happy as if they had good sense. Thereabout was an old fellow, a pipe in his mouth, his face as weather beaten by the sun and rain as a snag of driftwood that thrashed above the current, the ceaseless current of the Darling or Snowy River, as it ran its course to the Indian Ocean.

The ringers referred to the old one, with due respect, as the squatter. One woman, her hair in a bun tied in a blue bandana over which a drover's broad-brimmed, shapeless hat shaded her face and neck from the merciless sun, went about the chores of the camp. The stockmen had been in camp for a spell waiting for the steamer *Victoria*. Time was of little value here, a day or a week, what the heck. The brumbies were all mares that could be bred to thoroughbred stallions and foal hardy colts, which were in great demand round about the stock station and mining fields, both gold and tin. Even the railroad used them for grading and to pull skid pans that move earth. The wild horses had been mostly broken to halter and were hobbled so they could browse about yet be easily driven into the pole sty, or pen that the mates had thrown up close by the river. They were afraid of the noisy old steamer, having never seen one before. They reared and bolted, whined and stomped, raising a dust, but to no avail. The men soon had them calmed; they seemed to speak a common language. No better horsemen existed on the face of this earth than the men from the Snowy River area. They also trained stock dogs, heelers and border collies; perhaps some wild dingo blood flowed in their veins, although a full blood-dingo was much like this strange land, untamable.

Our captain had his hands full bringing his trusty launch to moor. He cut his power and let her drift to the bank. Sinbad stood on the bow, line in hand, waiting for a signal to cast it to a hand who had swum to the muddy bank. The captain rang a bell, and the rope or line uncoiled, sailing to the mate on the bank, who threw a loop around a stump before the slack was taken up by the drifting steamer. She was fast on the bow. Then the stern came about and another line was secured to a tree. The captain rang his bell again, and the loading boom powered by the steam winch swung the gangplank to the bank, making a growling sound that spooked the brumbies again. No sooner had the gangplank hit the bank than Sinbad had his "father's" trusty Sharps over and under shotgun. After greeting one of the ringers who was also an aborigine, he was off on a walkabout in search for some outlandish critter for milady's cook pot.

The captain strode ashore to greet Limon O'Leary, the man called the "squatter" because of his vast land holdings, of which the deeds were somewhat clouded as to title. Now old captain Fred, Yankee that he was, was no stranger to the squatter of Swanpool, having traded with him on several occasions. He had a sharp eye for horseflesh, or as a matter of fact, any flesh. His blue eyes settled upon a Welsh pony among the string of mounts which were at rest. Their withers trembled to flash the flies which gave them no rest. This pony, where had he seen it before? Where, oh where? There weren't that many like him. He was imported probably from Wales, the coal mining district of Britain, where ponies were compact, built strong, and could go into the mine shafts with ease. But here this one was out in the bush. Oh well, some gypsy horse trader probably traded him off as a pack beast. *Tighten up Fred. Your memory isn't that bad.*

Old Limon, the Snowy River horse trader, was glad to make this roundup as his brumbies were worthless unless he could get them to far off Adelaide or some other livestock market. Before they strolled over to the sty, which held twenty three of the nervous beasts, he made his guest welcome, commenting that his daughter was about the camp, preparing a dinner for tonight, at which he, the captain, was to be their honored guest. The young woman, Limon's daughter, was about her task. One of the men slowly turned the lamb over the campfire, and a Dutch oven was being filled with dough to bake into a hoe cake of bread. A keg of beer was about, but hot tea simmering in the billy kettles would steep for a while to gain strength. Strength was going to be in great demand after the sun, which had done its best to bake this godforsaken bight or drain, would give up and sink below the low mountain some distance in the west. The night would bring a chill that could even bring a frost. Sinbad was back in camp, having bagged a fine bird that was almost a load for his broad shoulders. The lad's unerring aim had downed the fowl as it called for its mates to roost in a break of dead gums which crowded the sparkling river. These large birds were ground birds, larger than a North American turkey. Their name was cassowary, and their flesh was held in great esteem by all who had tasted them, from the black natives to the Prince of Wales, the home turf of that pony tethered near by.

So tomorrow would be a feast for all. But my fellow travelers, our Yankee Captain will probably feast only his bright, old eyes that until recently only lit up at the sight of gold. Cupid, come down from that puffy little cloud that you drift about on with your bow in hand. Where did you get these little pointed-toed shoes that glitter with stardust? Please be careful with the powdery stuff; please don't get any in our hard-bitten captain's Yankee eyes. You stay on your bed of fluff, at least until we get back to Swanpool. But knowing you, you little imp, you have no respect for age, wealth, day or night, health or color. Please behave yourself, for once.

The stars were bright, the ringers were strumming an old ballad, which had no words until some swagman by the name of Peterson set a verse of words to it and named it "Waltzing Matilda." It looks like it will become Australia's national anthem. The mate may even be in this group, but never try to figure out a swagman. He can just evaporate into space, which is plentiful hereabout. The stars must be made of pure diamond, polished to perfection by the creator of this universe, and to top it off, add roasted lamb washed down with tea strong enough to walk about.

The camp cook had kept her back to the men and said nothing. She had retired to her tent, aglow with the feeble yellow light of a kerosene lamp. She shed her riding togs, untied her bandana letting her tresses fall as her flop brimmed felt hat lifted away. She slipped into a cotton frock, put on her stockings, lightly painted her lips, and put just a shade of rouge on her cheeks, very proper. But Cupid must have smiled his approval as she closed her compact, dropped it into her tucker bag, lifted her tent flap, and strolled to the bonfire to be introduced to the captain of the *Victoria* by her doting father in a proper manner, which was necessary before a lady could carry on a conversation with a strange man. Now this little filly had spied his highness, the captain, from afar and kept in the background of the camp until now. She curtsied very properly, tucking her skirts and bowing her bonny head before the captain. As her father spoke the words, "And may I present my baby daughter, Bridgett, a fair bit of the old sod, and may the old saint Patrick, by name, dance a jig at the sight of her fair face, and may the pipes wail if that sunny smile would be wiped from her bonny face!" Listen well, Yankee Captain.

The flames flickered and danced about the camp. Aye, methinks your seafaring days are about over. Don't spill that hot cup of tea. Yes, that is the Welsh pony that just whinnied. What are we going to do about your memory? Even the pony remembered the day on the cobblestone village street, and was that Cupid I heard laugh aloud? No, it was Bridgett. Maybe she has kissed the Blarney stone, which rests in a chapel in far away Ireland. The campfires burned low, the ashes glowed in the cool dry air. The stockmen's heads began to nod. Perhaps old Limon O'Leary, the squatter, excused himself to his tent, commenting that "These boots are killing me!" Deep down inside his wise old heart, he could see a quality or two beneath the grizzled beard and ill-fitting seaman's garb that our captain wore. He had hoped to see such a man of achievement, for he was no swagman, no drunkard, and he had a great strong body with those piercing blue eyes indicating that this Yankee had no fears for the paths unknown. Yes, daddy knew good breeding stock and here he sat, beside the glowing coals that cast dancing shadows on the faces about.

Look at Bridgett, if you will, with her bosom swinging to and fro beneath her blouse, as she raked the twinkling coals together, bending over as she worked with her fire stick. She knew that the captain was looking at more than the burned out ashes. He had filled his belly at the feast. Now he feasted his eyes on the endearing young charms of the lovely young woman who would, before long, be the heir of her dear father's vast acres and livestock on a thousand hills around about. Rest well, Captain Fred, on your hard old bunk in your cramped musty state room marked "Captain." Ah, how it needed the touch of a woman, a well heeled woman, if he had a choice, as he blew out the lamp and listened to the whisper of the river's current and the howling of the wild dingoes or dogs of this land down under.

Tomorrow, oh tomorrow, we must load the brumbies, sail or rather steam down stream to the auctions at Broken Hill, settle with old Limon, and perhaps see a Welsh pony, clipped so neat, tied to the hitching rail at the auction yard. Dream on, old pirate, but please don't take the sunny smile off the bonny face of your heartthrob. Why does the word hitching keep cropping up in your conniving old mind? You still have lots of miles on you. That is, if you repair that hissing steam in the boiler of the trusty ship *Victoria. Sleep well, you old "reprobate." Tomorrow is another day.*

Chapter III

First Walkabout

More and more the *Victoria* moved along the lush banks of the Darling River, where the railroad trestle was now completed, and the smokes that arose from the low lands were now not only from the river boats, but also from the noisy little railroad steam engines. Their brass fittings glistened in the sunlight. Their white-tire driving wheels were propelled by steel rods which relentlessly spun them to drag the obedient coaches along tracks of steel rails laid by sweating trackmen. These ribbons of wooden cross-ties bore the steel rails which were worn shiny by the flanged wheels of the trains that depended on them for a smooth ride and to direct them unerringly to the next settlement or town springing up beside these tracks.

The tracks just waited in silence for the next locomotive to sail down them with its whistles splitting the once silent Outback, bells tolling to announce its arrival and the fact that it was bigger, more powerful, and faster than any creature that lived hereabout before the tracks arrived. The settlers seemed to forget how helpless they would be if the tracks weren't there. Oh well, even I might, by chance, be fascinated by this new toy. I have heard that "the only difference between a man and a boy is the size of his toys."

Back to the Yankee Captain Frederick. He had trimmed his mustache, slicked his hair back, and donned his best suit. His gold watch chain was strung across his vest, leading to a gold watch as large as a biscuit. Even a silk tie was knotted around his sun-baked neck. Yes, our captain cut quite a figure this morning as he spoke to his adoptive son, Sinbad, telling him that he would be gone for a day or so as he was going to Swanpool, the home of the O'Learys, at their invitation to celebrate the bottling of last year's wine crop, which had aged in large barrels till now, the month of May.

Seasons are reversed in the southern hemisphere, and winter was just around the corner, but in the captain's heart it was spring. The thought of the lovely Bridgett O'Leary brought his calloused old heart into a virtual flower garden, as if it were spring eternal. Our Romeo couldn't have cared less how the wine tasted, but it had gotten him an invitation to the station of Limon O'Leary, father of this gorgeous creation who had become the apple of his eye. Frederick had never met Bridgett's mother, Mrs. O'Leary.

He boarded the railway coach at Gumba Station. Ticket in hand, he climbed aboard to select a seat beside a miner headed for Broken Hill, the jumping off place for prospectors. Two short shrieks of the little saddle tanker engine with its rinky dink bell tumbling atop the boiler, and they were off with a jerk that knocked Fred's pipe to the dusty floor. Hang on Captain, you have had many bone jerking rides during your adventures which we know little of. Here and now, you have set sail on a stormy sea. No one has a chart of the sea of matrimony, and you had better batten down the hatches or you may wash up again on a shore which won't be as friendly as that of Kangaroo Island, ten years ago.

The ride to Swanpool was short but not as smooth as the *Victoria*'s. But there he was standing on the station platform, carpetbag in hand and a lump in his throat. It wasn't fear. It was a strange feeling that reached down inside him and stung him to the gizzard. There was no brass band to meet him, only an aged ringer wearing baggy trousers the color of the dry earth under his booted feet, held up by a belt of well tanned leather. A loose shirt as blue as the wide sky above, a flop-brimmed suede felt hat which shaded his face that sixty blistering summers had done their best to bake to resemble ginger bread that had been left in the oven too long. He doffed his hat and asked the passenger if, by chance, he was the Yankee Captain. If so, he was very welcome to step around the corner of the depot for a ride to Dun Wallace station, the abode of the O'Leary clan. The cart which awaited them had only two spoked wheels, a driver's seat, and behind the shafts, two seats with a partition between them. Could you imagine in your wildest dream seeing a Welsh pony standing between the shafts with one hind foot cocked? He arched his well-clipped neck with his mane standing at attention. His nostrils flared to catch a scent that he recognized from the past. Yes, you guessed it right; it was Bridgett's Welsh pony.

All the way to the Dun Wallace station the captain's heart beat a rhythm much like the pony's hooves did on the hard dry road. Before long, he saw the rolling foothills of the Snowy Mountains, which rose in the distance to form a backdrop for the green paddocks. There were also many acres of grapevines that produced the wine, which, along with the brumbies and the fine continental stallions were the life blood of the O'Learys and their clan. The imposing house sat on a green hill. Made of wood, not stone, it commanded the landscape for miles. Sheep, cattle, bunkhouses, and cribs to master herds of horses or cattle dotted the distant hills and valleys. The captain's mouth dropped open as he took in the beauty of the land, which was as beautiful as Ireland. But he hadn't come for the scenery. Let's get down to the brass tacks of romance; those were the tacks he had come to drive. Water was our captain's element, not rolling hills. These landlubbers could have their mobs of animals, and choke in the brown dust they raised from a thousand hills. Come on now, old salt. Wasn't it you who now wanted a home ashore and a lovely lass to bathe your aching back and set a table of fine food for you?

Don't forget those long lonely nights you have spent in that cramped cubbyhole you call a stateroom, aboard the old vessel *Victoria*. Now, there isn't too much difference in a squatter and a pirate, so feel at home. Don't raid the coast and rape the women, just relax and hove to the coast, which is clear. You are a guest now, act like one.

Limon's handshake was firm as was the captain's. This handshake meant as a greeting of two friends, was actually the firm physical bond which was to shape many lives and blood lines of generations to come, even to the coach that we weary pilgrims, huddle about as I spin this yarn forty years later. There was no clap of thunder, no flash of lightning, no band to salute this handshake. Destiny was sealed as flesh met flesh. This was good strong flesh which knew that failure was not an option, only dogged work, a sweaty brow, with the only sure event being the sunrise and sunset and whatever moon shines to guide us through the dark nights. The stars above twinkled and trembled; maybe they knew the future.

We mortals know only the past and some of the present. Irish people are more resigned to keep the wind to their backs, to go with the current, to depend on the saints and fairies, to be content with only the necessities of life, to be fair. No disaster exists that a lilting fiddle on a sour note or a wailing pipe cannot improve, stirring the feet of both men and women who have never had a dancing lesson or cut a jig before. Some writer has written that the will of the Irish is indomitable, but woe be to the one who treads upon their feet or their freedom. The world is their stage and the curtain is never drawn. Their gene pool courses in the veins of every race, from the windswept tundra of the north, to the burning sands of the Sahara, to this small island continent of Australia and its odd flora and fauna. Only the hearty souls survive here, and two of the most capable well worn hands have just been clasped, a bond that I, the storyteller, who no doubt shares this blood line, will try to set the stage for, and the show will last the next one hundred and nine years. "Bless Pat, and begora!"

Where is the femme fatalist, the star of act one, the lass with the hair which shines even in the dark, the one with the skin as white as alabaster; the body which the master sculptors of old Italy could scarcely copy, the one who can see through a man to melt the hardest old heart; the apple of her aging old father's eye, the one who can see treasure in a chest even if the lid is bound by a steel strap and a padlock whose key has been lost for many tides. Come on, fair lass, your star is a shooting star which flashes across the sky to light the darkness. Tonight will bring new wine to the lips of the winemaker and his comrades, new hope to many a heart and maybe even a gold ring of engagement to a finger which has been bare long enough as the flesh is ripe for the harvest, much like golden grapes..

The night was young. The aborigines had drawn ancient pictures in the sand, and had seen the future as their gods were more generous with them than our gods are with us. The moon had risen. The wine had been poured and tasted. Old Limon had retired. The star of the evening I have described was Bridgett, as if you didn't know. She had played her part to perfection. She and the Yankee captain had become better acquainted. The wine, the charts of the natives and even the moon had cooperated. The lovely gown that she wore, she told him, was her mother's, who passed away at Bridgett's birth. She not only inherited the dress, but also the duties of the lady of the house as she grew older. Now, her 30th year was not far away. She had one older brother, who was a swagman or wanderer. The house had servants. The stock was her first love, the horses, cattle, sheep, and a Welsh pony named Boo, a birthday gift when she was only twelve. He, like her father, was aging, or perhaps only mellowing.

The old ringer who met the captain at the train depot tended the bonfire in the yard. He waited to escort the guest to his room in the guest house next to the bunkhouse. The fire began to flicker, and the shadows crept in. A dingo whined in the distance. The yard dogs, heelers, pricked their ears, and the cockatoos cackled on their roost. The newfound couple was in another world, their world.

Cupid's sharp arrows had struck their mark. Take a hint, lovers, the old man has raked the ashes twice and only coals are glowing. With a fond hug and a light kiss upon a cheek so fair, the day was finished. A door creaked and a figure slipped into the house. A good night was spoken, and a latch fell with a click. I couldn't hear all that was said, as I must have nodded because the hour was late, and it had really been a long day. The old ringer led Fred to his room, where the yellow glow of a lamp awaited the guest, and linen sheets were laid back by the hands unseen of a chambermaid, who longed to be a mother and a wife. Remove those dusty boots, Romeo. Hang your britches on the leather-bottomed chair. Make sure to hang your vest on the nail above without spilling the contents of the pockets, which still bulge with their valuable burdens. Pull up the covers. The chill of the night is settling in and you don't yet have your love to keep you warm. That lamp must be blown out, and you must sleep the dark away. Tomorrow will find you aboard a horse instead of your ship. Your mate won't be Sinbad to serve your every command. It will be your heartthrob Bridgett O'Leary, the fair one.

The morning was bright and clear. The breezes were sliding down the back side of the Coastal Mountains cooled by the snows of the lofty peaks which were only a purple haze in the distance. A mantel of white snow and ice covered them. Our Yankee Captain needed no crown to make him feel like a king, and soon he would have his love to warm his strong heart.

Breakfast was served on the long table that dominated the dining room paneled with select local gum boards. Old Limon sat at the head of the table with charts of his vast domain spread before him. His foremen gathered about deciding which paddock the mobs would be driven to by the drovers already in their saddles, as they had risen before the sun and had eaten their plain fare produced on the land.

Limon had two brothers who had joined him and worked with him in Australia. They lived nearby, and they and their wives and children galore had gathered that day to celebrate the bottling of last year's wine crop. They were a cheery family. Each tried to outtalk the others, the lilt of their laughter echoing to the open ceiling. This was a new world to the Yankee guest. His raising had been of a serious nature; children spoke when spoken to, adults smiled seldom. We could use the word "dour" and be close to correct. Words were clipped and few, and jokes were forbidden. Puritans frowned on laughter and mirth. They lived on a cold and somber rockbound coast, where the winters were long and bitter and the days were short. Seldom did the sun show its face. The flickering firesides and candles were the only weak light to drive the gloom away. The people reflected this way of life. Even their clothes were black or gray. They turned to the sea as a way of life, to fish, trade, or maybe even plunder. Our dear captain was thus endowed. Perhaps this laughter of the Irish was contagious, and he could come to the party.

Never far away, the old ringer, who had met the captain at the train depot, appeared in the yard before the home place. His name, our captain had learned, was Charlie McCook, a sidekick of Limon O'Leary. From the time they were but lads, they had ridden together. Charlie never found the right woman to become his wife. He loved to sleep beneath the stars and cook his meager meals by a campfire. He and Limon never separated. Now, semiretired, he lived in a shelter beside the main house. This was the only home he knew.

Since her mother passed many years ago, Bridgett had had no shortage of attention. Both, Limon and Charlie were doting fathers, one biological, one adoptive. Though she had no sister, she had had a female handmaid from childhood. The girl was the daughter of an indentured Italian family, who tended the vineyards and made the wine for which the station was noted. The girl, Bella, was one year older than Bridgett. The two girls had grown into young womanhood together, one a true Nordic specimen, the other a dark and somber Mediterranean girl, whose dark eyes could flash like flint when it struck to steel. It is said that opposites attract, and this certainly was the case. Bella had married a good hard-working Italian lad, who labored in Limon's vast vineyards. They had two bambinos who romped about the yard. Bella selected Bridgett's clothes, combed her crowning glory, the abundant mop of red hair which cascaded in waves about her smooth white shoulders, the shoulders she never allowed the sun to shine upon. Perhaps Bella and Bridgett shared some whispered intimacies of married life and even love.

Pardon me for stepping aside to acquaint you a bit with the ones who were the closest to our Bridgett. Back to the porch which wrapped around the station house. The rocking chairs were occupied this morning by the owner, however shaded his title was, and the dry-docked sailor, our captain, who was striving to act a new role, the suitor. Lord, Lord, boys. Fate has dealt a wild card to destiny's hand. Will his anchors hold? Or will he drift aground? Only I know the answer, as the gypsy woman has let me peer into her crystal ball.

As Charlie McCook led two piebald ponies of brumby decent, two empty saddles upon their strong backs, Limon arose to greet his old mate. Charlie glanced at the captain as he reached forwards to greet the newcomer. He had yet to decide whether this Yank would be fit to wed their fair colleen. Also, from the paddock nearest to the porch a pair of marbled blue eyes looked upon the men. They were the unblinking, slightly cloudy eyes of the aging Welsh pony Boo, who wondered why he had not been saddled, as he too loved the beautiful burden he had borne so many seasons. He also knew that change was in those cooling breezes which came with the change of seasons. He pawed the ground and whinnied his greeting to the other animals. They could accept change better than their human masters.

Charlie grunted and looped the reins over the worn hitching rail. He spit a long, liquid line of brown tobacco juice, the same brown as the dusty ground, probably stating his sentiments much better than carefully selected words could have done. Limon bid him adieu as he stepped forward to check the belly bands for tension. He grunted his approval and turned to smile at Fred, the intended. A grunt was not enough to state his approval of our Yankee Fred. He only mentioned that his daughter was one of the best horsewomen there in the Snowy Mountains. She was soon to join him in a walkabout of the station to break bread with a group of ringers and their Basque shepherds, far from this fair vale. Limon, his eyes narrowing to slits, suddenly gave a hoot and almost shouted. "Bless Pat, this man needs a duster and some chaps, maybe even a wide brimmed hat as he will catch his death in that seafaring garb."

One of Bella's lads was sent to the bunkhouse and returned with an old servant. After much ado, they smiled their approval upon the new image that stood before them. Fred only hoped the river men and barmaids never caught a glimpse of him, all dressed up like a ringer or a swagman. Cupid, I only hope you can recognize your target. Now let's be fair. Fred is no beginner with horseflesh. All boys are taught to ride and tend animals. Some have their master's degree, some just ride and others hit the dust. We will see.

The horses were impatient. The captain, even more so. His face began to flush. Yanks are an impatient lot. The two old Aussies, Limon and Charlie, winked at each other. Time there down under had little value. The tide which brought our captain up this creek had ebbed, and he was grounded there. The horses chomped at the bits, but Fred had no bit in his mouth yet. Why, he wondered, was the third mount brought up also empty saddled? Well, well, who are coming around the porch but two young women. Yes, two. One the well swaddled Bridgett, and lo and behold, the dark Bella, also in riding habit. Yes, tongues might waggle. Papa thought a chaperone was proper. After all, this was the couple's first walkabout. Who knows? A mount could go lame or Cupid could have administered an overdose to his love patient.

"Be off with ye!" old Limon shouted. The trio mounted the horses, the gate was swung open, the heelers leaped up from their unseen beds beneath the porch, and the party was out of the compound, leaving a cloud of dust which drifted to who knows where. The rolling hills soon enveloped the riders, and the road rose before them. Who would have ever thought the sea dog could ride as he did? But to be fair, Yankees have many capabilities that let them adapt to most any situation. If he could only impress his intended with more than his horsemanship. Round one, and he was still on his feet, or more properly, in his saddle. The ladies appeared to be a part of their horses with the wind in their faces. Soon the station O'Leary was but a dot.

As the trio rode by, the laborers in the vineyards, dumping buckets of grapes into their carts, stopped to wave. The oxen, now lying about, would pull the carts to the winery for the grapes to be pressed to release their sweet juice for next year's wine. The road led up from the valley of the Darling River. The hills became steeper, the valleys became gorges, and the rolling landscape became an undulating sea of long grass, punctuated only by an ancient baobab tree, which was home to many small creatures. Reptiles, lizards and serpents abounded. A mob of kangaroos thumped the ground with their stout tails as they bounded away.

Captain Fred's intentions were honorable, though they had not always been so. There are many more miles, or should we say knots, left on your carcass. You aren't old. You have just been about for a long time, thanks to Lady Luck, the only lady with whom you have ever been acquainted until your chance meeting with Bridgett that day on the cobblestone streets of Swanpool. There are many roads upon the face of this planet spinning through space. Maybe some day we could travel the roads of America, or more surely the sandy pine barrens of South Georgia, one of the United States. "United," let's remember this word as the future unfolds, much as this dusty red road did here in South Australia. Don't watch your boiling wake, Captain. Post your lookout high in the rigging and steer your ship away from the rocky reefs until you sing out, "Land ho!" Reef your main sails, wait for the tide and drift into port, don't breach and wash ashore. Now, this is the part for which you set sail so long ago from a far and distant port. The day is real, though, and you must live only one day at the time. This one seems to be nestled in your bony old hand, the hand which some day before long will clasp the graceful hand of the fair Bridgett. Come on!

The mounts were tiring and the land became wilder and steeper. The grazing animals, the sheep, cattle and horses, even rabbits, or hares as they were known here as they had been imported from Britain, browsed the coarse but nutritious grass. Since the beginning of time the great Creator had endowed the plants and creatures, birds and reptiles, to exist side by side in this ancient land, through dry seasons, wet seasons, storms and fire. When the aborigines arrived is still a mystery. The Europeans came only yesterday, when the sea rover Captain Cook stumbled upon this land, far off the beaten sea lanes of India and China.

The party drew up to a spring which had a stone curb about it to collect water into a tank for the stock to quench their thirst. Thirst was an ever present condition here, as if the Creator must have been running short of water the day he created this land down under. The women folk on the trip today let the mounts drink only enough to quench their thirst and wash the dust from their throats. The three drank from their bottles in the saddlebags and ate bits of bacon and biscuits. The winding road would lead them to the line camp and the cook wagon that followed the drovers on the undulating range. The riders knocked the dust from the tunics or dusters they rode in and chatted a while. The Latin woman packed the leftovers and checked the girths, belly bands and hooves of the now patient horses, giving them a lump of sugar or two. The love-smitten captain bubbled in his Yankee brogue with sugary words in a small talk which the European women found rather amusing. To say the least, the fair one especially laughed at things that weren't really funny. Perhaps Cupid's arrows had affected her funny bone. Her Irish lilt came to the surface and bubbled about her, much as the water of the roadside spring boiled to the surface of the tank to refresh the bodies of the riders and their trusty mounts, whose well brushed hides reflected that ever present sun which shone in abundance in this thirsty land. That thirst was not only for water, but also for love and companionship, as the Outback is one of the most sparsely populated lands on this earth.

Even the humor and spirit of the Irish wear thin at times, but not today. I must say that Bridgett's Latin friend Bella, although she spoke English, seldom spoke and was slow to laugh. She stood slightly apart from the couple, who found themselves more and more at ease together. It was not Bridgett who checked the gear, replaced the water bottles, checked the horses' hooves, and repacked the lunch. It was Bella, for her love was in the vineyard, her heart about her hearth, and her bambinos were soon going to be free men to grow their own vines and stamp their own wine. Perhaps Bridgett stood on that same threshold.

Chapter IV

The Proposal

The hour was late as noted by the watch that bulged in the pocket of the captain's vest. The bulge was matched by a second vest pocket which remained buttoned to hold its contents firmly in place. Mount up. That kitchen wagon is only an hour ahead as a passing ringer has informed Bella. The beans simmered in a copper pot, the tea water boiled in its billy, the tomatoes were being sliced, the biscuits were set to rise, and the oven was heating. Mount up, me dears, the romance that simmers in the hearts of our two lovers may come to boil if we tarry too long in the shade beside the bubbling spring of fresh pure water. May the winds be to your backs and your fates rest in the palms of your hands, which now hold the reins of the piebald ponies as they climb ever upward to the mountains that front the Indian Ocean and its moisture-laden winds. How in the name of St. Patrick did old Limon acquire all of this vast domain? Surely the title he acquired as the squatter had some truth about it, but surely he did a lot of squattering.

An hour's ride brought the riders to the line camp of the ringers. At this altitude the air was thin and much cooler, the grass was sparse but green, being adapted to this alpine climate, a rarity on this island continent. The Chinese cook waved his welcome to the riders as they dismounted. A vagabond or two always hung around a cattle mob and the stockmen. The vagabonds peeled potatoes, washed pots, played the banjos at night, gathered firewood, saddled the mounts, and spun the yarns of days gone by. As soon as our trio's boots hit the ground, one of these mates led their horses to the makeshift lot to rub them down, hang the saddles on a rail, hobble the beasts and turn them to graze. A cup of steaming tea was handed to the honored guests, the daughter of the squatter, the Captain, and her handmaid.

The Captain was the first to accompany Bridgett on a walkabout, a Yankee from the far USA, a land they had heard much about, but they had never seen a Yank in the flesh in the Snowy Mountains, and a seafarer at that. Word had spread that the riders were approaching the camp. The drovers seldom came about the camp till dusk, but just by chance, mind you, several happened to be near and felt obligated to sit a spell and welcome the guests to their range.

Most of the drovers had been raised here. Some were native aborigines, others had mixed blood. One was the older brother of our Bridgett, a strong young man, of slight build and a sandy complexion that the sun had blessed with a bountiful crop of freckles. He was old enough to have a long moustache, which gave him the appearance of being older. His blue eyes had the mischievous twinkle of youth. His name was Hiram O'Leary, but somehow he had acquired the nickname of "Sport," and that he was. He sailed from his mount and clasped the captain's hand in a viselike grip as he clapped his new acquaintance's back so hard that the scalding tea sloshed about and almost spilled. He doffed his flop hat to its throat band and gave his sister a kiss upon the hand and a hug about the neck. Not to ignore Bella, his one time playmate, he gave her a more restrained hug. Let us call this lad Sport as the others do, as he has rightfully earned it. I believe he is to be watched in the future, no doubt. That fair head and stout heart would bring sunshine to the darkest corner.

Bella made camp as our riders planned to camp about the kitchen wagon for the night, under a cold, star studded sky here below the equator where the southern cross dominated the constellations and seen only here in the southern hemisphere far from the New England fogs and smokes. Sport had fishing tackle in his duffel, which he referred to as "Matilda." He and Bridgett talked of the lake that nestled in a mountain vale an hour's ride above the shelf which the camp clung to. He told her and the Yankee, as he had taken the liberty to name the Captain, that the trout his father had transported to the lake years ago had thrived. He told them an afternoon of fishing was in store after a meal of rice and beans washed down with gulps of tea which will be so strong that a spoon would stand erect without touching the sides of the cup, and hot enough to make the devil himself hop into his own fiery pit only to cool off.

The stalwart captain could bear the joke, but did the lad, Sport, have to always clap him on the back at the end of each story, No doubt the lad was a kidder, a species much endangered in New England. Would he never shut up and stick to only the facts? Dream on, my captain, you have a lot to learn here in this far away land.

The men saddled the horses. One loaded a pack horse with fishing gear and placed a rifle in its scabbard placed across the pack's side, just in case some game animal should present itself. He also packed fishing equipment on the horse, such as fly rods, a book of hand-tied flies, and a wicker basket or creel to put the cleaned trout in. "Sport" wondered if they ought to take two creels along as he felt lucky as usual.

"No, Sport," Bridgett, the sensible one, admonished her brother. "We are only to catch our supper, not feed a regiment." Another outbreak of that infectious laughter and the captain braced himself for another clap on his aching back. He realized that his rank of captain had no weight here among his newfound friends. He had left it aboard the hissing old steamer docked in the Darling River in Sinbad's care.

Don't look now, but you are fast becoming a landlubber, my Yankee Captain, and you too will before long follow the advice of the fair lass who rides beside you on the twisting road to a lake that glistens as a rare jewel in its emerald setting, here on the roof of Australia this fall day.

Sport relieved the pack horse of his burden and hobbled it with the others that had already set to cropping the short green grass that carpeted the pleasant valley, which seemed almost as green as Ireland. Perhaps if a body searched enough, even a four leaf clover would grow about. A fire was built and the billy kettles whistled their shrill song, sung by the hissing steam eager to escape the confines of the copper kettles.

Sport and Bridgett assembled the fishing rods and selected the hand-tied flies, hoping they would fool the wary trout, which would find themselves lying row upon row in the moss-lined creel that was empty now. Our captain relaxed a bit as his legs were sore from the unfamiliar saddle. Sea legs, which have paced the decks of ships for so long, are different legs.

He watched the clever hand that now poured a steaming cup of strong tea. Bridgett had a sunny smile about her face, the face that had lured him to this mountain valley. He found himself quite under her spell as his past paraded before his vision. This vision, a peaceful and happy vision, intoxicated him. He snapped back to reality when the scalding tea burned his tongue. He wondered to himself how these carefree Aussies could pour boiling tea straight from the billy, take a long swig and never wince. No doubt their mouths were lined with heat resistant membrane. Drink up, lad. Take the fishing rod which has been thrust into your hand. Come along to the tune of the song which flows from the full smooth lips of Bridgett O'Leary.

A verse flowed straight to his heart. I do believe the lyrics were, "When Irish eyes are smiling, 'tis like the rose in May." Perhaps he thought she should have been named Rose, for no other was quite so fair as this wild Irish rose whose vines had entwined his rough old heart. Look, my friend, we came fishing, not to quote poetry. You have sworn enough, brawled enough, and laughed at henpecked husbands. Your time has arrived, and was it you who quoted another line of poetry, "Love is like a lizard, it will wrap around your heart and sting you to the gizzard." Ha-ha, not so funny now, is it?

You have your rod in your hand, show these children a thing or two about fishing. Your Yankee blood loves competition. It wouldn't look too good to be skunked by a lass. The flies dimpled the mirror-like surface of the cold mountain loch, excuse me, lake to a Yankee. A squeal of delight was heard as the lake surface boiled and Bridgett's rod bent into a quivering arc. She had caught a fat brown trout, a descendant of the ones her father, old Limon, brought up here in a sloshing barrel of water aboard a cart pulled by Bridgett's pony, Boo. She and her brother were wee ones at Limon's knees on a day much like today. Bridgett and the trout are adults, ready for harvest now.

The captain had fouled his line. A backlash as large as a bird's nest had to be untangled. That couldn't be Sport shouting as he set the hook in a fish that should have been mounted and hung above the fireplace long ago. Don't tell me, oh captain, that you are to eat tonight fish that a mere lass has brought to the creel, around a bonfire with a mob of mates. Maybe she could help you untangle your line, her fingers are so nimble. Must she hum a tune while she is about any task? Now hold on, strong one, don't let your hands tremble and your Yankee temper flair. Don't throw your tackle down and stomp it into the stony bank. Smile and take the rod into your hand and try again. Surely there is a one eyed hungry trout that you can lure to take your fly. Or maybe you are fishing for other fish. You seem to fare much better with the fair sex. You, yourself, seem to be hooked quite soundly! Could this be you? The captain's rod quivered, not his mouth, as he led a fish to the bank. It lay flopping about his feet. Did she have to smile that radiant smile and comment, "Only but a minnow, me dear."

"You just be calm, lass," the Captain said. "I am about to land a whale, which the pack horse that is biting the short green grass shorter, will have a struggle to tote back to your bivouac. His carcass will fit no pan, and the butcher will have to set upon him to pare it down to fit your laughing mouth."

Tread softly, my good man. The sun sets like a rock in these mountains. The trio soon had a mess of trout, which had been dressed and carefully packed in the wicker creel, lined with damp moss that only a few minutes ago grew on the rocks lining the lake shore. The fishers headed back to camp in a race with the sun, which was sinking in the west, as the cool mountain air flowed in, much as the tide does on the sea.

Meanwhile, back at the station house on the wraparound porch, Limon O'Leary and his friend Charlie patiently waited for the trio of riders to return from their trip the following day. His friend was a trusted friend, his mate, who rode with him when both were young and this territory was being settled with much upheaval. They could ask each other an opinion and expect a straight answer. Their pipes were lit and silence fell about them, a silence that the blue tobacco smoke of their pipes seemed to accentuate. Limon, a man not to waste words, broke the silence. "What do you make of Captain Barrick? Fair or foul?"

"The question is not fair, my friend, as I have but known him only lately. But he has the hands of a workman, and he will look at you in the eye, dead on, and the word is that in his dealing along the riverbank he has been honest, and his breath has not the scent of rum. His words are as clipped as his beard. These Yankees are a feisty lot, not given to mirth and song, and their dance is to be pitied. And, as you know they are not so fond of the Crown of England and have been a thorn in its side, much as we Irish are. So, old mate, you can weigh my opinion. He seems to have your darling daughter's affection, which I have found to smooth out many a jolt in the road of life. As you know, they are headstrong and won't be bossed, and a man must be the head of his household, as you and your own determined spirit well know."

Another long silence and another cloud of smoke arose. Finally only one word, "Aye," exited Limon's lips, set about his crook-stemmed pipe. In his mind, the mind which had weighed many a problem, he had already taken a liking to the man, who he thought would befit the apple of his eye, the offspring of his beloved Mollie, who died in childbirth. Yes, she needed a man of strength and will, not a swagman, a dandy, a fiddler, or one to nip upon a jug of Irish mist. She needed a man who would be so kind to his wife as to make her lug a large child, for there would always be a baby in the crib, bless Pat! Yes, the family needed a new blood line.

"This Yankee Captain," Limon finally said, "has a bit of quality about him, me thinks. I shall give this union me bonny blessing, and may all the saints bless them, amen! And begora!"

Old Charlie, not being an authority on matrimony as he had never married, withheld any advice on the matter. He did comment that a man should be dry behind the ears, have some experience, and be of a mature age as this was the custom in Ireland. He said that he rather liked theCaptain, despite the fact that he was a Yankee, and hoped he would learn to speak proper English and not be in such a hurry.

No more was spoken. When the sun had long since sunk below the foothill and the cold had begun to creep about the lowlands, they knocked out their pipes and rose to retire.

Back in the highlands, Sport and the packhorse led the couple toward home. The Captain sat very stiffly on his spotted mount. Bridgett pushed back her drover's hat to free her crowning glory which shown so bright. Each hair fell into its proper position, forming the molded waves that always looked as though a comb had just passed through them. She had forsaken the sidesaddle which she used on the streets of Swanpool. Here on the family station, she wore pantaloons much as her brother and the other ringers did, and a chemise of kangaroo hide of soft suede which hung loosely from her shoulders. Somehow the loose-fitting garments failed to mask completely the curves that lay beneath their folds. She rode high in her saddle, her weight in the stirrups which pocketed her crocodile hide boots and the knife scabbard built into the shanks that went close below her knees. She struck a grand and free flowing figure aboard her mount, which had quickened its pace to a gallop along with the others as they always did on the homeward leg of a journey. That feed bag of oats would be hung about their heads when they arrived at the line camp.

Bella, the fair handmaid, was dressed in her culottes and suede blouse with the shark teeth buttons. Her shining raven black hair plaited into a thick ponytail laced with colored wool yarns hung down her back. The triangular earrings dangled from her earlobes and twinkled in the setting sun. She had set the campfire before the tents strung between the slender eucalyptus trees, which grew in the grove a bit removed from the line camp where the ringers would no doubt soon be camping for the night beside the kitchen wagon and their campfires. When Bella spotted the rising red dust of her riders coming into camp, she walked to the road to meet and greet them in her mother tongue. Though her radiant smile bespoke her mind, the words puzzled the Captain. He dismounted first, dropping his reins as he struck the ground, then caught the bridle of Bridgett's horse. Bridgett swung to the ground and into his waiting arms which encircled her waist. They looked into each other's faces for but a moment and spoke not a word, as a word would have been a waste of breath. In a flash she recovered her feet and a smile broke across her face. Cupid also must also have smiled for his mission was accomplished. This bond was hammered together in the twinkling of the Irish and Yankee eyes. Sport, the future brother-in-law, gathered up the dangling reins and led the ponies away, as his world was the stock and the roving life of a drover. Some day, maybe, he would rope himself a bride, but only heavens above knew when.

The trout, which had been slit down the freshly scaled bellies, gutted and washed at the lake, were taken in their wicker creel to the flat stone that Bella used as a makeshift table. Now, mind you, Italians without a doubt excelled in their kitchen, and Bella was no exception. Her deft fingers and sharp knife soon had the fish filleted and rubbed with the salt and spices she had brought in her saddle bags. She robbed some glowing coals from the fire which burned brightly before the tents that sheltered the opened sleeping bags of goose down. Bella handed the Captain and Sport a mug of brandy to whet their appetite and cut the dust of the road from their throats. Bella and Bridgett chattered as only women can, both talking at the same time. Bridgett ducked into her tent to freshen up a bit while the men strolled down the road to become better acquainted and do the things that they do and say only to each other. It must have been pleasant as bursts of laughter rose into the dusk air. Soon it would be night as night comes swiftly in the mountains, much more so than on the plains. When they returned, the women had borrowed the metal grill from the drovers' cook nearby and the trout fish were slowly turning a golden brown as Bella basted them with a butter concoction, a family secret no doubt. Bridgett had slipped into a frock more comfortable for the fireside supper. She and Bella had some wine in a goblet and were giggling quite a bit. The evening star, Venus I believe, shone bright in the clear mountain air and twinkled its heart out, far above these earthbound mortals and their endless parade of birth, life, and reproduction, only to die and return to the dust which the Creator made them in the beginning. Who knows, he probably hung that star far above to watch over us mortals.

A fire had been kindled in the hearts of Bridgett and Frederick, and now burned quite brightly, although the night about was very dark, for love has a way of brightening the darkest corner. Bella, by the dancing light of the campfire, called the group of friends together, and being the good Catholic that she was, she gave thanks for the fish to the nourishment of their bodies and the sincerity of their bonds of friendship and relationship. This was perhaps the first time the Captain had ever doffed his hat and bowed his head to give thanks to God almighty, for he had worshiped other gods, gods of material goods, passing storms at sea and lust. He never had a doubt that some almighty power had brought him through thick and thin to this fireside. He never seemed to have time or direction to sink to his knees and bow his tousled old head, until now. Now he stands there with his rumpled hat in his left hand. The right hand dangled at his side only to be enfolded in a smooth young hand that twined around his fingers in a firm grip. Yes, my friends, the hand was Bridgett's. The words of the psalmist King David, which he had heard at his mother's knee long ago in far away Connecticut as a child, were fulfilled, "And his cup was filled, and runneth over."

Fred dropped his hat to the ground and groped the pocket of his vest, the one beside his gold watch, and brought forth a small box which was the cause of the other bulge in his vest. Freeing his hand for a moment, he opened this box and brought forth two rings; one was a ring of gold with a white diamond setting, the other, a band of gold. As he turned to face the young woman so fair, without a word he gathered that exploring smooth hand and located the slender ring finger which seemed to produce itself to him. Without a word, he slipped the ring, the one with the stone so rare, upon the finger so fair. The goddess of love is Venus, and her star suddenly shone much brighter to reflect the light which had traveled for millions of light years to this remote camp. The other stars twinkled their approval as well.

The couple embraced, and she, upon her tip-toes, turned her face up to meet his, and their lips met in a prolonged kiss. When it ended, they spoke to the silent witnesses, her brother, Sport, and her beloved handmaid, Bella. Bridgett shook back her hair, a glow of the fire upon her face, wreathed in a smile the angels in heaven would envy, and said, "Yes, my loves, this is the man I have given my heart to. Now, with the approval of my dear father, I shall take my vows to God above to be this strong man's lawful wedded wife, for as long as we may live and this eternal stone shall shine."

Then the Captain spoke, in a strong voice, clipping the letter "r" that all could hear. "Yes, this night forward my heart will belong to Bridgett, the fairest of ten thousand, as I intend to approach her father tomorrow to seal this matter. May I hope for his blessing, as I know that his daughter is of untold value and this diamond is but a token to him."

Bella dabbed a tear from her cheek, then embraced her fiancé, as Frederick shook the hand of the intended brother-in-law, Hiram "Sport" O'Leary, who gave a yell which caused the ponies to bolt and whinny. Supper was ready, and they gathered the trout from the grill, each with a strip of bacon laid upon them. Cups of steaming tea were poured, and the biscuits, so brown, were placed in a basket with a hand towel spread over the top. Bella and Bridgett set the food upon the flat rock and soon the jackaroos had their tin plates heaped and silence fell as they ate. Frederick was so excited he barely knew what he was eating, as he sat beside Bridgett, who chattered excitedly with Bella, not only her servant, but her best friend. A girl does need a friend at a time like this. The food, the crisp mountain air, and perhaps the sandman had dusted their eyes with sand, eyes which could hardly stay open. Sweet dreams that only lovers can dream would soon descend upon our friends, who were soon tucked in their sleeping bags of goose down. The fire didn't blaze as high, but the coals, which still glowed, kept the strange wild creatures at bay, until the sun peeped above the sleeping mountains to announce a new day being born, a day of many expectations and hopes to be fulfilled.

Chapter V

Back to Georgia

While things were as they should be in the Snowy Mountains in the long ago, perhaps we should let our loved ones have a few years to grow and be fruitful. The train that we are aboard tonight is about to arrive at its railhead in Georgia, and the past must wait.

The day was August 12, 1896. The Georgia & Florida Railroad had extended its tracks to Tootaville, Georgia, in order to accommodate a new settlement nearby. A boarding house of heart pine lumber had been built high atop a gentle hill. The railroad had built a track laid out in a "Y" alongside its main line. A brakeman uncoupled the engine from the coaches crowded with settlers from the North and boxcars containing their belongings: furniture, horses, pigs, chickens, even canned goods. They were all needed to set up new homes on this new land. The little steam engine ran around its own train, now at rest on the mainline. The trainmen lined the switches to the "Y" track, leading the puffer belly engine down the leg of the "Y," till it screeched to a stop on the stem of the "Y" track. upon the signal of the trainman to come ahead on the other leg of the "Y," only to have reversed the direction of its travel back to the North and points beyond. The boxcars carrying the settlers' belongings were uncoupled and parted from the coaches, then switched to a spur track further back to be unloaded into the wagon for the final leg of their journey from the North.

The weary travelers dragged themselves up to the porch of the boarding house that was built just for them here in the pine forest which before had heard only the sounds of the Creek Indians, passing traders, Government surveyors, and maybe even the armies of Andrew Jackson during the Indian wars early in the eighteen hundreds. The groups mostly traveled the post road or Coffee Road named for the popular General Coffee. This road was crossed by travelers going from the Georgia coast to Montgomery, Alabama, on to New Orleans and points west. They passed through on oxcarts, stagecoaches, buggies and by foot. This road was twenty miles south of the railhead at Tootaville. Sherman and his invading Yankee army had passed north of here. The area had been Indian Territory until a treaty in 1820 opened it to white settlement, but fever, both yellow and malaria, plagued this lowland and had discouraged settlement for years. Now, a new company had been formed in the Midwest. This company was the dream of a Union veteran to form a town of rather prosperous farmers, mostly Union Northern Veterans of the Civil War. Sherman's campaign, which had passed through Georgia on their march to the sea at Savannah, had broken the back of the Confederate armies led by General Robert E. Lee.

Tired of snow and ice and not as young as they once were, the Union veterans liked the climate and soils of the south. The founder and president of this Tribune Company was P.H. Fitzgerald himself, a well established newspaper editor and publisher in the state of Indiana, who sold many shares in the fledgling company. Each individual received land in proportion to the amount of shares that he had purchased. All of this project had been on paper awaiting Mr. Fitzgerald and his land agents, who had been searching in the pine lands of South Georgia. They had surveyed many properties. Finally, several thousand acres had been traded for and bought from large landowners along the western or Indian bank of the Ocmulgee River, a major stream originating just south of Atlanta, the capital city of Georgia. It flowed southeast, becoming a deep fast-flowing river at Macon, being navigable all the way to the port of Darien at the mouth of the Altamaha River. It nestled among the Golden Isles of the Georgia Coast of the Atlantic Ocean, where ships from all over the world docked to load heart pine lumber, naval stores, pine tar, cow hides, and that all important commodity, cotton, which was shipped worldwide. The Ocmulgee joined the Oconee River at a point known as the forks. The Oconee flowed down from the well-established Georgia towns of Athens and Milledgeville, once the capital city of the original state of Georgia. A trading post had operated in this area along the river since before the Revolutionary War with England, when the half-breed Indian woman, Mary Musgrove, her English husband, and a close friend of the founder of Georgia wrested it from the Spanish crown in the Battle of Bloody Marsh, near Brunswick. She established a trading post at the forks, trading deer hides, gunpowder and whisky with settlers and the Creek Indians. She had a talent for getting along with both the Indians and the English colonists, and perhaps was the mother of the colony of Georgia, as the blood that flowed in her veins was of both white and red origin. This was all well and good, but the settlers had intended to travel to the northern uplands of Georgia, above the fall line, where they would find less humidity, less mosquitoes, less fever, better cotton land, and less savage Indians. Now you have gone back to the beginning of the white settlement of the largest colony east of the great father of waters, the Mississippi River.

We, the latest band of settlers, were perhaps the last mass migration of true settlers to pack up and begin a new life here among the towering long leaf yellow pines, which only recently heard the ring of axes and the crash of trees hundreds of years old. When they were cut into cants or logs to be sawn into lumber to build the cities of the Northern States and Europe, many oxen were required to skid them to the creeks and rivers to be floated into booms or rafts to silently drift with the current of the Altamaha's tributaries. This tributaries surged together at the forks, meeting the churning steamboats bringing goods to the settlements and cities that had sprung up alongside the riverbanks, much like those of the Murry and Darling rivers of far away Australia that I spoke to our settlers on the midnight train last night.

I have tried to focus upon Shepard and Chasity Barrick, known as Shep and Chase to family and friends. Now perhaps is a good time to turn our spotlight on this family group of five. The father of Chase, Dan Cooper, the one with the full beard, was a saddler by trade. He was a Union cavalryman by conscription. He came along with his daughter, a logging camp cook. This family would probably never have joined this Tribune Company if Dan hadn't been reading a newspaper on a Sunday afternoon. This paper wrapped a package sent to a logger from his family in Indiana. Old Dan, a frugal man, had some savings tucked away in a Michigan bank, some of which he had brought to America when he migrated here with his parents before the Civil War. He had married Chase's mother, whose parents were descendants of pilgrim settlers who arrived in the Massachusetts Colony on the vessel Mayflower, stepping ashore on the Plymouth Rock. No doubt. Dan Cooper and his wife moved to the Cooper's homestead in Pennsylvania where his sisters lived.

Shortly, the Civil War began, and Dan went off to the war, leaving his wife expecting a child. It was in his good fortune to be on the winning side. The skills that he had brought from England had served him well in the Union Army. The cavalry unit to which he was attached had assigned him to mend the tack because of his ability to build and repair saddles, and to groom the horses. He never fired a shot as his tool wagon followed the troopers. After the battles were over his work began; strings of lame horses to doctor, and harnesses and saddles to repair. He was never a dyed in the wool Yankee, for he was still as he often stated, "A subject of the Queen, and long may she live!"

Please, my friends, the ones who listen to this unfolding drama of lands and people, don't forget this man and his direct, if not fiery, determination. Some might even call him hard nosed. As his troops of Pennsylvania Dragoons stormed the Georgia midlands, where they found cultured people, quiet towns, large cotton plantations, many pathetic slaves freed only to hunger and harassment, poor sharecroppers, and dirt farmers who had no slaves, Dan Cooper saw Atlanta burn to the ground. He saw widows who were trying to hold what meager belongings they had salvaged. The widows sent the older children to the thickets with the mule, the cow, and perhaps a sow with pigs to hide out till General Sherman and his invading army had passed. You could follow his path by the columns of smoke that rose to the sky. The General commanded his men to burn and pillage these settlers. He had no supply lines. His army was living off the land that lay ahead of them on their way to join the Union forces already in Savannah. His famous report to his Commander in Chief, President Abraham Lincoln, was, "When I leave Georgia, a crow will have to take his lunch if he follows my forces," and he pretty well fulfilled his report. Later, when asked about the hardship which was wrought upon the rural southern people, his only response was, "War is hell."

Our player, Dan Cooper, witnessed this burnt earth march to the sea. He only wished that someday, if he survived this hell, he could return to this pleasant land. After the war was over he, upon the horse that had been given to him by the army, made his way to his sisters' home in Pennsylvania. Dan Cooper rode down the lane at the homestead on a bay mare with "US" branded on its withers. There, for the first time, he saw his only child, a small toddler. Dan farmed the family land, and his sisters helped raise Chasity to young womanhood, schooling her and teaching her the ways of virtue. Dan wasn't enthusiastic about farming, but he wanted to be there so his sisters could help to raise his young daughter. By the time our Chasity Cooper had become a budding teen-aged girl, she was much like her father, in mind that is, as she had inherited his strong views, direct manner of speech, and a love for literature, reading and writing. She wasn't a gentle, demure girl, and even at that age she was the captain of her own ship, a ship that would visit many ports, a ship that set its course, come hell or high water! She loved her father very much and barely remembered her mother. She detested farm life and the drudgery it offered. She lived in a world of her books and papers. To her taste, those stuffy aunts and their lace bonnets, going to church every Sunday and to quilting bees, were "yuk." Horses were more to her taste, even if riding and grooming them was not ladylike. She felt more at home in overalls than she did in a pinafore.

The homestead seemed more like a prison to Chase, and Dan shared these feelings with her. Many evenings after they had washed the dishes and had some time to spend in front of the fire they dreamed of the day when they could move and live under their own roof in a new setting. Finally the day came when their dreams were realized. Chase gathered her few clothes and, to her aunts' horror, cut her hair short. Dan brought a buggy, hitched to it a strong old bay mare called Kate, and put his and his daughter's meager belongings in the back of the buggy. He had his savings in a money belt strapped about his waist. The contents were the long held savings he had withdrawn from the bank in Tuscarora, Pennsylvania.

Yes, destiny had taken this young woman by the hand. Perhaps the road beyond that peaceful lane would only present challenges, heartaches, disappointments and poverty. I can see that destiny had chosen her because her frail body, which housed an indomitable spirit, could overcome all of those hardships for nearly a century ahead. The hardships that life would bring only strengthened this bond. Dan, with a long beard and a bitter mind, again had someone to love and cherish, his own flesh and blood, child of the only woman he had ever loved. They would stay together the rest of their lives.

Chapter VI

To Sydney

My story left Australia thirty long years ago, half-way around this spinning globe, to stop here at the railroad boarding house, deep in the pine forests of the coastal plains of the state of Georgia, USA. Those thirty odd years saw many changes in modes of transportation. Railroads were being built in every nook and corner of the country. Steam power replaced oxen and horses, and telegraph wires stretched along the transcontinental rail lines from the Atlantic to the Pacific. Messages were sent by Morse code to anywhere, instantly. Yes, changes were in the wind. The scars of the Civil War gradually healed, as the veterans became fewer and fewer. A new generation was now at the helm of business and politics worldwide.

Many hearts had been broken. Babies and grandbabies played in new homesteads, both, here and in far away Australia. Fortunes had been made and lost. Now, my friends, this very morning, I will attempt to bring you up to date. We left a happy scene in South Australia in the shadow of the Snowy Mountains. A mature Yankee steamboat Captain asked a beautiful young Irish woman, heir to an empire along the Darling River with many vineyards, cattle, and sheep as far as the eye could see, to marry him. Bridgett O'Leary, and her friend and indentured servant, Bella, were dressing for the ride in the saddle back to the station house at Swanpool.

Bridgett pulled on her riding gloves of kangaroo to hide the ring. She hated to cover the diamond ring high on her third left finger. It was the ring that Captain Barrick, whose proposal she had accepted beneath the moon and stars so bright last night, had given her. She had asked her brother and her handmaid to just be a bit mum on the news until they, as a couple, spoke to her father back home and hopefully received his blessing. The women rode ahead to escape the dust of the horses' hooves as they traveled the dry ruts of the road back home. Fred Barrick and Bridgett's brother, Sport O'Leary, followed them some distance behind the leading pack horse, leaving their dust to drift off to the Outback. As the riders dismounted at the hitching post, Limon O'Leary doffed his sweat stained hat to the ladies and removed his crooked stemmed pipe from between his clinched teeth to cradle it in his hands, the hands that had wrested this station from the wilderness. They were hard hands when needed to be, to prove up his claims, hands that had buried his wife, hands which had shaken the Yankee's hand, hands which now trembled a mite. Little did Bridgett know that approval of this union had already been arrived given on this same veranda by her father and his sidekick, or mate, Charlie McCook, Limon's trusted balance wheel, as those wise old wranglers could tell at a glance what was afoot. They had been young once with roving eyes of blue.

Limon had heard the hoofbeats of the mounts approaching the station house as he sat in his office inside. Old Charlie also heard the hoof beats and had come to the hitching rail. He reached for the reins of the lathered horses and spoke in a tone that settled the beasts as the young women dismounted. He called for a groom to come and lead the four mounts away as the men were also approaching the rail.

The riders removed their dusters and hats, but Bridgett strangely failed to remove her riding glove. The dogs, now silent, went to their cool dirt beds beneath the porch. The ladies laughed and chatted with old Limon while the men brushed the road dust from their togs and tried to look solemn. Only a bit of a wrinkle showed about their mouths, which could break into a smile at the proper time. Rocking chairs were taken by the old man and the women. Bella waited for a nod of approval from Bridgett to be seated. Limon put his pipe back into his mouth and through clinched teeth said in Irish brogue, "Tis plain to see, me lass, so dear, the bulge beneath the leather, so sheer, upon the finger on the hand of your left which is the customary one to bear the rings of matrimony. And for the life of me, why did you not doff the glove as the others did?"

Sitting on the steps somewhat away, the men nudged each other, and the wrinkles about their mouths spread into broad silent grins. Bella looked away so her smile could not be seen.

Bridgett's face turned red in a fiery blush as she spoke, "Tis plain to see I can never pull the wool over the eyes of my father, so wise, or by chance may it be those spirits that hover about ye, the ones you tolled here from county Cork, the ones that see every secret that may dwell in my bosom." She removed her gloves to reveal the ring with the stone so bright. "So now, without the glove, feast your eyes upon the ring I wear to tell the world that I have made my selection of a bonny lad, stout enough to serve my every need."

A puff of blue smoke exited the mouth of her father and had nearly drifted away before a word was spoken. Only when the eyes ceased to flash, he smiled and said, "Bless Pat! You have the spunk of your mother about ye! And may never a man who walks this green earth wipe that spirit or smile from your face, so fair, and may God in heaven bless you and this lad you have selected from the mob of lads and lassies who have the spirit of the Irish, for life is no bed of roses, you may find. Tell me fair one, who is the lad on whom I have been asked to bestow my blessing? Couldn't he be the bloke who now rests his body upon my step riser? If so, tell him to raise himself, so I can shake his strong hand once again, and may he forever be welcome in my humble abode."

With that outburst, Fred, the Yankee Captain, arose, squared his broad shoulders, threw his hat down to the floor and strode forth to clasp the hand of his intended's father. In doing so, he spoke the words, "I appreciate your blessing. She will become my pride and joy forever. May God see fit for me to tread his earth."

The date of the wedding was set for a month away, on a weekend. Bella had actually become the sister Bridgett had never had. After a night's sleep, so sweet, she finally drifted off for forty winks. They had to plan the wedding. What type of wedding was it to be? A problem had already risen, as Bella and her family were devout Roman Catholic, but on Bridgett and her family's vast station, religion played little part in their lives. Old Limon was an "orange man," or Protestant Irish, the church of Christ, I believe, or best known as the Christian Church. This difference has rocked the very ancient foundations of the Emerald Isle, with the Catholic faith having deep roots there.

The followers of the Catholic faith were known as "green men." Much blood has been shed over this question of religion, and between the Irish it is as difficult to change the mind of an Irish man about religion as for a sheep to change its color. In fact, this perhaps was the reason Bridgett's family, three generations ago, loaded their poor belongings aboard a sailing ship and set out upon the shining Irish Sea for a long and perilous sea journey. They traveled around the Cape of Good Hope on the southern tip of Africa and continued to Australia beyond the Indian Ocean. They landed at Adelaide with a load of shipmates who had greater worries than the church they supported. So now, religion was seldom mentioned on the station. Now don't get me wrong, a Christian ceremony was necessary for a wedding, a baby's christening, or a funeral. So, you see, a man of the cloth had to be contacted and the date of his being in this area had to be arrived upon.

The booming mining center with the new rail line connected Broken Hill with Sydney, the great city and port of choice. With luck, a person could be reached, and a day's journey from Swanpool on the rail line or a wire on the telegraph would confirm a date. A rig would be waiting for the person and his party to bear witness to the ceremony and register it upon the county records, for the world to witness. There was no doubt that this wedding would be the social function of the decade, perhaps of the century. Old Limon had only one daughter, and he would never miss the money the wedding would cost. A hundred brumbies could be mustered to pay the bills, a cart of wine from his winery, maybe a wagon load of yellow tail gin to loosen the spirits of the ringers. Maybe even Peterson, the swagman of fame, and his banjo would be present. Who knows, the O'Leary name was well known even in Alice

Springs, so far away, and even the Ayres Rock may tremble a bit as it stands so dominant in the red desert of the forbidding Outback. The drums of the natives would vibrate their message of joy to the tropical jungles of the Northern territories, even to the city of Darwin, so far away. These wise old people had no need of telegraph wires or little men who sit before clicking keys pounding a typewriter and snatching a yellow sheet of paper from the printer to advise a date of importance.

The mysterious aborigines probably now knew the date and place of the festivities and would light their campfires in a grove of trees near the station house of Limon O'Leary, the one who sent them a mob of lambs when the land lay beneath a drought. They were always in touch. You might receive a message written with a stick in the sand before your steps, not in words, but pictures. Any half-breed can read for you. They may perform a wedding dance stark naked with tiger snakes between their teeth and their black skin painted in designs that can bring happiness, fertility or doom to a young couple. The land was theirs. Even the sun and moon were theirs. These whites were only guests whom they tolerated.

The river men would be there, too. Perhaps half the colony would arrive. The wedding dress, ah yes! Maybe Bella and Bridgett would board that noisy passenger train and rattle away to Sydney, to the dress shops and seamstresses who abound there. The question was how would the captain spend his bit of free time. He wouldn't get drunk as he was smitten by the beautiful wild Irish rose. Heavens to Betsy! He won't stray. Perhaps he needed to visit the Chinese tailor newly arrived from the British colony of Hong Kong, who had a shop under the bluff at Sydney. My guess is that he will suggest for the sea captain a suit of blue, complete with a vest, anchored with buttons of brass, and a jaunty cap with a black visor. The captain being a seaman, it is somehow beyond my imagination to see him involved in problems on land or wearing a business suit or a ringer's slouchy garb; perhaps a prisoner's suit, shirt and pants of black and white stripes, and leg irons put in place by a blacksmith, not a Chinese tailor fresh from Hong Kong. Oh well, he still remembers burying a sea chest on Kangaroo Island. Maybe he needs only a dory to set forth in a dark night. Grab a pair of oars and a lantern, and, old captain, don't forget a shovel. Be off with ye, old story teller, that chapter is closed.

Must I remind you, my friends, that Australia, the largest island on the globe, was chosen as far removed from the English Crown and its laws for people who had difficulties walking the straight and narrow paths of the law. Sheriffs were put on notice to arrest and hold in the jails all traitors, until such a number was assembled to fill the holds of the Crown's merchant ships for an outward passage to Australia. Troublesome thieves, pickpockets, debtors, prostitutes, beggars, gamblers, political activists, and protesters of the Royal

Court were sent to Australia. Pirates were to be hung on the spot, unless they preyed upon the Spanish merchantmen, then they were to be knighted. Soon the streets were safe and the gutters were unclogged. These policies were first conceived in earlier years with the penal colony of Georgia, in America, established to serve these purposes. But then in 1775, a rebellion occurred in the colonies in America, which resulted in their Declaration of Independence and the strength to back it up. This war left the Crown without the penal colony in Georgia. Australia was established in January 1788 and became the dumping ground for this motley lot.

No journals were needed, no guards to pay and food to buy, only a vast, desolate landscape, inhabited only by outlandish animals, deadly serpents, and roving bands of Stone Age humans wise only to the laws of nature. "Have a bloody good life, my renegades, but never come back to London town." The melting pot had been boiling for quite a while, and now, I am pleased to state, this breed of people has survived to be quite a capable lot. Our characters, Captain Fred and his beloved Bridgett, were programmed to meet head on the direful obstacles life may present. So hang on, loved ones, the band is playing, the stage lights are on, the house lights are dimmed and the curtain is about to be drawn on act two of this play.

The Captain had returned to his vessel, the *Victoria*, and his foster son. Sinbad, now a man, no less, had set about to make the aged steamer shipshape. He had her loaded with fuel, decks painted and the hull scraped. The crew of deck hands had rested and healed. The old toothless hag of a cook was replaced with a young Chinese man, a master of his profession. He spoke only pidgin English, but his menu was international: egg rolls and "ah-la-king" were his specialties. The holds were loaded with salted hides, bound for the tanneries' vats at Gumba-Gumba. The brine which leaked to the bilges only helped to preserve the keel and ribs of oak and the planking made of Philippine mahogany. She was still a stout old tub, almost as stout as the men who manned her and the muddy bosom of the Murry River, upon which she floated as the currents surged ever to the sea. What else could Captain Barrick desire? Business was good.

This one half-breed son could only have been sent by God alone. The captain's secrets of the past would be left undisturbed. His love life runneth over. Now, if only he could tie this knot of matrimony and have a family to share his good fortune. He was ready to shove off aboard his steamer and upon the stormy sea of romance. Tread lightly, old Captain, don't disturb these saints that have seen fit to bless you so abundantly.

The smoke boiled from the funnels of the *Victoria*, the whistle was sounded and echoed back from the bluffs above the river. The bells rang and lines were cast aboard. Gangplanks rested on the forward deck. The rudder obeyed the cables attached to the steering wheel. High above the deck in the wheel or pilot house, the Captain spun the large upright wheel with the hand knobs above the rim. The vessel drifted into the current, and at the Captain's ringing of the bell, Sinbad obeyed the signal and eased the throttle to one-half speed forward, and the paddle wheels churned the muddy water. The steamer came to life, and once more his ship left a wake that formed waves, which raced to the shore to crash against the river bank and slosh back, only to make the restless waters more cloudy.

He, our Captain, truly is the master of *Victoria* now. Can he master the will of the Irish woman to whom he is betrothed? Only fleeting time will tell. Yes, mind me, your lifetime and the lifetime of the wee ones who patiently await their wake up call deep inside Bridgett's belly now so flat. They will come forth, grow, and develop to take their place on this green earth as your heirs to whatever fortune they may inherit when your name is called up yonder and the bells in the steeple atop the church of Christ toll the news that you have gone to meet your deeds. Sail on, oh captain, watch the currents of the river and the stars which twinkle high above. Keep them in good alignment. Bon Voyage!

The Captain had a good crew that had been with him for many voyages. He felt safe enough to relax now that the ship had negotiated the narrow channel under the railroad trestle over the river. The main line was now complete with a fine harbor on the south shore of Australia. The railroad line connected Sydney to this coast, opening much inhabitable land soon to be settled by immigrants from far away Europe. With Sinbad at the wheel, Captain Fred let his mind drift like the heavily laden *Victoria* did with the seemingly endless current; a current that could wash him and his ship laden with a valuable cargo upon a sandbar or snag. Someone with knowledge of the river and its currents must stand at the wheel and steer her, to hold the channel which would take her and the cargo to safe harbor.

He, the Captain, also was about to set sail on the stormy sea of matrimony, a sea riddled with snags and even whirlpools. His captain's papers would not be valid on this sea. He must stand at a wheel which would steer not only him, but his beautiful bride through the storms of life. Their course must be kept in the channel that would lead to health, happiness, and possibly wealth.

Suddenly, he realized he had to prepare a home for his bride. It had to be in his element. He would never be a drover. He liked the foam and spray of the river and ocean much better than the dust and saddle sores of the Outback. When this cruise was over he would search for a bungalow high upon a bluff, so he could sit upon his porch and with his spyglass scan the horizon for the tall ships, to read their colors and note their home port. He had enough tucked away to live on. The river traffic had been profitable. Sinbad could master the *Victoria*, Bridgett could keep the books, and he could rule the roost.

Dream on, my captain, or should I say bridegroom. Only fate or perhaps destiny knows whose hand will rest upon the pilot wheel, whose hand will rock the cradle, whose hand will hold the purse strings or whose hand will prevail in times of peril. Yes, my friend, even the best of players can run amuck, you old skinflint. I am going to find that gypsy camp about some town and lift the flap of a stripped tent with the string of lame blind ponies bunched about, to place a few shillings in the unnerved hand of the old woman with the crystal ball and the eyes that at birth were covered by a veil of skin, so thin. Her vision can plainly see into the future that is reflected in that glass sphere, so clear. The captain had little faith in the gypsy women. Their skirts were so full that they swished about. They wore necklaces of gold chains and medals of Fatima, and gold rings upon each finger. Their eyes pierced and flashed and could see much clearer in the presence of gold and silver, especially when it was placed in their palms by a Yankee.

Bridgett and Bella stepped down from the railroad carriage onto the stepstool that the young conductor had set upon the station platform in Sydney town. He set their luggage aside and with a bow took the ladies' hands in a gesture of grace so they would not stumble and sprain their slim ankles. A hack was summoned, a driver stowed their bags aloft, and they were helped to their seats in the cab. A crack of the whip and the horse leaned into his collar. The driver in his seat so high held the reins. Through his speaking tube he asked, "To where me dears?"

"To the Balmoral House, the home of ladies away from home," Bridgett answered the man. "No doubt you know the way direct. Touch that nag of yours up a bit as I will permit no dalliance, my good man." Bella only smiled as her Italian accent was of no value in these streets so crowded.

The driver was cockney and he knew the bloody Irish and their nature. He pulled up beside the hotel in the heart of the garment district. He honked the hand horn beside his seat, tied the reins about, jumped down, opened the carriage door and assisted the ladies to the sidewalk, where a doorman sallied forth to man the bags down.

Bella had the purse. Bridgett was not the Bridgett we saw out on the range and bush in ringer's garb. Here uptown she was the lady of means. Her three-pointed hat of black felt nestled atop the coiffure of red hair, which was lightly held by hairpins and still wanted to march about her head in waves so perfect. The ribbons of green silk were tied in a bow to hide the hairpins. Her suit of tweed was tailored to perfection. The dickey of Irish lace choked her perfect chin. Her waist was so slim below the generous bust and flared again below the narrow black belt of leather. The flare was quite pronounced. Obviously she had her waist cincher about her body. The skirt followed her contour, forming a figure much resembling an hourglass. Her button-up boots made of black calfskin with high heels were shined to glisten in the dimmest ray of light. The tweed skirt reached to her ankles with gores that ended in a slit that let her boots flash as she walked about in measured steps. Her green velvet handbag with beaded fringe hung on a strap of black leather from her left forearm. The diamond ring sparkled on her ring finger, which she held rather prominently at just the right moment. She wore a large opal set in gold upon her right hand. On her lapel was a brooch bearing the coat of arms of the Clan O'Leary. She carried a folding fan in her hand and constantly unfolded it to shield her face as she spoke to the servant. I was about to forget the prissy parasol with ruffles. She handled no luggage and paid no tips, only signed the register at the desk with a flair for herself and her lady in attendance.

Old Limon would have been proud of this moment. Only yesterday she was a child upon her pony Boo. Now, with Boo retired in his paddock, Limon O'Leary was not the only one to be proud. Bridgett herself this very morning aboard the first class railroad carriage, with its ample ladies' room had, with the help of Bella, styled her beautiful hair which would not obey the desires of the ladies. Having a mind of its own, it fell as it pleased, not like Bella's long coarse Mediterranean hair, which loved to hang loose or obey the plaiting. It had hung loose since childhood. Heaven knows the problem it would have been to plait that red wavy mane with which Bridgett had been so blessed.

Bridgett had stood before the full length mirror between the jerks and jolts of the train, a slow smile of satisfaction spreading on her face. She was a proud woman, well aware of her many charms. Only she and Bella knew the struggle and wiggles, deep breaths and Irish oaths it took to pour her charms, so abundant, into that corset, which Bella had laced so tight. But man, oh man, every penny that old dad had spent on that foundation garment and the Hong Kong tailor who had fitted it to her was well spent. Let those eyes pop downtown. They could look but never touch the fair one.

Bella was no slouch herself. Bridgett was good and kind to her, but here and now you must know who took the limelight. My, my, how generous can the good Lord be to some people. Perhaps the gypsy woman can tell us now the matter of a wedding dress for the bride to be. Bella, I must trust you not to let our lady we love so much go, shall we say, overboard. You hold the bank note signed by the squatter O'Leary to outfit the bride and her trousseau. He trusts you more than his own flesh and blood.

The two women arose early the next morning and had only coffee and toast for breakfast. They dressed in their traveling togs and walked to the street. The doorman hailed a carriage and away they scurried to the garment district, where they were directed to a bridal shop, whose manager was an aging German-Jewish woman who only spoke broken English. As the women alighted from the carriage, Bella gave the chauffeur the fare and a shilling tip, and with a bow he was off. The shop was small. The show window upon the sidewalk was just large enough for one mannequin, gracefully posed, dressed in a white wedding gown. Bridgett, the fiancée she was, let out a sigh and her heart skipped a beat. Suddenly, she saw herself as a bride. Her vision made her aware of the step she was taking, from a girl to a woman, and all the changes that this step would bring upon her. Here on this sidewalk in Sydney town, she was aware that one chapter of her young life was soon to end. She would then become a wife and mother, by the grace of God almighty. A tear or two welled in her eyes so blue, not tears of fear, but tears of joy. She dabbed her eyes with the lace handkerchief that was stuffed in her blouse cuff. Bridgett had never shed many tears, and she herself was surprised at how easily they could flow. Bella took her by the arm and gave her hand a quick squeeze. Suddenly, the little old dressmaker burst outside the door upon the sidewalk. The two women stood in a trance, gazing at the gown, so white, in the show window. The gown denoted the purity of the one who wore it, announcing it to the world, much as the snow which capped the Snowy Mountains of home, high above Swanpool.

Now the dresser was listening to Bella. The little old lady was bent from the years of stooping over the sewing machine, which had fed and clothed her family for years. She was Mrs. Kassen, a widow immigrant from Germany to Sydney town, down under. She knew the sewing business, and she knew the whims and moods of brides to be and the latest fashions. Our ladies had been most fortunate to land upon Mrs. Kassen's threshold. As she ushered her prospective customers into her cramped sewing shop and its fitting room in the rear of the narrow building, a kettle or billy sang a merry tune upon a small stove. She reached up on a shelf and set cups and saucers upon a tiny table in a corner, seating the ladies in small, dainty chairs. The cups were filled from the singing billy with strong, hot tea. There was a tray of freshly baked tea cakes between a tiny pitcher of cream and a miniature sugar bowl of fine chinaware.

The ladies exchanged introductions as they enjoyed the tea and cakes. The wise old seamstress, behind her chattering, evaluated Bridgett and her companion. From her experience, she judged her customer, her station in life, her manners about the tea table and how she held her teacup. She read Bridgett's expressions and chatter, which would denote if she was a lady of means or a wench all dressed up. At a glance, Mrs. Kassen estimated the young girl's girth and weight and ascertained that her bulges were in the right location about her body; the material which would flatter her complexion and the yardage required for a gown and train and what she would need if the wedding was to be in the judge's chambers or a church house. She speculated about the number of bridesmaids and whether, by chance, this was the girl's first marriage.

As they sipped tea and nibbled the cakes, the date of the ceremony was named and some indication of the price range was discussed. The wise old Jewish lady could see at a glance the fact that the handmaid Bella could be relied upon to stay, shall we say, within the realm of reality, so scarce here in this colony so far from the culture of civilized Europe. Rising from her chair, Mrs. Kassen withdrew her tape measure from her apron pocket to indicate that the lady with the hair of red was, without a doubt, her next labor of love, and that she would transform this budding woman into a bride.

Bridgett had the body and style. The seamstress had the skill and materials to create a gown long to be remembered down in Swanpool town. Samples were shown and measurements taken. Bella spoke often, softly telling the old one that the mother of the bride had gone to her reward at Bridgett's birth and that she herself was married and from a family of class in Italy. She produced the bank note of Limon O'Leary, which she carried in her handbag, only to prove the ability to foot the bill.

The morning was gone when the young women said their farewells and hailed a hack. To the hotel they galloped. When the swaying carriage came to a screeching halt before the shoppers' quarters, the doorman leaped to open the door and assist the ladies to the walk. Bella paid the fare. She and her mistress were much too excited to sit at the dining table for lunch. They went to their room, collected their baggage, and rang the hand bell in the hall. The bell man mounted the stairs to assist the guests and their bags to the lobby below. The bill was settled and the doorman hailed a hack. A bow was made, directions were given to the driver, a tip of a shilling was given and away they went to the train station to board the westbound Limited which was soon loading on the station track number nine. They had their tickets in hand, and a red cap beside them to wheel the luggage to the waiting carriage. The handsome conductor punched the blue tickets and tore away the portion for his record, leaving Bella holding the stub which stated the destination: Swanpool, a six-hour journey.

The train ride back to the station at Swanpool was quite nice. On the journey home, they talked about their bridal selection – a white satin dress featuring a pearl and crystal lace bodice, fashioned with long sleeves with a cuff of four pearl buttons on the wrist. The gown would be complemented with a full-length veil of white tulle with scattered pearls and crystal beads.

Bridgett dropped off a telegram at a station in a town west of Sydney advising that she and Bella would arrive at their destination around midnight and would overnight with friends near the railroad station. Perhaps Mr. McCook could drive into town around 10:00 a.m. tomorrow morning.

Having done this, Bridgett watched the landscape slide past the carriage windows. She had time to think of her future, which would include the Captain and the home she would share with him, wherever he might desire. Deep in her heart she was restless to see what lay beyond her father's fences.

Captain Fred, no less concerned than his fiancée, thought of his future as he half-heartedly watched the Chinese coolies unload the green salted cow hides from below deck. His mind wandered about the past, which he kept to himself, a dark chapter now closed. As age crept upon him, he needed a future more secure. He wondered where he would take his bride after the ceremony, a honeymoon I believe it was called. He had talked to Sinbad at length. Even the natives along the riverbank had told him of the new "ma-ma" he would soon have. The primitive ones had instincts and knowledge that civilized people would never comprehend, and wasn't he, Sinbad, with his swagman father and native mother born to share the best of the worlds? The Captain over time had come to love the dusky lad with the broad shoulders, blue eyes, rusty wool upon his head, a flat nose with flaring nostrils and last but not least, a heart as big and kind as the entire Outback. Perhaps Sinbad laughed and told the Captain that he would love to see the woman he had not met, who was but a scant five years older than he was, come aboard and become a member of the crew of the *Victoria*.

The two men, one a Yankee, and the other a "half-breed," at the urging of the younger decided to clean the old tub. It had become a home to both of them; the older man in his crowded state room with the word "Captain" painted in bold letters upon the door of hand-carved teakwood, the younger man in his nook. Behind the boiler were his quarters, for he never wished for a shelter above his head as his mother had never had one. They had to go under a rock when an occasional storm burst forth. A partition in the above deck could be knocked out to achieve a quite comfortable room. Its door would be exchanged for the door of the deck below, on which the word "Captain" was written.

The walls could be painted pea green, and they could place a single bed with a brand new mosquito net draped from the low ceiling. Windows would be placed on each side to view the changing scenery they passed along the bank when the craft was under way. Shutteres could be added for privacy and perhaps a toilet installed and a dressing table with a large mirror. Yes, we will dry dock the old girl if we have to steam her to Adelaide. There the shipmates would spare no pains to refit her, even her leaking seams about the boiler. Yes, those lads could work wonders with a hull as sound as hers. The captain would spare no cost to make her the Queen of the River Murry and the sparkling Darling River. He might even retire the name she now bore and after the wedding, rechristen her the *Bridgett O'Leary*. As you know, gold, if you have enough, can accomplish many things. Perhaps people say, "It can't buy happiness." True, but it can certainly be a good down payment on it. I have noticed that.

These improvements would take some time, perhaps a month or two. Let the Christmas holidays pass. Time in this world down under is cheap, no one is in a rush to change. The Captain and his intended had to speak of these matters which crowded his mind. Somehow his thoughts were brighter and his steps had become younger. He shaved more often and his moustache was groomed and trimmed. The new cook from China saw a change in his appetite. His waistline became slimmer and he wore a tie. He changed his clothes every week. What had love wrought?

The *Victoria* had been loaded with hard-worn items down river; picks and shovels for the gold miners, rifles and balls for the ringers, Scotch whisky for the bars, and what was this with stickers upon the wooden crates reading, "Fragile, handle with care"? The labels read "Limon O'Leary." They were empty wine bottles to be filled from the cask that Bella's family tended, aging the wine until the following fall, then to be bottled. This new love of Frederick and Bridgett had to do the same, for only time can mellow things to so rare a flavor.

The *Victoria* had to be made ready. The gown of matrimony had to be made in Sydney. Some say that the ship should be renamed the *Love Boat*. Perhaps those Irish blokes could be a little more respectful to this couple, so prominent. Keep your bloody jokes to yourself, you scums. Mend your own fences. You don't want to rile a Yankee Captain, for hell knoweth no fury like a Yankee when he is angry.

Chapter VII

Festivities in Town

The river was swift, and the throttle at full speed. The fire within the firebox surged with each exhaust of the engines. Sinbad heaved more firewood into the firebox, banking the flames. He then filled the boiler with water, as the injectors screeched when the cold water was forced into the hot boiler. He knew the river as well as the Captain standing before the wheel in the pilot house, high above. The railroad trestle loomed ahead. The steamer slowed to a steady pace. The Captain went to the engine room below. He then reached his hand above his head to grasp the cord that led to the brass whistle just ahead of the smoke stack. This stack belched clouds of black smoke drifting harmlessly down the river channel, which was trying to calm itself from the thrashing that the rotating paddle wheel had churned it into, only to splash onto the muddy bank.

The water calmed as it raced to the Indian Ocean. The black smoke began to dissipate to again admit the ever-shining sunlight illuminating the blue sky above. Yes, the river quickly went back to its quiet self as if no steamer had ever disturbed its ageless passage, now tolerating such a machine, so noisy and dirty, piloted by a Yankee Captain so far from his own rock-bound coast in far away America. Distance and time were two elements not even a Yank could change. His hand grasped the whistle cord, which he pulled down with a mighty force. The whistle valve obeyed the pressure from below, and a cloud of white steam under 160 lbs of pressure shot in an ever billowing column, skyward, creating a deep mellow wail as it passed the throat of the whistle, resounding to the bluff above which the town of Swanpool nestled.

The wooden trestle allowed the puffing engines to drag their carriages and wagons each day to Broken Hill town, and eventually to Pine Harbor on the south shore. The melodious sound of the steamer awakened the town's people and the dock stevedores, letting them know that a steamboat was coming. It was the *Victoria*, a very special ship to a very special young red-headed woman sitting in a cart pulled by a spotted Welsh pony, now about blind, but still alert, with its mane clipped to a crop. Yes, my friends, it was Bridgett O'Leary and her pet pony Boo, until recently the love of her life. Move over, Boo. You may always be her love, but for now, you must play, shall we say, second fiddle. The channel was negotiated and the steamer was fast ashore. The engines had eased their labors, only some hissing steam escaped from them. The gangplank was swinging to the dock, the mail was delivered to waiting hands, and merchants claimed their shipments of goods from the wholesale stores down river. In all, the arrival was a joyful occasion for a river town.

Sinbad was first to spy the lady who still sat upon the driver's seat of the cart hitched to the Welsh pony. The Captain, after attending to the formalities of landing, set his cap of blue with the brass miniature anchor at a slightly more jaunty angle upon his mop of hair. For the life of me, why doesn't the bloke visit his barber more often? Perhaps he needs someone to remind him. That someone, Bridgett O'Leary, did not rush and fling herself into the arms of the burly figure that strode up the bank and across the common toward her and her pony. A slow smile shone about her face. The pony pricked his ears. His nostrils had picked up the Captain's scent, a scent he remembered well. There was a moment of silence as their eyes met. He extended his hand to grasp the dainty hand with the fingers so long, one of which bore a diamond ring that had not faded in the least.

Bridgett looped the reins about the seat and rose as he assisted her to the cobblestone pavement of the common. One fond embrace ensued. Her head tilted back and to the crew's delight, he planted a kiss so firm upon the red lips that were only partly closed, not so tightly as her eyes. The pony whined and stirred in his traces. His eyes were not that dim. A hundred other eyes turned to gaze upon this scene and a cheer of "tallyho!" rose from the bystanders. When the embrace was broken, our Captain, in one liquid motion of his powerful arms, swept up the girl into his clutch. As her skirts swirled, the lace of her petticoats strived to cover the calves of her shapely legs. The broad-brimmed hat was bound to her delicate neck by its throatlatch. Her purse dangled from her arm, and a cascade of wavy red hair flowed at gravity's call, as her hairpins failed under their burdens. Somehow the finger which bore the stone, so rare, seemed to catch the light so bright, and it too seemed to flash a silent cheer!

Great strides were taken by the man in blue wearing the jaunty cap. The stiff black brim reflected the sunlight with each stride toward his steamship. Who might that be, me dears, up in the wheelhouse high above the crowd with his hand upon that whistle cord. Could it be Sinbad, by chance? As the strong man mounted the gangplank with his lovely burden, with only one slipper on her feet, the other slipper now held close by an onlooker, the whistle was pulled.

A cloud of steam exited the whistle valve and gave a shrill blast which made the river surface tremble. The mist from the billowing steam fell upon the crowd. Yes, it was that devilish Sinbad, his Irish eyes shining, giving salute after salute of the vessel's whistle. To everyone's delight, the ship gave a lurch as the river current changed and the Captain skipped a step, danced about, and his wiggling burden was no help. Suddenly, he and his darling lunged with a great splash into the river Darling, which only sang the song that its current had always murmured, from time immemorial.

Beware Captain, that river can claim your dusty butt whenever it chooses. Sinbad roared nearly as loudly as the now dripping whistle above. Don't laugh now, my lad, your father will probably demote you to deck hand, if he ever quits sputtering as he holds his lady fair above the current. The river vagabonds and the stevedores dropped their burdens of cargo and hoisted the couple to terra firma. A lad, who was fishing from the bank, cast his line and hooked the hat that only moments ago had sat upon the head of our Romeo Captain. It just so happened that a bevy of whores, who served the needs of the crew, had pitched their tent of red canvas with the bar in front lined with bottles of spirits, all in a row. The wenches quickly spread a blanket about the shivering form of our ladylove and bore her into the tent, so red. They kindled a fire and changed her wet clothes for a dress donated by a lady above the bluff and delivered by a runner on a bicycle. The lady was warm, the crew even warmer. A wise old codger from his seat upon the loafers bench only chuckled as he packed his pipe, and was heard to say, "Tis but right, the old reprobate needed to be baptized, and now he knows what she looks like before she sits before the mirror upon her dressing table."

The deck hands slapped their captain's back to stop his coughing and sputtering. He drew a deep breath and emitted an oath that would have made the paint peel from the ship's hull, if any paint were there. The cook rushed a bowl of chicken noodle soup still steaming to the red tent and to the stateroom marked "Captain." The now dripping man, the bearer of the dignified title, stood in a puddle which grew even wider as the water flowed from his frame.

When Sinbad approached, the Captain drew back his fist and swung at the boy, now a man, who ducked quicker than a tiger snake could strike. With a laugh he spoke in his pidgin English.

After the Captain had regained his balance, his drooping mustache dripping even more, he spoke again with a civil tongue, "I might have known that blasted Irish true father of yours, wherever he may roam, would be proud of you, whose hand has rested upon my whistle cord, when only I, as a captain, have that privilege. Thanks to you, the only love of my life may return the ring she now wears. I should throw you overboard to fill the bellies of the crocodiles, which would more than likely die of food poisoning!"

The ladies of the night did a quick repair to Bridgett. They had makeup to spare and were masters at quick repair as their livelihood depended upon deceit. The cook from China soon had the Captain dried and dressed. Our Yankee Fred marched down the deck to the cheers of the river rats and the winks of a few of the members of the oldest profession. This approach to the gangplank was somewhat different. Bridgett in a Mother Hubbard dress, barefooted, a towel forming a turban about her head, and a smile upon her face, took the hand of her true love and they mounted the plank, this time to stride upon the well worn deck, hand in hand. The deckhands doffed their caps. Sinbad in shorts, the only garment he ever wore, his calloused feet set apart, bowed low, so low his gold earrings tumbled to his cheeks, and gave a smile so bonny the angels in heaven must have blushed and strummed upon their harps of gold. Here and now, a bond was forged between the two young people which only death could break. She curtsied and held forth her hand on which he placed a kiss. "Yes," she thought to herself, "I, myself, am marrying a ready-made family."

Sinbad straightened his body and his face, and spoke softly. "At your service, milady. Welcome aboard our humble ship." He took her for a tour of the steamer, which now was at rest along the river bank and only hissed and rocked a bit, groaning at her moorings. If the craft could have spoken, she too would have sworn to be at the lady's aid, but ships speak, only through their masters, God rest their souls.

When at last the touring party climbed the steps to the pilot house, the Captain, gentleman that he had become, with a humble bow presented her with the now limp whistle cord, which upon the command of Sinbad had created the scene of pandemonium. Now the cord obeyed the hand of Bridgett O'Leary, soon to become Bridgett Barrick. The white steam again shot from the whistle valve, and again the shrill blast deepened into a melodious echo, as Bridgett slowly released the cord and the valve closed. The crowd roared their approval. A few pistol shots were fired into the air, and the flock of cockatoos that were at rest in a dead tree, screamed their shrill call and flushed into flight only to circle the steamer and land upon their tree again. "A good omen," the natives quietly said, as everything that happened was observed by the elders. Through natural events their gods had spoken to them through the ages before any steamboat ever chugged up the Darling River, a river so dear to their primitive hearts, a river they did not own, but used only to sustain their lives for so many generations.

The wedding drew nearer with every brilliant sunset. The date on the calendar was agreed upon, when the spring commenced in October. The couple would stand before the man of the cloth, friends, family, servants, and yes, even the natives, on a porch at the station house near Swanpool. The house Bridgett was born in and where she lost the mother she never knew, who had lived a short but happy season there, may God rest her soul.

Word had reached the station of the happening of the morning. Bella and old Limon O'Leary had set forth in a buggy, or rather a carriage led by ponies stepping so high, carrying dry clothes and shoes for Bridgett. They too joined the unplanned festivities, as an uninvited mob had crowded about the common and wharf below the bank of Swanpool. The whores had done a brisk business at their portable bar. The drinks they poured of watered-down whisky and rye loosened tongues and purse strings, and the gathering had grown into a roaring party. Some fool was sawing upon a fiddle. The young people were dancing a jig upon the common. The old people were clapping their hands to the sour tune of the fiddle. The red tent with the flap which covered the entrance now opened on occasion to eject a lad with tousled hair, the shirt tail barely tucked into his pants, a weak smile upon his face, and a carrying a lighter poke, which once held a bit of silver, nuggets of gold fresh dug or an ounce of gold dust which would never reach the bank, now safe in the bosom of the fat madam rocking away in her rocking chair. Her black bouncer pouring the weak drinks, and her hand was upon her strong cane of oak.

Forgive me for leading you astray from the now reunited couple of our intentions. Bridgett, you must understand, was never allowed below the bluff of Swanpool, because that was where the hooligans held forth. She had been sheltered from life's other side. Being the lady that she was, she had only ventured below to meet her love, now her protector. The vagabonds, the tarnished ladies of the night, pimps, gamblers, and drunks who were often referred to as the scum of the earth seemed to accumulate around steamboat landings to prey upon innocent newcomers to this land of newfound opportunity. The foam and flotsam of the river always accumulates in eddy waters, much as human flotsam does.

Our Bridgett in her exposure to life's other side was not so naïve as some might think. She had always been protected by her loved ones, and now the Yankee Captain had become one of them. These people, the ones who lived upon the weakness of their fellow men, were well acquainted with the Captain and his legendary wrath and showed their best sides to him and his lady, so fair, who was so rare along the waterfront. The mob scattered away from the carriage of Limon and Bella, who alighted before the gangplank of the *Victoria* moored to the wharf. They joined the couple, and ascended to the Captain's quarters. The mate Sinbad led the way.

Limon laughed at his daughter and commented, "Aye, me dear, you appear as the wreck of the Hesperus. The leap you have just taken will, no doubt, not be your last, my bonny lass." After he lit his pipe, he told Bella to see if she could put his daughter in repair. He then joined the Captain and Sinbad in a stroll to the ship's saloon, where the cook, Wong by name, was setting the captain's table for the mess dinner aboard the vessel. The men laughed about the ducking as they sipped some brandy. Then, the captain told Sinbad to find himself a blouse, and put himself in some kind of shape to be in the presence of a lady who would, in a few moons, be his stepmother, no less. "Tighten up, my lad, and only speak when you are spoken to," he said.

Upon Sinbad's departure, the Captain and Limon in the quiet setting of the ship's saloon turned their conversation to business and the cold, hard facts of life, the life that was unfolding before their eyes, a melting pot of humanity. They somehow had to steer their ships of destiny through this life to win the race and the victor's crown. Limon, with his wisdom and many years of experience, expressed his feelings of trust to this man his daughter had selected for a life mate. They would be the parents of his grandchildren, he said, whom he hoped would live and thrive upon the lands, vineyards, and livestock he had wrested from this fickle land. The land had waited so long for hands that could tame and cultivate it into blossom, to make a home and livelihood for his offspring, who now stood upon the threshold of maturity.

The door to opportunity opens only to the ones who are stouthearted, to those who can laugh when everything goes wrong until they survive to come forth again. With a grin Limon added, as he lit his pipe and blew out the match, "We have done so much and this opportunity opened up to us."

The Captain thought for a spell and doffed his cap on the table with a flurry of his mustache. Now standing erect, his broad shoulders squared, he spoke, "By the rock-bound coast of my homeland and my ancestors, who threw off the yoke of oppression, by the grace of the God that has guided me to this table, I hereby swear to uphold and protect your daughter as long as I may draw breath upon this green earth of his."

Upon this oath, the two men raised their glasses and drank a toast to the names O'Leary and Barrick. They drained their glasses as the bottoms went up. Before too long, Bridgett and Bella entered the saloon escorted by a bowing deck hand. Chairs were set before them, and they were seated at the table soon to be joined by the smiling Sinbad, clothed in more proper attire. He stood behind his chair, using the manners that his white stepfather had tried to teach him: how to handle silverware, how to wait to be served, how to keep his voice down. For now, his shining hour had arrived. Please Sinbad, don't belch, or gnaw a bone, or spit upon the floor. You have made giant strides from savage to civilized.

The captain rang his hand bell to summon the cook from the galley. The chow was ready to serve. A steaming platter was set upon the table, a goose baked golden brown on another platter surrounded by stir-fried vegetables, a large bowl of sauce made from the giblets of the bird and another platter of his famous egg rolls. Table wine was poured and plates were served, as a smiling Wong silently stepped back to observe the diners as they helped their plates. Yes, the Captain's crew had met this unplanned occasion with a flair so brilliant that he himself could not have envisioned it.

Sinbad tucked his napkin about his neck, flashed his best Irish smile, ate with proper use of silver, and never missed a move, thanks to the saints above. Limon, sport that he was, joked that the captain's goose would soon be cooked, too. He only hoped it would be good. An air of friendship and unity was born right there within the saloon of the aging *Victoria*, chaffing at her mooring at rest upon the bosom of the river Darling, which had set the stage for the show that was just beginning to be acted out. The players were taking their places on a stage as wide as two continents on opposite sides of this green earth, little to the knowledge of the players, known only to the gypsy woman and her ball of crystal, inside her striped tent.

One day, perhaps, I could prevail upon the Yankee and the Aussie woman soon to become his wife to come with me to this tent beside the quaint caravan of the Romanians who pledge no allegiance to any land. This one, the one born with the veil over her eyes, will take the hand of the bridegroom and with her gnarled old finger trace the lifeline engraved by the creator deep in his palm to predict his fortune. I wouldn't have to be a gypsy to read the look that would spread about her old face to know that she had seen a future she would not speak of, for fear of having her fee of silver revoked from her apron pocket. She shall polish her crystal ball with a purple cloth of velvet, then take the hand of the bride and smile, because the picture within would be much clearer. Her lifeline would reach to her wrist. This scene has taken place only in my mind's eye, so be off with you, spirits of gloom, this is a happy occasion to be enjoyed by all.

The party of O'Learys departed the dock. The Welsh pony Boo was asleep on his feet on the common of Swanpool. Bridgett and Bella mounted the cart and untied the reins. The cart rumbled down the road to the station house, closely followed by the carriage of the father of the bride-to-be, his heart in tune to the changes to come, as they were certain to arrive, just as certain as the spring comes about. May we leave these people to their thoughts and plans, the moons to rise over the coastal mountains, and the sun to bake the deserts beyond.

Yes, as the Captain had planned, the *Victoria* was dry-docked. She was being refitted as she should have been long ago. The ladies would roll away on the smutty little steam train to far away Sydney and the Jewish seamstress who would fit the wedding dress to Bridgett, according to Bella's wishes.

The thoughts of the father of the bride-to-be turned to his future son-in-law. You must understand, good men were few and far apart in this young country, especially responsible men, mature enough to have sowed their wild oats and survived their harvest, so to speak. Yes, the man was a Yankee not turned to fun and frolic as the Irish and Italians. Yes, his heart had a soft spot that his Bridgett had located, and she, with her many young charms so endearing, had enlarged a broad entrance to let a bit of sunshine illuminate his other good qualities. In fact, he had few really bad qualities, if only he could mellow a little more and not be so crabby. How else could he have achieved the station in life he occupied?

The old man held the reins to the high stepping mare that was single-footing at a brisk clip toward his vast station. Had not he too been a bit, shall we say, ornery in his younger days? "Yes," he thought, "my lass has her father's good judgment about her sunny self."

With a slap of the reins the carriage disappeared into a cloud of red dust. Well behind that red cloud, came the two-wheeled side cart bearing the lady of the station and her beloved friend and servant. The women spoke of Sinbad, the ward of the captain. The term son didn't set too well with the fair one. She told Bella that he was a bit coarse, a bit uncouth, but his smile was so tender she was glad it was his feet that had such calluses andt not his heart. For she could see, in his Irish eyes, that his love for the captain was as big as all New South Wales. Yes, she would accept the overgrown laddie who seemed to be placed in their life and future. She wondered where he fit in the scheme of things.

With a lilting laugh, Bridgett slapped the reins that ran to the bit that Boo despised so much. "Get about," she shouted to him. "The sun will set upon us on this dusty trail. If you could tighten up a bit, you would be worth your oats." Boo's stiff old legs limbered a bit, and soon the light-hearted colleens drove to the waiting hands of Charlie McCook, who waited for Boo with a bag of food and a fond greeting. The young ladies mounted the steps and disappeared into the shadows of their home, sweet home, upon the range.

Chapter VIII

Going to Meet Him

The steamer *Victoria*, with her long overdue overhaul, rested upon the dollies of the dry dock in Adelaide town. The Captain, Sinbad, and their cook Wong, rented a cottage nearby. Wong cooked and was their houseboy. The tailor from Hong Kong set about designing a new suit for Frederick and suitable attire for the now young man at his side, Sinbad. A suit of European style was out of the question for him. The tailor knew the fashions of the South Pacific. He designed a tunic of silk, a floral design he had seen in the Fiji Islands. This shirt-like garment had a long tail that hung below a generous loincloth with a sash knotted about his waist.

No shoes would fit his enormous feet, as they had spread so wide and the soles of his feet had become hardened and leather-like. The tailor sent for a cobbler who fashioned the good fellow a pair of leather sandals with brass buckles, and then upon his wooly head he formed a turban which wound about it, giving some height to the somewhat "squat" figure he possessed from his native blood, perhaps. He then sent the lad down the lane to the jeweler for him to pierce his ears and fit him with gold earrings.

Upon his return the next day, Sinbad was outfitted in his new wedding costume, and there he stood. "Shiver me timbers!" He looked as though he had just stepped out of "The Arabian Nights." He was a dead ringer for his namesake, Sinbad the sailor, from the long, long ago. So good that he was not crammed into Western clothes. Now, if only the gifted tailor with the slanted eyes could transform the salty Captain into a handsome bridegroom. This is quite an order, but the groom, if his gold holds out, will probably fair as well as his man.

The captain's credit was good as his name was known far and wide. Time had flown, and the winter or rather the dry, as it was called here down under, was passing quickly. The rains had come, and the snow high above in the mountains was soon to melt. Shipwrights, as talented as the tailor down the lane, refitted the steamer. The Captain paid the bills and workers knocked away the chocks that held the dollies upon the dry dock ways, which had held the weary steamer. With a cheer and a splash the *Victoria* slid into the river Murray. She rocked a bit then settled gracefully upon the bosom of the water. The Captain mustered a crew with no problem, as the dock was crowded with deckhands, anxious to sign aboard a vessel so grand. The crew kindled the fires and loaded the ship with firewood. They filled the boilers with water, fresh drawn from the river. The Chinese cook was about his new kitchen. Sinbad had tried the whistle, and deckhands had stowed their gear in their quarters. The Captain, beneath his grumbles, was proud of his spacious new quarters which would soon be fitted with lace curtains and the bridal bed, for which he had paid a handsome price, but any woman would be proud to grace such a craft.

His first cargo was a mob of Italian laborers, masons, I believe, who were needed to build permanent buildings of brick in the shack town that the gold strike had spawned up river. The men would camp on deck, with their tools and hardware below with the mail and express packages. The hour had come for departure. Steam was built up and lines were cast off. The whistle blew. Bells rang. The throttle was opened, and after some hissing and groaning of the engines, the paddle wheels began to turn, and the steamer glided with a lurch to mount the current of the swollen Murray River. Slowly, the *Victoria* and her cargo of men and materials began her maiden voyage as a newly overhauled steamer under the command of Captain Frederick Barrick. She flew the flag of the British Empire, only to be commanded by a Yankee whose fate had brought him to the other side of the world to seek his fortune and now to take himself a bride, who without a doubt, was the finest of them all. Here in Australia, she too was a transplant from the Emerald Isle, the old sod of Ireland. We must wait patiently for the wedding day, not far away. Catch the incoming tide, Skipper, stoke the fire, advance the throttle, and set your course for Swanpool town where you are expected.

The stage was set, the stage lamps were lighted, and the players awaited the curtain to be drawn. The captain, as he stood before the wheel of the proud newly fitted steamer, decided, if things were going as planned, there would be a ceremony to rechristen this once grimy steamer, work horse that she was, to the Bridgett O'Leary now that her appearance befitted such an honor. Steer well, my man, a few more bends of the clear cold river Darling, and a long whistle sounded as the railroad trestle loomed ahead. The town of Swanpool would awaken to the cry of "steamboat ahoy!" The cry would travel afar, as only Captain Barrick could blow a steam whistle with such flair.

The natives would send the word on their hollow log drums soon after the launching of the boat. They also loved Sinbad, their brother. At each river landing, a few, maybe only one naked black man would appear smeared with different shades of wet clay designs that bespoke his name, rank and tribe. He would never speak but would give a nod which Sinbad quickly acknowledged. The runners would then turn and vanish into the bush. When the moon was in its correct position, the drummer would beat with sticks upon the log so hollow, resulting in booming resonant sounds that carried for many miles upon the still cold night air, a drumming done in a code so old no one remembered when first it was heard, long, long before the birth of the savior, away in a manger.

You see, Sinbad's mother follows his every movement, little to the knowledge of the white people. The Captain's hand which pulled that whistle cord was still about the wheel handles when a dark figure tapped upon the back door of the station O'Leary and smiled to the cook, also of aborigine blood. No word was spoken, no need. She went directly to the house of Bella Monsorretti, if you must know her full name. Bella put her own house in order, dressed and went straight to the bedroom of Bridgett O'Leary. Bridgett, about her bath, grabbed her dressing gown and flung open the door that Bella had just tapped upon. Bella, the serious one that she was, flashed that Latin smile and said, "Before the sun sets, you, my dear, will hear the distant sound of the steamer *Victoria*, as she blows for the town of Menindee."

An embrace followed a squeal emitted by the woman with the abundant hair of red. "Make you ready, my Bella dear, as I must, for my appearance should be my best foot forward, you see. Tell my father to shake the dust from his frame to go to the landing, as a knight in shining armor is about to set foot on this fair shore."

Soon the household was in a dither. Horses stood to be hitched to a chaise to seat six passengers, the driver above. This chaise or carriage was used on rare, important occasions. A team of two matched geldings gaited the rack. Quite an appearance they made with none other than Charlie McCook seated in the driver's seat above. Sure enough, a lad burst into the compound, and with a shout, "there she blows!" The chaise was brought to the steps of the porch. Bridgett and Bella, assisted by Limon himself, swung aboard. With old Charlie mounted in the seat of the driver, the horses stamped and snorted, ready to strut their stuff. Charlie lifted the reins, released the brake and away they went with a cheer from the household servants. The dogs ran ahead baying away, only to stop at the station gate hung wide by a lad they called the gateman. Many eyes unseen followed their progress along the winding road to Swanpool town. Under the bluff they went to the landing common and the gathering crowd about the wharf. The steamer blew her whistle again. Shouts of welcome were heard. Children danced. The bottles of grog were set about the bar. The painted ladies, their trade to ply, lounged about their camp, as they had heard that the cargo today was the Italian masons, so far from home. Perhaps they could cheer them a bit.

Limon and Charlie hitched the team and put their oat bags about their snouts. The ladies remained in their leather upholstered seats, as the men went in steps so measured to where the gangplank was to land and the ship to moor. There would be no performance today upon the gangplank, as happened before. This welcome would be more to suit the dignity of people of means, shall we say.

As the *Victoria* cleared the channel beneath the railroad trestle, a hush fell over the crowd assembled upon the dock. Then a murmur arose. Have we made a mistake that by chance a steamer so fine, has gotten ahead of the old *Victoria*? The murmur rose to a roar as the boom, all set to lower the gangplank, kissed the dock as it had done so many times before.

Was that Sinbad in his new shorts, a shirt about his body, and a cap of blue upon his wooly head, the cap of a first mate? And could that by chance be his new sandals upon his feet, so wide? Yes, my dear, it was Sinbad. He, like the steamer, had a new hold on life. The whistle sounded again. Yes, no doubt it was the *Victoria*. The dark-skinned Italian passengers let out a greeting cheer. Those lads about the shipyard in Adelaide must have not only been shipwrights, they must have been magicians.

Old Limon spoke to Charlie McCook. Bridgett's gloved hand covered her ruby lips. She loosened the ribbons which strained to hold her tresses beneath the bonnet, all trimmed with lace. Her glee was vented with a deep sigh, and to her friend Bella she said, "My ship has arrived, me dear. Can you believe how beautiful she rides upon the water. The paint has done wonders for the old girl. I only feel a bit of pride, may I say, as it swells upon my bosom."

"Yes," Bella replied, "I only hope she is as sturdy as she is beautiful. You must remember *mia amica*, beauty is but skin deep. What is beneath that paint is *più importante*," meaning more important. She mentioned that with the boss of masons she had to speak the name "Monsorretti," in the village of "Dominico," away in old Italy, as many of her family still tended vineyards which climbed the mountains much as they do here in Australia, her adopted home now.

Bella, the rather plain stately young woman that she was, made clear to Limon O'Leary her wishes to communicate in a very proper manner with the older Italian lead mason. Limon, being the gentleman that he was, spoke to the lead mason who spoke but little English. That was never much of a barrier to an Irish man, who knew well the jealous nature of Italian men, and used his better judgment. He approached the lead mason, not a young man, perhaps fifty years of age. The two men shook hands. A welcome was extended after Limon informed the man, Pedro Ingratta, that his station was but a short drive away. He told them to camp temporarily hereabout the river bank, and the following day he would send two wagons driven by two of the Italian men who worked upon his vineyards and winery to transport the men and their belongings to camp among their fellow men.

Upon this news, Bella was delighted for she longed for news from Italy. Bridgett and her party awaited the unloading of the masons.

In the formalities of the landing, papers had to be signed, money exchanged for the passage, and mail delivered to the postman. Sinbad stood aboard with his arms folded about his barrel chest and a smile upon his face. He saw the ladies still sitting in the chaise, only after the crowd had thinned and the captain stepped forth, walked his gangplank and shook the extended hand of Limon O'Leary, with whom he then had a hearty *abbraccio* or hug. One of the men was in his prime, the other was beginning to bend under the burden of age, that inevitable burden that becomes heavier with each year passing, until it is no longer bearable. The two men loved the daughter and the wife-to-be. Blood, as you know my friends, is thicker than water. A blood bond can never be denied, but first a bond must come about, a water bond. Then and only then can a new blood bond be created, such as this bond we are witnessing upon this grassy river bank. At times the captain grieved for the money he had spent on his faithful river boat, now glistening in the relentless sun, the sun which seemed to delight in baking every creation upon this remote land, animate or inanimate. The reptiles had learned to go under the surface of the land. The animals fed at night, sleeping in what shade they could find, a rock or cliff face, but a ship had no refuge. She had to only endure the burning rays of the midday sun.

Today our Captain was proud of the refitted steamboat and the investment that was long overdue, which he could well afford. The captain bid his mate to mind the ship, stoke the fires, and maintain the water level of the boilers, as she could explode unattended. As the men approached the rig, Charlie McCook was still perched upon the high driver's seat. The ladies, so proper, were still seated upon the leather-upholstered seats, their umbrellas held over their heads, chattering as only two females can. They ceased their chatter, and turned their faces to meet the gentlemen, so dear, as they neared the chaise. Our captain on his best manners extended his hand after a bow, so low, to the lovely hand which reached forth to grasp his. The connection was made and a current flowed. Only lovers know the feeling. He nodded to Bella who returned a proper smile. Charlie spoke a crisp, "Good day, Captain."

Bridgett collected her wits as only the Irish can, and spoke, so clear, "Aye, Captain, and when did you trade that old tub you and your man Sinbad did master? Or did you shanghai this bonny floating palace from some failing duke or prince? Perhaps only you, that crew of ruffians who now man this dreamboat which lies at rest here about, the name plate *Victoria* and the whistle, so brash, remain. Even your mate on your deck himself cuts quite a wake."

A Yankee can, if need be, express without an oath flowers upon his tongue, especially to his ladylove. He gave a reply to fit the occasion, and with another bow, he spoke simply. "I and my mate have spent our time and means upon the old tub that you mentioned, in a feeble effort to please me lady's eyes, so blue. No, we did not steal her from a prince, we only strove to fit her for a queen, whose hand I now hold so firm, and pray she finds it to her approval."

Well spoken, old Captain. May you always handle the storms and tempests of life as well. At this point, Bridgett pushed her bonnet back, folded her frilled umbrella, threw her loving arms about the strong square shoulders before her and planted a kiss upon the whiskered face of the Yankee Captain. Bella frowned. Charlie spit a stream of tobacco juice. Old Limon smiled as he kicked the dust from his battered boots. "May I suggest, my children, that we retire to a place more private. There is a pub upon the hill, where the tea can be poured and the stew is bubbling in a pot so black. Let's leave this muddy bank and the scum that floats ashore. Be off, my fine friends."

The men climbed aboard the rig, and the driver cracked his whip. The team sprang ahead, and with a wave to the crowd our party soon mounted the bluff and drew up at the park. Charlie leaped from his seat above to assist the ladies to unload, hitched the team, joined the group, and opened the door. A barmaid bid them a fond welcome. With a curtsy to the ladies and a bow to the men, she led them to a table beside the fireplace which filled one wall.

The flicker of a fire, coals aglow, and pots hung from cranes of iron decorated the place. Teakettles cheerfully whistled as a plume of steam escaped their spouts. When all her guests were comfortably seated about, she smiled and spoke, "And what will it be, me friends? May you rest your weary bones and allow my humble self to spoil you but a bit. Ladies, I will show you the powder room and you gents may find your way to the outhouse at the rear. Now perhaps a glass of stout will settle the dust which rests upon your throats. My porridge is famous hereabout, and my pastries are fit for a king."

"A shot of whisky for me," old Limon ordered.

"The same for me," Charlie added. "The ladies would like a goblet of wine, perhaps."

The mutton stew was served. The Captain his tea did sip, as he had eaten aboard his vessel. The whisky and wine did loosen the tongues of the Aussies. A frolic about the floor was made, and hearts were softened, even the Yankee one. Plans were made and dates were set. At daybreak steam would be made aboard the ship. They enjoyed the fellowship and food of the pub. The *Victoria* was now being loaded with cargo. No more salted cowhide. Now a cargo of wool bales, fleeces of Merino sheep that the swagmen had shorn, bound for the mills of England, so far, were being stowed aboard. One more voyage to make a wedding gown to fit Bridgett. The Italian masons would settle in at the gold strike shack town up river and return to Swanpool when their work there was finished. A grand wedding would take place upon a porch of a securely deeded homestead set upon 5,000 acres of the lushest grazing land along the river Darling. Stretching for many miles beyond Swanpool were Limon's vast land holdings on which he held squatter rights and to which the deeds were, shall we say, somewhat clouded.

Chapter IX

Making Preparations

Bridgett and the faithful Bella sat upon the railroad station bench awaiting the little passenger train, which would chug its way over the long high ridge of the Blue Mountains where the city of Sydney lay beside the bay of many coves, the city where the dressmaker awaited, her labors now finished. The trip was long. The train stopped often for fuel and water and to load and discharge passengers.

When a woman is young and in love, the hardships of the day are but a trifle. The women set out on this journey in a festive mood. With the wedding date was not far away, Bridgett thought of many things. Among those thoughts were the strong shoulders of her husband to be, his rough hands, so skilled, his bearded face, trimmed so neat, his handlebar moustache, all waxed, the fire that flashed in his deep blue eyes, the quick way he always assisted her, and last but not least, his ability to pay his bills. Didn't he own outright that beautiful steamer, now so fit? And the half-breed boy almost a man was so quick to learn. Could she fit into his life and become the lady of the house, or should we more properly say the ship? For everything must be shipshape if a smooth voyage comes about. She, her will so strong, had managed her life so far even without a mother's care. Hadn't she set her cap to win the Yankee Captain's heart, and now his name?

Bella, so close to her age, had never been a mother to her. She had been more like the sister Bridgett had never had. She had only that roughneck ringer, her older brother, Sport. The family Monsorretti, the Italian family, labored in the vineyards and winery to settle their debt to her father, as he had paid their passage from the crowded shores of Italy many years ago. Limon had built them houses and garden plots and furnished the necessities of life. In return, they set their hands to carve a beautiful farm from a desert, borrowing the life giving waters of the River Darling to quench the dry but fertile sands thirst. Italians posses a love for family and home life, a love they have taken around the world wherever fate may plant them. They take root and become fruitful. This family, of which Bella was a member, had extended its love to the motherless Irish rose, who had never known the lack of family affection. Limon, the squatter, never a fool, let this relationship blossom and mature, but now the fruit was ripe, and the season for harvest had arrived. Bella had already been harvested by a hardworking husband devoted to her and her young family.

Yes, the season was late. Bridgett's fields had to be plowed and her crops planted. A surge of excitement flooded her heart, goose bumps rose upon the nape of her neck and along her thighs. She said to herself, "Will this day, my dear, never arrive?" She twirled the ring, the one set with the diamond so clear upon the finger of her left hand, which told the world of her betrothal to the blustery captain. Soon her marriage ceremony would be performed, and the little band of gold would be placed on her finger to announce that to the world as well, and may the saints in heaven bless this union. She had gone out upon a shaky limb, so to say, selecting a seaman almost overripe.

The little engine of the train on which Bridgett and Bella were riding to Sydney was built in Liverpool, England, some years ago, and packed upon a tall sailing ship for a passage to the Island Continent of Australia. Perhaps four long dreary months at sea, channels to negotiate, tempests to brave, and calms to endure were required, only to be unloaded one fair day on this far shore. The little engine never missed a stroke as it pulled the passenger cars on which our ladies relaxed over the high passes that the Irish track laborers had blasted and shoveled, the passes which men with no vision had said could never be built. The day was late, and the sun was setting behind the dividing Coastal Mountains' crest. There, before their eyes far below, lay Sydney, the city by the bay. This great harbor is said to be one of the most beautiful spots upon this earth. It is said that it could harbor a thousand ships in perfect safety.

For a moment Bridgett remembered something of Australia's founding as a colony of Britain. Australia had been discovered by the British explorer of fame, Captain Cook, in 1770. He had landed at a bay a few miles south of the bay at what was now Sydney, which he called Botany Bay. There he claimed Australia for the British Crown, after Britain lost its American colonies in their war of Independence in 1774-1783, including its debtors' colony of Georgia. The British Crown needed another outlet to house its prison population and so established a penal colony in Australia at Botany Bay in January 1788. The larger area of the colony was named New South Wales. It was soon discovered that a harbor superior to Botany Bay lay a short distance north, and there the capital of New South Wales was established and named Sydney, after Sir Philip Sydney, an English soldier, courtier, poet, and writer.

The little puffer belly engine ground to a stop at Sydney station. Bags were unloaded. A taxi was hailed and driven to a hotel near the garment district and the sewing shop of the Jewish seamstress, so skilled. Soon upon their arrival, a generous bedroom with a view of the bay, no less, was waiting for them. Baths were drawn, clothes soiled by the soot and smoke of the engine which climbed the mountains were brushed and hung about. Bella unpacked the street clothes, packed so neat, both for herself and Bridgett. She was first to bathe as Bridgett, now in love and bubbling, hummed a tune and danced about the room, only to fling herself across her bed, clothed only in her underwear which strained to cover her charms so voluptuous. After a bit, Bella emerged from her bath. A sash tied in a bow with a flair held her brocade bathrobe firmly about her waist. She leaned over, letting her hip-length hair which had never been cut and was as shiny black as ravens hang down. She shook the droplets of water from the shining mane with a toss of her head, gave it a quick twist, and wrapped a towel about her head. Then Bella, her English so poor, spoke to the one upon the bed, "Your bath, milady, awaits your highness. Maybe the cold water will bring you back to Earth."

The ladies awoke the next morning to the hustle of the street traffic. After the hot tea and sweet muffins that the maid delivered to their door, they powdered their noses and away they went to the little shop of the seamstress. Greetings were exchanged, and the woman ushered them to the fitting room in the rear of her shop. There upon a rack hung the wedding gown of white satin with white lace trim. The bodice was off shoulder with long tapered sleeves, and the gown had buttons in the back and on the cuffs of the sleeves. Bella fussed about the fit of the gown, she would accept only perfection. Finally, a bank draft was signed, a receipt was written, and many fond farewells were made. Off to the cobblers they went for slippers to fit her feet. A boy was hired to help with the packages. The day was spent, and again the sun sank behind the dividing Blue Mountains. The streetlights were lit. Back in their room, they relaxed a bit, chattering away in excitement of their day's purchases.

Now mind you, many Italians had migrated to Sydney town, many to open cafes in the neighborhoods where they settled. Bella, as all Italians, was close knit and on inquiry she sent a runner to her relatives' house nearby. Soon a carriage arrived at the hotel doors, and a dignified man stepped to the sidewalk. A handsome man he was, his manners so perfect. "Signor Ingratta, at your service," he said. Yes, it was a cousin of Bella's.

After a fond greeting in Italian, introductions were made. Bridgett looked odd, to say the least, standing with these dark-skinned people who spoke such a flowing language, constantly using their hands. They climbed into the carriage. The horses' hooves clopped upon the pavement down dark narrow streets. The carriage rolled until it stopped at a gate which was flung open to admit the coach to a courtyard with a gushing fountain dominating the center, from which water splashed into a pool. The family Ingratta rushed into the yard. The gates were closed. Hugs and kisses, sighs and laughter amused the Irish lass, for she might as well have been in Naples. The walls about shut out the world she knew. Bella, for once, was beside herself and among her relatives. Finally they turned their attention to Bridgett, calling her the *sposa*, their word for bride.

They set a large table and brought dusty wine bottles from the cellar, chilled in bowls of silver full of ice. The popping of corks was heard, candles were lit, and toasts were made to their families and to the long and happy life of the *sposa*. Before too long, great bowls of spaghetti making a cloud of steam were brought from the kitchen. A bowl of tomato sauce with spices galore followed. Wine glasses were filled, a blessing was said, and the plates were served. A meal and great fellowship was enjoyed by all, although our Irish rose understood little that was said. Back at the hotel, they were tired but happy after a day never to be forgotten.

Aboard the *Victoria*, now docked at a river town named Wentworth near the confluence of the Darling and the Murry rivers, supplies and wood were taken aboard. Young Sinbad was given more responsibilities of deck duties, relieving the Captain somewhat. He now had more time to record his accounts and just to prop his feet up on a rail. One of his peeves was the fact that the Murry River was the state boundary between New South Wales and Victoria, the state to the south. Taxes and landing fees were to be paid to whichever bank he landed on. He had never liked the officials in Victoria State. It seemed that they discriminated against him for not being a citizen. For this reason, he had definitely decided to change the name of his ship from *Victoria* to the name of the lady soon to become his wife. The overhaul had changed her appearance, so now was the appropriate time to change the name of the ship to the *Bridgett O'Leary*. The admiralty had to be notified in advance. That night the forms would be filled out and the following day mailed to Adelaide, to register the new name on the date of the ceremony of marriage.

With a faraway look in his eyes, the Captain dreamed of the lady of his intentions. Her regal carriage, her hair as red as the setting sun, her heaving bosom white as snow, the flair to her hips which her corset struggled to control, the lilt of her laughter, the clip of her speech, all rolled into one delectable package that now wore his diamond ring of engagement. He was proud of the remodeled stateroom that would be their home for now. He did not wish for her to look upon the room until he carried her over its threshold. He had made no effort to decorate the room, providing only a handsome bed of mahogany which he had traded for and a dressing-table with a large mirror. His bride would add a woman's touch.

Limon O'Leary, who had spoken to the Italian lead mason at the Swanpool landing, made preparations to receive his guests here at his station. Bella's father, a good man, was no longer indentured to Limon. Now he was somewhat of a partner in the vineyard and winery. Benito Monsorretti, by name, was glad to assist his fellow immigrants from Italy. The two men,

Limon and Benito, decided on an area which had a large shed and a nearby spring of clear water. They agreed the men could camp about the shed. Limon could supply horses and carts for their transportation, and his commissary would supply staple groceries.

They would have the company of their fellow countrymen, who at times grew lonely for company. Don't forget old Limon never missed an opportunity to feather his nest. Two wagons were hitched and rattled away to the river landing. Benito and Humberto, Bella's husband, were at the reins. The newly arrived Italians crowded about their campfire as the cool morning air settled to the river bottom. Coffee mugs were in their hands to wash down the hard bread they munched upon. They had had quite a frolic the previous night. The wine had flowed. The ladies of the night had tried hard to welcome the group. Their madam was counting her take.

There was no song and dance to be heard as the sun peeped over the mountains. The hoofbeats of horses were heard upon the bluff road, soon to pull up at the river bank camp. The morning air was rent with greetings, acquaintances were made, and belongings loaded in one wagon. The other wagon was soon crowded with strong young workmen, whose future was uncertain as most of them would never return to their beloved Italy. The horses strained into their harnesses. Hooves clawed the earth of the bluff road. Some men leaped out to push the wagon and help the struggling team. Soon level ground was gained, and away they went to vanish in clouds of red dust. Dust seemed to lie awaiting to be stirred by feet or wind, only to boil up in clouds that obscured the sun. Limon saw the approaching dust clouds as he sat upon his shady porch. A satisfied smile came upon his face, upon which time and weather had left their prints. Bridgett and Bella joined him to greet the newcomers. The greeting was made, and the yard was clear. Bridgett told her father that she planned to have her wedding ceremony performed upon the station house porch, the same porch where her mother was brought as a bride, the porch upon which she and Bella had played house with their dolls scattered about. Could he perhaps, on his next trip to the growing town of Menindee, engage a parson, a man-of-the-cloth, to perform the ceremony of holy wedlock?

"Ay, me daughter, you have asked me for so little of life's goods, and me duty is to bear the experience of this occasion so near. I would be honored to comply with your every whim. This porch we now sit upon is as you say steeped in many memories, both sad and glad. I commit myself to make this occasion one to be long remembered here in the valley of the river Darling. Just as soon as my teams are free, I myself will journey to my mill at Menindee to fetch the lumber and my carpenters to enlarge this porch we sit upon which is much too small for the wedding party. My men will build a gazebo so ample that no elbow will nudge my ribs."

He knocked the ashes from his pipe, stood erect to take his daughter in his arms, and placed a grizzled kiss upon her rosy cheek. He then spoke in a voice with a tremble, "This new addition will endure the ravages of time to stand as a witness to the day of this union, to whomever it may concern."

Bridgett flung her arms about the father she adored. Her eyes were twinkling like the stars twinkle at night. She spoke a pledge in a voice so sweet on the name of the saints above to always cherish his name and honor the vows she was about to make.

In a few days time the carpenters' hammers did ring. The sawdust did fly upon the breeze. The painters painted the whole station house a gleaming white and the gazebo with its ginger bread trim decorating every corner. There was none equal in all the valley. Bridgett and Bella could only draw deep breaths. Bella shifted to her mother tongue to say, "*Grazie a Dio, che bella!*" meaning, thank God, how beautiful. The dogs, which always lay beneath the porch, had returned from the barns to look in puzzlement at the new building situated at the corner of the porch.

Back on the River Murry, up river at a booming town named Albany, about as far as the Captain could push his lovely steamer, he loaded a cargo of wheat bound for the flour mills down river at Remark Town, far below, then to broker a cargo for up river Menindee, oh so close to Swanpool. There they would moor, empty and knock out her fires, and sit upon the clear waters of the River Darling to await a very special cargo. Yes, my loves, the wedding party and a bride so radiant, and a new name for both, the bride and the steamer, which would bear not only a new name but a co-owner. It would then become our steamer, no doubt!

You may, by now, realize that this was no run of the mill occasion. The bride was from a long line of Irish people that went as far back as the Vikings, perhaps even to the king of the Vikings of the north, who raided the coasts of Iceland, raping the women and enslaving the men. After a thousand years, who knows to the contrary? The Viking blood brought the red hair, fair skin, indomitable will, even the sure manners to the bride-to-be, Bridgett O'Leary.

When I gaze upon her body, so perfect, the crowning glory of her red hair and a freckle or two danced about her face when she smiled. She had a regal carriage. Why she herself could have been the Queen of Eric the Red, King of the Vikings, standing in the bow of his long boat as he approached the misty shores of Ireland, sword in hand. What whim of fate had brought her to this altar upon this distant shore, on the other side of the globe, in New South Wales, to soon be united in holy matrimony to this blustering swearing seaman, the Yankee Captain Frederick Barrick? He was of mongrel stock, perhaps one of Attila the Hun's ruthless warriors, or some Roman soldier, a member of Julius Caesar's legions, which conquered the British Isles and the uncivilized tribes that called them home.

Yankee Fred himself had pledged no allegiance to king or flag, being of a rather ruthless nature himself. Even his title of Captain was self-endowed. He had no papers with the seal of a king stamped upon them. He had, most of his life been, if not a pirate, a freebooter. Yes, I like the latter title as I would pray that you be well informed of the two soon to be united by the powers invested in the parson, the representative of God almighty on this earth, whether it would be on a desert of the Australian Outback, or the rock-bound coast of New England, in North America. Be patient my good people, the cards have been shuffled in the hands of fate, soon to be dealt once more to the players in this game of life on the table we call Earth.

The gypsy woman sat in her tent so tattered with the faded stripes. She was born with the veil upon her eyes, which gave her the power to see the future as it was reflected in her crystal ball upon the table she sat behind. Hold out your wrinkled hand, and I will place the coins which make your vision so clear. Polish your crystal ball, for so if the full moon does rise behind the Coastal Mountains, so high, as the blazing sun retreats beneath the burning Outback desert horizon, so flat, I perhaps shall raise your tent flap to let your vision turn to our couple to see their future. I have the silver money if your vision is dim. Back to this day, old dreamer. The future will never arrive if today is wasted.

The steamer was being loaded with lumber from the coastal forest, so lush, to be delivered to the hands of the carpenters who were building a city at Broken Hill, the mining town where so many prospectors had rushed to seek their fleeting fortunes in the desolate gold fields, searching for the gold that lay hidden in the bowels of the red earth. Their tools and hard work showed the sweat of their brows in the sweltering heat. The lure of quick fortune had brought many to the north to a barren ridge of rock and sand, where life was hard for mortal men. Only the birds and serpents, so deadly, and lizards so fleet, had evolved to survive this uninviting land, the ridge which the creator had seeded with generous clusters of opals unmatched for size and beauty. The miners called this land Lightning Ridge.

Dig away, me lads. Some had left with fortunes; others hadn't and the dingoes had gnawed their bleaching bones which lay scattered upon the sun-baked desert floor. Gold had a magic lure. The zinc, tin, lead, and yes, silver, perhaps, were the true treasures concealed in the same area which would bring fortune to the miners, the ones who were not in such a hurry to collect riches.

Captain Barrick's steamer was loaded with eucalyptus lumber, stacked on the decks with barely a path open for the deck hand. He, at the wheel, set his course for the settlement of Wilcannia just above Swanpool town on the river Darling. It was a challenging passage as the river divided to two runs, barely affording a channel passage, but the natives had told him, after a gift of rum, that the river was flooding. The passage was safe, or possible, at best.

"Full steam ahead!" the captain said. "We can unload at Wilcannia, and then drift down to Swanpool on the full of the moon, the date of the wedding ceremony."

May Lady Luck come aboard your vessel, Captain. There are channels to negotiate, snags and sandbars to avoid the temptations of the shore. Oh yes! The perils did exist to entrap the weak, but our players were strong. Perhaps they were born under the correct stars. which God Almighty set in the heavens above the earth, where no mortal man can adjust his course to suit his whim! This wedding, so close at hand, was becoming the talk of the community, especially the Italian community. English and Yankees don't scratch the surface of romance, music, flowers, or sensuality that Italian and Spanish people possess. The Scotts were dour, the English were pompous and proper. The Yankees, oh those Yankees, they hadn't been in existence long enough to really have a culture. They had struggled just to survive life's hardships.

Perhaps they would soften up and laugh a bit more, as their puritan blood was diluted by Irish blood, after they fled their homeland and English rule. The Irish would never overcome the potato famine which had settled upon the Emerald Isle, which had them migrating by the boatload. I fear they would never become Yankees no more than they could become English. Here in Australia, there was a melting pot of nationalities: Italians, English, Irish, and a little of aborigine. The Chinese stayed to themselves. The Spanish were in the far-away Philippine Islands. The stew with its many flavors should be quite unique. Stir well, Mother Nature, for the ingredients you are about to add to your stew.

Bridgett and her dashing Yankee Captain soon would stand before this altar on this remote livestock station, set upon the verdant bank of the river Darling. Charlie McCook was busy about the paddock with several jackaroos and apprentice stockmen, grooming and training a team of iron gray horses, which would pull the vintage carriage that he would drive. Only Charlie would deliver Bridgett in all her bridal splendor from wherever bride's retreat for their arrival to the altar.

The father of the bride, Limon O'Leary, with the help of the Monsorretti men from his vineyards, worked about the gazebo, placing an altar and decorating the porch with garlands of greenery and ribbons. The yards were swept. Tables were set under the arbors to bear the refreshments and the wedding cake for the reception that would follow the ceremony.

The Captain, ah yes! Who, by the grace of the loving horn spoon, would act as his valet? Sinbad perhaps? Yankees were pretty self-sufficient. His Hong Kong tailor, being well paid, had done well. The Captain could dress himself and Sinbad. He had decided to ask Sinbad to be his best man, as he looked quite handsome in his Island garb. The Captain had been too busy to make friends, as he was a very busy man, never staying long in one location. He was a rolling stone, but he had acquired a lot of "moss." Until he met Bridgett, by chance, upon the Welsh pony Boo, he never really trusted anyone. His gruff manner never won friends, and he never influenced people by his abilities and hard fist, only to let a frail slip of a girl melt his heart of stone.

He would go to the livery stable and rent a carriage and team at Swanpool town. He and Sinbad could drive to the station with no problem. The people who called the dives beneath the bluff of the river landing home, the ones with few scruples, shall we say, the ones who would never be welcomed above the bluff, know their place in society and with few exceptions stay in that place. The Captain had often spoken a Yankee proverb: "There is so much good in the worst of us, and so much bad in the best of us, that it doesn't behoove any of us to talk about the rest of us."

The madam offered to press his new suit. The girls offered to tie his tie, and the gamblers gave him a new deck of cards. The shoeshine boy wanted to shine his new boots. The bartender offered a free set of drinks to the wedding party, and a stiff one for the road. The deck hands cut throats all aboard the *Victoria* and moaned about these dens of iniquity. They would give their worthless lives to protect her.

Enjoy your name, sleeping steamer, for the day after the wedding your name plate upon your bow will be ripped away, and a fresh painted plate bearing the name the *Bridgett O'Leary* will grace your bow. Your stern will proclaim Swanpool as your homeport, registered upon the ship registry at Adelaide town, South Australia, fees paid in full. This was a giant step for two proud people, a step not taken lightly by either. Bridgett's brother, Sport O'Leary, would give her away, as her father had vowed never to give away his darling daughter.

"She may have my blessing, but she is no 'gift,'" he vowed. Never argue with an Irish man, for your case will only fall on deaf ears.

Bella was in a dither, as the day would soon be upon them. Her children would be flower girls and ring bearer. She wished that the wedding would be of the Catholic faith, as she was devout, but if wishes were horses, beggars would ride. She could give the *sposa* a rosary to hang upon her bridal bed. Holy water could be thrown upon the couple to receive the blessings of all the saints, not to mention the Virgin Mother herself. Bella only crossed herself and busied herself with the clothes and hair styles.

By the way, mysterious things can happen during the night so dark, when the moon is but a sliver of a crescent in a starlit sky. Yes, things that have no explanation occur. When Bridgett awoke after a fitful night, there upon the pillow beside her head, rested a small metal box embossed with gold, locked with a tiny key that hung on a chain. She sat upright in puzzlement and, with hands which trembled a bit, she fit the tiny key in the lid's keyhole to release the lid, revealing a silver tiara to fit upon her head. Engraved upon the base were Latin words, *semper fidelis* (always faithful). No one had been seen to enter her chamber; all heads shook negative to her questions.

Her father only smiled and said, "Never question a gift-hand, me lass, a spell could be broken, only treasure it. Ah! What a gift to see ourselves as others see us."

With those words he lit his pipe and blew a cloud of blue smoke, cackled a bit and said, "Be off with ye." Bella gasped at its glitter as she fit it to the *sposa*'s head. A smile of satisfaction spread across her olive-complexioned face, so sincere. Its plainness mirrored her simple beauty, a beauty which would never fade as the years passed. Yes, perhaps she would mature to a more beautiful old lady than she was in her youth. Few of us do this, but Bella will, no doubt.

The ringers had mustered their mobs, and left some jackaroos at the line camps. Sport and his mates arrived at the station gates followed by a gust cloud of red dust which drifted back to the Outback from whence it came. A keg of beer was opened at the bunkhouse, banjos and fiddles wailed, cheers and toasts rang out, and several gunshots were heard.

Ole Charlie had to put a hard hand on these free-wheeling blokes. Enough is enough. This isn't the bush, you know. We have a bride who must not be disturbed. Her beauty sleep was most important. She had a reputation to uphold here about, as her beauty was most respected, pure as the snows which mantle the towering mountains beyond these foothills, mind you. Save yourselves for the formal ties at hand, then perhaps a bit of horseplay will be OK. As the steamer sets forth from Swanpool landing, there your riots will be more appreciated, shall we say.

I have failed to inform you of the activities of the ever-present, but seldom seen, aborigines. They clung to their old ways. The elders told age-old stories, as they had no written history, only paintings on rocks about the skills of haunting and the never-ending panorama that nature had provided for them.

Australia is a land of contrast. There is tropical vegetation in the north, beautiful beaches, fish aplenty, coral reefs unmatched, snow-capped mountains, coastal forests with forty species of eucalyptus trees, baobab trees standing as sentinels in the deserts, kangaroos from wallabies to animals standing on giant hind legs, higher than a man's head. There are flocks of parrots of many varieties, white cockatoos, masters of flight, screaming their shrill call as they approach a waterhole, snakes so deadly only a prayer can be said to save your soul, crocodiles called "salties," as they go from fresh to salt water, rivers, called billabongs, which flow in the wet season, only to dry to a trickle during the dry season.

Life is hard, to say the least. The people who survived these hardships, the aborigines, had a tolerance for hardships that more fortunate people never developed. They migrated with the seasons, and now with the civilization that the Europeans had brought to their doorsteps. They were amused with the lack of knowledge the newcomers had of nature's ways. They had watched old Limon over the years and saw his good nature and generosity. This land had given them their bare necessities of life as they knew them, but in times of the plague of drought this bounty was taken away. At those times Limon had let them wander his lands, never harassing them. He had been their white brother. They never, except in dire need, took his stock. The rains had come, perhaps with their powers unknown, and Bridgett was a goddess to them. They knew of the wedding and had watched the wane of the moon, their deity.

Now their camp was near the station. They silently crept into the bushes about the yard to watch the ceremonies and nod their approval. They knew Sinbad would be there. Perhaps if you looked at the ground the next day, you would see the pictures they had drawn in the sand, pictures which would express their evaluation of the couple and their future. It might be a year before rain erased these drawings. As sure as I am standing here telling this account, Old Limon will stroll over after the wedding is over, after the people are gone, to study the drawings in the sand, probably with one of the old natives who sat around his campfires. The message of what lay ahead for his children, fortune, fame, sadness or even death, would be recorded in the red sands of Swanpool station.

Never underestimate the spiral connection and this power that primitive people possess. The vision with which they could see this may have been the one thing which permitted them to survive the earth scattering growing pains which beset this developing planet. Civilization has a way of blinding modern man to these powers. May I quote the words of an old ballad, "After the ball is over, after the sun has risen, many a heart is broken, many a heart is sad." The wheels of fortune were spinning two stories which would become one, on the opposite sides of the world, oceans apart, and unfolding before our eyes.

Chapter X

Those Wedding Bells Are Ringing

The wedding day dawned. The roosters crowed, the cows lowed, the roosting cockatoos flew from their roosts shrieking their good morning to the sun, which would once more endeavor to bake this land and the creatures that struggled to survive until the life giving-rains returned. Aboard the steamer *Victoria*, the deck hands began their daily routine, swabbing the decks with mops wet with water from the river Darling. The fire in the firebox was banked, the water level in the boilers was checked, and the valves of the engine were oiled. The cook was in his galley. The aroma of bacon drifted on the early morning vapors. Hen eggs were broken, and the golden yolks dropped into a bowl. Tomatoes were sliced, and orange juice was squeezed into a pitcher. A newspaper had been thrown upon the deck. The milkman had delivered fresh milk from the cows, which he carried astride his donkey's back in a hollow gourd, now being dipped into the cook's pail to be boiled. Sinbad, the ever-smiling lad, awoke the captain and reported the day's weather as he had read it in the sky and clouds. "Today," he shouted, the news written across his broad features, his eyes gleaming, "is the day I am to have a new mother."

"Yes, yes, contain yourself, lad," the captain said, "none of your Irish shenanigans. Speak when you are spoken to. Be seen not heard, or you will receive the hard hand of your benefactor, and by the way, go just a mite slow on this mother bit. Don't let me have to remind you again, lad. You look quite handsome in your new attire. Now don't let me down, make me proud of you. Mind the manners I have strived to teach you, and don't be chewing that tobacco you seem to always have tucked in you cheek. There is a time and place for all things. All you have to remember is to stand erect, smile, and drive the horses I will rent. Drive them back to the boat, return the rig to the livery stable, keep curiosity seekers off the deck, pull the gangplank, and keep your hands off that damned whistle cord. May peace and quiet prevail. Tomorrow the ceremonies will continue. The ship will be re-christened *The Bridgett O'Leary* as the new nameplate will proclaim. The old name *Victoria* will be retired forever. Understand?"

A snappy salute and a crisp "aye, aye, sir" was returned, but still that devilish Irish smile and the twinkle in his blue eyes, which should have been black, sent another message, oh so subtle.

Breakfast was served. The deck hands, devils they may have been, loved the Captain and jumped at his command. They lined up and were handed their chow, then retired to their quarters. They themselves were in a festive mood. As the news had spread of the wedding, other steamers had tied up along the riverbank. The dens of sin were closed. The miserable people who plied their wicked trades were sleeping till noon and counting the take of the night before. Perhaps tonight would be good because the other steamers had people and crews aboard, and the festivities of the wedding and the re-christening would occur. Fresh people, fresh money, and gold fresh dug. Fill the bottles, water the whisky, smear on the rouge, shorten the shirts, heist the breast, a little advertising never hurt business, shall we say, "The fleet is in."

Make hay or gold while the sun is shining. A new skipper and his bride would stand in the pilot house of the new paddled wheeler, she to change her name to Barrick. Everyone on shore would be drinking a toast to that, even the steamer with her new mistress and namesake. She would feel the bottle of O'Leary wine as the glass bottle would shatter against her bow, and the contents would flow down her hull planks to mix with the ice cold waters of the river Darling and join the flood which would take it to the Indian Ocean, perhaps even to a swell or a breaker which would roll ashore on some Atlantic beach in North America, so far away.

Back to the Captain, who was trying to read his newspaper and sip his hot tea, as usual. He found his mind was only upon his love and the commitments he was to make this very evening, before the sun sank too low. He hoped to God above he would not tremble. Perhaps his neatly trimmed beard and mustache would cover any weakness his face might register, when he and Bridgett stood before the parson. Would he be able to collect himself to say in a strong voice, so all can hear, the words, "I do," so simple; and when asked if there is a ring, would he take it from the ring bearer without his hand trembling and place it upon the finger of his bride, dressed in her fine gown?

Surely his Yankee spirit was strong, which in severe times would arise to meet any occasion that may occur. Be as steady as the *Victoria* navigating the surging river floods and the coastal reefs just waiting to snare her and her cargo.

This is only a wedding, mind you, old skipper. The cook, the Chinese man, happened to be quite skilled with the talent of tending clothing, and had washed and bleached the captain's shorts, pressing them with a hot iron. He could have been a valet, as well as a cook, as he had helped him into his suit, tied his tie, and dusted his boots only to back off and survey his captain. He bowed and laughed his little laugh, clapped his hands, backed away to turn in the door, and vanished into his galley.

The Captain strode down his deck to the gangplank. A cheer arose from the mob that had gathered about the rented rig drawn up before the gangplank. The team of horses shone from their grooming, chewing at their bits in their mouths. Sinbad was wearing his turban high upon his head, his flowered silk shirt, the sash of his loincloth hanging to his knees, and the generous gold earrings hanging from his floppy ears. He looked as though he had just stepped from a storybook. A surge of pride went through Frederick Barrick's body as he climbed to the cushioned seat of the rig, the best one the livery man possessed. The horses surged ahead as they clawed the earth, and up the bluff of the river Darling through the cobbled streets they clopped along. A cheering crowd followed the handsome rig down the lane. The shopkeeper and his ladies stopped their walk to wave and throw a kiss or two upon the passing carriage. The Captain waved back. The village dogs came from under the porches to chase the two men, adding their barking to the din of the people.

Sinbad reached for the whip that stood in its holder beside his seat. With a vigorous cast, the pop of the whip sent a message to the team as they broke into a gallop down the red dirt road, which led to the station O'Leary. There a crowd of different types of people, good people, waited; the stockmen, the men of the Outback, the ringers, the swagmen, the jackaroos, the blacksmiths, the vintners, the Italians, yes, even a vagabond with a banjo strapped to his back with a song upon his lips. There, removed a bit to the bush, a group of primitive aborigines, black naked people, huddled about leaning upon their staffs. Even the old one had come from afar. These were all the friends of old Limon O'Leary, the squatter, who was still just as Irish as if he was in Killarney, so far away.

The gates to the station had been flung wide. The cloud of red dust that settled down the dirt road seemed to cheer the passing rig and the hooves which pounded the dry red earth. Glasses were raised and groomsmen ran to gather the reins of the team. The driver, best man for a day, Sinbad, and the groom alighted to the sod of the paddock before the station house. The crowd parted to make a path for the father of the bride, to walk slowly through the opening before him. He removed his pipe from his mouth, knocked the ashes to the ground with his pocket knife, removed his hat from his head, tucked it under his left arm, and extended his right hand to shake the hand of his elegant son-in-law to be. Sinbad joined the well-wishers and waved to his kinsmen, who returned the wave and began a chant low and soulful. Some of the younger ones leaped up and down in dance to honor the occasion. The parson prayer with his book in hand and a ribbon marking the place of his scripture, his head so bald and face so solemn, waited in the shade of the newly built gazebo, which was all decked out in greenery and roses of pure white. The flower girls, the children of Bella and her Italian friends played about in their frilly white organdy dresses. The ring bearer, in a white suit, held a pillow of white satin to bear the ring of gold, which the groom had in a small box in his pocket. The bride's maids, in their dresses of pink all alike, fussed with their black hair. Sport, the brother of the bride, stood in a dark suit, a bit tight, and fingered a black bow tie that seemed to choke him. He seemed tipsy and had had a dram of whisky to steady his nerves, no doubt.

Where is the bride? Will she be late? The hour had arrived, but where under the blazing sun was she? A low buzz arose from the eager crowd. Where, oh where, could the bride be lurking? Was this some Irish prank? Would she arrive? Would the Captain continue to mop his brow and pull the gold watch by the chain draped across his chest, holding it to his ear to be sure it was ticking? Charlie McCook had left the stable in the family carriage, hitched to the pair of iron gray horses since mid-morning. Had a wheel wrung off the rig, had the horses run away? Why was the Welsh pony Boo not in his paddock? There were speculations among the restless wedding party, and rumors flew wildly.. Even Sinbad had ceased to smile.

Only Limon O'Leary calmly stared into the hazy distance. He called to one of his half-blood ringers blessed with unknown vision, from his native mother no doubt. He mounted himself high upon a haystack, shaded his eyes from the sun, and stared into the distance for what seemed to be an eternity to the Captain, who wondered how he had arrived at a point in his life where he had absolutely no control over it. How, by the great horn spoon, had he allowed himself to let a slip of an Irish girl take the wind from his sails? Was every eye in the state of New South Wales cast upon him? These Irish were a bit slippery. Matie, don't begin to swear, the parson is about. Why wasn't Limon fidgeting? He only had his eyes cast upon the lookout high upon the haystack. He was frozen in a trance, it seemed. If he couldn't spot the dust cloud afar, no mortal could.

Suddenly, his arm rose to point, no word was spoken. He had seen a plume of the ever-present red dust which arose on the parched plain. Could it be the tardy bride? A cheer arose from the milling crowd. Yes!

The lookout called that he could see the iron grays at a steady gallop, old Charlie in the driver's seat, reins in his hands. The seat behind him was occupied, as was the one behind it. A receiving line was formed at the driveway. Sport O'Leary stood at attention as the carriage drew to a stop. Bella alighted from the rear seat, soon surrounded by her family and bridesmaids dressed in their matching finery. The radiant bride, dressed in her white full-length bridal dress, remained seated. Charlie's stable hand led the blind Welsh pony, by the name of Boo, with a side-saddle upon his back. Yes, his nostrils' flair caught the scent of his mistress, the special child who always had a lump of hard sugar in her pocket just for him. Sport extended his arm to steady his sister as she rose to step to the ground. Bella and the bevy of bridesmaids adjusted her tiara, the one from the gold box of her dear mother, who had to leave her as a baby. They swept up her gown and hoisted her into the waiting sidesaddle, after the lump of sugar had been given to Boo. Perhaps this was the last time he would feel her weight upon his back, which had a bit of a sway. They made a handsome pair as Sport led the pony toward the gazebo.

The Captain and his best man were standing beside the parson under the arbor, upon the gazebo, which had been hand decorated with white roses and green ivy. The brid,e assisted by her father and his old sidekick, Charlie McCook, mounted the steps of the gazebo. Bella, maid of honor, carefully lifted her train and followed her up the steps. Close behind came the five bridesmaids. The flower girls carried baskets of rose petals. Last was the ring bearer, carrying a satin pillow upon which rested two gold bands provided by the Captain. Old Limon, father of the bride stood under the arbor in his regular Outback clothes to witness the wedding ceremony.

The bride had been handed her bouquet of white roses with streamers of white ribbons. The bridesmaids' bouquets were identical to the bride's. The groom stepped forward to take the bride's arm as they now, arm in arm, moved to stand before the parson. The wedding party was thus assembled from the porch, and the singers performed the notes of an old Irish love song, "The Wild Irish Rose," accompanied by the strumming of a banjo carried by the swagman. The parson performed the double ring ceremony. His stern words proclaimed the vows to which the Captain responded the familiar words, "I do," in sickness or health, richness or poverty, for better or worse, so long as he might live.

After these words were spoken, and Bridgett repeated the words, "I do," the parson then asked, "Is there a ring?" The ring bearer stepped forward to present the satin pillow on which the two bands of gold rested. The groom reached for one, and as the bride extended her left hand, he placed it upon her ring finger. She, the bride, reached for the remaining ring upon the pillow and placed it upon the left ring finger of the groom. They were then told by the parson that the groom could kiss the bride, who tilted her head back to meet the lips of her groom. The parson spoke his blessings upon the couple, with the power of God that he possesses to proclaim to the world and whom it may concern, as no objections were heard, that the couple before him was now man and wife, and may no man set them asunder. With these words, a pistol was fired, and a cheer rose from the spectators. The singers burst into the familiar strains of "Waltzing Matilda."

The newlyweds were a handsome vision. She, with the hair so red, which had so many waves you might become seasick if you stared too long. He, in his crisp uniform, so blue, had buttons of brass each with a tiny anchor engraved upon them. Sinbad, with his exotic South Seas garb, turban upon his wooly head, still stood beside the only father he had ever known, the Captain.

The Captain stood by his wife-mate for life, the lovely Bridgett Barrick. He had pledged allegiance to this woman, a woman one in ten thousand. She perhaps was the only creation of God almighty that had his pledge, with the exception of Sinbad.

He now had a ring upon his ring finger. The thought kept recurring to his mind as it would for the rest of his life, however long it might run. The vision of the pure white gown she wore and the graceful hand she had extended for him to place the wedding band upon her ring finger, the sleeve upon her arm, and the cuff with the small pearl buttons which held it in place upon her wrist would always be with him. Four buttons of pearls, why four? Why did his vision lock upon the buttons, so small, with all the beauty in them? Was Fate, that fickle force, trying to send him a message? You, oh Captain, are not a superstitious man. That is for ignorant lesser beings. You always said, "People make their own fate." Have you let these Irish blokes' silly ways creep into your Yankee stamina?

The wine is flowing, the music is lilting, your bride is beautiful, and your father-in-law is rich. You have a strong lad, Sinbad, dreamer he may be, to bear your burdens. Bow to the toast being raised to you and yours. The lambs had been roasting over the coals for a day and were being served to the mob of well-wishers. Could that be the Lord Mayor of Mildora, His Honor, standing beside your father-in-law, Limon O'Leary? You have come far, old Yankee, laugh for once. Your face won't crack. You, me lad, have hit the jackpot. You and your missus stroll down the receiving line which has formed just to shake your hand in congratulations.

Could that be a table being set with candles and a cake, three layers it seems, with two small likenesses of you and Bridgett? These Italians loved a festive occasion, and they had spared no effort to create a happy atmosphere, here, thousands of miles from Italy. Bella and the bridesmaids sliced the wedding cake, and Bella insisted that the groom feed the first slice to the bride. With trembling hands he fed the first bite to his new bride. Cheers arose, wine was poured, and more toasts were made. The bride also fed her new husband a slice of the ceremonial cake, symbolic of the life they would launch upon the stormy sea of matrimony, its reefs and rocky shores, and peaceful harbors to navigate.

To be quite fair, Bridgett had, herself, done quite well. The Captain had, to say the least, kept his head above the water. He had in the face of dreadful odds, steered his life upon these wild shores. Didn't he salvage some of his treasures buried who knows where? He possessed a fine strong body, and he had escaped the ravages of strong drink and maladies that have ruined lesser men. And let's not forget the steamer *Victoria*, moored at Swanpool town.

Good men were not often to be found here on the frontier. Bridgett was no giddy butterfly to flit about from one flower to the next. Perhaps her mother so long dead gave her these qualities she had, more than the striking beauty and her crowning glory of red hair she certainly didn't get from her father. He gave her common sense, patience, humor, and the indomitable will of the Irish people. Yes, Fate had dealt the newlyweds quite a good hand. The cards could be read. How well would they be played? Only time would tell. Would they win the race and the victor's crown? Or would they take the wrong road at the forks and one day, come to the road's end or to an ugly snag?

Come on back to the festivities, old storyteller! The reception was in full swing. Plates were served, music was played, songs were sung. The groom had paid the preacher with one of his gold pieces. The bride had thrown her bouquet, and the children had soiled their clothes. Sinbad had slipped away to greet his kinsmen, who had given him a potion to ward off evil spirits, and had drawn their picture prophecies in the sand before leaving the paddock. The only sad face to be seen was upon the graying face of the old Welsh pony Boo. He too was wise. He knew his playmate and mistress was leaving. His legs that once would frolic were now stiff, and his teeth were worn and gone. But hadn't he carried her to the altar, today? Perhaps he too would leave this station before too many moons passed. Go back to sleep, old mount.

The Australian sun, which seemed hotter and more brilliant, had begun to sink into the west, only to rise on the American shore. Back in Swanpool, below the bluff where our steamer was moored, a crowd had gathered along the wharf. A deck hand had removed the nameplate *Victoria* from the steamer's bow, and it was now hanging above the bar of the bordello. The crowd that had gathered was not of the kind of people who were at the station house of the O'Learys. These people were also well wishers, but were the ones who perhaps had taken the wrong forks on the road of life; it may be short, but has many attractions to the unwary, sins of the flesh, false attractions to lure a body to take the wrong road. These people were pretty well lit, and demon rum loved a celebration! The fiddlers had rosined their bows; the ladies of the night had their paint dabbed much too heavily on their tired faces; and the gamblers shuffled their cards marked so cleverly, and rolled their dice, loaded to win. The traders spread their wares. The medicine men, with their formulas in hand, filled their bottles with a brew, an elixir of youth and health, to cure any ailment.

Yes, they loved old Yankee Fred, for wasn't he the one who brought them their customers? They were jackaroos so green and homesick, the miners who arrived to seek their fortune in the gold fields, the immigrants fresh from Europe who kept their life savings in their carpet bags. Yes, they were all grist for the gin mills. Did I by chance forget the Irish railroad trackmen, who were building the railroad to Pine Harbor, and the train crews who needed a little female attention, shall we say? The poor blokes were so far from home, and a body could become a bit lonesome, especially on payday, when the pay train ran from Sydney town. Yes, the Captain and his crew brought the lifeblood to these shores.

That couldn't be the gypsy troupe, their wagon drawn about in a circle, the flag with the new moon and the evening star mounted above. Yes, there was the striped tent of the fortuneteller, her crystal ball set before her. She, too, had heard of the wedding and awaited the return of the bridal couple, so happy. In fact, she had the newlyweds' images in her crystal ball.

Before leaving the station, Bridgett returned to her quarters. She went to slip into her going away outfit, with Bella's assistance. They carefully packed away her bridal gown, the one adorned with four pearl buttons. The heirloom tiara was placed back in her mother's gold box to await the next generation, so it be the will of God almighty! Next, they packed her steamer trunk, as she would need her personal apparel and effects. Bridgett was pulling up her stakes so to speak. Here at the station, Bella would now be the lady of the house. She would move her family to these quarters, and run the household for Limon, who was very fortunate to have her services.

He was a fair man, mind you. Yes, in his younger days he did squat a bit on land that wasn't being used, but he would pat where he had been patted. For, you see, he was a kindly old ringer and a respected man. The Captain himself had gained respectability by being accepted into this prominent family.

Sinbad was not in this group. He was with the station mates and commoners. Bella had instructed him to load Bridgett's trunk onto the rear of their getaway carriage. Before long, the bride, now dressed for the road in her riding habit, emerged on to the porch. Immediately the groom took her arm. Rice was thrown by the bridal party, children, and a host of well wishers. This custom had been handed down from generations as a symbol of life and perhaps fertility.

I, the storyteller, have myself become quite weary of the word "fate." Everything hereabout had been changed on this memorable day, here on the valley of the river Darling. Things would never be quite the same. May we now adopt a new world to follow the Barricks, Frederick and Bridgett, and, oh yes, Sinbad, now the ward of the new couple. His mixture of blood had turned out very good. He had the best traits of both, the Irish and the mysterious aborigines. The three climbed aboard the rented rig. Sinbad held the reins in his hands. The newlyweds, trying to shake the rice grains from their clothing, settled into the padded passenger's seat. The trunk was strapped behind the seat. "Be off," Limon shouted.

Sinbad braced his feet and slapped the reins upon the horses' haunches. They sprang forward, but the carriage remained in its tracks. The spoked wheels never turned. Sinbad lurched forward to land upon his face in the dusty road. The red dust of Australia rose once more. The horses were grabbed by the halters. The ringers, who stood about the road, soon had the team in their traces and hitched back to the rig.

A roar of laughter rose as Sinbad realized that some Irish bloke had pulled the kingpin from the hitch. Sinbad had been hoisted to their shoulders. After being dusted off and his turban placed once more upon his wooly head, the ringers hoisted him to his driver's seat, once again. He was sputtering some seaman's oaths the men had never heard. They, the men of the Outback, just couldn't let a seaman sailor that he was, come into their realm without an invitation. It was a prank, but now he would be one of them, one of the ringers. Old Limon looked quite innocent about the whole charade, a little too innocent. He lighted that infernal pipe once more and held the yard dogs' leashes.

Remind me to ask the gypsy fortuneteller to tell me the whole story and who pulled that all important kingpin that was in someone's pants pocket. Shall we, the wedding party, once again, try a departure? Shall we hope more luck? This time Sinbad, rumpled and dusty, glanced to see if the harness was, shall we say, shipshape. This attempt was as it should have been before, smooth. The well-trained team broke into a fast, even walking gait that could cover the ground to the steamboat landing at Swanpool, under the bluff of the Darling River. The shouts of "tallyho" had died out at the station. A change had settled upon the station house and the green paddock which surrounded it, nourished by the river, and the arid plain which seemed to stretch endlessly to the western horizon. Only the undulating hills broke the monotony.

Old Limon had strolled to the paddock. There stood the pony named Boo that had been a companion to the growing child who had become a beautiful bride, who had just sped away sitting beside a gruff Yankee sea captain, who perhaps should have remained on the bounding main, never to have steamed up the Darling River to take Boo's darling mistress away. Hadn't the pony been a faithful pal? Hadn't he pulled her cart to market down the dusty road to Swanpool town? Hadn't he nuzzled her pockets to get the lump of sugar she always gave him? Yes, Boo had.

He had smelled Limon as he neared the fence of his paddock. He followed his nose to receive the time-worn hands which now gave him a sugar lump, a tear-stained lump. "Yes, the flower of our station is gone. We knew one day she would drive away, old pony. She is destiny's child, old one, by the saints above, but she shall return one fair day. It may be only my and your spirits that witness her return, but she was ours for a season, now the season to bear fruit has come about. You know old pony, one day you left Wales to land upon this shore. Now we must value our memories, so tighten up, old one, and I shall do the same. I will bring you a lump of sugar upon occasion. One sunny day, yes, one sunny day, if the saints so will it be, she shall return to this sod."

Hurry on, spirited team. The Captain, now the bridegroom, had paid his gold for your services. Break that gait you walk and start to gallop. Darkness shall not overtake you on this road to Swanpool. Sinbad popped his whip and the carriage continued down the road. Sinbad was holding his turban upon his head with one hand and the horses' reins with the other one. Now they could see the bonfires which had been built to chase the lengthening shadows that the sinking sun had flung. Yes, my dear Bridgett, bride that you are. Your day before the altar is coming to an end, not before a gala evening about the dock. The crowd of river people await to welcome you to their world, so different from your sheltered, shall we say, life at the station. Sinbad had his welcome, painful as it was. Now you, my dear, are to become the Captain's lady. These characters I have told of before, the ones a bit tarnished, perhaps can, with a bit of polish, shine once more. They will love and respect you as they do the Captain of the steamer. Tonight it will become your new home. Your bridal bed is set in order. That Chinese steward cook will perhaps take the place of Bella. Please don't underestimate Wong. He will be your servant to smooth the bumps that roughen the new road that you have taken today.

You, my dear bride, were not informed as the crowd was. This evening, the steamer which rests upon the bosom of the river moored to the dock, she too, my dear Bridgett, before that slip of the full moon rises beyond the Snowy Mountains, will have a new name. The nameplate, so freshly painted, "The Bridgett O'Leary" in letters so bold, and a large bottle of your father's wine, await the christening ceremony. The dock master and the honorable Mayor of Swanpool town are now standing on a newly built platform before the freshly painted bow of the steamer. You and your husband, get familiar with that word however awkward it may seem, are mounting the platform. Remove that riding hat and the ribbon which holds it upon your head and let your tresses fall free.

The Mayor, in suit and tie with a white wig upon his head, the symbol of his position, handed Bridgett the bottle of wine. A deck hand, holding a hammer and nails, a bit drunken maybe, was placing the new nameplate in its place, high upon the bow so all could see. The hammer rang as the nails were driven home by the unerring aim of the deck hand. The Lord Mayor read his speech from a scroll that he unrolled before the now silent crowd: "By the powers invested in me by her Majesty, the Queen of England, I hereby proclaim that the packet steamer before me, on this day of our Lord, no longer will bear the name *Victoria* upon her bow, but will be entered upon the ships registry as *The Bridgett O'Leary*. May the grace of God bless the name and never again will she be known as the *Victoria*. Now may the bottle of wine be burst upon the bow plate by the honoree herself."

With that introduction Bridgett was handed the bottle of wine and with a mighty swing of her arm, the bottle was shattered. Its contents flowed down the gunnels and into the river Darling on which the steamer floated. From high above in the pilot house, Sinbad with the hand that had held the reins of the horses now held the whistle cord. At the signal from below, he pulled with all his young might upon the cord. A cloud of white steam formed as the valve released upon the whistle throat wailed a high pitched shriek into the twilight, soon to be followed by a deep-throated bass note that made ripples on the surface of the clear cold river water.

Would he never release the cord? Someone else might like to speak. Yes, the bride and namesake of the refitted vessel, now dropped the neck of the broken wine bottle, shook her hair to her back, and dried her hands with the towel that was handed to her. Her voice pierced the crisp evening air, "Yes," she said, "I accepted this man beside me this very day as my husband, and I accept this boat named in my honor. I only hope you, the lifeblood of the river, will accept my humble efforts to become a fit mistress and wife aboard *The Bridgett O'Leary*. May God record my words."

With her speech the whistle boomed again, and flags of Australia and the state of New South Wales were raised. The crowd went wild. The night fell and the bonfires became glowing embers. Slowly, the crowd drifted back to their abodes. The day had ended, a day never to be forgotten.

Bridgett had not seen the stateroom which had been remodeled and redecorated for her. It was compact. The bed was ample with mosquito netting draped about it. The closets would barely hold her wardrobe. Perhaps a woman's touch would help. She did appreciate his effort. To be frank, he did a better job than she had expected. Perhaps Wong, the Chinese steward cook, had helped in a pinch. All that could be heard were the sounds of the river, the gurgles of the current, the night birds, the bell which rang the hour, and the sound of feet padding the deck. She had changed into her nightgown after bathing at a washstand, upon which sat a large china bowl and a pitcher of clean water. This she was used to, as she had no running water at the station house. Her gown was made of pale blue silk with spaghetti straps over her shoulders. She was waiting in her gown and negligee with silk slippers to match. When his duties aboard ship had been secured and the night watchman was standing on the fog shrouded river, her husband would join her in their stateroom,.

The cockatoos had flown their roost, and their shrieks had faded. The revelers of the night before, now silent, slowly awoke and rubbed their heads to stop the throbbing. Sinbad and the deck hands swabbed the deck. Their fireman stoked the firebox and smoke rolled from the *Bridgett's* stack. Steam was being built. The smoke mixed with the morning fog, only to soil it into a dirty gray cloud that the sun had difficulty piercing. Wong, the cook, was preparing breakfast, soon to be served. An oath was heard, and the stateroom door burst open. Captain Barrick had overslept, and it wasn't funny to him as it was to the crew. His mop of hair, which had lain so smooth only yesterday, was now tousled. His blue suit was wrinkled and his boots needed a shine. He glanced toward the bluff the gypsies had left. He had meant to have his fortune told, but that could wait. He ordered all hands to cast off down river as a cargo bound for the coast waited at Mildura.

Wong had the Barricks' breakfast on a silver tray. He knocked on the stateroom door, and a cheery voice rang out, "Come in," at which Wong entered to see the lovely woman who now sat among the satin pillows brushing her abundant red hair. She had slipped into the dressing gown that Bella had packed for her. She rose to receive Wong and the tray of food. She smiled a "thank you." He bowed low, spoke a few words in Chinese, turned to leave and at the door bowed once more. He smiled, closing the door as he left.

Alone with her thoughts at last, she was happy. She was eager to see more of the outside world and less of the dreary Outback. Her husband was, beneath that crust and bluster, gentle and kind to her. Yes, she loved him, crust and all. She heard the whistle blow, and a shout from Sinbad, "All ashore that are going ashore."

Quickly, she tied her hair with ribbons, slipped on her slippers, opened the door marked "Captain," and stepped to the deck rail, to wave goodbye to the crowd that had gathered there on the bluff of Swanpool. Was her father standing by the cart that was hers? Old Boo, the Welsh pony, was standing in the shafts with his head once again erect. The ship paddled, and the wheel slowly turned as the current of the river turned her bow to display the name *Bridgett O'Leary.*

Yes, she did see Limon and Boo. Limon was waving his floppy hat in great arcs over his head in a fond farewell. She danced and waved. She was never going to forget the two of them standing upon the rise of the bluff, with the sun's rays dancing about the billowing fog.

Another pair of eyes saw the two old characters who stood upon the bluff. The Captain's hand reached for the whistle cord, while his chin trembled slightly. As he pulled it down, a column of white steam left the boat to send a salute of musical thunder to echo across the river valley. Goodbye, old man. Goodbye, old Welsh pony. Farewell to fond memories. A new day had dawned and new players would come upon the stage of life. Weep not, milady, the show has just begun. The curtain has been drawn on act two!

Chapter XI

Fitzgerald Town

Act two takes place in Tootaville, Georgia, USA, thirty-six years later. If you remember, a tired group of settlers from the Northern states had ridden through the night on a steam passenger train of the Georgia and Florida railroad company and arrived at its railhead in Tootaville, Georgia. The settlers had bought into a land development scheme, hoping to escape the hard winters of the north and to make a new start. One family had caught our eye. It was Shepard Barrick, Bridgett's son, his wife Chase, two boys, Bob and Dan, and Chase's father, the Civil War Veteran. They spent the night here at Tootaville, several miles from the land development area and the town to be named "Fitzgerald," after the founder and president of the development company. After a hearty breakfast had been enjoyed by the settlers, I approached the man who had impressed me on the train trip of yesterday. Yes, he said he was Shep Barrick.

After telling him that thirty-six years ago I had made the acquaintance of a Captain Frederick Barrick, I asked could he, by chance, be related to the captain? He then shook my hand and paused. After a long stare into space he said, "Sit down, old man, whoever you are, and I will bring you up to date on that rascal 'Yankee Fred,' as he was known all over South Australia. He was my father, God rest his soul. His river steamer was named for my mother, who till this day lives in a fine house in New South Wales, Australia, in a town named Swanpool. My grandfather, who now is a very old man, goes by the name of Limon O'Leary. My uncle Hiram, known as Sport O'Leary, is now the master of the family station. My mother has a fleet of coastal steamers and riverboats. My brother and a half-breed known as Sinbad, operate the boat line which has prospered no end, as my mother is as wise as she is beautiful. She is the brains of the company. My brother Limon, a quiet family man, much like old Limon, our grandfather, has a hand in the machinery, and Sinbad is now a cripple as he lost a leg in an accident. Yes, the man has some years upon him. He is a wonder at handling the deck hands. His sense of humor is perhaps the best in South Australia."

"This is great news," I said, "but, my new found friend, you have not spoken of your father, Captain Fred, the Yankee."

"My father, I never knew, only the stories my grandfather told me as a lad. My mother lived then in a fine house over the bluff at Swanpool, as she had a child, my brother Limon, and was carrying me in her womb. My father, never to be beaten, was in a race with a new fast steamboat that threatened to outrun the steamer he commanded, the *Bridgett O'Leary*. At full steam, the *Bridgett* was being overtaken by the new packet *Adelaide*. My father ordered his mate, Sinbad, to tie down the relief valve. 'Go to the hold, get two salt sow bellies, cast them into the firebox, then open the throttle to full speed ahead.' She, the *Bridgett*, sprang to life and held her place above the *Adelaide*, so new. Then, my friend, an awful explosion was heard to echo down the river valley. A jacket sheet, which had leaked steam for years, parted and the boiler exploded. My father at the wheel above was killed, and the *Bridgett* was blown to flinders, never to sail again. What a pity, a cargo was lost, the Captain was killed, the Chinese cook was found dazed as he was blown into a tree along the shore."

"What of Sinbad?" I asked.

"Several mates were blown away to heaven knows where, possibly to the Outback. We never knew as the explosion was awful! Ah! Sinbad, the lucky bloke, he lost only his turban and the lower part of his leg. He happened to be in the head toilet answering the call of nature, may we say. Sinbad now has a peg leg of wood, and never misses a step. He says he will never suffer a snakebite upon that leg! He loves my mother, he is a good and faithful servant to her, and spent much time with me as a child.

"My grandfather Limon told me much of the events before my birth. He, with his Irish ways, had seen the omen not so good for the captain. The aborigines had drawn pictures in the sand on the day of the wedding, signs which showed a short life for the Captain. And yes, the gypsy woman had taken him by the hand, the fortuneteller she was, the one with the crystal ball. She had told him soon after the ceremony, so gay, the picture she had seen in her crystal ball. She saw the lower part of a woman's hand, a satin cuff with four small pearl buttons, a button for each year that remained for the Captain. Yes, the explosion came almost to the day. Four years they were married.

"He, my grandfather, tried to tell the hard-headed Yankee to remember the date, but he only said that the natives were ignorant, and that old hag of a fortune teller was only after a gold piece. He held no stock in such and the like."

"My mother, the young Barrick, told me he had insured the steamer and its cargo as she too felt impending doom. She loved the Captain but as a fact, he was a bit hard to live with. 'Hellfire and damnation,' he often yelled. She never married again. She and her old friend Bella sit now in my mother's parlor, and sip tea and nibble on teacake. She, now a bit stout, is still a handsome woman. Her red hair now has streaks of gray. Bella's is white as snow. She is a mother and a grandmother to a flock of beautiful children. Life at the station has been good to her and her husband. Their wine is famous all over the world.

"Sport, now known as Hiram O'Leary, finally settled down. His ancient father doesn't know how many sheep and cattle roam the green valley of the Darling River. Their horses bred from the brumby stock have won many races and steeplechases. O'Leary's horses have become a breed to themselves! Perhaps the question has occurred, why, I, my father's youngest son, don't share a comfortable position there at Swanpool. To begin with, let me make myself clear. I, being a true son of Yankee Fred conceived aboard a riverboat, longed to see what lay around the next bend of the river, and mix and mingle with people from all walks of life.

"Yes, I was truly my father's son. My mother saved her genes for her first son, whose red hair refuses to lie flat. You could pick my older brother Limon, bearing the name of his grandfather, amongst a crowd his red hair stands out like the sun setting in the west. He, today, sits at a desk in my mother's office in Swanpool town. My uncle Sport and that Italian wife of his are trying to populate the Outback with O'Leary brats. Sport is a ringer for sure and will always be an Irish man, always some prank to bear with.

"My grandfather will never retire. He still rides out to the Outback land to sit at the fires of the aborigines. Perhaps he runs naked with them. They are wise in the ways of nature. Many of them look as old and tough as the Ayres Rock, yonder in the red desert. Old Limon perhaps takes one of their youth potions daily. He must be one hundred years old, and he still smokes his pipe as I do.

"As a lad growing up, a jackaroo and apprentice stockman I was. I did have the old man's gift of horsemanship. Many times he said, 'Shep, me lad, a fine stockman some day you will be. That lass of mine, your mother, gave you quite a proper name. A Shepard you are, for a fact.' He taught me how to train a brumby, how to relieve the colic, and how to mix an ointment to heal a bruise or chaff where a harness rested, and how to build a saddle. Yes, he educated me to be a stockman, which I am to this day. I am never far from my horses. That was my position at the logging camps. Oh, I could handle an axe with the best of the fellers, but with the horses, oxen, and the skidder, I came into my own. For days and weeks, when but a teenager, I would vanish on walkabouts. Charlie McCook, my grandfather's old foreman and friend, was quite a man to challenge all comers in a bout of fisticuffs. The Irish love a scrap fight, and he was no exception. I had the strength of my father. My knuckles were hard as rocks, and quick I was upon my feet. My mother wise as she was, let me take my knocks, so to speak. She rather liked to see me rebel. Perhaps this was the attraction she admired in my father, the Captain, as she always referred to him. He died as I have told you, trying to win a race. He lost his last race, but to this day, a battered steamer nameplate, *The Bridgett O'Leary*, has a place of prominence upon her office wall, testifying to his dogged determination.

"At eighteen years of age, I had earned a name as a boxer who had lost few matches. I picked up quite a few purses, enough to pay my fare as I wandered about the mining camps and stations. I had no address as I moved often. There was a bout or match fair. I fought a lad who was famous at fighting and from a very prominent family. Six rounds I went with him, to the deck I went, once for a count of six. He himself had an eye that had swollen shut from my bare fist. When it looked as though the match would end in a draw a friend of his, with a wager so large, handed him a pair of brass knuckles to lay upon my head. My strength prevailed, and a blow to his head sent him to sleep. The knucks fell from his fist.

"I took my purse and caught the next train to Broken Hill town, to the Outback I trekked. One day a drover at a pub, a friend he was, told me of a letter he had seen addressed to Shepard Barrick, somewhere south of Lighting Ridge. It had the wax seal of the sheriff upon it. My friend said the lad I had sent to sleep never woke up! That night I caught the train to Port Pine, about as south as Australia extended. There a whaler had docked for supplies and to discharge a cargo of whale oil and whale bone. A Yankee vessel she was, flying the flag of the USA. I signed aboard as a cooper as I knew how to build barrels to stow the oil of the whales. I had learned this trade as a lad at the winery of my grandfather O'Leary. The anchor was weighed. We sailed on the tide and stayed at sea for over a year.

"One fair day, we sailed into the harbor of Seattle, Washington, USA, loaded to the gunnels with barrels of oil. I went upon shore. At that point, a shipmate, a true friend who made his home there, smuggled my clothes and purse from that last boat ashore hiding them in his own sea bag. I jumped ship, recovered my belongings, and bought a train ticket for a town two thousand miles east, a city named Milwaukee, Wisconsin. The railroad was, to my amusement, named The Great Northern. What an adventure I had survived. My education, which was quite short, had been extended. I now had a degree in the hard knocks of life on the run. My destiny lay before me with each clickety-clack of that railroad track. I felt a little safer from that sheriff on the other side of the world, in New South Wales, Australia, the home I would never return to!"

As I listened to the man relate his life story, I asked him to continue his experiences and the events which had brought him to be on the midnight passenger train of the Georgia and Florida railroad, deep in the south of the USA, a stronghold of the now defeated rebel south, defeated by the Yankee northern states. Few Yankees remained as the armies and carpetbaggers had long since returned to the now prospering northern states. How in thunderation did he expect to support a growing family, as it was obvious his wife Chase was far along in her pregnancy, and there were also two sons and a weary looking hobbling father-in-law, Mr. Cooper. He looked as though he should have been in the old soldiers' home, up north, but here they were at a hastily built hotel, at a railhead at a camp named Tootaville, you might say only ninety miles north of Spanish Florida. Only a few years ago, it was the territory of the Creek Indians, now vanquished to Oklahoma, and a few remnants, the Seminoles, led by Chief Billy Bowlegs, still on the run. No Australian sheriff will ever find you, for you are an Aussie by birth, now an alien immigrant. Australia might as well be on the moon. Breathe easy, only the gnats, mosquitoes, and rattlesnakes will harass you now.

The town had been surveyed to the satisfaction of Mr. P.H. Fitzgerald, president and treasurer of the Tribune Company. These people who were pouring in by train and in wagons covered with canvas were carrying chickens in crates, draft horses, oxen, milk cows, pigs, furniture, family portraits, even window sashes and panel doors. She, Chase, a frail woman with a limp resulting from a fall on the ice one winter, had borne her two boys, Bob and Dan, in Michigan with only a midwife to deliver them by lamplight. Luckily, they were healthy babies, much like their father, strong and fearless. The Barrick family had moved before from upper Michigan and its logging camps where the young couple was married. They had left Michigan as the northern forests were beginning to vanish before the axe. To Pennsylvania they moved. Her father, Mr. Cooper, the Civil War Veteran, had family in Lancaster County, Pennsylvania.

The Coopers, English pilgrims, landed on Plymouth Rock after a difficult passage on the historic ship the *Mayflower*. The Coopers, tradesmen they were, were almost as stern as the rockbound Massachusetts coast they landed on. David Cooper, by trade a saddlemaker, as you know, had his only daughter, Chasity. Her mother had been a Pelton of English descent and of pilgrim origin. She had died when Chase was a child. After some years in the North Woods the forests had been depleted. Dan Cooper needed a home, so he returned to the family farm in Pennsylvania. Shep, Chase, and their two sons accompanied him. They farmed the land for some years, and Shep acquired a team of Belgian Percheron draft horses, which he loved very much and spent long hours feeding, grooming, and training. They became his pride and joy. Perhaps he was still a stockman and not a farmer.

Shep Barrick despised the cold winters, the snow, and ice he never knew in Australia. Dan Cooper came to agree with his son-in-law. Chase also was intrigued by the south and its gentle climate. They remembered the newspaper advertisement of a while back, and wrote a letter to the Fitzgerald Land Development Company. They sold the farm, bought shares from Mr. Fitzgerald, and loaded a boxcar with their unassembled wagon, their household goods, livestock, and hay and corn to feed the stock en route. They made beds upon the hay for the boys, and after three days, they arrived at

Tootaville, Ga., six miles from the beehive of activity of laying out streets, parks, cutting timber, and digging stumps where the town was being built.

Can you picture perhaps three thousand people from the North and Midwest? Work gangs and carpenters built temporary shacks of slabs and tarpaper, the reason why the settlement was nicknamed "Shack Town." Drawings were held, and new arrivals were assigned to their lots as their shares were numbered. Actually, it was a drawing in which you only had a ticket with a number on it. If you had bought several tickets, the numbers ran consecutively, as your plots of land did. You could not pick and choose. The surveyors long ago, shortly after a treaty with the Creek Indians in 1820, had surveyed this vast area south of the fall line and west of the Ocmulgee River, beyond the forks where the Oconee joined the Ocmulgee, forming the largest river system in the state of Georgia, the Altamaha River.

The treaty land included the west bank of this mighty river to the Atlantic Ocean, with the town of Darien, Ga., being the port town. This treaty with the Indians opened a vast area to settlement westward to Alabama land. The large counties' boundaries were now defined by state surveys, then divided into militia districts. Maps of the new counties were filed in the county seats. Upon these county maps, land lots were defined and numbered, and each land lot was surveyed to contain 490 acres, more or less.

Renegade Indians, malaria, yellow and typhoid fever, and vast swamps with their dark interior known only to renegade Indians were hazards that discouraged settlement. Runaway slaves, outlaws both English and Spanish from Florida, and American colonists or settlers had set up a homestead on this wild land. The Civil War also delayed formal settlement of this vast area. General Sherman detoured north of the area, as little of the interior had any value to his army, which was living off the fat of the land. The only things fat on this Indian bank were the fat pine stumps and pine snags found among the vast longleaf yellow pine forests.

These forests stretched westward across to the Mississippi River, all the way to East Texas. Literally, millions of acres were covered with stately pine forests, which stood upon the gently undulating hills, pockets or bays, clothed in cypress and hardwood, poplar, bay, magnolia, red maple, tupelo, holly and oak trees of many varieties. Clear ponds choked with reeds and water lilies were populated with fish. There were perches of all varieties: bowfin, bass, jackfish, chain pickerel, garfish, frogs, and untold reptiles, deadly and beautiful. Alligators grew to sixteen feet, awaiting any creature they could subdue. There were several varieties of snakes, such as cotton mouths, moccasins, eastern diamond back rattlers, the largest poisonous snakes in North America, and their cousins, the bog loving canebrake rattler, and the seldom seen, colorful coral snakes, cousins to the cobra of India, and the tiger snake of Australia.

The lowland swamps at night during warm seasons vibrated with the croaking of bull frogs, tree frogs, and toads. The pine ridges supported a carpet of wiregrass, which supported several herds of horses and cattle, even sheep, descendant of the Spanish stock that the old Admiral Christopher Columbus and the Spanish settlers, who followed him to Florida, brought to this land. This stock probably escaped or was stolen by the Indians over the last two centuries.

The European traders were adventurers, even back to the first white man to explore and map this subtropical corner of southeast North America. Hernando DeSoto, marched his soldiers in search of the fabled fountain of youth, in St. Augustine, Florida, westward to the father of all waters, the Mississippi River. Steamboats much like the ones Shepard Barrick's father had operated upon the Murry River in far away Australia, had been running up to Macon, Georgia, on the Ocmulgee River, past the forks. The settlements or trading posts, founded by the half-breed Indian woman, Mary Musgrove long ago, were located from Darien to the mouth of the mighty Altamaha River, main stream of travel and commerce in South Georgia, before the advent of the railroads shortly before the tragic Civil War, which left Georgia in a state of dire destruction and chaos. Plantations were burned, crops destroyed, and vast numbers of slaves set free to fend for themselves at the mercy of carpetbaggers, people who followed the Yankee army south only to prey upon these poor survivors of war, both white and black.

This was the scene that kept recurring in the mind of Daniel Cooper, veteran of the march through Georgia years before when he was a strong man, riding with the Yankee cavalry through the virgin land, a land of new opportunity and no snow. Hadn't the newspaper advertisement, the one of Mr. Fitzgerald, the land promoter, lauded, "Throw away your overcoat and burn your snow shovel. No need to barn your stock, and grow a garden the year around. Have running water all year, even two field crops a year, fruit trees loaded with luscious fruits year around, even go bathing in the creek on Christmas day! There's fertile land and plentiful timber. Railroads are being built to connect the infant town of Fitzgerald in the heart of this, till now, undiscovered utopia; with the capital of Atlanta, the fastest growing town in the south; with the port of Brunswick, Georgia, and even close by Jacksonville and Tampa, Florida, the sunshine state. Don't delay. Send your money to the Fitzgerald Soldiers Tribune Company and become a shareholder at Fitzgerald, Georgia, soon to be the home of ten thousand contented landowners, professional business men, lawyers, and gentlemen of leisure. Your land is waiting for you." End quote in the Indiana newspaper, circa 1894.

After much thought and deliberation, Daniel Cooper, a man of some means, his beloved daughter Chasity, her hard working husband, Shepard

Barrick, their two boys, Robert, the oldest, and Daniel but a year younger, and the unborn that should arrive in February decided to move. These were the family roots so far, and this was the dawning of their new life, there in that new town. As I watched the Barricks and the old man, Daniel Cooper, leave the porch of the boarding house or hotel, as the sign proclaimed, they walked to the boxcar which held their worldly belongings parked on a team track, there beneath the towering pines. They had to assemble their wagon, food, water, and their draft horses. They depended upon this team to make a living from the virgin soil they had to clear during the winter and plant in the spring. They had taken the choice of two twenty-acre tracts of rural land, northeast of the neatly laid out lots of the town proper. Yes, two parcels they bought, sight unseen of the fertile land, so touted in the newspaper in far away Pennsylvania.

The Barricks were excited as they loaded their now assembled sturdy wagon, and hitched their muscular Belgian draft team, so glad to graze the green grass which grew so lush beneath the splendid pines. The water trough beside the hotel was filled from a spring of crystal clear water. Yes, the water was good as the advertisement stated. It gushed to the spring head to spill into a creek, House Creek, they were told. Tootaville did in fact seem a restful respite from the bustling cities of the north. What a wonderful place to raise a family! Even crusty old Daniel Cooper, a faultfinder at heart, could find no complaint. The warm autumn soon relieved the rheumatism that made life miserable for him. Perhaps sleeping on the cold ground when he was a soldier in the war, some forty years ago, contributed to this condition.

Yes, load that wagon, boys., Be careful not to damage the furniture they have brought from the north. The railroad company had allowed them two free days to unload their possessions. Hopefully it wouldn't rain for a week or so. The fall here in the south was the driest season of the year, almost as arid as it was in Australia, and great to harvest the bountiful crop they hoped to harvest. Shep Barrick was not a farmer, but the old man was, and a good one. They had a large tent of canvas to pitch upon their land, forty acres no less. Perhaps they would gather as bountiful a crop as they had been assured of, even with no fertilizer, as the virgin soil was deep and fertile. It said so clearly on the claim ticket Chase, the mother, had in her handbag she had held so close to her bosom.

Their land was nearly ten miles from the land office at the center of the proposed town of Fitzgerald. The road was crowded with people, black and white. The blacks reminded Shep of the native people of Australia. However these people wore clothes and spoke a strange, almost unclear English dialect, strange to his ear. The English that Shep spoke was the Aussies' slang modified with the Yankee brogue. He ended in a sharp, heavy sound which fell upon the ears of the native Georgia crackers as a foreign language, most strange.

These people upon the road from Tootaville to Fitzgerald could have belonged to a circus troupe. There were odd wagons, bicycles, carts, wheelbarrows, fine buggies, and people walking, take your pick. There was an Irish gang of trackmen building a railroad right-of-way. Shep could converse with them and was directed to the drivers of the town. Smoke arose from the clearing. They were rolling logs to piles which burned day and night, log rollers they were. Through the din of axes and saws, the glistening black men were wet with sweat, and the swearing farmers were striding about. There in the center of the clearing, with flags and banners flying in the breeze, was the land office with a huge sign saying, "Welcome to Fitzgerald." People from all states were welcome to this settlement.

Yes, it was truly a time to forgive and forget. Here beneath the pines, the virgin land had not been stained by the blood which had flowed so freely. Veterans, now graying, saw their sons and daughters rolling up their sleeves, pitching in to the tasks of building a town to be proud of. Their blood had mingled on the battlefields of Vicksburg, Shilo, Gettysburg and Antietam. Now in friendship, old differences were not forgotten, but laid aside. Soon the next generation, their sons and daughters, busy about the everyday chores, and even the unborn offspring would forget the bitter times. They would laugh and play, go to school together in schools yet unbuilt. Youth looks to the future, seldom behind. They would stand before the altars and take vows. Their blood would mingle in love and harmony. Yes, perhaps this town would in the future stand as a monument to forgiveness, tolerance, and even love.

The seeds of these values were being planted there that day in Fitzgerald. That day our friend Shepard Barrick, calling himself a subject of the Queen of England, not a Yankee, just a passerby in the northern states, had very little sentiment over wars which had been fought here in the USA. He was an Aussie and well proud of it. Work camps of free-wheeling stockmen, even squatters, pubs, dens of iniquity, outlaws, immigrants, and even gypsies, were an everyday scene in his native Australia. This town was much like Broken Hill, in New South Wales. His father, he was told, made his fortune dealing with just such itinerate swagmen and tradesmen, the same crowd he was raised with.

After the Civil War, in which brothers fought brothers, widows and children were left destitute to fend for themselves. Shep was quite familiar with black people, the natives of Australia, simple superstitious beings and their nomadic lives, who lived mostly in peace wandering a vast Outback. They had no one to fight; just to survive the extreme elements took all their effort. Here in Georgia, the blacks had been bought in bondage from their brothers. They had been sold by British, and yes, Yankee slave traders. Perhaps some Portuguese dealt in human flesh, too. The Spanish had an inexhaustible supply of American Indians to enslave, why buy black people?

Here in the South, the old South, the settled South, north of Macon, Georgia, many slaves had been freed to fend for themselves. Some went north to get jobs, many knew no skills except agriculture, timber, labor, and saw mills. They depended on their strong backs. Naval stores and pine turpentine distilled from the sap of the endless pine forest were the main source of employment for them. They had flocked to the site of the new town, which was under construction, and the railroad tracks which were being laid to serve Fitzgerald. This town was springing from the clearings as no railroad existed before Mr. Fitzgerald and his agents bought the tract that let sunlight flood into the shadows of the big pine trees, which now laid in piles, waiting their turn to be devoured by the dancing flames of the fires which never went out.

Daniel Cooper, Shep Barrick's father-in-law, being the Yankee veteran that he was, was asked on occasion if he was offended to be called a Yankee. He only quietly said, "You may call me a Yankee, but mind you never to call me a damn Yankee," as some southerners referred to everyone north of the Mason-Dixon line, far north of this awakening corner of Georgia, not far from the Atlantic ocean or the Gulf of Mexico. In fact, the waters that fell to the east of Fitzgerald town went to the Atlantic, and those to the west of town went to the Gulf of Mexico. A slight rise of land divided the drainage between the Alapaha River and the the Ocmulgee River.

Back to Daniel, he drew his monthly pension from the Federal government. He went about his business seldom mentioning politics and avoided people who wanted to pick a fight. He was here to help his daughter and her family to make a home, plant a crop, and spend his last days in the sun to warm his worn joints. The two had left Chase and the boys in the sturdy wagon, which was loaded with the most important everyday equipment. The all important milk cow with a rope to her halter and her calf by her side were tied to the rear of the wagon. Chase waited as her men folks wiped the mud from their boots on the mat before the steps of the land office. She only scoffed and thought to herself as she was an intelligent young woman, "Shaw, I have my doubts about all this forgive and forget. All this white trash and black people far outnumber these old veterans, and I don't trust that scamp old man, Fitzgerald. He doesn't give a flip for brotherhood and harmony. He and that brother of his are but a pair of high flying shysters. I don't intend to hobnob with these ignorant hot-blooded southern scum. I hope they don't think I will shake their hands. I have more important things to do. My parents taught me to have more respect for myself. These sentiments of mine are extended to these Africans, all smiles and with hands open for a handout. I hope both varieties of southerners stay in the forest with the other varmints. I do wish Shep and my father would hurry, my morning sickness is upon me. What will I do when this baby I carry decides to see where we have taken it? Pray tell!"

The two men were told that Mr. Fitzgerald was not in at the moment, and that he was out with his survey team, but should be in the office later that day. Poor man, he was so busy! "But I am his agent. Welcome you and your family to our fast developing settlement soon to be the largest town in all South Georgia, south of Macon. We welcomed over one hundred families this week, all from those northern and western states. If you gentlemen will come to the map room, I myself will assign you to your two tracts of twenty acres each. The numbers you have drawn are located only four miles northwest of town, a lovely pair of tracts, only recently surveyed. It is land just waiting for the plow, so to speak.

"Here at the boundary of the city, take the road still under construction to Arbor Church. Continue north by Mr. Clearance Sydney's estate and gristmill. Go two miles north on the two path trail to the markers which denote your tract. The foremen of the work crew, who are grading that trail, will direct you to your land with no problem. The deeds to your tracts are in escrow here in the office to be recorded when Mr. Peacock, our building constructo,r completes the new Court House, here in Fitzgerald, as you have probably heard. Mr. Fitzgerald and Governor Northern have formed a new county out of Irwin, the new county being named Musgrove County in honor of an early settler here on the Ocmulgee River, the proprietor of a trading post at the forks of the rivers Ocmulgee and Oconee. Good luck, gentlemen. God speed. Drop in for your deeds in two months as the new Court House will dominate the eastern skyline of Fitzgerald." With that, he ushered them out as other settlers were arriving. Poor man, he was being run to his death.

The children were hungry as the breakfast at Tootaville was early. Now at midday, they looked for a café among the shacks of tarpaper and slabs. Down the muddy street was a two-story building with the sign "St. James Hotel" hanging in front. A crowd of laborers stood in the vacant lot. A group of black men were behind the building, and a smaller group of white men had gathered. An older woman was stirring a steaming wash pot hung over a blazing fire of pine knots from a pile so large. The team was hitched to the hitching rail, after they had drunk deeply from the water trough which had been made from a huge cypress log.

The Barrick boys leaped to the ground, their first time to set foot in this town, if it could be called that. The old woman, who was stirring the contents of the black iron pot, rested her paddle on the pot rim and went to the wagon to help Chase Barrick to the ground. She introduced herself as Mrs. Cora Lee, proprietress of the St. James Hotel, the first hotel in Fitzgerald. She told the Barricks she was from Iowa and a widow. She had a room vacant on the ground floor, and ladies and gentlemen could be seated in her dining room.

Her black cook had fresh catfish fried in hog lard. She herself had a pot of Irish stew for the laborers. Gangs of day laborers and Irish and Italian masons had their own bowls to be dipped with a ladle filling the bowls to the brim. They also had a slab of cornbread and a pitcher of cane syrup to pour over it. The black gangs wanted fried pork belly, beans, and cornbread with cane syrup. They retreated to the shade of a Chinaberry tree to eat their fill. The foreman paid Mrs. Lee the bill, which would be deducted from each man's pay at the end of the long days of labor. These people lived from hand to mouth, day by day. They got drunk on Saturday nights and slept on Sunday. That was their way of life there in Fitzgerald.

The Barricks had some money to soften their move there. A room was rented for the mother, another for the men and boys as they needed rest. Travel was not easy on this late blooming frontier. After a full dinner, such as it was, Chase retired to her room to bathe and rest. The men and gleeful boys climbed into the wagon. Shep let the oldest boy, Robert, or Bob as they called him, drive the team. They asked directions from the workmen along the rutted mud holes, called streets, to the corner of the town. Then the land agent directed them to the estate of Clearance Sydney. They found him on the porch of his mansion, which overlooked a large field being harvested of corn. "A good crop," he said.

He himself was a nobleman by birth in his native England who had been banished by the court from English soil, never to return. He never stated his crime but was still every inch a nobleman. He never took a tool into his hand. Groups of black servants little better than slaves worked in his fields and mills, living in the cabins down a lane he called his quarters. Yes, he had built himself an English manor here in the middle of nowhere. His handsome appearance, his long white beard, his clean-cut profile, expensive clothes, the beaver hat, and necktie only complemented his regal posture. Yes, Clearance Sydney, no doubt, was a nobleman, Lord of all that he surveyed. He had no wife. Lady Clair was absent. He did have a small nervous lady, his secretary and housekeeper. She, with the help of several black women, managed his business affairs and manor.

He, Sydney, remained aloof of the commoners, northern or southern. He was, no doubt, the captain of his own ship or estate. He had arrived here in Musgrove County as one of the first arrivals and had purchased his vast holdings adjacent to the town lands from the original southern owners. The land was cheap. Four hundred and ninety acre land lots had been sold for the price of one double barrel shotgun or a milk cow.

In post-war, the Civil War, Georgia, land that didn't affront a navigable river or railroad could be bought for a song and you could sing it! Money, hard money, was nearly non-existent. Money that was issued by the Confederacy was backed by gold, which was buried by the president of the Confederate states before he left Virginia to go to Montgomery, Alabama.

The site where he was captured in Irwin County, Georgia, was barely twenty miles from Sydney's estate. The gold lay buried no one knows where, perhaps under the feet of Shepard Barrick, or on the forty acres he and his paw-in-law had bought. The location of the buried gold died with the president, much like the gold that Shep's father, Frederick, the Yankee Captain, had buried on Kangaroo Island, off the coast of New South Wales. Neither Jeff Davis nor the Yankee Captain knew what awaited them. To this day people dig and speculate where these fortunes lie. It was only stumbled upon by some lucky bloke, and then could become a curse to him!

A life friendship was forged between Clearance Sydney and the strong Aussie with the handlebar mustache and the piercing blue eyes. He too was a subject of the English Queen, thousands of miles away from sheriffs of their beloved Queen. They both had secrets, brothers under the skin, one with five thousand acres, the other, younger, and with only forty.

Most people here didn't give a hoot why they were there. Many of them had skeletons in their family closets, and only hoped for a new chance here in this perhaps last frontier. Let the axes ring and the ancient pines crash to the ground. Lay the rails, lay the bricks, and build fine buildings. Here the long arm of the law was weak at best, nearly non-existent. Few questions were asked. Jails didn't have top priority in a new settlement. There were crude shacks to shelter the pilgrims, as the crackers named them, from rain and sun, snow and ice. Criminals, murderers, rapists, thieves, white or black, most likely could find themselves dangling from a low limb by a rope, a noose knot hung about their necks.

Yes, justice was swift and effective. No one had time to hear fancy lawyers plead cases days on end. Courthouses were few and capital crimes were mostly self-evident. A man holding a smoking gun had to be guilty. Yes, justice was swift. The night riders with the hoods over their heads, perhaps your neighbors, were a great deterrent to crime. Sins of the flesh, gambling, prostitution, stump liquor, and bootlegging, were looked upon as professions or recreation. Insults to yourself or a lady's name were settled by duels between two gentlemen. Whoever was the best shot or owned the best pistols won the argument to the satisfaction of the witnesses. Yes, Southern justice kept most people upon the straight and narrow walk of life. A man's word, perhaps a handshake, was his bond, his signature sealed the fact. Judges existed far away, but their dockets were short.

Clearance Sydney invited Daniel and Shep to visit him or to pass upon his land at will or pleasure. Their land, the forty acres, joined his estate. As Shep Barrick and the old man Cooper drove the beautiful Belgian team down Sydney's lane, he, Sydney, knew that the land the newcomers had drawn was sandy and poor and would support only pine trees and wiregrass. The high land terrapins or gophers dug deep tunnels in the loose soil. Gophers dug holes to protect them from the sun and winter's cold. Also their neighbors shared their tunnels, namely the huge diamond back rattlesnakes, their strikes as swift as lightning. Indigo snakes and skunks often raided hen houses for eggs.

Mr. Fitzgerald in far away Indiana should have looked a little closer at some of the land parcels that he touted so highly. For a fact, some good land existed upon his map. The northern tracts had fine timber, but the soil left much to be desired for row crops. Clearance Sydney himself had picked up many tracts which bordered his land from settlers who simply packed up and left for greener pastures. He made them offers they could not refuse as there were no other bidders, only enough money for a few supplies and a train ticket to Atlanta or Florida. Boomers they were.

Chapter XII

The Forty Acres

The Barricks found the tract numbers on a board nailed to a pine tree, which matched their papers' numbers. Axe blazes on trees marked their land lines. The wagon trail ended at the tract. A stream trickled from a spring at the foot of a hill. The land was high and well drained. A lot of hard work lay between that land and a homestead. Hadn't the Barricks camped in forests darker than these far away in the North Woods of upper Michigan? They had lived in tents and shacks, army camps, and with armies on short rations. Hardship had been the lot of the Coopers and the Barricks of Australia. This was but another challenge to be mounted and it was their land. They could clear it and make it bloom. They had enough money left to buy the necessities of life until the town of Fitzgerald prospered. Hadn't they only today seen the progress which was being made toward a fine town with the vision of thousands of colonists just like themselves? Shep was young. The old man Cooper was wise and experienced in the ways of the world, and anyway, wasn't Mr. Fitzgerald an honest man to stand behind his word? Success was guaranteed by him and his bondsmen in Indiana. It said so right in the fine print in the land papers which vouched these facts paid in full.

Sharpen your axes. Let the chips fly with your teams. Clear the lands and plant your fields. It is only six miles to town, Fitzgerald by name. Those did seem like long miles, didn't they? The boys, Bob and Dan, drank from the spring. The horses grazed upon the green grass after a deep drink from the branch or creek, as the old man called it. Shep decided upon a home site and unloaded the wagon with the help of the boys and his father-in-law whom he called "Pop." They hitched the team once more. The horses, glad to be free of stalls built of boards inside the boxcar of the railroad, pranced and whinnied. They seemed to like their new home, unaware of the hard days ahead. Their bulging muscles would be put to the test, but that was a horse's lot. The wagon rattled along the trail, now empty of its burden of doors and windows, boards and shingles, which were left behind at the site of the homestead on that lonely forty acres, soon to be home to the growing Barricks family. They hoped this would be the last of the many moves they had made. Yes, they were anxious to put down roots here in the south. They passed and met many wagons upon the road that led back to town, such as it was.

They hitched the wagon by the boxcar and walked to the hotel, the St.

James Hotel, to be greeted by Mrs. Lee. She seemed to be the welcoming angel to weary travelers. Her smile and cheerful chatter did much to chirk up a body. Had not she and her family trekked the entire distance in covered wagons, camping at night along the road from the plains of the Dakota Territory? Her table was set. Food steaming hot did much to brighten the spirits of travelers.

Chase came down the steps, quite a chore for a woman with a lame hip and five months with child. Her smile was bright. The rest had restored her spirit. She was a strong young woman, tempered by many trials and hardships in the north. She had learned from her father, so dear to her, to live only one day at a time. She had patience and fortitude inside her frail body. Trials of the mind and body were an everyday occurrence to her. Truly, Chase Barrick was a rock. She had pitched her lot with the strong Australian stockman as he called himself, now matured into a man of many skills, the best of which was the way he had with animals, their care and training.

Yes, his grandfather, old Limon O'Leary, had given him a gift, and the ringers of the Outback in far away Australia had trained him well. Here, he could be put to the test, now in southern Georgia, their home to be. Time, that fleeting factor, waits for no one. It was Shepard Barrick's time to step up to the plate in this game of life. Now for the sake of your family and the unborn, please don't strike out. The bases are loaded; a home run is in order if you are to win!

The family became acquainted with many settlers from many northern states, not many from New England states, but mostly from Ohio, Indiana, Illinois, Iowa, Pennsylvania, Kansas, the Dakotas, and Wisconsin; a good stock of hard-working people, farm people, tradesmen, stockmen, and a few immigrants, Irish and German mostly, not down east Yankees, the seafaring stock. These were good people only seeking a homestead or small farm in the sunny south. They brought with them many professions, skills, and a patriotic spirit, as many of them were veterans of the Civil War.

Daniel Cooper and his daughter Chase meshed nicely with this class of colonists, but Shepard Barrick didn't fit the mold. He had a mop of curly hair, wore baggy pants, no collar or tie, and a pipe in his mouth above which loomed a thick out of proportion mustache. His slowly drawled words were unfamiliar to American ears. He had a generous nature, a love of animals and flowers, a strong back, good health, good teeth, no religion, and was drawn to the sport of bare knuckle boxing. He was a good woodworker, not a carpenter, but a cooper. Also he was very talented with hardwood and hand tools. He still had a little cash money and was not lazy. The old man, his paw-in-law, was still quite well heeled from the sale of the farm back in Pennsylvania, and probably their most valuable possession was the fine young team of draft horses.

Some of the colonists were quite rich, some just comfortable. Others were butchers, bakers, candlestick makers, barbers, lawyers, preachers, metal smiths, builders, all the trades necessary to make a new town self sufficient. The Barricks were not the first wave of colonists, nor were they the last. This project, Fitzgerald, had a lot of steam behind it. Yes, I must give Mr. Fitzgerald credit. Although seldom seen there, he sure knew how to beat a drum and raise a crowd. He must have taken lessons from Napoleon Bonaparte, the French general who conquered all Europe. Trainloads of eager people had unloaded their worldly possessions at Tootaville to travel the well-worn rutted excuse for a road to the site of Fitzgerald.

Perhaps this would be a good time, as this is our second day here, to explain the layout of the projected city, which only a year ago stood in virgin forest. The surveyors did an impressive job, quite a work of art. Most towns just sprang up beside rivers, railroads, or trading posts. Streets followed cow paths, Indian roads, even wild animals' migration routes, as animals seem to have an instinct to follow the ways, and to know where good water holes existed. Mr. Fitzgerald, being the frugal business man he was, spent months here, he and his land agents. They first considered tracts with frontage on the Ocmulgee River, which gave access to river traffic, the main stream of traffic from middle Georgia to the port city of Darien at the mouth of the Altamaha River. This land could not be bought for a song. Other lands with a sprinkling of farms and sawmills closer to the new railroad, which was soon to diminish river traffic, also demanded a premium price.

The decision was made to buy this three thousand acres in the middle of nowhere, where there was only a turpentine still and a commissary or company store operated by a prominent family. Black families blazed the pine trees to collect the sap. The sap flowed into tin cups that hung below the streaks that bled this valuable sap. When distilled, it would become spirits of turpentine used as paint thinner and medicine. The residue that was left in the vats was known as rosin, used in many ways to waterproof ropes. Tar, as it was called, had a worldwide market, too. This was the only industry other than sawmills that moved about the margins of the pine barrens, as this area was known to the native settlers, who eked an existence from its interior. People who held the titles to vast acreages farmed only enough to supply grain corn. For the staff of life of the original settlers, there were corn, grits and corn meal to feed themselves and the freed black men, who at best led a primitive existence in these virgin forests. The forest sheltered the wiregrass that piney woods cows, and razor back hogs roamed upon the open range to survive, much as wild animals had from time immortal. The hardwood bottoms abounded in wild turkeys, white tail deer and quail. The streams and sink holes supported a bounty of fine fish, there for the taking.

A man named Benny Helton, resident of a river village north of a large tract of this forest land, owned a watermill built upon a spring-ed creek, which ground the corn of the early settlers for free or a share of the grits. He ran a store nearby a railroad that ran from Alabama to Savannah on the coast. He had agreed to build a spur line ten miles south to his settlement at Helton's Mill, so remote, which was the site of the last conflict of the state militia and the Creek Indians. Several militiamen were killed, but the Indians retreated to Florida, never to return.

Mr. Helton, visionary and shrewd businessman that he was, agreed to let the seaboard railroad extend its tracks across his beautiful mill pond with crystal clear water dotted with lily pads, which held their beautiful petaled flowers upon the surface. Spanish moss hung on cypress trees surrounding the pond, and there was a right away through his forest to Tootaville. Yes, he sold Mr. Fitzgerald the three thousand acres he wanted just south of the railhead. The price was agreed upon, and the surveyors set about their work. The tract was four hundred ninety acres, mostly on high ground, seven eighths of a mile, and square bounded on all four sides by a generous drive.

If only the dreams of the developers could be realized, and the muscles of the colonists could hold out, Fitzgerald would without a doubt become a model city here in the middle of nowhere. Several other towns and villages had sprung up as the potential of the area was realized, now that the fevers malaria, yellow and typhoid had been controlled. There was good farmland, timber unlimited, and no ice and snow to contend with. Yes, it certainly had possibilities. Outside the border drives of the town, five acre tracts were surveyed. The newly formed city was attempting to build and maintain roads leading from Fitzgerald to neighboring towns. It was a rule that the owners of land adjacent to public roads would donate their labor or pay the wages of a laborer once a year to maintain the road. Outlaws sentenced to hard labor were placed in prison camps to work out their time on work gangs known as chain gangs, working in shackles to pay their debts to society. These wretched men in striped suits did a lot of the public labor. It is not for me to judge, but I hope to obey the laws and stay off that gang!

The last we saw of the Barrick family, the men and boys had returned to the St. James Hotel to reunite with Chasity Barrick, now rested and ready to return to the spur track at Tootaville, to unpack her household goods and the tent that would serve as their shelter deep in the forest. It would not only shelter her family, but also the furniture and personal effects so dear to her. Her books were her treasures, as she had been quite well educated by her loving family of good puritan stock, as you remember, English to the core. Perhaps she was one of the best-educated of the colonists. In this wilderness she loved the challenges of travel. She had followed her father Dan Cooper since she was knee high to a grasshopper, camping in the forest and cooking for workmen. She was also well educated in camp life and the care of animals. Now the mother of two growing boys and crippled, she was pregnant once more. She was not as healthy as she once was. The wear of the years and hard work had begun to show on her frail body. Her spirits were strong, and she would do her best to build a new home here in the south. Hadn't they bet their fortune on Fitzgerald? In fact, she rather enjoyed life's challenges.

Her husband, Shep, is strong and capable, but the Irish from his mother's side of the O'Learys had followed him from Australia here to Georgia. His free-hearted nature, his slouchy dress, his love of a challenge, his ability to select his friends and associates were part of that O'Leary blood. Well, now the fellow needed a balance wheel to moderate his personality, and Chase, as she was called, wore the pants in the family. She was the one who could set him in his place, so to speak. Why didn't he inherit the business sense both his father and his mother possessed, both of whom were achievers? The boy was a dreamer, a wanderer. The Australian term swagman fit him well. Perhaps that was why he had ended up here in this town. He really needed to set his cap and realize that he was the father of two boys and soon to become a father again. Are we speaking of responsibility?

Barricks' team of horses pulled up at the dray track to unload more of their belongings. The tent was almost a load, with a few dishes, pots, and pans to cook in. Yes, the camp must first be set up. The milk cow and her calf, which would follow its mother, were tied to the rear of the loaded wagon. The youngest boy stayed at Tootaville to sort the goods while Shep and the oldest boy Bob made the trip to their forty acres. Clearance Sydney had told Shep of a trail over his lands which would save him several miles as the two men had formed a friendship that would continue to the grave, both being subjects of the Queen of England. These Yankees and southern crackers could tout their harmony all they pleased but, hey, the two of them were of another blood and they would march to their own drummer.

The trail was rough fording a creek. The horses almost had to swim, but soon they arrived at the farm, their farm. They unloaded the pots, pans, and dishes and pitched the tent. Shep had the clearing looking like a camp in a short time. He instructed the lad Bob to stay with the camp. He gave him an axe and told him to cut fire wood from the fallen logs until he returned that afternoon with the rest of their belongings and the family, as they were to spend their first night of many to come on their own land, here in Georgia. The boy was a bit apprehensive, or down right afraid, but he dared not cross his stern father. Shep Barrick's good nature was not wasted on his boys; he saved it for others. Boys grew up fast here in Georgia, and Bob and his brother would be no exception.

Back at Tootaville, Dan Cooper had accompanied his daughter Chase and her younger son to the store and bought the staple groceries and household items they would need to survive for a week or more. The old man settled the bill with Mr. Helton, a kindly southern man of the old school. He suggested things they would need, the necessities of camp life, as he had out fitted hundreds of new arrivals. Why, perhaps twenty five hundred people had moved in, and each train brought another wave of colonists. That Mr. Fitzgerald sure knew how to beat a drum. Was the whole north going to load up and move here to the piney woods? "Let them come," Benny Helton said, "My cash boxes will hold their money."

Chase had trimmed her father's generous beard and hair. A colored wash-woman had washed their soiled clothes, just glad to get the silver dollar the old man gave her. Help was plentiful as the camp followers flocked about the newcomers like flies to sugar. With this new activity, the town builders brought many people not only to Tootaville, but to the river landings on the Ocmulgee River. The steamboats, which plied the river's muddy currents, unloaded at Lampkin Oldfield and Camp Eveleyn, where tram roads, narrow-gauge railroads, led out to settlements and sawmills throughout the area. Many people came from Macon and Savannah by steamer to be met by draymen, who made their living hiring their wagons and labor to settle newcomers moving into Shack Town, as it had been dubbed.

Shep Barrick's empty wagon rattled into the settlement at Tootaville. He was glad to have avoided that beehive of activity at the town site. The family loaded their furniture, tools, plows, cultivators, seeds, and other items into the big wagon along with their new bought provisions from the store, even some side meat and syrup, cane syrup, not their familiar maple syrup, unknown here in the south.

Shep helped Chase up to the driver's seat. The grandpa and his grandson, named after him, climbed atop their precious cargo, which hopefully would sustain their lives and give them the strength to hew a new life here in this town. Chase loved to drive the team. She slapped the lines against the broad rumps of the faithful horses as they surged into their collars, and away they went, leaving an empty boxcar to go back north only to return with other settlers as they liked to be called.

Did we leave Lady Luck and destiny forty years ago in Australia on the other side of this spinning globe we call Earth? I wonder, oh how I wonder, will they succeed, or will they fail? They were not happy in Michigan and restless in Pennsylvania. Now only time will tell, because they are off again. Someone has quoted a saying. I believe the words were, "A rolling stone gathers no moss."

What future waited the child that grew in the womb of the woman who held the reins of the Belgians, which strained in their harnesses to keep the wagon and its cargo rolling along the trail, deep in Lord Sydney's untouched forest. The grazing cattle were branded on their hips with a crown, the brand of the Sydney estate. The deer held their white tails high, the quail flushed from the hedges, the squirrels barked an alarm, and the buzzards circled in the blue sky to feast on some poor critter that had met its fate. Life goes on, you know. The sun sank into the west, only to rise on the red soil of Australia. Who knows what it beheld of the relatives there?

The boy Bob had succeeded in building a fire, which felt rather good. The chill of the fall night had begun to creep in. Their milk cow, Becky, had been milked; the calf was sucking the teat. She was stubbed out on a chain so she wouldn't stray. To Bob's delight, his mother had brought him a sack of hard candy. Chances had been taken and rewards received.

The wagon was quickly unloaded. The weather was fair, and the flames leaped high, only to burn down to glowing coals. A Dutch oven was put into the coals. Dan Cooper, a master camp cook, put his dough into the cast-iron oven. A pot of Irish potatoes was set to boil in the clear spring water that providence had provided them. These decent British people brew and drink strong hot tea with their meals. The kettle was whistling, tea was soon brewed, mugs were filled, bread broken in bowls of fresh sweet milk, and boiled potatoes buttered. Yes, settlers get very hungry. Not a scrap was left. If they had had a dog, he would have just gone hungry tonight. After some tales of long ago and far away were told by the adults, the family crawled into their sleeping bags. The campfire was banked for the night. A wash pot of water was moved close to the coals as warm water would be needed at daybreak, their first day on their land.

The others were soon snoring but Shep lay awake. He did have thoughts of his young life there upon the Darling River, the stern old Captain he never knew, and the beautiful mother he left behind. He was suddenly snapped back to Georgia by the far away mournful howl of a southern gray wolf, calling for its mate. He had hoped that he had left these bloodthirsty critters back in northern Michigan. He remembered how to build a wolf trap. Tomorrow he would build one on the far boundary of the land which was now theirs.

The day arrived with a burst of sunlight. The warmth that it brought soon melted the frost that had cloaked the meadow below the spring in white. Yes, Jack Frost had arrived. Winter could not be far behind. Peter Painter had painted the red and yellow leaves of the swamp maples and poplar trees that grew along the creek, which seemed more brilliant before the background of pines so green. It seemed almost a shame to clear this land of its native growth to be replaced with rows of corn, but the livestock must be fed and a living must be made.

Chase was the first to stir from her sleeping bag of goose down. She, the only woman in the camp, soon had the fire poked up and a tea pot simmering as she had two men and a pair of growing boys to feed. Camp life was a way of life to her. Perhaps before too long she would have a house to make into a home, a home for the girl she hoped to birth after the New Year arrived. There she could hang curtains at the windows and cook on a kitchen stove with an oven. Yes, a girl child would be nice because she was growing tired of this nomadic life she had shared first with her father, now with Shep, her husband, and the boys. She had no close friends to confide in, no relatives to help her. In fact, she and her father were loners until she and Shep had married. Shep had left his family far across the Pacific Ocean; Dan Cooper had taken his daughter and run. These colonists were birds of a feather, all adults flocked together here to stand on their own feet, perhaps never to see their relatives again, far flung as they were.

This situation did have its merits, no prying questions to answer, no one to please, no visitors to feed. They had landed in a beehive of activity here in the once silent pine forest, which had only heard the calls of the birds, the rush of water, the bellow of the bull frogs, the alligators, the wood peckers pounding on a tree that lightning had struck during a thunder storm, even the wolf that called for a mate. The Indians made few sounds unless they were on the war path. Their feet were shod in deer hide moccasins, which could carry them through the forest with no sound. They blended with their surroundings, even their dialects were soft and bird like.

However, these settlers were a noisy lot. Their tools broke the silence, as well as their shouts of instructions to work gangs, the singing of the black people at their tasks, and the steam locomotives and river steamboats which could be heard for miles. Yes, the sounds of progress were never far away, except on Sunday when church bells rang and preachers shouted the words they read from their tattered Bibles to the men who created so much noise all week and were now silent, many of them sound asleep in their pews. Sunday was a day of rest, wasn't it? Was there ever a better or safer place to take a nap than at church?

Back at the Barricks' camp, eggs and bacon were served. A hoecake of bread from the Dutch oven was broken by eager fingers, washed down by strong hot tea with plenty of sugar. Yes, they would need the energy that breakfast would give them. Trees were to be cut, the giant pines girded to die, rails to be split, and fences and a shack to be built. Much elbow grease is needed to change a primeval forest into a homestead. Shep Barrick accepted this challenge as he was strong and young. He had helpmates, two sons and a good father-in-law, one he could confide in and one with some money and a lot of experience with men and animals. He was the father that Shep never knew. Now, women were another experience that obviously he had flunked out on. Perhaps Bella, who now was the house keeper with her daughters, had been more of a mother to him than Bridgett, business and beauty being her main endeavor. She had been thrown into the position of breadwinner when the steamboat had exploded. Sinbad had trained him as a lad with the skills of the seamen and the operation of steam engines. His grandfather, Limon, had taught him the skills of a stockman and a horse trader. With these skills he had been a good student, and they would follow him the rest of his life.

Shep had learned how to trap animals while a timberjack in the north woods of Michigan. Now he had to apply that skill to trap the wolves that ranged the pine forests of Georgia. Mr. Fitzgerald had failed to mention the wolves in his flowery description of the lands.

First, Shep dug a deep pit with the help of his boys, a wolf pit as it was called, so deep and steep no wolf could jump out. Then he pivoted a strong board half over the bottom of the pit. On the end over the pit he set a rag soaked in bacon grease. When a passing wolf scented the bacon, he would follow it to the site of the pit. Not knowing much of the laws of gravity, he would "tiptoe" out on the trigger board, his weight tilting the board and dumping him into the recess of the pit. The trap would reset itself to await the next curious wolf, which would also get a course in the laws of gravity, then await the hunter or trapper who would dispatch it to the happy hunting ground, as the Indians referred to the great beyond. Wolves, clever as they were, were soon extinct here in Georgia by this and other methods. For many years, several of nature's most elegant creatures would become extinct or nearly so, as their habitat and that of civilized man were much different. Some adapted to the changes, others never could. Perhaps Mr. Fitzgerald in far away Indiana couldn't have cared less for the ecology of the longleaf pine ecosystem. He seemed to think only of the money to be made for himself. Oh well. If he hadn't triggered this development, someone else would have, as the same changes were taking place all over America. Perhaps we should blame Christopher Columbus and his Queen Isabella. The winds of change began to blow when he waded ashore in the New World, and they were still blowing a gale here in Georgia, four hundred and four years later!

Chapter XIII

The Birth

One quote that I have heard, "Footprints in the sands of time are not made by sitting down," was self evident here on the Barrick homestead of forty acres. The fall weather was all they could hope for, cool nights and warm days. Thanksgiving came and went. Christmas had been a season of good will as southern neighbors, the Hoovers, had stopped to visit and brought a gallon of cane syrup as a gift of friendship. These people were humble and kind, although a bit lazy, and had murdered the queen's English. They had no education. The black people lived their simple lives, one jump ahead of poverty and want.

Chase's father had given his only daughter a used buggy he had traded for down in Fitzgerald, which had grown by leaps and bounds. Most of the streets were open to traffic and shops and stores were going up every day. Shep put his skills at trading horses to good use — a "hoss trader" as these crackers said. He had traded a gold brooch of his mother's for a blind racehorse to pull the buggy. This rig was the property of Chase, who had to be helped into her buggy by her father who was never far from her. She could, with her younger son Daniel, drive to town to trade. The horse was a fast high stepper named Peggy, retired from the racetrack. Her vision was so poor she would never run away and wreck the buggy. She depended on her nose and the reins of the driver, always Chase Barrick, and best you don't get in her road as she would surely run you down in a heartbeat. When Chase drove to town, soon the pedestrians and street people would cry, "Here comes Miss. Barrick and that blind hoss. Gang way. Don't be there!"

Man, that Peggy could put them down and pick them up. At the hands of Shep, Peggy was soon sleek and her chestnut hair gleamed. Those oats he gave her made her shine, and the lumps of sugar and the pop of a training whip overcame her affliction. Horses don't have the best eyesight. They see only movement. Their noses and their hearing are very acute, even more so when their eyesight is dim. That Shep was a master at training a horse. His soft voice calmed them down. Blind horses were his favorite pupils, as they were cheap. His eyes could see for them. Yes, he was truly a stockman, one that his grandfather, wherever he was, would smile upon.

Chase Barrick's trips to town became fewer now in February as her time was near, and the weather was cold, not as balmy as the land he had touted.

The men and boys, her men, had built a frame house with rough heart pine lumber, and the windows and doors were now swung. It was not a fine house, but comfortable. A lean-to barn was built for the horses, two cows, and a young bull they now owned. There were chickens in the yard, and a bred sow pig. Yes, things looked good for now. By spring a new baby would be in the crib, a vegetable garden would be growing and a crop would be planted in the new ground fields.

Christmas wasn't much, mainly an excuse for the Irish and the black people to get drunk. A few churches had sprung up, mostly arbors of brush and tents for now. Pine trees were cut and decorated with popcorn and paper chains. Fruit vendors set up stands to sell oranges, apples, and Brazil nuts. Children looked for Santa Claus to bring dolls and slingshots. Some rich kids might get bicycles. Stands sold fireworks that lit the night sky and startled the horses. The railroad had been opened to Fitzgerald and more merchandise was on the shelves of the town stores.

Yes, it was a sight to see how businesses had sprung up. This town had overnight become a boomtown in the wilderness. People celebrated holidays to overcome their hardships. This was an unfolding drama of once enemies, local pioneer families, freed slaves, and immigrants from Europe, even one from Australia. They seemed to have their shoulders to the yoke and to the wheels of progress. Their labors were beginning to make a showing even if Mr. Fitzgerald was seldom seen!

The holidays passed. January was cold, and frost turned the fields white. The Barricks wished they had their winter clothes that they had left in Pennsylvania. Chase told the men folks that if she ever saw that smooth talking shyster by the name of Fitzgerald she would give him a piece of her mind. The woodpile was a constant chore. The axe was well worn. Shep was good at wood chopping, and the stews the old man stirred reminded them of the logging camp days far north of there.

February brought rain and wind and labor pains for Chase. Her child kicked within her. The boys were excited about the new baby. Shep kept the fires going. The cold didn't seem to bother him much. He was not lazy, and he worked everyone around him. "The boys," as he called them, seldom had free time. They grumbled that they thought the slaves had been freed.

One morning, late in February, Chase cried out, "My contractions are coming regular. Go for the doctor or old Mrs. Player, the midwife who lives on the northwest side of Fitzgerald. She has delivered many babies, and the colored helper she has is the best. I don't care for that old Dr. Bussell. He is too old to make the trip out here, and we will have to feed him for a day or two. Go fetch Mrs. Player. I can relate with her. Five dollars will content her."

With that, Shep hitched Peggy to the buggy and headed for the house beneath a giant cedar tree. Mrs. Player soon had her bag packed and had sent one of her boys on his bicycle to the east side of Fitzgerald to the black quarters to tell Mary, her helper, to come quickly. Shepard Barrick waited for what seemed an eternity. He went to Mrs. Player's barn and hitched her horse to her buggy, and loaded her things aboard. Mary had arrived on a mule. Shep led her mule to Mrs. Player's lot and barn. Peggy, the blind horse, stood still, her nostrils flaring at the scent of the other animals. Mrs. Player and Mary climbed into the buggy and followed Shep Barrick to the farm.

The sun was low in the western sky as the two buggies pulled into the yard of the home place. Daniel Cooper sat upon the porch of the house. He quickly arose to meet Shep and the midwife in a long coat and a stocking cap over her head. Mary was bundled in woolen clothes and a hat. She grabbed a black bag from the buggy and was soon in Chase's bedroom. Mrs. Player spoke some words of reassurance to the writhing form that lay beneath the quilts. Dan Cooper had plenty of hot water waiting on the cook stove. He had been through births before, and after all, this was his own flesh and blood. Mary asked the men and boys to go on about their chores as she and Mrs. Player had everything under control.

Shep sharpened his axe. Daniel paced the porch floor. The boys shucked corn at the barn, hoping the new child would be a baby boy who could help them with the chores, maybe even milk the cow on cold mornings. When Chase cried out, the men looked at one another, not commenting.

The sun was setting when Mrs. Player opened the front door and called to the men and boys, who scurried to appear before her. Only then she smiled a broad smile and in measured words said, "The baby is here." They could hear it crying now. Mrs. Player seemed to enjoy the announcement of a new baby. Yes, she loved her work.

"Must I ask of you, my lady," Shep asked, "is it a girl or man child?"

After a pause that seemed another eternity, her tight lips parted to form the words, "Mr. Barrick, you are the father of a fine baby girl, of perhaps 7 pounds, and as you can hear, her lungs are clear. I will, with your permission, stay about your wife during the night as she is still under my and Mary's care. Her contractions have ceased, but she still has some pain. I had rather keep an eye on her for the night as she is weak. Your daughter will be at her mother's breast shortly, and you may speak to her and view your daughter."

Mrs. Player went back ihnto the house, and the men tended the horses, did their chores, and put Mrs. Player's horse in the lot with Peggy to spend the night. The draft horses in the pasture came about Peggy's lot to get acquainted with the new horse. Mr. Cooper soon had a hearty supper on the table. Mrs. Player and Mary ate together, and the men and the boys ate after the women had retired to the bedroom where Chase lay with her newborn daughter snuggled beside her. Somehow she couldn't get comfortable. The men had visited with her and peeked at the girl child, and names had been mentioned.

Mary made a pallet on the floor beside the bed, where Chase and the child lay. Mrs. Player was to sleep on a cot in the sitting room. The men and boys would sleep in the hayloft as the night was mild and the heat of the manure and the breath of the horses took the chill from the air. There was no plumbing in the house, only chamber pots of clay to be emptied at the outhouse or privy the next morning, one of the chores that the boys hated but nearly everyone else did the same.

This wasn't New York City or Boston, this was the Pine Barrens. The kerosene lamps gave a dim yellow light when turned low at night, not much better when turned up. Lamps had been turned low. Fires were banked in the cook stove and fireplace. One thing they were blessed with was firewood, and now a baby girl. Shep wondered how she would fit in this working, Spartan household. He had never been around a girl child, as he had no sister, although his brother Limon back home had been somewhat of a sissy, not a stockman as he always was.

Shep's first playmate was old Boo, the ancient Welsh pony that his mother, Bridgett, had loved so much as a girl long ago. Now he was the father of a girl, perhaps she could help her mother about the house and marry a stockman some day, or maybe a prize fighter, a champ, no doubt.

Dan Cooper, having loved his daughter Chase so dearly, was in his heart happy to welcome another daughter, a granddaughter, into his heart. Around midnight Mary, the nurse, holding a lantern in her black hand awoke Shep. "Mr. Barrick," her soft voice spoke not to awake the others. "Mrs. Player sent me for you to come to the house quick as your feet can carry you. You done bees da paw of another baby girl. Yas, sur, you done an got two 'gulls,' twins da be, one big un and one bitsy one. Come see!"

Shep already dressed, grabbed his boots, ran barefooted, and jumped the front steps only to meet Mrs. Player in her nightgown and house robe, with a pan of bloody water to fling out the open door. Shep sank down in a cane bottom chair to pull his boots on. His face was blank. He said, "What in heaven's name, woman?"

Mrs. Player smiled to ease his anxiety, "Yes, Mary has told you, I see," she said. She can never keep news under her bonnet. Mrs. Barrick was uncomfortable, pains returning, I thought it was the after birth that had failed to pass. I wasn't satisfied last evening. She hadn't cleaned up to my satisfaction, which was the reason I wanted to pass the night by her side. She called for the chamber pot to relieve herself. With a cry from her, I heard a splash within the chamber, and there with another placenta, was a tiny child, perfect in every respect, a doll she was. Red hair she had, and quite a mop. I could hold her in the palms of my hands tiny as she was. I wiped the small body clean. She only weighed a couple or three pounds. Mr. Barrick, she is fine, now sucking hungrily at your wife's breast. Oh yes, sir, a strange thing other than the fact I might have thrown her out with the afterbirth, was a clear membrane over her eyes. I wiped it away to clean her eyes of the deepest blue I have never seen in a newborn as eye color develops, but not hers. She is a very special girl. Mind my word, Mr. Barrick, this is a once in a lifetime experience for a weary old woman who thought she had seen everything. All three, mother and twin girls, are fine. She is sleeping now. The morning will come, sleep now. Mary and I have everything under control. You are a lucky man. Mary will have a hot breakfast for the lot of us as we have had a busy time. Now sleep."

Mary turned the lamp down and saw Shep, bewildered as he walked to the door and closed it behind him. He stumbled back to the barn where he awoke his paw-in-law to tell the wide-eyed old man the latest news. All old Dan said was, "Damn!" Soon the rooster would crow, the nighthawks and bullbats would give their raspy cries, and the bobwhite quail would whistle. The sun would peek through the lofty pines to melt the frost of the night, and not one but two newborn girls would try out their lungs; one loud, and one but a chirp like a bird.

Now, this matter of the veil that covered the wee one's eyes, and her eyes so blue and her hair so red intrigued Shep. The gypsy woman in Australia had told Shep that the veil meant that she would be able to see into the future. Why had destiny chosen him to be the father of a freak? Yes, he had some fear in his heart. Fear that he seldom had, but this was supernatural, and he hoped Chase and the others had never heard this omen. Was he afraid of his own flesh and blood which could sit in the palm of his hand? He would examine her himself, closely, come daylight. How could Mrs. Player, the midwife at so many births, be so calm?

Shep's stepbrother, Sinbad, a half-breed, told him of the superstitions of primitive people, who lived closer to the spirits than white people did. Yes, he had seen the look of fear in the eyes of Mary, the black woman, only a generation from Africa, like Australia, the home of many spirits and gods. He will for sure corner Mary in the morning and demand she tell him of this veil that his daughter had been born with at the midnight hour, unexpected at that!

The words of the kindly midwife, Mrs. Player, continued to echo in Shep's mind. Lucky! How lucky can a man get? They were barely getting by, now two, not one, baby girl to raise. Mrs. Player asked for her horse to be hitched, and gathered the tools of her profession into her bag. Shep brought her rig to the front gate of the homestead and helped the women into the buggy. He withdrew his pocketbook asking for her bill. "Well," she said, "you know, Mr. Barrick, I have to file a birth certificate at the court house, which I will do for you. Then you must enter the names of the infants and pay the county the remainder. My fee is five dollars per baby, and being as you have two babies, the bill is ten dollars." Chase, weak as she was, named the first-born girl Olive. The second little girl, the one with the veil over her eyes, was named Anna.

He said nothing as he opened his leather purse and handed her a ten dollar gold piece of hard earned money. Bank notes were worthless these days. Thanks were exchanged as she dropped the heavy coin into her bosom, "clucked" to her horse, and away they went. Shep Barrick stood stunned as the ladies' buggy grew smaller and smaller down the three path road that led back to Fitzgerald, the city that had just been born, now bursting its bounds.

He didn't speak as there was no one to hear his words, but silently he hoped it would be a long time before Mrs. Player and Mary would darken his door again. What about the tiny baby girl who clung to just a spark of life? She perhaps was the lucky one. She had nearly been flung away with the slop. Why had that membrane covered her tiny eyes of blue, and also the mop of red hair, wet and plastered to her doll-like head? It just dawned on him she was the spitting image of her grandmother, Bridgett O'Leary, bless her money-making soul in far away Australia. Perhaps he should write and tell her of her granddaughters. There were many things he should have done, but his education was not in writing and reading. His brother Limon was the bookworm.

Shep had excelled in stockmanship and boxing, not to mention wandering the world over. Now he was a family man with five mouths to feed, in addition to his own and Mr. Cooper's. This sandy ridge would never give his brood anything but a bare existence. He knew that, but for now, they had a roof over their heads, even the tiny, newborn head, which had been sent to him along with the healthy bouncing baby girl whom he could hear bawling in the house.

He saddled Peggy and rode to a black settlement named Kingsland, to hire a black woman to cook and work for Chase, until her strength returned and the babies were on their schedules. She could sleep in the loft room, and he still had a little money left. Now that the new babies were bathed, nursed and diapered, they had to be named and educated by their parents and family. They were not identical or one twins. Why, in fact, they didn't even resemble each other. The big, dark complexioned, black-eyed, brown-haired girl was named Olive Marie Barrick. The other girl, the small, delicate-featured one, with the copper red hair, fair skin, and blue eyes, after much deliberation was named Anna Theresa Barrick, to be called Anna, and her sister to be called Olive.

Chase, the proud mother that she was, loved her girls. She would only shake her head in wonderment and stare into the bewitching blue eyes of Anna, possibly the only features she possessed that approached normal size. Her little chin, what there was of it, would wrinkle and tremble a bit before a weak wail would exit her rosebud lips, but if I may repeat, those eyes followed every movement in the room and possessed their own mute language.

Anna was not as content a baby as Olive, who ate and slept a lot, accepting her lot in life. Yes, already although half the size of her twin sister, Anna was the dominant one, to remain so for life. Chase was quick to realize this fact. Perhaps she inherited this nature from Chase herself, who felt she was as good as anyone, and perhaps some better than a lot. She had to fend for herself in the post Civil War period of much upheaval and rampant politics which dominated that era. She had educated herself mostly with the tutorage of her father, himself, a man of letters. Daniel Cooper had taught his daughter's quick mind to learn. Books, not dolls, were her playthings as a child. In fact, she was better educated than many young women, maturing early, being a grown woman at sixteen. Now twenty-eight years old, she was mature, the mother of four, two big boys and two infant girls, one normal size, the other just a wee spark of life in size, but a full dose of shall we say, spirit.

Chase didn't care for the black woman, Mollie, and as soon as Chase was on her feet, she sent her scooting back to the Kingsland settlement. These black Americans were new to Chase. She had only seen a few passing through the northern states to Canada on the underground railroad to freedom. She abhorred slavery, but she had been disappointed by their ways and language. She thought they could have done better now that they were free men. Perhaps she set too high a standard for the down trodden black people who toiled under the burning sun of summer and shivered through the cold southern nights in shacks not fit for human beings.

Mrs. Barrick was a bit hard on them, more so than the southern people who were more tolerant. Few, if any of the white people here in south Georgia, had owned slaves. They were too poor. The slave owners were along the coast on huge plantations which were old when the Indians and traders inhabited this area of Georgia. They, the white settlers, lived off the land, forests and rivers, and had existed much as the natives had, although a little better than Indians or slaves. Hardship was a hard master; sickness, death, starvation, wars, were an everyday occurrence beneath these towering pines and rushing rivers.

Chase and her father were always a good team. They the household chores shared and raised a fine garden in the sandy, well drained soil. Much of the barnyard manure was dumped upon the garden plot. Irish potatoes grew well, as did turnips, rutabagas, field peas, green beans, okra, tomatoes, and corn. The father and daughter tended the garden with the help of the boys, Bob and Daniel. The huge pines that Shepard had girdled with an axe were now just dead snags, letting the light of the sun flood down on the virgin earth which had never felt the fall of a hoe. Shep hired a gang of black field hands to plant corn with hoes among the snags, which did well as the rains were regular. The ashes of the winter fires fertilized young corn plants. He also scattered the crude rows with a sack of nitrate of soda at his side and a bottle cap in his hand. As he passed each plant he flung a cap full of the nitrate fertilizer at the base of each corn plant. He then laid it by and the sun and the rain did the rest. The boys hoed the field peas which ran their vines upon the corn stalks, weeds, and grass.

Lo and behold, five acres of fine stock feed was made. The ears of corn would be put up for the team of horses and for the saddle horse, Peggy. Shep had seen this done in Australia, a sloppy way of farming, but after all, weren't Australians just a bit sloppy? Shep's way of dressing only fortified that fact. Why, I doubt that he owned a formal suit of clothes or wore shirt and tie. Yes, he was a stockman to the hilt, no more, no less, unless some ill-advised blockhead would care to go a few rounds in a boxing ring and a purse to be taken by the winner!

All through this unfolding story, luck, fate, destiny, even Cupid's romance, the aborigines' visions, the gypsy woman's crystal ball, and the nonsense of veiled eyes, have reoccurred. Now a new spirit had stepped forward, here in primeval Georgia. She was known as Lady Enterprise and had taken the reins of development. Who has ever heard of a town being surveyed to such perfect dimensions, deep in a sparsely populated forest in Indian Territory, not on a navigable river or bay of an ocean to form a harbor, poor forest soil, and no main trails or roads? No through railroads, no telegraph lines, only the sighing pines swayed as the wind sang a sad song, as it passed through the boughs that supported the longest needles that white men had ever seen.

Other settlements had been started with trading stores, saw mills, turpentine stills, cow pens, and river landings. Few survived the sweltering summers, cold winter nights, and malaria fever, which the swarms of mosquitoes passed among the white people, sapping them of their strength and vigor. Poor diet and laziness did the rest to sap the vigor and ambition of the white settlers, who seemed satisfied with mere existence. Now bands played and hastily laid railroads connected people and merchandise to a thriving new city, named for a visionary Yankee in far away Indiana, a Mr. Fitzgerald, his name fast becoming a legend. The city would soon possess an Opera House seating twelve hundred people, two through railroads connecting Atlanta and Florida, not to mention Savannah, the port; a hotel four stories high, the largest wood frame building in Georgia; a coal-fired steam electric generating plant, owned by the city; sanitary sewage system and flush toilets; schools of brick on the four sides of the city; a high school with stately Greek columns; even a race track with stands and stables for thoroughbred racehorses.

Wake up, you sleepy villages south of Macon, or you will be left in the dust and smoke that these Yankees colonists are raising. They were a determined crowd of hard working people, who never entertained the thought of failure. They and their ingenuity, linked with that of a few southern bankers and men of vision, were being attracted to the smell of money and business opportunities. Even black labor and businessmen, barbers, tailors, teamsters, cooks, grave diggers; work was here. Streets were being paved, fine houses built, mules and horse traders coming form Texas and Oklahoma where the winds blew free. Here in Fitzgerald the winds of change were blowing a gale, and Lady Enterprise was fanning them, if you believe in spirits. Others believed in the sweat of strong men's brows, and the hands that rocks the cradle.

The city now had been incorporated and had elected a mayor and councilmen and established a fire department, police force and a jail house. There was a courthouse with a dome on top and a clock to strike the hour; churches, fine churches of all denominations, even a Roman Catholic Church, not common here. Over night, it seemed that railroad depots had risen to receive the scheduled passenger trains that ran daily to unload more people from the north, immigrants with their families, with only their shirts upon their backs and their strong arms to lay bricks and build mills of all kinds. The first wave of colonists had torn down the shacks that first sheltered them, now to live in brick homes, styled after the ones in the north.

Shep Barrick was no dummy. He and his wife and her father sat by the open fireplace late into the night to discuss their future. The children were asleep and the lamp turned down to a flicker. The pine knots, which Shep had thrown into the flames of the fireplace, were rich with sap and the fire leaped to consume it. The eager flames cast dancing light upon the grim faces of the three. This farm was not what they thought it to be. Mr. Sydney was correct. The sandy land was soon exhausted, only dog fennel thrived, and spring was undependable. After the trees were destroyed the water table sank. They were not broke. The pension the old man, Dan, drew from the Union Army could feed them, but barely. Chase wouldn't consider spending their nest egg of money she had nursed so carefully all the way from Pennsylvania. That lady could stretch a dollar!

Shep found plenty of public work in town. He and the Belgian team of draft horses could earn their way any day on the streets of Fitzgerald. The Barricks were not desperate. They only wanted more than the southern farmer who eked out an existence from the worn out, eroded fields. The old man Cooper was now showing his age. His once black beard was gray and grizzled, and his joints were stiff. The girls needed to enter school soon. That little doll of a girl, Anna, as she was called, always had her nose stuck in a book. Her red hair was beginning to fall in waves, exactly as the waves cascaded to the shoulders of the grandmother she would never know in far away Australia, if by chance she was still alive, who knows? The other girl, Olive, was strong, healthy and free hearted, a Barrick to the bone. Chase had twins but she for certain had two individual children.

The boys, Bob and Daniel, had been schooled at a one-room schoolhouse by a teacher and a helper, but they could read and write well. Daniel, the younger, was quick to learn like his mother. Rob looked like he would be a stockman or mechanic, much like his father, but without the mustache and that crooked stem pipe always in his mouth or cupped in his left hand. Lit or unlit, it was without a doubt his father's crutch. Chase despised it and was quick to say so.

The three grownups talked far into the night. The flames ceased to dance upon the board walls, unpainted as they were. Chase, always the thrifty one, complained that they were only burning the midnight oil, the kerosene they had to buy at ten cents a gallon. It was delivered by the tank wagon with "Standard Oil Co." emblazoned on the sides and pulled by a team of mules.

Shep was fascinated by these mules, much larger than any farm mules. Upon each hoof of these splendid mules was engraved the letters "J. D. R." Shep always pointed out this singular method of branding an animal. These mules he said belonged to Mr. John D. Rockefeller, the owner of Standard Oil Co, and half of the USA. In fact, those were Missouri Mules, the top of the mule line, and Shep knew horse and mule flesh, along with camels and oxen back home, as he always referred to his young days in Australia.

Before the lamplight was blown out, Chase and her father had convinced Shep that they had to leave this poor farm and move to town, which grew each day as though some magic wand had been passed over it, becoming a city. Shep was the last one to agree to another move. Chase argued that he spent more time there than he did on the homestead with her and the children, not to mention with her aging father, who bore the drudgery at the end of the road, while he and the horses pranced around town.

Shep was not a bad man, not one to raise a ruckus. He was rather mild and agreeable. "Yes," he said, "I will string along. Chase, you are the one with the gumption and brains. I can be content anywhere I can have my stock, and I am no farmer. Tomorrow if you will go with me to Clearance Sydney's estate, we will discuss this matter with him, as he is my trusted friend and advisor."

With that pledge Chase blew out the lamp and tucked a quilt about her father by the glow of the embers of the fireplace, as he was sound asleep in his easy chair. The baby girls slept through the night in their cribs beside Shep and Chase. The rooster that crowed had awakened Anna, the smaller of the twins. Chase gave the baby her every attention. The other girl, baby Olive, only needed a bath and a clean diaper.

The old man always cooked a hearty breakfast, perhaps different from the native people as he cooked no grits. Hash browned potatoes, scrambled eggs, and coffee were made, but Shep by his raising always wanted hot tea, very strong. Chase allowed her youngest son, Daniel, to stay out of school to mind his baby sisters. Her father would oversee the field hands, day laborers, milk the cow, and feed the sow and chickens. Chase combed and brushed her long hair, balled it up, put on her best dress, and slipped her bonnet over her head. She carefully placed the important papers, deeds, and tax receipts into her handbag. Shep had Peggy hitched to the buggy. The Belgians could rest today as they had earned a rest, for it was they who had become the bread winners for the Barrick family.

The beautiful spring morning almost put a song in Chase's heart. A move always brightened her heart. Shep drove up to the front gate. Peggy and the buggy looked good, wheels greased, leather seats, as well as the harness, dressed with neat's-foot oil. Peggy was curried and clipped and her tail bunched in a neat bun.

However, Shep seemed to have forgotten to groom himself. His thick head of hair was a mop. He wore a cap he must have saved from the whaling ship in which he spent over a year and the same old baggy pants. His shirt was wrinkled and stained with tobacco juice. He smelled of horses and their lot. The pipe smoke mixed with the other odors settled upon him. Chase made a face and questioned his appearance, to say the least. He only blew a cloud of tobacco smoke, climbed into the driver's seat, clucked to Peggy, and away they went on another venture.

The warm spring morning had cheered Sydney up, and at his side, puttering in his rose garden, was his black manservant and gardener he called Green. Shep hitched Peggy to the ring in the hand of a statue of a small black man dressed as a groom in a space reserved for guests. The two men shook hands firmly, one dressed to perfection, as a landed Lord upon his English estate; the other as an Australian stockman, both subjects of the Queen of Buckingham Palace in London town. The two men were very satisfied in their images and spent their lives as such. Mr. Fitzgerald's town was the least of their worries. Sydney didn't trust this promoter and openly called him a shyster.

"Have no more dealings with him, Shepard. I think he has hightailed it to California. He never intends to repay you your initial purchase money if you homestead as the agreement stated. A man's agreement is no stronger than his purse." Chase stayed in the background as a lady should when men discussed business. Lord Sydney told Shep that only a day or so ago a German immigrant by the name of Manfred had stopped at his office to inquire of a small farm. He had bought six lots on Federal Street, a front location, but he was unhappy with the traffic and the railroad had laid their tracks too close to his home. There was one acre of pasture and a barn close in town, and the new ward school was close by. It was a great location for a stockman, and the land had city water, sewerage, and electricity. The German wanted to put in a dairy and raise strawberries, grapes and chicken. Their children were taught to work, not frolic city streets and those dens of the devil which lined the street.

"He gave his name and address, which my secretary will furnish you with," Mr. Sydney said. "Now go to his door and you have my blessing upon you and your family. Keep an eye upon those Yanks and their schemes. Come to me when you like, as we English must remain loyal to each other and the crown." Chase herself of good English stock, didn't disagree with Mr. Sydney. There were a lot of under the table deals that left honest people stranded and penniless.

Chase went into the Sydney office and obtained the address of the Manfred family. Peggy's hooves beat upon the wooden floor of a stout bridge over a large creek, Gladys Creek it was. Traffic was brisk on the street that led to the business district of Fitzgerald. Yes, there was the pasture and the vacant lots, six of them. On the corner lot to the south was a large house of recent structure. In fact, no building was more than three years old as it was 1899, only one year shy of 1900. Could you believe a new century was close at hand?

Shep liked the huge barn with many stalls and the street frontage. Chase eyed the house over. It needed paint and porches and shutters at the windows, but yes, it would do. "Play it cool, Shep. Don't let the people know you like it," Chase said. "You know how to trade horses, let me trade with the Germans. I am well acquainted with them and their frugal ways. They were my neighbors in the Dutch settlement of Pennsylvania when I was but a girl. I even speak some German."

The yard dogs rushed out to nip at Peggy's hooves. She only tossed her blind head and came to a halt when Shep said, "Whoa!" He stayed in the buggy as Chase mounted the steps that led to the unfinished porch, cluttered with scrap boards and saw horses. The front door was open and footsteps approached. A smiling stout woman in her mid-thirties wished Chase a good day, "I'm Mrs. Manfred, lady of the house. May I help you?"

"Yes, I am Chase Barrick. My husband Shepard Barrick and I are neighbors and friends of Clearance Sydney. Mr. Sydney informed us that by chance a one-horse farm could perhaps be more to your liking than the home you have here in town. Perhaps we could have a word with you and Mr. Manfred and arrive at a trade of property that would be to our mutual satisfaction."

"Mr. Manfred," she said, "is today riding the area in search of just such a property as we were truck farmers and dairymen in the old country. I will inform him upon his return of your visit and offer, Mrs. Barrick. He knows the way to the Sydney estate and he can meet your husband there at 9:00 A.M.

I am quite sure you may come in our house and look about, and your husband can survey the premises, if it so pleases him. The dogs won't bite and the gates are unlocked."

Chase rather liked the woman and her house. What it lacked in workmanship it made up in space and comfort, with even a toilet with a flush commode and electric lights that came on with that flip of a switch by the door. After eyeballing the property, the Barricks bid the German woman good day. The men folks would meet the following day at the estate of Clearance Sydney. That night around the supper table, trades were discussed. The boys were excited as farm life was from dawn till dark, and the pay was just a living.

Next morning, Shep was up with the sun. He told the boys to tidy the yard, milk the cow, gather the eggs, feed the team, and put them in the pasture as a prospective buyer was coming at mid-morning, and would more than likely have the midday meal with them. "Please make me proud of you and the farm," he told them. As he swung into the saddle that his father-in-law had built for him, Peggy came to her gate. Shep felt she could see a bit. A black buggy and a horse waited at the Sydney gate. Shep pulled Peggy to a stop, tipped his hat, removed his pipe from his mouth, and bid the stranger good morning. Could you be Mr. Manfred?

"Yes," the man said in a thick Germanic brogue, "I am Max Manfred and you no doubt are Shepard Barrick." The men shook hands as was the custom. "I was told of your visit to my cramped quarters in town. I expected a tract of land, but the land company said I was too late as the forty-acre tracts had been drawn. I had no choice but to take the town lots you saw yesterday. I am anxious to get back to a small farm as I am a man of the soil, and this traffic is not for me."

"Be my guest, Mr. Manfred," Shep said. "We are but half an hour from my homestead where traffic is almost non existent, and the soil is ideal for truck farming. I myself am not a farmer, neither Yank nor Rebel, as I am Australian, a stockman, and cooper by trade."

The German followed Peggy and Shep along the paths of a road to the gate of the Barrick homestead into the yard swept clean before the frame house, not much more than a year old, not yet bleached grey by the southern sun or northern winds. The garden beside the house shone in the spring sun. Cabbage, turnips, English peas, radishes, and Irish potatoes were ready to harvest. Shep's son, Bob, took Mr. Manfred's horse and buggy to the water trough and cared for the horse.

The men spoke to Chase, and made the guest acquainted with Mr. Cooper and the children. The twin girls held their rag dolls and clung to their mother's skirt. The men made a tour of the perimeter of the forty acres. The pines which stood along the creek bottom sighed their sad song in the spring breeze, as wondering what lay ahead for them under a new landlord, as so many had passed beneath their spreading limbs since the Indians had left there forever.

A hearty dinner was set before the men by Chase. They drank tea and peach cobbler was served to Mr. Manfred's delight.

The bargaining went on until the sun began to sink. A bargain was struck to the satisfaction of both parties. A bit of debt was still owed on the town property to be assumed by the Barricks. The German wanted the team of Belgians, but no way would Shep part with them. He got all the stock, but the sow and pigs and a heifer calf soon to come fresh. Max Manfred was an honest man. His title proved good as did the Barricks'. A handshake sealed the deal. The agreement was to make the move in two weeks.

Chapter XIV

The Federal Street Home

The Belgian Percheron horses, the team that Shepard Barrick was so proud of, pranced into the boomtown of Fitzgerald. The team driven by Shep arched their necks to form crescents of their clipped manes. Their hooves, large as water buckets and shod with steel horseshoes, pounded the sandy soil of the street that had become the main thoroughfare of Fitzgerald, the town that many southern natives had predicted to fail, pure folly! The Barrick household goods were stacked high in the big wagon. Chase and her father sat on the buggy's leather upholstered seat. The twin girls, Anna and Olive, sat in their grandfather's arms, wrapped in cotton blankets. The boys, Bob and Daniel, were left behind to mind the place, the place of hard labor and disappointment beneath the sighing pines. The Manfreds were welcome to it.

The swap had brought new vigor to both families. Chase Barrick thought to herself, "Many men of many minds." Max Manfred, his wife and children, had most of their belongings moved to the shed and barn ready to be loaded. Perhaps the prediction of the local people would have come about if it hadn't been for the spirit of these immigrants, their will to succeed, and the spirit to help one another. Shep, being the big-hearted fellow that he was, had offered to haul the Manfred goods. A swap of labor was common in the city, why they pitched right in. Max's boys soon had Shep's wagon emptied and had begun to load their possessions aboard for the return journey to the country, the forty acres.

Clearance Sydney sat upon the veranda of his manor house and watched the movers. He stroked his white beard and chuckled to himself, poor soil, skitters, flies, rattlers, and hot dry summers will break those Germans, and those forty acres upon his land plot would soon have one of his blue thumb tacks stuck square in the middle, his mark of possession all clear and legal, purchased for a song, and he would sing it. The English and Germans were never loving neighbors in Europe or here in Georgia. Rock on, your Lordship, time will tell the rest of the story.

Chase Barrick set up light housekeeping in a room of the spacious house that would soon be her new home. Her neighbors would no longer be hoot owls and white trash or those black field hands. She now could send her children to the brick school which was being built on the city's western border. There was a Christian Church of "granite" blocks being built by the town's leading builder, Mr. Peacock, he himself of the Christian faith. Chase, herself, hadn't attended service in years, years of upheaval and moving from camp to camp, farm to farm, but she wanted their children to have religious instruction and association with decent people.

Now, Shep, she had lost hope for him. He was not a choir boy or deacon. None of his people here remembered his father, the Captain. They seemed too busy to stop and sit among a group of wailing fancy dans. Australia was sparsely settled. Churches were few and far between. This boomtown scene was old hat to Shep. Hadn't he seen Broken Hill rise from the red dust of the Australian Outback with the gold strike and passage of the cross-country railroad? What about Lightning Ridge, the mining camp, serving the opal strike? This was just another boomtown, Fitzgerald it was called, the same crowd, the same surnames, and same goals.

Shep only lived for today. Tomorrow some other town would be surveyed out, and the rush would be on again. This Fitzgerald rush, the one Shep and his family were caught up in now, astounded even an old timer like himself. Rich people, mostly northern work gangs, Irish, black, and Italian masons, were laying the streets in the business district with red paving bricks which the new railroad had brought in from Macon, Georgia. Streets were crowded with traffic, wagons, buggies, bicycles, peddlers on foot, and Jewish merchants whose dry goods were packed in trunks, drummers they called them. These drummers traveled from town to town by any means of transport. Some even had their wares on their backs as they walked a path beside the tracks. Chase hoped Shep wouldn't see these drummers. Under some trees there were the wagons and tents of, yes, you guessed it, gypsies, and their strings of horses to be traded. The word gypped, meaning to be cheated, derived from these people, the ones who could see into the future, your future, for a fee.

Yes, this strip of vacant lots by the bridge which crossed the creek's dark waters and the rambling frame house with the big barn and fenced lot would become the perfect home for a stockman and his family, if Shep could only keep his head. Perhaps Chase would have to put a bit in his mouth beneath the bushy mustache and the crooked stemmed pipe. The move was completed. Daniel Cooper had his own room. The boys didn't want a room in the house. They liked the barn and the quarters their father fixed for them. They, father and sons, called it the bunkhouse. It had a stove, its metal pipe stuck through a small window supported by hay wire, which was plentiful around the lot.

The Belgian team had stalls and a grassy paddock, and a large cement water trough filled with clear cool water, city water from a spigot you could open and close with a twist of the wrist. The boys were relieved at this because water would not have to be drawn from the spring or hauled when it didn't rain. The toilet was not in the house, but in an outhouse on the alley.

There was running water at another spigot on the back porch behind the kitchen. Washtubs hung on nails driven into the wall of the unpainted house. Never had they had such conveniences. Why, a body could get lazy. An iceman delivered ice every other day in a yellow wagon. He even put it in their icebox. Milk could be stored, and they could have ice water in summer. Homemade ice cream could be made in a crank churn. Stores were on most corners up town, no more long trips in a wagon to town. They were already there all the time.

Chase furnished a room as a nursery for the twins. Her father bought her a new cook stove with an oven and a hot water jacket. A plumber came and piped it to a wash room on the porch. She liked to do her own housework as servants never seemed to please her. A few horseless carriages, automobiles, and dump trucks appeared on the streets. A horse-drawn fire pumper wagon and a crew of firemen had moved to a new brick fire station. There was a city hall just over the railroad tracks, which had been extended straight through the city, from east to west by the Fitzgerald power and light plant. The railroad cars delivered loads of coal to fire the light plant's boilers to generate alternating current to light the city's streets and homes. The passenger train came sailing in to the new depot twice a day, connecting Fitzgerald to the cities north of it.

Several tram roads had been consolidated and improved to accommodate even Pullman coaches and private coaches belonging to wealthy people in the northern states, linking the tourist traffic to Thomasville, Georgia, and Florida. The new colonists and tradesmen, not to mention traveling salesmen, came in the crowded day coaches, one for white passengers and one for black. A train whistle was heard often, blowing day or night. Four or five years ago, there was only the wind whispering a sad song through the pine tops or the lowing of woods cows. Their bells rang as they chewed their cuds.

It is hard to believe that one man by the name of Fitzgerald could promote such a town. Some said he was a con man. His land office was vacant and the pledge to refund the purchase price of a land tract or lot upon development had never been honored. The town loafers around the card table outside the blacksmith shop said he was in Panama, promoting a city on the banks of Teddy Roosevelt's canal! Whatever he did, he had lit a fire here which had grown into a roaring inferno that only burned brighter by the day.

Chase looked better and dressed better. She strolled around town. Her girls, the twins, even the tiny one, Anna, were walking. Olive was still larger than Anna, but not as active, why Anna ran on her tiptoes everywhere, so light on her small feet. Her eyes were as blue as the Georgia sky, and she didn't miss a trick. People stopped on the sidewalk to marvel on how her copper-colored hair lay in perfect waves, tight as coiled copper wire, only a stray finger curl hung on her brow. Her abundant hair made her pale face appear smaller than it actually was. Her chin, but a button, quivered when she was frightened, happy or angry, which wasn't too often, as she was of an open disposition and seemed to love attention and music.

She and her sister could sing a duet already, and they were only toddlers. They could sit up in that buggy with their mother as old Peggy strode down the crowded streets. Pedestrians had learned to clear a path for Mrs. Barrick and the girls, as Peggy was blind and she would stop only when commanded to do so by Shep or Chase.

By the way, Shep was doing much better now that he had left the farm. His seafaring days were paying off. He had learned as a deckhand on that whaling ship he left Australia on, how to operate hand winches that raised anchors and ten-ton whales. With the help of a blacksmith, he built himself a winch that could be turned by a small horse hitched to a long wooden boom. It gained much leverage as the beast walked a circle around the winch and the spool of cable, hitched to its payload, stump logs or even a house mounted on wooden "dollies" or rollers set upon boards. He would anchor the winch to the earth by driving steel rods, mostly buggy axles, into the ground at full cable length from the burden. Then as the pony walked its path around the winch, which gathered its cable onto its geared down spool or reel, the burden was drawn forward inch by inch, the distance growing as the dollies' wheels rolled upon the track of heavy wooden boards. Shep greased the dollies' wheels with Octagon soap, and soon learned that a blind pony didn't get drunk as it walked its circle until the cable was wound and the house sat before the winch. Then the men pulled the pins that anchored the winch.

A team dragged the machine of Shep's design one hundred feet farther down the road or field, to its new address, be it ten miles or one city block. Many houses and barns had been built around the area, and many had been abandoned as better buildings were built. The old structures were in demand for tenant houses on farms, or people who just wanted to move, house and all. Yes, Shep had a good business, as labor was cheap, and didn't he have two strong lads of his own? The vagrant life of a house mover, who camped beside his burden, appealed to him as it did to the old time Australian swagman who never knew where he would hang his hat next, by the billabong or by the rocks of the Outback. Many tales were told around the campfires; even a few boxing matches were held beneath the Georgia pines.

The new freight wagon Shep purchased had the words "Barrick House Movers. No job too small or large. Shepard Barrick and Sons. Owner. Fitzgerald, Ga." painted on the sides.

Chase Barrick was pregnant once more. Her lifestyle had changed. She no longer lived the life of a vagabond, sleeping in a tent, cooking for work gangs and clearing new ground. Her father sat on the porch most days, tending his granddaughters, telling them stories of his youth, the Civil War, and the farm they had left in Pennsylvania. This left Chase some leisure time to read newspapers, local and statewide, which the train delivered to Fitzgerald each morning. She managed the books and finances of the moving company. Her frugal ways kept some money in the bank, and already she had paid off the mortgage on their new property, painted it, fenced the vacant lots, cut the brush and planted trees and grass. Perhaps the Barrick place, as it was known, was one of the outstanding home places on that side, the north side of Fitzgerald.

Shepard Barrick's appearance showed no improvement. His personal appearance was the least of his concern. The barn was his dominion. Hay was stored in the loft, corn in a crib. He considered himself a sharp trader. He traded horses well, and the lot was full of horses whose next home would have been the glue factory. To him, it was a challenge to get them back to health and work. This he was good at. His remedies and salves, the ones old Limon O'Leary, his grandfather back in New South Wales, taught him to mix and apply, worked wonders on the poor critters. Shep's main fault was his soft heart. He was a sucker for a sad story. Why, he was just as apt to give one of these animals to someone he pitied or liked. These freeloaders flocked about him as bees about honey. He would buy things he had no use for just to help someone. A soft touch he was, and the word was out. Many free meals were handed out to tramps, and Shep looked little better than they did.

Chase realized his weakness and rode his case hard. She relieved him of what cash he had in his pockets when he returned from a job. She felt that she and the children shouldn't go to bed hungry when those plugs, his horses in the "hospital" lot, were full of hay and corn bought with his hard earned money. She dreaded to see a gypsy camp at the corner of the drive. She knew that Shep would invariably come in with a string of limping or blind horses and a smile on his face. The gypsy men laughed openly after he left their camp.

Unknown to Chase who scoffed at gypsy fortune tellers, Shep slipped into the tent, the one with the sign of the open palm and the new moon with the star above it. He told the old gypsy woman behind the crystal ball of his tiny daughter, Anna, and the veil upon her eyes at birth. The woman upon hearing of the child became quiet and only stared into her crystal ball. After a long silence she solemnly told him to bring this child to her tent. Shep dared not to tell his wife of this encounter with the gypsy woman, but he couldn't get it off his mind.

The bars which lined the streets and the floozies who danced with the customers held no attraction for Shep. That racetrack having been built on the west end of Fitzgerald by a group of wealthy northerners was his weakness. He could pick winners, which he was quick to do for friends, even strangers, as his knowledge of horseflesh was uncanny. He even entered a few of his restored patients and won quite a few wagers. To him, the money was of little importance. The race itself was his fascination.

Back at the Barrick's home, Chase was heavy with child and her time was near. It looked like Daniel Cooper was going to outlive many of his fellow Civil War veterans. He lived with his daughter and Shepard, and split fat pine splinters to kindle fires on cold mornings. He tended the animals, but was quite feeble, although he still was the rock that his daughter clung to. Shepard was off on a moving job when Chase delivered a baby boy, refusing a doctor, sending for her trusted midwife, Mrs. Player, and Mary, the black assistant. When Shep arrived, he was thrilled with the fact that he had a new son to bear the name of his father, the Yankee Captain Frederick, who had perished long ago in the explosion of the steamer *Bridgett O'Leary* upon the Darling River.

The child, Fred, as the family called him, was the play pretty of the twins, Anna and Olive, now about to start school. They dressed him as a girl and curled his hair. Surely he would be spoiled or at least a sissy.

Why, pray tell, would the twins be so musical? Why, they were singing before they could talk very well. The larger of the two, Olive, was well named as her complexion confirmed the name. Her mind was one straight avenue, easy to negotiate. No sweeter child, a disposition so placid, body so well formed, Olive was easy to describe. Anna's copper red hair fell in waves upon her frail shoulders like a seashore and the watery waves that caressed the sandy beach. Her shining sky-blue eyes dominated her face, and her chin would tremble when her thoughts grew deep or emotions swelled in her tiny bosom. Her mind had many avenues, crooks, and curves. Yes, Anna was a complex child.

Chase enjoyed her younger children as she had more leisure time now, and, to her relief, Mrs. Player had informed her that her child-bearing days were over. Shepard spent more and more time on the bustling streets of Fitzgerald, whose population had soared to around six thousand souls, some northern original colonists, immigrants, craftsmen, camp followers, and many colored people who found employment about town. He had about turned the moving business over to his hard working sons and a bunch of roustabouts. He had a position as a groomer and trainer for the horses which were stabled behind the fire station.

These horses were a carefully chosen lot, each bearing the approval of Mr. Barrick, trainer and veterinary of the city stock, including the mules the city used to grade the streets and pull the garbage and sanitary wagons. He had a crew of men to groom and feed the animals, but those fire wagon horses were his pride and joy. He trained them to the point that when the fire alarm sounded its wailful sound, the team, three fine animals side by side, pulled the wagon through the streets at a full gallop, with firemen clinging to the wagon's footboards. The team would rush to their stall gates and upon release the three would stand beneath the harnesses that hung from the ceiling before the pumper wagon. The driver of the wagon dropped the harnesses upon their backs, and they were hitched in no time flat. Yes, Shepard Barrick came to his own when he looked a horse in the eye.

People came from far and wide to see these fire wagon teams perform. Shep still smelled of horse manure and pipe smoke, and wore the same baggy britches held up by yellow galluses, still an Aussie to his strong core. Chase had long ago given up on changing him into a gentleman. A stockman he was, not much of a homebody was he.

The railroad which served Fitzgerald had grown almost as fast as the town and needed a terminal to service its locomotives and rolling stock, a round house and a twin table to change the direction a locomotive would travel, and a back shop where locomotives or engines could be completely overhauled, if these railroads were to become first class railroads. The old Georgia and Florida line had been sold out as had many other short lines or tram log roads. Their most valuable asset was the rights of way they possessed. These had been pieced together to form the through lines that now connected Fitzgerald to northern cities and Florida.

Officials of the railroad had watched the phenomenal growth of Fitzgerald. They called a meeting with the elected city fathers and prospering businessmen, mostly local men of vision. Mr. Fitzgerald had long since vanished from the scene. The railroad officials asked for a large tract of land east of the city, but close enough to be served by the city's electric lines and convenient to the work force to man the shops and the switch yard and to consolidate trains. The County Commissioners, City of Fitzgerald Councilmen, the Mayor, and several prominent businessmen, both northern and southern, gave several hundred acres of land. The land was what the railroad desired. The company, now known as the Atlanta and Atlantic, brought all its forces together and built permanent buildings to house machine shops, yard offices, round houses, storerooms, coach sheds, even the main mechanical office of the road. They called the vast complex Westwood Shops. Fitzgerald was made the nerve center of the system as the dispatcher's office, where train orders were issued regulating the traffic over the five hundred miles that the system operated. The Superintendent's office was housed in a magnificent building.

All the ceremonies of the city's brotherhood had to take a back seat to about a thousand overall clad, greasy mechanics and mostly country boys, who came to town, black and white boys. Blacksmiths labored on their well-paid jobs, to keep a fleet of vintage and rebuilt steam locomotives streaking along the newly constructed tracks, which became the life blood of Fitzgerald. Fortune had smiled on this town, now to become a railroad town, the envy of several other sleepy towns that were bypassed. Other industries followed the rails to Fitzgerald, among which was a cotton mill, spinning yarns and weaving cloth for a worldwide market. This mill, which employed several hundred families, sprang up on the north perimeter of the town, which had become a city so quickly. There was scarcely a vacant lot within the original drives. Schools and churches had been built as fine as could be found in Georgia.

Chapter XV

Title?

Old Daniel Cooper, one of the last Union Veterans of the Civil War now history, had been buried in the plot reserved for War Veterans, now nearly full of neat rows of government headstones. Shepard and Chasity Barrick attended the funeral with their family. The daughters of the American Revolution, local chapter of the D.A. R's, as they were known, represented the Union faction, and the southern veterans' representative, the U. D. C. or "United Daughters of the Confederacy" group, both had a few words to say to the gathered group of mourners assembled at the cemetery. The group of aged men with gray beards and crutches, or in wheel chairs, were at attention once more, as the city band played "The Battle Hymn of the Republic," only to be followed by the lilting strains of "Dixie." Yes, this display of unity was typical of the founders of Fitzgerald. Bitterness and hatred had been buried there long ago and today. The Barricks had lost their father and grandfather. Chase loved him as he was not only her family, but the rock she had leaned on most of her adult life. She was not one to weep, so she kept a staunch stance, but behind her black satin dress and black veil her heart was broken. Shep Barrick, his hat removed to reveal his combed hair and trimmed mustache, had his pipe in his coat pocket. Shep had not only lost his true, if not best friend with the passing of his "paw-in-law," but perhaps the one stabilizing factor in his marriage and home. His shiftless ways which riled Chase, no end, were smoothed over by her father's steady course of everyday life. Shep's face was wet with salty tears, as his soft heart and emotions that dwelled just beneath his skin were hard to mask, as his wife Chase could. Yes, beneath that rough old hide Shep was a "soft" target, a champion of the down trod who was quick to recognize, I can't say "fault," but more a nature to be fair to the aging "Aussie" stockman.

Chase had often commented that Shep was more thoughtful of horses and "dead beats" than he was of his own family. He would buy feed for some old plug horse, or spend his last dollar to buy some animal which needed a good home. Their children at times went to bed with only a stomach full of boiled potatoes and whatever happened to be in the cupboard. Shep's boys had not had the best of relations with their father. They had the notion that they would have to face the hard knocks which life would send them, much as their father had to do in his vagabond youth. He had taught the two boys the rough and tumble of breaking mustang ponies, the skill of bare knuckle boxing and wrestling, not to mention back breaking labor, the labor of men when they were but lads. He saw no need of formal schooling. As soon as the boys could read and write, add and subtract, they and their axes and shovels were loaded on to the "tool wagon" and sent to "the job." Yes, they had learned the hard facts of life when other boys were playing ball on the vacant lots of early Fitzgerald town.

Shep had "extended" himself several times on the streets. Once, when he was at the fire station, a drunken farmer emerged from the bars which lined the street just south of the fire station. The man mounted to the driver's seat of his wagon and yelled at the team of mules. The mules panicked at the driver's frenzy yells, and only balked not to move, as was the nature of the critters when their burden was too heavy or their nerves were "frayed." The farmer dismounted with his plaited leather whip in hand to give his mules a good "thrashing." Shep watched the piteous animals stand for the lash. He slowly walked across the park that divided the two lane street, put his pipe in the coat pocket which he slipped out of and laid on the grass of the park. The men at the fire station, young strong men, called to Shep, "Come back, Mr. Barrick, that is the meanest man in the County. He will drive you into the ground as if you were a wooden stake. That is Rufus Corbitt. No one crosses his path, especially when he is drunk as he is today."

Shep never looked back. He walked a straight line to the man who was cursing and laying his lash with all his might on the mules harnessed to the wagon tied to a post, only standing to take the farmer's wrath which the whisky had set on fire. Shep had his knuckles clinched and his mind locked in his fighting days, the reason he was in Fitzgerald and not Australia this very day. He asked the man to lay his lash away, and not to strike the mules again. A look of astonishment came upon the man's face, not a stranger to Shep, as his reputation was known far and wide. His family was large land owners and had political "pull" with sheriffs and police. Mr. Corbitt studied the intruder's face and bare knuckles, only to say, "Yes old fellow, I will lay the whip aside." The mules stood trembling in their harnesses. He lurched to the wagon "bed," tossed the whip aside, and with a curse upon Shep's mother he grabbed a new hickory axe handle he had just purchased only that morning. A crowd emerged from the "honky tonks" and bar rooms; painted women and their pimps, and card sharks and gamblers who preyed upon farmers and railroad men. They sensed that a street fight would soon erupt before their eyes. Shepard Barrick easily side stepped the mighty swing of the axe handle, which cut an arc in the air, only to throw the man with the terrible reputation off balance. Like lighting, Shepard fist landed a blow to the side of the man's head, knocking him to the hard brick pavement with a resounding thud. Shep only danced about the slowly rising figure of Mr. Corbitt, who was reaching into his overall pocket to withdraw a switch blade knife. Shep let him lurch to his feet and press the knife's release button. A blade of razor sharp steel reflected the light of the sun in a flash. The bearer of the deadly knife spoke in slurred words, "As the good doctor sews you up, remember my name, you 'damned Yankee.' I am tired of your high and mighty kind meddling in my business." Another blow of Shep's left fist above the man's belt and right to his chin put Mr. Corbitt to sleep. This time the man awoke lying in his own wagon bed, being driven home by a deputy sheriff. Once again, Shep's fist had gotten him in trouble. He was hauled to jail by another police man driving the "black Maria" or jail wagon. Once again his love of animals had taken precedent over humans. The "burly" young police man who charged Shep with "disturbing the peace" was met at the jail by a group of witnesses, the men of the fire house. The Chief of Police, Captain Smitts, tore the charges that the young policeman had written to small pieces and let them trickle to the floor of the jail. He looked at Shep in the eye and calmly said, "In the future, please don't take the law in your own hands, Shep, as that is what I am here for. Good day, Mr. Barrick."

Two things came of this incident. Shep's fists were famous around town, and he had made an enemy of the young cop who would hold an "axe to grind" against the old man, even to his grave and beyond. Now, Shep was not that old, he looked old, and he was not a "Yankee," much less a damn Yankee. He had straightened out that fact, and had cleared his mother's name. Those questions were answered for good. His Queen would have been proud of him. The firemen handed him his coat and he lit his pipe once more. Clearance Sydney heard of the incident, and had his secretary, now his wife, write him a letter of congratulations! Chase, after the death of her father, had lost not only a father but her confident, not only to her, but to her children. He had been around to smooth the path of her life. His Veteran pension stopped. Many times in the past it had helped make "ends meet." Mr. Cooper's life savings were exhausted. Chase had settled his estate and bought a piano, and enrolled the twins in a music school that a Mrs. Ebenspeager, a German widow woman, held in her home. Chase had purchased a three seated "rig" and a bay mare to pull it. Shep had taken great interest in this purchase, but the money to purchase it came from her father's estate. Somehow, in spite of all his efforts, Shep never seemed to accumulate much cash, let alone a bank account. Peggy, the blind race horse, had died in spite of Shep's best efforts. Old age is hard to cure! The new mare named "Maud" was in the lot with the Belgians, now retired. Maud was well broken and gentle with the children. The older boys would hitch her to the "shay" and she could be driven by the twins, even delicate little Anna would grab the reins to drive. She would shout, "Get up Maud!" and her chin would tremble a bit. She would drive the "rig" to school each morning stopping to pick up the neighborhood students, until the surrey was overflowing with happy children of all ages.

In the early spring, the wet season, the creeks would flood the streets of Fitzgerald in spite of the promises of the promoters of the town, who lauded the well drained site which had been selected to build the city on. Perhaps Mr. Fitzgerald had never been here in early spring. Maud would wade into the water to ford the creek between the Barrick's home street and the two story brick school on the west side of town. This was quite a "lark" for the young passengers and they would cheer Anna and Maud on until Maud would have to swim, and the wagon high built as it was, would be flooded to the floor boards. Where did that tiny red headed girl get the "spunk" she had? Only her chin showed her fear. The other children were quick to notice Anna's leadership abilities and skills with the reins, but children can be cruel with the "nick names" they give their playmates, so as you might expect, little Anna ended up being called, even by her best friends, "Tremble Chin," a name she despised but was "stuck" with. Shep had taken great interest in this horse and "rig," perhaps more in the surrey and horse than in the children. He was kind to them, but he lacked a close relationship with them. Perhaps his favorite was Anna, called "Tremble Chin" by her playmates. Her fortitude and bright countenance, not to mention her delicate beauty and wavy red hair, never failed to bring memories of his mother.

Chapter XVI

Rural South Georgia

The years passed rapidly, especially in a boomtown, which Fitzgerald had become. Times had been both good and bad. After the initial building boom began to fizzle, many carpenters and movers were unemployed. The city fathers blessed them. Businessmen rallied and displayed a seldom seen spirit of cooperation in the struggling new town. Public work projects were commissioned and drainage ditches dug. The St. Paul Hotel had been completed. A building was built for expositions and agricultural fairs. Tourists stopped here en route to Florida on the railroad and some in touring automobiles on the Dixie Highway, which was being developed. Some climbed to the observation deck of the St. Paul with a domed upper story from where, on a clear day, they could survey the sprawling town with its checkerboard streets. They could even see the water mill and the three hundred acre Minnie Mill Pond five miles away, which was old when Mr. Binidict made his land purchase.

Old timers said that the dam that impounded the beautiful lake was built by slave labor and mules pulling skid pans of earth. A pavilion had been built by Dr. Alewine, the current owner. This structure was a favorite gathering spot for courting couples and picnics. A tram railroad, the Osceola Southern, ran an ancient passenger coach on the line that wandered south to Smith Crossing, Osceola town, Hat Creek settlement and Mariana Lake recreation site on the Alapaha River. It ended at the last of the great sawmills which were turning the giant longleaf pines into heart pine lumber, sawed from the huge logs with which the dinky railroad supplied the mills.

The sleepy saw mill villages and agricultural towns had mostly been owned by generations of landed gentry, who had a long tradition of fine homes in the towns and farms. They were worked by sharecroppers, both black and white, turpentine men and their "wood riders." The black hands worked the pine tree faces or chipped grooves, which bled the valuable sap of the trees to fill cups positioned below the streaks, which the men had to cut anew each week during the warm months of the year. They lived their itinerant lives in villages of simple cabins owned by the white landowners and known as quarters. They had evolved into enclaves of a specialized labor force. They were woodsmen proud of their profession, capable workers and were paid by the barrels of sap or gum that their crop of faces yielded to the dippers. They were specialized workers who also scouted through the forest to collect the gum or scrape in hand-held dip buckets. When these buckets were filled, they were dumped into large wooden barrels, and set in a wagon bed pulled by a well-trained mule, which followed the calls of the dippers down the wagon trails on the ridges.

Blacks lived out of the commissary stores at the quarters and seldom went to town, as they held themselves apart from town people. Their women folks kept house for them, bore their children, packed their simple lunches of biscuits and bacon, syrup and water in lard buckets and washed their clothes. They wore blue overalls, seldom a shirt, except in cold weather, when they wore some denim overall jackets. Their clothes were soon plastered with the gum of the pines that were their livelihood, simple as it was. Rain only cooled them. Molded rubber boots waterproofed to perfection with no socks were their badges, which were soon coated with gum. They wore felt hats with brims to protect their heads and faces from the chips which rained down as the faces on the trees were pulled out to keep the sap flowing as the tree tried to heal itself.

The Man, as the men called the white operator or land owner, on his truck wagon hauled them to their far flung crops, and delivered them back in groups to their quarters and the hot suppers that awaited them in their humble shanties. They and their sharp cutters, the blades which cut the bark and inner layer of wood from the trees, and the glistening black muscles that wielded them so skillfully, gave them much respect among their fellow black neighbors. By this time, few pine trees had escaped these men and their blades. Nearly every log was harvested for the mills, with their high-pitched whining-toned gang saws. Their shrill steam whistles blew at daybreak, for lunch time, and at dark or quittin' time.

These logs had to be junk butted, and cut above the base just above the cat face. It was a scarred scene of many deep cut streaks and sixteen penny steel nails that had been driven into their trunks to hang the boxes where the gum collected. Yes, that was a way of life in the piney woods of South Georgia, below the fall line.

In my experience, I never knew of a hand being bitten by a rattlesnake or cottonmouth moccasin, which shared the forest with these men who always followed the same paths among the trees. There was no malaria fever, which plagued the white people; the mosquitoes evidently didn't like the fumes of the fresh bled sap of the pines, or the smoldering fires the woodsmen built around their quarters at night. The smoke formed a blue haze or skeeter smoke, as they called the haze. Fitzgerald had its turpentine stills and its quarters, but the railroad, the Atlanta & Coast; the sprawling cotton mill, the cotton oil mills and the cotton storage warehouses, livestock, sawmills, tourists and stores run by Jewish merchants, generated huge payrolls to a second generation population, which had nearly forgotten the Civil War. Getting a job and establishing a home was the cry now; go to Fitzgerald, get a job and maybe even a Model T Ford, which was appearing in growing numbers.

Back to Shep and Chase Barrick. Our original settlers or colonists, as they liked to be called, had no babies in the cribs. Bob had married and left home. Daniel still dropped in on them, as he was active in the family house moving business, working so hard he hadn't taken time to marry. The twins were teenagers. Now even little Anna was nearly five feet tall, and perhaps weighed seventy-five pounds. Her hair was the most outstanding thing about her, truly her crowning glory, much like that of her grandmother, Bridgett O'Leary, who had passed in Australia long ago.

Now, Anna had told in her bird-like voice, with a far away look in her unblinking blue eyes, of things to pass, mostly sad things. Her grandfather's passing she had predicted. She seemed old for her years. When she spoke of things beyond her years, Chase feared her words and at times would clasp a hand over Anna's little mouth and say, "Anna, you are no gypsy fortune teller." But even Chase knew her little daughter was special. Some spark the other child didn't possess glowed in those blue eyes. She spent much time at the piano she loved, and played the hymns she had learned at church. She even played the piano at Sunday school services. She had a recital at Mrs. Ebenspeager's house, being her top performing student. Even her father, Shep, cleaned up a bit and attended the girl's recital. Olive, who loved and helped Anna, had more interest in sewing and cooking, and was her mother's helper around the home. Books and verses crowded the developing mind of Anna. She could quote long poems by memory. Both girls had quit school, as they got little encouragement from their parents, less from Shep, the stockman, not much of a family man.

For the last few years, the railroad had run a special train, consisting of a dozen or more passenger coaches, pulled by a sleek passenger engine, purchased from the New York Central railroad. It was second hand but refitted to burn coal, and it was freshly painted. This special was chartered by the Union Veteran Old Soldiers Tribune Society of the Civil War, to go to Andersonville, a national cemetery on Decoration Day, the Yankee Memorial Day in the month of May. The central of Georgia railroad crossed the Atlanta & Atlantic sixty-five miles north of Fitzgerald at the town of Oglethorpe, Georgia. There the sleek little engine had its coaches loaded with northern families and a few surviving Union vets. The Fitzgerald City Band members, in their faded blue uniforms and short-billed blue caps, practiced their polished brass instruments and steamed away for the short ride to the station at the village of Andersonville. There they marched in mass to the National Cemetery and the notorious prison camp. There they heard speeches and martial music from other groups form all over the northern states.

Chase Barrick, her father now deceased, and her children had each year faithfully made this pilgrimage to Andersonville. Shep, her husband, never went as the Civil War was American history and was of little interest to him. Australia had no wars. He was quite content to stay with his horses and the people upon the streets of Fitzgerald. The fire station couldn't operate without him, he thought. Besides, the excursion to Andersonville was not free, and tickets had to be bought and small children to be carried. He would have to bathe and dress himself for the occasion. He had rather spend his money on horse feed!

This Memorial Day Chase dressed well as her daughter Olive was an accomplished seamstress. She had stitched her mother and sister Anna very stylish outfits. The older boys had other interests around Fitzgerald. This left only Chase, the twins, and young Frederick, a big boy now, to board the excursion train at the Fitzgerald railroad station. Chase had bought the tickets herself. Her oldest son, Bob, the one close to his mother, had driven the surrey to the station house, where a large crowd of people in a holiday spirit were waiting for the special train to back from Westwood yard to load its festive passengers, band, banners and flags, picnic baskets, and courting couples, all dressed in their finery. Bob saw them aboard the coach reserved for veterans and their families, promising to meet the train upon its return to Fitzgerald in the wee hours of the next morning. He was a good young man, still single and more help to Chase than his father ever hoped to be. She, with her cane to lean upon, would have a struggle to walk to the parade ground and speaker's podium erected for the occasion, one fourth of a mile from the sleepy village of Andersonville and its southern citizens, who had their Southern Memorial Holiday later in May.

You understand, not all Georgia towns and cities had the relationship that the northern and southern citizens of Fitzgerald had. Other special trains arrived from the north — Ohio, Illinois, Iowa, — pure unadulterated Yankees, once again invading the poor defeated state of Georgia. The people of Andersonville, poor as they were, only hoped to provide some services to the revelers. Buggies driven by local boys, perhaps I should say taxies or shuttles, were returning to the prison park and cemetery with its elegant marble statues, memorials to the fallen sons of the windswept north, who now slept beneath the soil of the prison camp where they had suffered malnutrition, sickness, and death. Each state of the Union had a monument erected upon these hallowed grounds, now decorated with wreaths and banners placed there by these pilgrims close by the spur track, where the trains parked to await the return of the mourners to carry them back to their homes and jobs.

A young man, a small fellow of perhaps eighteen years of age, was hoping to relieve some of the prosperous visitors of a few precious dollars,

Yankee dollars, silver dollars with the eagle on them. He was too poor to have a horse and buggy to haul the visitors. His mother was a widow woman, and he was the baby of eight children, who had to scramble to put food on the table and clothes on their backs. This young fellow, with the straw hat on his head, a white apron tied about his waist, standing in a fifty-cent pair of Sears Robuck patent leather shoes was Teddie Newton. He was the sole proprietor of a hastily built lemonade stand decorated with blue crepe paper. Yes, blue. He was standing behind his washtub of lemonade with penny wheel cookies from the store, lemons on credit from the store and ice he had borrowed from the railroad track gang. He was a bright lad, small for his years, looking as though he should be in knee pants. His voice was full grown as he shouted to the Yanks as they paraded by, "Ice cold lemonade, made in the shade and stirred with a spade, five cents a glass, cookies two cents."

Yes, he was in business. He even had an employee, a small black boy washing jelly glasses in another tub, smiling a big smile as he dried them on a terry cloth towel. Business was good that hot day. He couldn't care less about the cause of the civil conflict. Let those eagles fly, tomorrow they would come to roost in a bank in his name, the name you must remember, Teddie Newton, named for Teddy Roosevelt, leader of the Rough Riders down in Cuba. Don't look now, but a pair of blue eyes rests its vision upon the young businessman stirring lemonade with a spade, filling his cigar box with hard cash. The eyes of blue, the ones that were covered by the veil at birth, knew in a glance that her future would include him. His name was unimportant, his politics of no interest. She pointed him out to her sister and whispered, "Look, Olive, and you will see the man of my dreams." Chase snapped at the girls to hold their little brother's hand, and not to loiter around any white trash that waited like buzzards to swoop down on decent citizens who tarried in this poor village of Andersonville, or sat on benches in front of the store on the rickety porch which sheltered them from the hot sun of this Decoration Day.

As the sun sank and shadows lengthened, the mourners meandered back to the station house to board their trains. The fireman was shoveling coal into the firebox of the jaunty locomotive that belched black smoke into the evening air. Its tender had been filled with water from a high water tank beside the track, drawn from Camp Creek, the run off of Providence Spring, which had sprung from the red clay hills and furnished water for the thousands of Northern prisoners. Some said it was an answer to their prayers. Now it quenched the thirst of the steam engines that handled the trains which brought the northerners here, and the ones from Fitzgerald, Georgia, only a four-hour ride from this place.

Anna, Olive and Frederick stood with Chase at the gate of the cemetery. Her hip, the one she had broken in the fall on the ice years ago, had failed her. Chase and her children needed a ride back to the station. A kindly man, an old man with gray beard and wearing overalls, was driving a farm wagon with a wobbly wheel and spokes pulled by a mule, which had ribs you could count, poor as a washboard. The mule answered the man's command to "Whoa!"

"Lady," the man said in a drawling voice, "could I offer you and your children a ride as I am passing that way?" Chase in her desperate plight, thanked him. The girls were glad their mother had accepted the man's generosity, and quickly hoisted their brother, sleepy as he was, and the picnic basket into the wagon. Then they helped their mother to sit on the tailgate of the wagon. The mule pranced ahead and soon they were unloading the wagon to board the coach, where the conductor helped Chase and her brood up the steps and to her double seat, which accommodated her and the tired sleepy young ones.

Olive giggled and teased Anna that the lemonade man had closed shop, and that she would never see her prince charming with the cigar box full of money again, ever again. Anna only smiled her knowing little smile, trembled her chin a bit and spoke to her sister, "Just you wait and see. I have eyes for no other, but please don't speak of this to our mother and never to Papa!"

The engineer of the train, his name was Homer Fairfield, checked his watch, or compared it with the watch of the conductor, who handed him his train orders typed on green tissue paper, telegraphed from the dispatcher of the central of Georgia railroad in Macon, Ga. That engine number 112 would run extra from Andersonville to Oglethorpe, there to transfer to the tracks of the Atlanta & Atlantic railroad south bound to Fitzgerald, mile post number 659. All overdue regular trains had run. With this clearance he threw his long-spouted oil can, which he would use to oil around the hissing little fast passenger engine, to the gangway between the engine and its tender. He mounted to the grab irons and climbed to the cab of the eight-wheeler. He blew one whistle note and set his air brakes to make a standing brake test. He watched his gauges as the needles beneath the glass covers climbed and fell to indicate that the brakes were operating as they should.

Then he spoke to his fireman, a lean strong black man in blue overalls, with a tall starched jacket and cloth cap that only railroad men wore. His goggles, as were the engineer's, were lowered to cover his eyes from the smoke and cinders which would shower from the locomotive as the throttle was opened. "John," the engineer spoke to his fireman, "read these orders if you can and look for the conductor's high ball and all aboard call. Tell me the minute when the flagman lines the mainline switch and waves his lantern. Get your fire right and put water in the boiler, 'cause I am going to take these Yankees to ride. Hang on, old man. If that dispatcher doesn't put us in the pass track hole for some midnight local, I will have us sitting at the station in Fitzgerald before midnight."

The signal came from the conductor. The engineer blew two short whistle blows, opened the engine's throttle with a gloved hand and released his brakes, which whistled as the air reservoir equalized. He leaned out the engine cab window to see the last coach turn through the switch which led the train onto the main line. The high ball signal came from the flagman as he ran to catch the last coach, his station on the train, his lantern swinging in circles. No word other than "main line" was repeated from fireman to engineer. The fireman took his shovel into his hand and slid it into the coal that tumbled onto the steel deck of the engine from the tender. He heaved one shovel full of coal to each corner of the dancing fire as his foot pressed the pedal which activated the butterfly doors, which swung open to admit the coal that slid from the shovel bit to replace the coal which was now glowing embers.

Darkness had fallen when the Special Extra 112 South arrived at Oglethorpe to transfer to its home road. The dispatcher was good to the extra south as he and he alone regulated the traffic upon the shining rails. All these sleeping passengers and the train crew's lives and welfare were in his hands, until the train sat on the track before his second story office in Fitzgerald station, mile post number 659, which only fifteen years ago had been virgin forest, and eighty years ago, the hunting grounds of the crafty Creek Indians and their squaws with papooses strapped to their backs.

Sure as his word, Bob Barrick had the surrey pulled by the bay mare sitting in the station yard as the train sailed into the station. Its air brakes brought the steel wheels up on their steel rails to a grinding halt. Doors were opened, and stepstools dropped to the concrete loading platform. Tired people carrying sleeping children and empty picnic baskets stepped to the platform and hailed taxis. Horse-drawn buggies were loaded, and the people disappeared into the night to their homes and rooms at the St. Paul Hotel, if they could afford the rate, which many could.

Bob helped his mother to a seat in the surrey. The girls drug their little brother to the rig and climbed to a seat. Away to their home on Federal Street they went. Shep came on to the porch to greet them. His pipe in his mouth, he made more over his son Frederick than the girls. He only tipped his hat to Chase and them. He didn't seem to know how to greet his own women folks.

Chase and Shep went to the kitchen to have a cup of hot tea. She told him of the trip and the ceremony, and only wished her father could have lived to have seen the new monument to honor the soldiers from Pennsylvania. Shep was more interested in how the Italian stonecutters had moved the huge slab of marble which had arrived at the park on a rail way flat car, to be positioned correctly and sculpted into an angel with spreading wings.

The twins had put their brother to bed and were now in their room, getting into their nightclothes before they switched off the ceiling light which hung by a twisted electric wire. Anna spoke of the fellow at the lemonade stand, the one who was only a bit taller than she stood in her stocking feet.

She wished she knew his name. The important thing was the fact that he existed, not too far away, and he didn't have her power to see into the future. She told her inner self that he would step in obedience to this supernatural power.

Anna had slipped her dress over her head and stood before the mirror, brushing her wavy red hair, which fell back into place with each sweep of the brush. She was nearly seventeen. Next February she would have her birthday, the same as Olive. It was time for them to think of their future and a husband should be in that future, for sure! She turned to face her sister and stared at her a moment. "Aren't you going to admit that you had eyes for that handsome young engineer who handled our train with such skill? I saw you two eyeing each other over on the station platform, while he and the conductor were comparing watches. I wasn't born yesterday and my eyes don't lie to me."

Her sister's face flushed beneath her olive complexion and she blurted, "Yes, the fresh thing tried to flirt with me. He must be five or six years older than I am, and probably has a wife and baby on the other end of the line. You know how railroad men are. I wouldn't have him on a Christmas tree, no sirree."

"But, Olive," Anna countered, "I have seen it. It won't be on a Christmas tree. You will have him right here in Fitzgerald. I even went to the train register book opened in the station waiting room and read where he signed his name on the crew line up. His bold handwriting, to be read by all concerned, said 'Homer Fairfield, engineer, extra north #112.'"

Chapter XVII

Fourth of July

The following spring Anna had turned seventeen as had her sister Olive, who was a good steady girl, much larger framed than Anna. Anna, still "bird like," was very talented at the piano, as Olive was at singing. Bob, Chase's anchor man, had left home to marry a southern girl. He still worked at the house moving trade, as did his younger brother, who still lived in the bunkhouse. Shep was now slowing down somewhat as he was fully middle aged, but he was still proud and walked upright, and often bunked with his son. Chase and her daughters sheltered Frederick, the baby of the Barrick family. He would never be a stockman as he was doing well in grade school, and would probably be the first member of the family to graduate from Fitzgerald High. He was even showing interest in baseball.

Anna or Tremble Chin, as the family began to know her, spent long periods of time with a far away look in her eyes. Chase noticed the change in the girl who seemed different from her other children, who ate like horses. The older boys grew fast and could stand their ground when they were barely in their teens. Olive, perhaps a bit oversized, was an open minded young lady, very domestic, happy, and a pleasure to be around. Frederick was quick to learn and outspoken of his own mind, as much as Chase was. But Tremble Chin, a child-woman, ate like a bird and thought she was an eagle. She possessed fear, but she had the fortitude of a giant. She had musical talent, a well proportioned body and that red hair she groomed so carefully. If only her chin wouldn't tremble. But didn't her salty old grandfather, Captain Fred, the castaway, have the same affliction?

Chase weighed all these qualities her children possessed. Anna's strange powers of insight and her ability to foresee the future set her aside from the others. It was something she couldn't put her finger on, but yes, it was there. Many times she had come to Chase's knee to predict things, good and bad. Now as she stood on the threshold of womanhood, Chase herself wondered. Anna no longer came to her mother's knee with her visions, especially if they were not good. Finally, Chase drew the girl aside and asked her, point blank, "Child, have you seen a bad omen?"

Anna raised her eyes to meet her mother's and spoke in a low voice. "It isn't very clear, but at times I hear the crackle of flames and the smell of smoke. Perhaps it is only Papa burning trash at the lot." She said no more. She dared not mention that also the vision of the lemonade man at Andersonville haunted her, and the dashing locomotive engineer who had eyes for Olive occupied many of the girl's thoughts and dreams. Yes, she was a dreamer and the other children knew that. Cheer up, Anna, the Fourth of July is nearly here!

The Fourth of July was a day of celebration in the city of Fitzgerald. Firecrackers exploded and parades marched. What remained of the Union veterans assembled to celebrate Independence Day. The northern faction was very patriotic. Some families could trace their ancestry back to Bunker Hill, even the Boston tea party, and were quick to cheer the flag of the Union, although it was never mentioned. Southern people had other memories. Most of them were poor men of the farms and forest, independent by nature and necessity, and Abraham Lincoln was no hero to them.

The colored population was always ready for a holiday and a little celebrating. It was just another Saturday night to them. Regardless of their political leanings, a large crowd of people would assemble at the generous center square of Fitzgerald to witness the activities of the day, hear the band play the national anthem, listen to a welcome address by the mayor of the city, elect a beauty queen, and pray for unity and America the Beautiful. The bootleggers did a land office business.

One of the activities that was staged upon the square was a water fight. Two teams were chosen, strong young men, older men, teams of whites and teams of blacks, who carried fire hoses connected to the fire plugs that existed on each side of the square, paved with dark red bricks which were slick when wet. A fireman with a wrench herded the crowd back to the sidewalks. One team of a dozen men on the east side of the square faced a like team on the west side. Both teams had a firm grip on the limp hose with its brass nozzle, which they pointed at the other team of hardies at a signal from the fire chief. The hydrants were opened by the men with the wrenches, and the hoses instantly sprang to life, the water pressure causing them to writhe like a great snake. A geyser of water erupted from the nozzles of the opposing teams, and a flood of water surged across the brick square, knocking team members down and washing them to the street curb. The strongest men on the nozzles, striving to keep their footing and the powerful flow of water aimed at the opposing team, did their utmost to wash their opponents away in a surge of water which turned and rolled them to the side lines. The team that remained on their feet when the wrench men closed the fire hydrants and the water subsided, was the proud winner of some small prize and the cheers of the crowd. The Southerners and the colored people loved the event. Maybe Miss Fitzgerald would place a kiss on the winners' cheeks.

The other attraction was more, should we say, bloody or sporting. A boxing ring had been dragged by a team of horses, the Barrick team as a matter of fact, now as their master was a bit over the hill, but still strong. The horses were nearly thirty years old, and their trainer more like fifty years old. The ring had ropes and a canvas floor, a bell to ring the rounds, and a referee in a white shirt and a bow tie. When the contenders climbed through the ropes of the ring, the cheering crowd went wild. The fighters went to their corners where their trainers waited with a bottle of water in their hands and a towel to put over their shoulders. Now this was to be a bare knuckle fight, no gloves, ten rounds, no less, and may the best man win! The men were bare to the waist, tights below. The contenders went to the center to shake hands, and a murmur went through the crowd.

Little Anna was there, as was Chase and others. Could it be? Yes, the one with the straight broad shoulders and the mustache was in fact Shepard Barrick, long time champ. The other, by the name of George Lawford, was the powerful young policeman who had recently charged old man Barrick with disturbing the peace of Fitzgerald when he gave the bully of the town, Mr. Corbitt, a thrashing on River Street. Corbitt had kept patrolman Lawford supplied in stump liquor he manufactured for his protection upon the streets of Fitzgerald. Chase looked at Anna, whose chin was trembling and her head was shaking a negative signal. Chase, the wife of the contender, who had a small chance against a man twenty years younger than him, quick and mean as he was known to be, herded her brood to the surrey and headed home.

Shep was good, in fact great, as he out-danced George. He had to depend on footwork. The first round ended with the clang of the bell. Both men went to their corners unscathed. The gamblers were making book. So far it was a draw. I don't know whether Shep was careless or too sure of his abilities, but George landed a blow to Shep's chin which shook him. He bounced back to pound Lawford's body, which stood like a rock in the center of the ring. He was saving himself as he knew he could take a lot of blows in his stride, but these blows would grow weaker as the rounds passed. Shep began to slow down in the fifth round and Lawford came to life, landing blow after blow on the old champ.

In the sixth round the referee called the fight. Shep was beaten, still on his feet and bleeding about the face. Lawford had settled the score he held against Shepard Barrick. The prize was high. The champ's hearing was gone. He was carried from the ring, and the crowd dispersed. Shep would never be the same. His boxing career was over. Even his mind was slow and his steps measured. People on the street, the streets he loved so much, whispered the words, "The old man Barrick is punchy, deaf as a post for the remainder of his life."

Shep stayed around his animals and was respected by the street people. His boys, Bob and Daniel, were now the acting managers of Barrick Movers. Chase did what she could for Shep. She had made few friends in the neighborhood and secretly longed to leave Fitzgerald and the people who jammed the sidewalks up town. The train whistles that resounded through Fitzgerald were a call for her to leave, but she was faithful to her children. Bob and Daniel needed her. Shep had withdrawn and left the bunkhouse only to eat his meals. He seemed to be able to communicate with his horses, now his companions. He walked to the firehouse each morning and sat in a sunny spot on a curbstone with some of his friends from the past, who also had seen better days.

Speaking of better days, Anna and Olive had had their seventeenth birthday and were popular girls. They went to church, had girl friends, even among the Southern girls. Good girls they were, who had been taught good manners, music and the true values of life. Often a group of neighborhood girls walked to downtown Fitzgerald to shop or drink a soda at the drugstore. Anna, small as she was, stood out in a group of girls, as her hair was unusually beautiful and her personality one to be envied — timid she wasn't.

The main line of the Atlanta & Atlantic railroad went through Fitzgerald on Gloshester Street, and crossed Federal Street, perhaps now the busiest crossing in town. Automobiles had replaced much horse-drawn traffic, and a flagman was stationed at the crossing to warn pedestrians and traffic of oncoming trains and the switch engine that shuttled about town. The old man at the crossing, the flagman, was a friend and neighbor of the Barrick family, and a special friend of the twins, Anna and Olive, as they often passed his shack by the crossing.

Now, the freight depot of the railroad company had a long platform where a gang of men unloaded freight to be delivered to stores uptown.

True to Anna's prediction, not to her surprise, she grabbed her best friend Millie Knight and confided into her ear, "There, Millie, is the man of my dreams. I knew he would one day appear before my eyes, and there he is, with a clipboard in his hands. Isn't he cute? I will only smile at him as I have never been introduced to him. I only saw him once before, when we went to Andersonville on Decoration Day. I hope he sees me. Yes, he is looking. Oh, Millie. I hope my chin doesn't tremble, not now. I am happy!"

Sure enough, the young man let his eyes leave his clipboard and the waybills it held. He smiled broadly at the passing girls, who smiled at him.. Then he pushed his hat back and bowed a bit to say, "Good day, ladies," and smiled a winning smile, so warm.

"Oh, Millie, my knees are knocking. I am so thrilled. I must not rush to him unintroduced. He must make the first move." As the girls passed on, Teddie Newton walked over to the crossing flagman, Mr. Morris, withdrew a dollar bill from his pocket and smiled. Then he spoke, "Morris, do you know my brother Charlie Newton, agent for the railroad company? I am his younger brother, from Andersonville, now living with him and his wife Lillie. I am single and learning agency work under my brother, and I will soon have a good job, as I am good on the Morse Code Key. I hope to soon be a telegraph operator and station agent and hope to meet a young girl or two. Do you know the small one with the red hair you've just spoken to? I will give you this dollar if you will make me acquainted with her, a proper introduction, as I can see she is a lady and my last desire is to offend her."

The wise old flagman reached for the money and pocketed it. With a chuckle he said, "Yes, I have watched you, Newton. I am well acquainted with the redhead, Anna Barrick. She is a daughter of good people, even though they are Yankees. Her father is Australian, a true friend of mine. Her mother is a bit to herself, but I myself will have a word with her. I like you. You be near, as she will return within the hour, as she would never let dark catch her on the streets, as these street walkers do. Don't be far, Teddie!"

Teddie was twenty-two years old. He was from a railroad family, not farmers. His father and grandfather were Irish immigrants who had been trackmen and hard workers. He had five uncles who survived the Civil War, Tennessee volunteers in the Confederate army. His father had been too young to go, so he stayed in the mountains. He hid out for weeks with their livestock to save them from the Union army. He had married a girl orphaned by the war, Sally Ann Appleton, adopted by a returning Union soldier walking back to West Virginia. She didn't even know her family name. She was so young and had lost her entire family. The kindly veteran gave her his name, put her with his kids, and raised her to the age of thirteen. Then she married William Newton and followed him and his track gang to Mobile, Alabama. She bore him eight children, two girls and six boys.

Teddie was the baby and runt of the lot. He, like Anna Barrick, got a double share of grit and fortitude. His sisters and two brothers, the frail ones, became telegraphers. The husky ones became trackmen, section foremen as the hard-working father had been. They left Alabama when Teddie was in knee pants to relocate at Andersonville, where the father was section foremen on the Central of Georgia Railroad. His section was the track between Andersonville and Oglethorpe, the very track the special train had passed over the day Anna saw Teddie for the first time as a lemonade vendor! He had learned to telegraph from a kindly woman agent telegrapher there at the depot in Andersonville. He had tried farming, as Shep Barrick had, and gave it up as a hard dollar. His older brother, Charlie Newton, was a railroad agent at Fitzgerald, and had offered to train Teddie to become an agent, some day, somewhere. The only condition was he must not marry until he had a paying job, a paycheck, and a shelter over his head, and must never marry one of these Yankee girls who abounded in Fitzgerald, an enclave of Yanks here in sun-kissed south Georgia, far from their homeland in the frozen north.

Teddie, not one to lend himself to others' wishes, played with fire eyeing over these Northern girls. Teddie watched the old crossing guard closely and after an hour or so, the girls returned, laughing and teasing one another. Anna could hardly wait to get to the tracks to see if the young man was still about his work. Millie, her confidant, was first to spy Teddie, "There he is, Anna. Don't panic. A train is passing and we must wait till it has gone, giving you an excuse to stop a while."

Mr. Morris, the flagman at the crossing, turned to greet the young ladies, who always passed the time of day with him. He spoke to Anna in a low tone. "Miss Barrick, I have a young friend, an admirer of yours, he is a fine young fellow and attends church where I do. By chance, could I make you acquainted with him, as he is single and new in town, anxious to meet the young people? May I call him over?"

"I have seen him before, Mr. Morris. Last May it was, as he had a cold drink stand along the tracks where we left the train to attend the memorial services. He seems to be a hard worker, and I hate to stop him from his work."

"Oh, he won't mind," Mr. Morris replied. "Oh, Teddie, do you have a moment? It would be my pleasure to introduce you to Miss Anna Barrick. Her parents are dear friends of mine. Anna, this young man is Mr. Teddie Newton, new in town, soon to be employed by the Atlanta & Atlantic railroad, and this, Teddie, is Millie Knight, her closest friend."

Teddie stuck his clipboard in the flagman's shack and strolled away with the girls, telling them of his plans and hopes. Then, out of the blue, Teddie blurted, "Anna, you don't mind if I take the liberty to call you 'Anna'? Could I have permission to call on you at your home? I know you live in the large house down Federal Street before the bridge. I would like to meet your parents and become better acquainted." Anna looked into his eyes and, to her relief, her heart, not her chin, began to tremble.

Teddie thought Sunday would never come. His brother Charlie gave the young man many duties around the office, from sweeping to balancing the books. Even on Sundays duties awaited him, but Sunday evenings were his. Charlie's wife, Lillie, was good to Teddie. She herself had two small children and made her home in a small rented house in perhaps the best neighborhood in Fitzgerald. Charlie Newton had been Teddie's protector since their father had died of typhoid fever, which struck the rail gang of which he was a foreman. Sally Ann Newton, their mother, fell upon hard times as a widow. The hard-working older boys and girls of the Newton family were not lazy and soon fanned out all over Georgia. Their devotion to duty and perfection in their work rewarded them well, and they didn't forget their widowed mother and little Teddie, now a man in a boy's body.

Teddie loved his mother back in Andersonville, but knew he had to seek his fortune, and fortune seemed to love Fitzgerald and its thriving railroads, which were hiring people and paying wages far above those of agricultural workers. Fitzgerald was the place to go, and Charlie Newton had a good job as agent operator in the new depot of the Atlanta & Atlantic Railroad, connecting with all the major railroads out of Atlanta and the Plant System railroads that dominated Florida and its port cities. Soon it would also have a line to the port city of Brunswick on the Atlantic coast, only a hundred and thirty miles distant from Fitzgerald.

More and more Charlie had depended on his young brother to perform his duties at the agency. Teddie had no bad habits other than tobacco, but Charlie had begun to spend more time at the pool room and bars which abounded on East River Street, not to mention the Sweet Water Street location of Wilma Littletrees and her house of ill repute, featuring fallen women, both white and black, anxious to satisfy the sexual needs of the male gentry of Fitzgerald. Teddie could see his brother sliding into the gutter if some changes were not made. Teddie had followed the other course of life. He went to church and Sunday school, making many friends among the better class young people of Fitzgerald, both of Northern and Southern extraction. This Anna Barrick, outstanding as she was, had kind of knocked the props, so to speak, from under him. He could hardly wait to call on her and meet her parents.

Sunday arrived. Teddie arose from his cot with the rising sun, helped Lillie with the children as Charlie had never come home, then went to the railroad office to check the message hook for telegrams advising of special movements or livestock to be fed or watered en route to Florida or Texas. He breathed a sigh of relief that the message book was empty, no impending movements or derailments. You do understand, a railroad knows no day or hour, three hundred and sixty-five days of the year. That traffic never stops. An employee lucky enough to have such a good job must protect it, twenty-four hours a day, seven days a week, although Sunday was a light day. Yes, it appeared that Teddie had inherited his older brother's job, all but the paycheck every two weeks, which Lillie usually managed to get her hands on to run the Charlie Newton home.

Teddie usually rode a bicycle to the office and church, but he had side jobs that Charlie didn't know about. One was to clean the stalls at the livery stable of George Block, who paid him a few dollars along to help him with the horses and buggies he rented to people on occasions. Teddie, after a quick midday lunch, hitched one of Mr. Block's harness horses to a livery or rental buggy and away he went in some style to the Barricks' home on Federal Street, before the wooden bridge over Gladys Creek.

Now if Teddie Newton had a shortcoming or perhaps a quality, the young scamp would take a chance or blow his own horn. He longed to be a big shooter, and he would try most any route to become one. Yes, that clean-shaven mite of a young man driving up to the Barricks' hitching post was Teddie Newton, no less.

Shep Barrick and his son Bob were sitting on their front porch. Shep, now deaf and slow to speak and think, spoke slowly to his elder son, "Bob, who could that be driving George Block's best buggy and Kate?" Kate was the iron gray mare that he had broken to harness long ago for Mr. Block. Shep still knew the horses about the streets of Fitzgerald, that sense was still awake in his battered head.

Bob told his father, "Well, Papa, I'll be a horn-toed-biddy if it isn't that new fellow down at the railroad freight station. They call him Teddie. He is older than he looks." Bob arose from his chair on the porch to greet the well-dressed fellow, as Teddie stepped to the ground from the driver's seat. "Hello, Teddie. What brings you to our door?"

"Good day, Bob. This perhaps is your father, Mr. Barrick of the fire station? I was introduced to your sister, Anna, by your neighbor, Mr. Morris, at the crossing where I work."

Shep slowly rose from his seat upon the steps to extend his hand to Teddie. He removed his pipe from his mouth and spoke in measured words, "Yes, my friend spoke to me recently and told me to expect you to come calling on my daughter, Anna, as I would not let just any bloke call on her!" He could not hear Teddie's reply, so he handed him a small pad and a stub pencil.

Teddie took the pad and wrote, "My name is Teddie Newton, and I hope you will permit her to ride about town with me this afternoon."

"Yes, on one condition, that her twin Olive goes along," Shep wrote in reply. Chase had also spoken with Mr. Morris and on his recommendations had told both girls to get ready as they had never had a date before, and he was somewhat of a stranger and a Southerner at that, not from a family of Fitzgerald that she knew. In all probability Shep Barrick took more interest in the iron gray mare Teddie had hitched to the buggy than he did in the young man, who was about to drive off with his twin daughters. Chase studied Teddie's face through the window and liked him, but she didn't like the way he butchered the Queen's English or his tacky Southern drawl. Why couldn't these people go ahead and spit out what they had to say? Why, for the land of Goshen, couldn't Anna have fallen for a northern lad of a good family? A banker perhaps, not an apprentice railroad man trying to make an impression on her girls by driving up in a rented rig.

The twins were dressed and coming down the stairs. They had on their best Sunday clothes, which were in good taste and style, midi blouses and pleated skirts to their ankles. They were surprised but thrilled to see the horse and buggy that Teddie somehow was driving. Their giggles ceased as they stepped to the porch to welcome Teddie, who didn't realize Anna had a twin sister, to whom he now was introduced. Teddie was quite handsome, white shirt, celluloid collar and bow tie, suit of clothes and shined shoes, a very different image than the Barrick men, as they were working men, stockmen, blue collar or no collar. In fact, Teddie was quite a dandy and attended church and Sunday school every week, unless duty called him to the railroad. The girls, especially Anna, were tired of coarse men, fisticuffs, horse manure, shouting, and swearing, simply tired of it.

Anna wanted a gentler home for her babies to come up in, a regular paycheck, singing about the piano at night, dinner parties at the St. Paul Hotel, band concerts in the parks, and perhaps a Model T Ford automobile in the driveway of a bungalow on a lot in a quiet neighborhood, maybe even on West Central Avenue, near the mansion being built by Captain Jack Jacobs, the lumber baron. Yes, the child-woman with the vision for the future could not and would not settle for the rag-a-ma-tag life style that her mother had shared with Shepard Barrick. This Teddie seemed to have his wagon hitched to a star, and she intended to be at his side in that wagon, whatever life would bring!

Chase came out on the porch to meet Teddie. She shook his hand after wiping her hands on her apron. Her first impression of him was good. He certainly wasn't the average lad. His handshake was firm, his smile happy, and his breath did not have the odor of strong drink. Shep liked the way Teddie handled the mare, his straightforward nature, and the look that fell upon his face when he saw Anna.

Don't think for a minute that Shep didn't want the best for his daughter. I hope I have been fair with old Shep. He was not an evil man, only an Australian swagman.

The buggy seat was designed for two grown people. Olive, being the only full-sized person of the three, had plenty of room as they all sat in the buggy seat with room to spare. About town they drove, waving and calling to the other Sunday evening promenaders upon the streets and sidewalks. They saw window shoppers and even passed a baseball game on a vacant lot. Down Central Avenue they went. Not far west of the post office, Anna pointed to a fine vacant lot near the home of Mrs. Ebenspeager, her beloved music teacher. That strange stare crossed her young face, and then she calmly spoke, "My home will stand here some day."

Olive laughed her carefree laugh and spoke, "Anna, my dear sister, that lot belongs to the widow Sasser, and there isn't enough money in the Exchange Bank to make her part with that lot. Paving is being put down, even sidewalks. Why, we couldn't even pay the taxes on that lot. Besides you could buy three lots on Swan Street for the price of that lot!"

Anna stared straight ahead and softly said, "Wait and see, my dear."

Teddie turned the horse about as the house he shared with Charlie and

Lillie was only two blocks farther west. To change the subject, he quipped, "We are not in the real estate ventures. We are out on a lark." He slapped the reins across the generous rump of the iron gray mare. She broke into a canter, and he steered her and the happy young people away to the south end of Federal Street and the Dixie Highway, which led to Osceola.

The sisters asked where he was headed, and he said nothing for a bit. Then he told them he was taking them to Minnie Mill Pond to walk the ancient dam beyond the watermill, to the second spillway, where the millpond poured its run-off water, when the mill was not running. The twins squealed in excitement as they had never been there, and if the mare would step up, they could return home before evening church services started.

The horse, at the urgings of Teddie, soon covered the four miles to the mill and the store which fronted the highway soon to be paved. It was just a drive through the country and a stroll upon a dam, but, oh, what it seemed to Anna! As Teddie held her hand, Olive said she was tired and sat on the bench to give her sister and her new beau a bit of privacy. Teddie was a gentleman and didn't leave Olive on the bench too long. He did softly mention that perhaps the following Sunday they could attend the band concert in the Tribune park, and he had a friend, a young fireman and extra board engineer on the Atlanta & Atlantic railroad, a good young man, a member of his youth group at the Methodist Church, his church. He was lonely and if he wasn't on a run he could date Olive as a blind date.

Anna was quick to reply, "I will be ready and Olive also would like to meet a proper young man. I will speak to you at the crossing early into next week. Now we must get Olive and hurry home as my people expect us home early." They rejoined Olive, and Teddie, splurger that he was, jingled the change in his pocket and bought the girls a cherry cola and a moon pie at the store. They laughed and talked all the way back to the Federal Street house of the Barrick sisters, just as the sun sank below the horizon.

Chapter XVIII

The Fire

Autumn followed summer in Fitzgerald. Thanksgiving had come and gone. December had begun a season of cheer and happiness. Teddie and Anna spent many hours together. Olive had met Homer Fairfield, her blind date, to her delight and his satisfaction. Could you believe? He was the dashing locomotive engineer who handled the throttle of the #112, the eight-wheeler that pulled the special train to Andersonville. He was now a regular engineer on the Thomasville branch and waved to Olive each day as his train crossed Federal Street. Anna passed the time of day with Teddie Newton, now a chief clerk at the railroad agency. Charlie, his brother, had lost his job as an agent. The wicked temptations which life's other side offered in booming Fitzgerald had been too much temptation for a country boy. He had sold a bale of cotton off the depot platform to a farmer to cover a debt he had at a gambling den at the Davis Hotel. When he left Fitzgerald, Teddie assumed the vacancy and a debt at the Exchange Bank to pay for the bale of missing cotton; his good name was his only collateral. Charlie had secured a job on the Seaboard Railroad in Ocala, Florida, never to return to Georgia. His move left Teddie homeless. He rented a room in a boarding house a block above the Barrick home on Federal Street, close to his job and close to Anna.

Homer Fairfield and Olive Barrick had eloped and rented a small house on Swan Street. He made good money on the railroad, which Olive shared with Anna, her twin, and her family. Then one night, just after Christmas, a bolt of lighting during a dry thunderstorm slammed into the two-story Barrick house. Even old Shep heard the bang of lighting bolt and the roll of thunder that followed. The electric lights were shot but a lustrous glow came from the wood-shingled roof of the heart-pine house. A lamp was lit and Anna rushed down the stairs to her mother's room, with her brother Frederick by her side, rubbing his sleepy eyes. She went to shake Chase awake. "The house is on fire, I smell the same smoke and hear the flames as they crackle on the roof that I heard in my vision, only tonight they are real. Get what you can and dress yourself quickly. Get my brother outside and I will awake Papa and Daniel out in the bunkhouse."

Shep and Daniel were already in the lot, as the horses, the old Belgians stiff and blind as they were, had smelled smoke. The bay had already whinnied and broken the gate down. Soon the men and Anna, her chin in a tremble, had all the stock loose from their stalls, even the blind ponies in another barn nearby, farther away from the flames that danced their deadly dance upon the roof of the house. Daniel had left barefooted to run to the fire station to alert the firemen, who were now blowing the fire sirens, which wailed atop the city hall. Shep knew that the three fine horses that stood beneath their harnesses at that alarm would soon be running at full tilt down Federal Street. The pumper wagon rumbled through the night with firemen clinging to its sides and rear.

The barn was saved, but as the sun sent its first rays into the fog and smoke, all that remained of the large house, home to Chase and her brood, was only smoldering ashes. Shep was ok. Bob and Daniel saved a few personal items and clothes, a picture album, and Chase's father's portrait. Shep, despite his affliction, was relieved that his barn and stock were saved by the firemen and all his friends. Anna had only the clothes on her back, as she could never return to her burnt room. Olive came as soon as the alarm had sounded and had her mother and sister moved by the neighbors to her house, only two blocks away on Swan Street.

They never returned to the Federal Street home. Shep was embittered and continued to live in the bunkhouse, sometimes alone in his own silent world, thinking of his horses and livestock and his family. He milked his cow, tended a vegetable garden that supplied the neighbors with vegetables, and doctored a few sick or abused horses which were in about the same shape he was in.

Homer Fairfield made good money and Olive had a Model T-Ford car, which she drove about town, taking Anna and her mother to the store and to the Christian Church. Teddie Newton, a tireless worker, had soon been promoted to stationmaster, with a staff of clerks and laborers and a pay raise as he was on the railroad payroll now. He and Anna eloped a month after the house burned. They were secretly married by the justice of the peace, Bill Smith, and Millie Knight was a witness. Anna was a tight-fisted little business woman, as she was fed up with sloppy bookkeeping and poor business practices like Shep's; or perhaps she inherited her frugal ways from the beautiful grandmother she never knew in far away Australia, Bridgett O'Leary Barrick; or perhaps from the old squatter, her great-grandfather, who amassed an empire along the Darling River on the other side of the world.

Anna managed Teddie's finances, even purchasing the marriage license from old Mrs. Lathem at the Courthouse. The newlyweds set up housekeeping in one room of an early settlement church house, sharing the kitchen and bathroom with two other young couples. Teddie was strapped with the debts that his brother had left around Fitzgerald. Somehow Anna stretched Teddie's paychecks to feed them, pay the rent, and drop a few coins in the collection plate at church. Anna even sent her mother a dollar bill every week. Olive sewed for her, and every morning at daybreak someone left on Anna's porch a bottle of fresh buttermilk, a mold of fresh-churned butter and a generous bundle of splinters to start fires. Anna was suspicious of who the kind person might be, and true to her notions, one morning before day a bent figure with a heavy mustache smoking a crooked-stemmed pipe strode across the street in the dawn's early light to place his burden on her and Teddie's doorstep. Yes, it was her papa, Shepard Barrick!

The fire in the night, which came as no surprise to Anna, had a profound effect on the Barrick family. Never again would things be as they had been in settlement days. Not only the fire but time had its effects also. Shep and Chase would never live under the same roof again. The older boys had their families now. The twins had married, and the youngest child was soon to graduate from high school at the head of his class, and he had a steady girlfriend. He and his mother lived with Olive, who somehow had held onto what family unity had been left. Olive was heavy with child to the delight of Homer Fairfield. It seemed as if the railroad had brought not only Fitzgerald prosperity, but also to the twins two responsible husbands. Their jobs, although different, demanded a person dedicated to duty and demanded perfection. The men were rewarded with a bi-monthly paycheck well above the standard pay around town. Anna and Teddie joined the Methodist Church. They were soon to be fire victims again, as the old rooming house where they lived caught fire. They escaped in their bedclothes and with their Bible, the one they hoped would become their family Bible. Anna stood by Teddie, watching the flames' dancing glow and their meager possessions go up in black smoke.

The prancing team, Shep's pupils, had been replaced by a big red fire truck with a high steering wheel, which came to contain the flames. Yes, progress had retired the horses as it had their trainer, who lived in a bunkhouse alone in a silent world, with his memories of a boyhood in Australia, the years at sea, and life as a lumberjack in the North Woods. He had witnessed the growth of the railroads, the coming of the gasoline-powered automobiles, the roaring days of the town of Fitzgerald, not to mention the boxing ring, the same epic of Broken Hill, New South Wales. Yes, he had watched two cities spring from the ground; one stepped to the tune of gold, the second to the tune of a bloody Civil War. Yes, Shep was not alone. He had his memories. He bore the scars of his boxing bouts. His beautiful Belgian team had passed on, as old Peggy had. He still walked to the fire station to pass his time. He still saw the fine horses he had trained so well, as they had been sold to the Fitzgerald Ice Company to pull their ice delivery wagons each morning. Wherever they might be upon the streets, their ears would prick and their heads would turn to whinny a greeting to their old trainer, Shep Barrick. Whatever he had lost in life, he would always be a subject of the Queen and an Australian stockman, two things that fire and time could never change.

Sit in the sun, smoke your pipe, and spin your yarns of the long ago, old man. You are rich in memories. Now let your offspring have their lives and children. The show must go on, only now new actors have appeared upon the stage of life. The curtain is raised. Who will be the star performers?

The spotlight was turned on Teddie and Anna standing alone staring at the ashes of what little they had possessed. Teddie relied on Anna's calm resoluteness. A smile came across her face, a smile that stopped her chin from trembling. "Teddie," she said, "Mama and Olive have a suit of clothes that my brother Frederick had planned to wear to his graduation exercise next spring. Olive will have it altered to fit you by sunup. You will be dressed in it and sitting behind your desk at the depot when it opens. Your credit is excellent as you have nearly paid off your brother's debts, and I am well. Although I have failed to mention to you that I have missed my last two periods. I will find us a room for tonight. I was tired of this wretched old rooming house. We will somehow buy that lot on Central Avenue. You see old Mrs. Sasser. I will bump thunder with you, and we will get that old black carpenter, Coleman Layfield, to build us a nice home on our lot, the one I claimed on our first promenade. I remember you didn't own that varnished buggy pulled by that iron gray mare, but we rode in it. Where is the gumption that shone so when you first called on me? Get going, you will soon have a wife and baby to support. Your job didn't burn up, and I will always be right behind you to weather the storms of life!"

Homer was out on his run. Olive had taken the Newton couple to her house. By sunup they, Mamma and the twins, had Teddie dressed even better than before the fire. Frederick would just have to wear his old suit to graduation exercises. When the railroad station opened to the public at 8:00 a.m., who do you think was sitting behind the desk marked "stationmaster," with a black shoeshine boy popping his shoe polish rag on a borrowed pair of shoes? You got it. It was Teddie Newton reading the *Atlanta Journal* newspaper. He was open for business as usual.

The day was a busy one for Anna as several people came by to leave clothes and sympathies. Old Shep came over leading a gaunt old horse, a gift for them, not to mention a jug of milk. Her brother knew of a little house that had been given to them if they would move it. Anna thanked him, but said no. She told him to move it over to the vacant lot her papa owned, next to where their home had burned, and set it up as a good tight home for their father, a decent place for him to spend his last days. This they did. Olive pledged to wash his clothes and look in on him, for Chase now was too frail and crippled to do heavy house work and spent much time reading and writing letters. Shep was rather hard to live with and seemed to enjoy his solitude, pipe, and a few old nags plus a good milk cow. He was still able to tend his vegetable garden, mostly giving the produce to neighbors and passers by. Yes, he was too good for his own good, still the target for a sad story. Too bad his family hadn't had all the money he had failed to collect or just given away.

That evening when Teddie returned from his job, Anna was dressed in give-away clothes and had sold the gift horse her father had given her for fifty dollars cash. Her red hair crowned her head in waves and curls. "Come on, Teddie. Don't sit down. Supper can wait! We are about to walk over to old Mrs. Sasser's home on Lea Street and approach her to sell us 'our' lot over on Central Avenue."

Teddie only laughed, "How in the name of heaven can a penniless boy buy one of the best lots in the most prestigious neighborhood of Fitzgerald?" he inquired.

"I have one of my feelings, dear one," Anna said, "Mrs. Sasser is a staunch member of the Christian Church, the one I was raised in. My 'natures' have told me not to tarry. As the sun sets, you, Teddie Newton, dressed in the fine suit my sister burned the midnight oil to fit you and the donated shoes will mount the steps of that old gray stone mansion over by my church on Lee Street, will ring Mrs. Sasser's doorbell with me, wait for her maid to open it, and wait for her in the dusty old parlor, and you, my love, will ask her to sell lot number 320 on Central Avenue to you and I!"

"But, darling Anna, I am tired and hungry and you in your delicate condition don't need to be walking clear across town in the dark."

Hearing his words, Olive shoved the young couple out the front door of her home. It looked as though Teddie had to step in obedience to Anna's wish, or possibly, was it the spirit of Bridgett, Anna's grandmother, which came from the long ago? Who knows? But true to Anna's vision, Teddie's hand twisted the doorbell of Mrs. Sasser's mansion. The creaking door slowly opened and Mrs. Sasser's black maid stood there, remaining to see who had rung the bell, which seldom rang. Mrs. Sasser in her dressing gown put her eyeglass on to recognize the young couple who stood in the center of her parlor. A smile broke her stare as she recognized Anna. "Anna Barrick, the piano player at church! What brings you and this young fellow to my door this evening? Please, have a seat and tell me of yourself."

Anna, at her best, looked at Mrs. Sasser straight in the eye and said, "This is my husband Teddie Newton, the new stationmaster for the railroad. He and I have been married for some months now. We have been burned out of our rooming house, and we would like to approach you on the matter of buying your vacant lot on West Central Avenue."

Mrs. Sasser studied them for a long moment, then spoke slowly, "Not to offend you, my dear, but you have selected one of my most expensive lots. I am asking five hundred dollars for it as the location is one of the best and the title is clear. Can you afford this lot, as I have others that may better fit your price range."

"Thank you, Mrs. Sasser," Anna protested never batting an eye, "I have fifty dollars in my purse to pay down on the lot."

Teddie's head snapped back, his eyes opened wider, and he almost dropped his fedora hat, creased lengthwise and with a rolled brim upon the sides.

"My husband Teddie has paid off quite a sizable note at the bank you have interest in, and his credit is as good as his paycheck is."

Silence fell heavily upon the musty room, which was seldom used. That silence was finally broken by Mrs. Sasser's deep voice, "Your family have been good sober people, never lazy, never partaking of strong drink. You were raised in my church, and you are talented at the piano. I have had my eyes on you for quite some time, and evidently your husband has shown responsibility on the railroad. You give me those fifty dollars as a down payment and I will direct my lawyer Mr. McArnold, to draw a deed and a note for four hundred fifty dollars to my estate, and wish you two the best of luck. Now, I will excuse you."

Teddie and Anna thanked the old lady and found themselves in the dark street, with nothing but their love and resolve to head them back to their bed in the old neighborhood.

Both of them were hungry and tired. The pit of Teddie's stomach had gnawed to his backbone. "Do you care to tell me, my dear wife, did one of the spirits that dwell in that soul of yours, perhaps your fairy godmother, give you those fifty dollars I didn't know were in your purse?"

"No, Teddie. My papa gave me one of his horses to help us in this time of need, and I sold it to a farmer. Tomorrow I will contact Clearance Sydney or his wife for a loan, as he is old and fickle, and he and my papa have for years been friends. When the home place burned, he sent his condolences and offered to help. You, my dear, no later than tomorrow, will approach this new banker, Mr. Oldcomer, concerning a house mortgage. I hope Clearance Sydney will cosign with you and me, as we will soon have a deed to 'our' lot. Perhaps it was my fairy godmother who pointed it out to me, or if you believe in spirits, it was perhaps my great-grandfather, the talented land grabber, Old Limon O'Leary, surely now on the other side of the river of life. You do, my love, have a meal ticket at the railroad station, Union News Café, and you, my landed husband, are about to take your pregnant wife out to supper."

Teddie laughed, swept her into his arms, and said, "Dynamite comes in small packages. Let's go Mrs. 'Got Rocks!'"

Teddie had all he could handle at the railroad station, although he did think Anna was correct in her thoughts to improve their station in life. The baby, who was on the way, deserved a more secure life than either of them had experienced. Olive didn't have enough room for all of them.

Teddie told Anna to locate an apartment, which she did with an old widow woman, Mrs. Willaford, near the new elementary school house on Swan Street. The rent was twelve dollars a month, which they could afford. It was close to Teddie's work. Small as she was, Anna carried the baby well and they were happy in the small, furnished apartment.

Things didn't go quite as smoothly for Teddie at Mr. Oldcomer's bank. The banker listened to him and would have liked to loan him money to construct a home, but Teddie had no collateral and the unpaid lot could hardly secure a loan for perhaps twenty-five hundred dollars, even though Teddie had a good name and a railroad job. Mr. Oldcomer told Teddie to return as soon as he had paid off the lot, and he would review his loan application. Anna took this news in her stride as her appeal for a loan from Clearance Sydney had also fallen on deaf ears. The old lord was destitute thanks to his young son's escapades. Still the young couple was happy. They had many friends among the young couples at the church, and Homer and Olive had helped them over their rough spots, two devastating fires within two years.

Sundays belonged to them. Teddie now had a clerk to protect the railroad interest on Sundays, and unless there was a derailment or several carloads of livestock to be fed and watered, he could spend the long summer evenings with Anna and their friends. The era of the tram railroads, short lines owned by sawmills or wealthy businessmen had seen their heyday, but still the Ocilla, Broxton & Southern OBS was in operation and interchanged with the Atlanta Birmingham and Coast (AB&C) at Hooker Street crossing in Fitzgerald. The powerful little shay steam locomotive, now an antique, was in tri-weekly service. The line was standard gauge, and boxcars of the two lines could negotiate the primitive track which crossed the Alapaha River at a popular resort spot named "Mariana Lake," featuring a swimming pool, dance hall, and concession stand. Roads were poor, automobiles few, and the distance of twenty-five miles rather difficult for horse-drawn buggies and wagons.

Teddie and Anna, now showing her pregnancy, were popular with the young people of Fitzgerald, and longed to go on outings and picnics, which were high on the list of entertainment. Picnic baskets were filled with fried chicken, southern-style potato salad, banana pudding, and don't forget the chocolate cake. These carefree young people would pack a lunch, and Teddie and Homer would knock on the door of the old man who was the engineer aboard the old shay engine parked down on Hooker Street, as it didn't operate on Sundays, and the happy crowd would wait down by the tracks. Homer, being an engineman himself, had fired for the old veteran engineer, Mr. Dykes. Teddie, good at approaching people, would make Mr. Dykes, who was famous for his appetite and especially fried chicken, a proposition: a free picnic dinner if he would let the boys fire up the shay and Homer operate the little engine. All he would have to do was ride and eat.

Mr. Dykes, being a good-natured old fellow, would quickly agree. Who could refuse all those pretty young girls and overstuffed picnic lunch baskets? The gleeful crowd soon had steam built and the fire roaring. Homer was at the throttle, and Mr. Dykes sitting in the fireman's seat. Teddie manned the foot board of the engine. He had a switch key and could unlock the switch which led to the interchange track. There he would couple to an empty boxcar, and return to the tracks of the OBS. line. The empty wooden boxcar with its wide side door wide open would soon be loaded with young men and their dates and wives, not to mention quilts to sit upon and spread the food on the banks of the Alapaha River, which would echo the laughter and singing of a carefree crowd of hard-working young people from Fitzgerald.

The track was uneven, and tree limbs dragged the side of the boxcar of the dinky little shay engine, which on week days hauled giant pine logs on flatcars not nearly as wide as boxcars were. The whistle blew to clear the way of free-ranging cattle and goats. The shrill shrieking whistle and the chugging engine exhaust muffled the joyful voices from the boxcar stenciled with the Atlanta Birmingham and Coast. That Teddie would try most anything, and Anna wasn't far behind!

Chapter XIX

The Baby

Time had flown. Anna bore her first child, and Teddie worked hard. The railroad officials demanded a lot, and he gave them a lot. Anna had a hard delivery, but Chase and Olive had called old Dr. Bussell and he had sat by her bedside all night. Finally a baby girl was crying to the top of her lungs. Olive, already the mother of a daughter, was a godsend for Anna. Anna was moved to Olive's house, and Teddie ate on the streets and slept very little at their apartment. Anna had one of her dark visions of the baby girl they named Dorothy. She felt something was wrong with the tiny girl, who slept fitfully and often turned a bluish cast.

As usual, Anna was right. She woke to nurse the child now two weeks old and found her dead in her crib. Too late to call Dr. Bussell, she was gone. Anna had a strong constitution and sent for Mr. Littlefield, the undertaker. Teddie was at the railroad station and ran all the way to Olive's house. He was devastated. He held the dead baby to his breast and wept. Anna quoted one of her poems to him, which seemed to calm him. Olive cooked for the mourners, and Chase counseled with Teddie. Friends and neighbors rallied around them, even Shep sat on the porch to keep Teddie company. Teddie didn't have the money to purchase a cemetery lot, so the dead child's grandmother, Chase Barrick, offered her lot for a burial spot for little Dorothy Newton.

At the cemetery, Teddie and Anna stood by the little mound of red Georgia clay, until Chase hobbled to their side and told them it was time to go home, that the baby was gone and they had to pick up the pieces of their lives and greet a new tomorrow. Anna perhaps bore sorrow better than Teddie. She straightened her face, took Teddie by the hand, and led him to the waiting T Model Ford with Olive at the wheel. As the mourners drove through the wrought iron gates of the cemetery, once again they had only each other.

Now Dr. Bussell and the undertaker, Mr. Littlefield, had to be paid. They did, by the way, have a vacant lot on West Central Avenue nearly paid off, and Charlie Newton's unpaid bills, and the bale of cotton which he had stolen had been settled. Teddie had carried quite a load, but though small, he was a giant in his own way. The businessmen of Fitzgerald had watched him, as the officials of the Atlanta Birmingham and Coast railroad had. His books were always balanced and his agency on the company's honor rolls each month.

Anna was in demand to play the piano and give Bible lessons at the missionary meetings. She even looked in on elderly people in need of spiritual encouragement. She seemed to have a special way about her. She saw to it that her papa had the necessities of life and tobacco for his pipe. Old Shep, the years now a heavy burden to him, didn't require much of life's goods, just his freedom to wander the streets and communicate with any old plug horse he might encounter. He would always smile when he saw Anna coming. I do believe she, and she alone, put him in mind of his mother Bridgett, long, long ago, when he was a headstrong lad in a far away land down under.

Daniel had taken over the house moving business. I don't know what happened to Robert and his wife, but he, being his mother's first born, had a special place in her heart. He and Shep had seldom agreed on things. Chase had always been of the mind that no roof was large enough for two women. With no word for anyone, she packed her bags and Robert picked his mother up in a taxi at Olive's house. She and Bob, as he was known, caught the afternoon train and left Fitzgerald and its crowded streets for Miami, Florida, never to live in Fitzgerald again.

Frederick had a job with the railroad. In fact, Teddie landed the bright young man a job in his office force. He soon married a Northern girl and saw little of the others. Shep's memory failed him, and he spent many hours sitting on his small porch, now a kindly old man, seemingly contented with his simple lot. Teddie buckled down to work, went to church every time the door was opened, and joined the Mason's order. He was neat in dress and met the public well.

One day he and an automobile salesman drove up to his and Anna's door on Swan Street, and Teddie announced to her that he had just bought her a brand new Ford.

Anna's chin began to tremble and her hands rested on her hips, she still had a stirring spoon in one hand. She marched down the walk to the street and hell knoweth no fury such as that little redhead threatening the smiling man with her wooden spoon.

The salesman spoke first, "Oh, Mrs. Newton, I have practically given Teddie this fine new car."

Teddie knew that they both, he and the glib salesman, were in deep trouble.

Anna ignored the salesman and swung the spoon toward Teddie, as she shouted, "Get yourself out of that flivver and march yourself in to your dinner. You know we can't afford an automobile. You have a perfectly good bicycle and a note to pay at the bank." She grabbed the bill of sale from the salesman and tore it to shreds, which the wind tumbled down Swan Street. The car drove off and Teddie, crestfallen, sat down to eat his lunch in silence.

Two paydays passed and Teddie walked the walkway with an envelope in his hand, his hat set way back on his head. Anna met him at the door as usual. He grinned as he handed her the envelope from the lawyer McArnold. It contained a paid-off deed to the Central Avenue lot, the lot of her dreams. She hugged his neck and her copper tresses cascaded down her back. He assured her that the construction loan would be approved soon,and she had best be selecting some house plans for their new home. Blue skies were here. Anna didn't walk anywhere, she ran about on her tiptoes.

As Teddie had promised her, their loan was approved. She selected her plans, and Coleman Layfield and his helper drove stakes on the lot. Teddie was sharp to recognize a good deal, and as the railroad company was transporting the paving materials for the paving of Central Avenue below the St. Paul Hotel, the contractor, as a favor for the good service Teddie Newton had offered him and his supplies, had his men fill and grade their lot, and lay a cement sidewalk scot-free. Perhaps now the lot was worth twice what they had paid Mrs. Sasser for it, and the new houses, uptown houses, were springing up all around a new neighborhood, no less.

Woodrow Wilson had been elected president, and war clouds were gathering over Europe. Anna had born Teddie a baby boy, and they had moved into their new home, a stylish bungalow. They named the bouncing baby Mayhew Newton. He seemed much stronger than their first child had been. Anna was still close to her twin sister, who spent much time with her and Mayhew, dressing him in handmade sun suits and rompers.

Teddie was doing well on the job and even picked up a little extra money cleaning railroad cars and feeding transit livestock for the railroad, as he had employed a gang of colored laborers to do these contract jobs. Now there was a shiny automobile sitting in the new house's driveway, and Anna drove everywhere with Mayhew, now a toddler.

Anna felt a cloud of doom hanging over their lives. She somehow felt something bad waited to fall upon her and Teddie. She hadn't mentioned this feeling to him as he was gone before day, and many nights it was ten o'clock when he came to 320 West Central Avenue.

This night it was later when Anna heard his footsteps upon the porch. Olive and her child were spending the night with them. The two children had played the evening away, and the sisters had put Mayhew and his cousin to bed early. They had put Mayhew in his crib and heard his prayers, "Now lay me down to sleep, if I should die before I wake, I pray the Lord my soul to keep."

Olive and Anna sewed until Teddie came from work, as Homer Fairfield was out on his run. The twins had both married good hard-working men, and the fruits of their labors had begun to ripen. Teddie, as usual upon his arrival, had stepped into the bedroom to look at Mayhew and place a kiss upon the sleeping child's brow. He snapped the bed lamp on and as he approached his beloved son's crib. Terror struck him when he saw the child's head buried in his pillow. When Teddie touched his son's lifeless little body and he failed to stir, he turned him over to see his open eyes staring at the ceiling. He knew the worst had happened. He called out to Anna to come quickly.

Olive was first to stand beside the crib with Teddie. In the bat of an eye she snatched the child's body to her breast, and, barefooted as she was, ran past Anna with Mayhew in her arms out the front door to Dr. Bussell's house, two blocks distant. Olive was still barefooted and breathless when Teddie and Anna arrived with Olive's baby. Dr. Bussell worked over the small boy's form. Anna had a strange look in her eyes. Teddie pushed past the women and heard the old doctor sigh. He took Teddie by the arm.

"Teddie, I wish there was something I could do, but Mayhew is gone, and you've got to buck up. He smothered in his sleep. I will give Anna a dose of ammonia and try to break her from the trance she seems to be in. I wish she would cry and stop her trembling. I will call Mr. Littlefield to bathe and prepare his fine little body."

Thankfully, Olive was a strong woman, and as surely as she had run her fatal sprint, she took charge of her distraught relatives and her own baby. Anna stayed under the care of the doctor until the following morning. At daybreak, friends and neighbors again took the young couple under their wings. Teddie went into a depression, as was his nature, and destroyed all Mayhew's playthings and pictures. He even took down the white wreath the undertaker had hung on their door. He swore never to love another child and prayed to God to die himself.

Anna now was the strong one, small as she was. She comforted Teddie once more with her poems of faith and strength. No tears, only a tremble of her chin. The child was buried beside his sister, Dorothy, in his Grandmother Chase's burial plot. Chase caught the train in Miami, Florida and arrived two days after the funeral. She stayed with her daughters and was a good counselor for Teddie. She was at Olive's house on Swan Street when Shepard Barrick visited as he often did. They spoke, but Shep couldn't hear. He had been at the funeral but being so deaf he was difficult to communicate with, and he soon drifted back to his Federal Street house and barn. Chase asked no questions, only said her children were grown and their problems belonged to them now, not her. She soon packed her things and caught the train back to Florida.

Slowly, Teddie got back into harness and went back to the station and church. He bought Anna a piano. She played and friends came in, and they sang and laughed, but their hearts still bled. The funeral bills, car payment, house payment, and piano payment caused the couple to tighten their belts. Anna was a wizard with the money Teddie brought in, and soon they were on their feet again, but the empty cradle weighed heavily on Anna's mind, and regardless of Teddie's admonitions, she intended to have another child. In her vision, she saw another little boy only waiting to fill her womb.

The war in Europe was eminent. Woodrow Wilson, president of the USA, vowed that American boys would never be involved in Europe's wars. Time passed, and Fitzgerald continued to prosper, now having all the amenities of larger cities. The railroad, the Atlanta Birmingham And Coast, had become a prosperous railroad employing many people. The old cry of the Civil War soldiers, now neighbors, who had laid down their arms to be as one, had dimmed with time and the passing of the old Union and Confederate veterans. The new generation was more interested in automobiles, brick homes, movie theaters, and big bands. But that war in Europe just wouldn't go away.

Chapter XX

Lenard, 1917

Two years passed before Anna conceived a child. She was still very small, and her childbearing had not been easy. The event which crushed her was the death of Olive. Healthy as she had always been, one day out of the blue, Anna felt that she should visit her sister on Swan Street. Homer had a worried look on his face as he answered the door bell. "I laid off my run, this trip, as Olive has a serious stomachache and I have to take care of my children, Becky and Emmet."

Anna hurried to Olive's bedside to find her doubled up in pain.

"Just something I ate didn't agree with my stomach, I will be all right tomorrow," she said. But she wasn't. She lay a corpse in Mr. Littlefield's funeral parlor the next night. Teddie sat up all night with her body and stood by Homer Fairfield, who was shocked and grieved.

Anna again went into one of her trances, "I knew it was a bad omen I had, but I never dreamed she would die. I always felt I would be the first to cross the river, but wait, I should have known. I saw her sitting in a boat, a strange man at the oars. I had written Mama about this, but she doesn't hold with such and the like always calling it witchcraft and tells me to keep my bad dreams to myself. So I did. Papa is not much help at times like this. He will shed a tear or two and drift back into his dreams of Australia and his own adventures. That last fight almost ended his serious thinking. He is childlike, as age also has taken a toll."

Chase came once more on the train to attend Olive's funeral. She was informed that Olive had died of a ruptured appendix. She thought she would be OK, but peritonitis had run its deadly course and taken Olive to her grave in forty-eight hours, leaving Homer Fairfield and his two children with no wife and mother. Anna and Chase saw that he in his grief would leave Fitzgerald just as he had come, on a wailing passenger train, this time back to Indiana where he had come from as he had family there.

Yes, he did just that, caught the passenger train and he and his children said goodbye to Teddie and Anna. Chase was sitting in the car, her bags packed to catch the southbound train away from the sorrows of Fitzgerald. They never heard from Fairfield again, only the memories of the past. Anna's babies and now her twin sister had left her here in Fitzgerald, with their childhood memories of settlement days, muddy streets, the shay pulled by good old Peggy, the blind race horse that her papa had trained so well, the laughing children who crowded aboard for a ride to school, the creek they forded, which was now a bustling city street, the trips to Andersonville on Decoration Day, and the young men of the railroad with whom they cast their lots, just penniless boys but willing to work and establish homes.

Time already had taken its toll. Her family had scattered to the four winds. Teddie's mother, Sallie Ann Newton, had died suddenly. It seemed that Teddie was dogged by death. He accepted bad news as it had come so often lately. Perhaps he had matured a bit. This time he boarded the train to bury his mother, the idol of his life, in the little cemetery beside a log church on a red clay hillside on the outskirts of Andersonville.

He stood on a freezing day with what was left of his family, with an aching heart and many boyhood memories, one of which haunted him now. His mother had called him when he was a boy of twelve years to come quickly with his twenty-two rifle as a snake was crawling along a rafter in her open-ceilinged kitchen. Teddie, quite a sure shot, soon brought the writhing snake to the floor of the kitchen. Then, as he reloaded the short barreled rifle, it discharged its load of lead into his groin. His older sister had stuck her finger into the wound until his mother sent for the doctor some miles away. Teddie was out like a light until the old doctor arrived in his horse-drawn buggy. He opened his black bag, placed the unconscious boy on the dining table, and sewed the wound up. Teddie woke up the next day but had to lie still on his back for a month. He healed well, and walked with a crutch for a long time, never to care much for guns again. The leg he shot did not grow as fast as the other, and he had a slight limp all his life. He carried that bullet to his grave eighty years later. Open graves seemed to be the young man's lot.

Anna, being in her ninth month of pregnancy, had delivered another baby boy, this time at the new hospital just below the 320 Central Avenue home of theirs. A new doctor by the name of Dare had delivered the baby and sent Teddie a telegram while he was still on the train. The conductor, Sims Barnes, a long time friend of Teddie's, smiled and handed him the yellow typewritten telegram. Barnes had already read the message and was grinning from ear to ear. "Teddie, we are pouring on the coal. The stork has beaten you to Fitzgerald. Why, boy, you are a papa again!"

Teddie, not yet over the shock of his mother's death, only turned pale and swallowed hard. How much could he bear? Anna stayed in the hospital that night. Teddie had arrived back in Fitzgerald after visiting hours, but was admitted to the maternity ward to find Anna reading a novel and looking beautiful. Her girlhood friends had just left her bedside. She even had fresh flowers. Teddie got a first peep at his new son they hadn't named yet. He had sworn not to pour his love out so freely, and that this time he would be more reserved, but he soon found that love comes with the child. He was relieved that Anna was fine and the boy was healthy.

The people of Fitzgerald would rally to a cause, and this couple was special. Dr. Dare himself delivered Anna's bundle from heaven under his own care, assisted by his nurse, Mellie Fitch, a registered nurse and a special friend to the Barrick family, as her mother was from the north and a dear friend of Anna's mother, Chase. Teddie took them back home. Anna reclined with her son, who began to nurse greedily. Teddie seemed afraid of the infant but soon held him and sang softly, "Anna and me and the baby, make three in my blue heaven." All the sorrow and heartache of the past seemed to fly away. They decided to name him Charles Lenard Newton, and they would call him Lenard Newton.

Teddie was a lot of help around the house. He washed diapers, cooked breakfast and swept the floors before he went to the railroad station. Soon Mellie Fitch was dismissed. Anna, what she lacked in size she made up in pure old grit, because she knew how much Teddie depended on her to stabilize his life. She never let him see a tear in her eyes, and her ability to handle grief and sorrow was inspiration to all. Religion was something that dwelled deep inside her bosom. She had a quiet calm nature, and could build a wall to insulate her from the trials and tribulations that life might confront her with.

"Tomorrow" was the world she lived in. She would sing a little song to Teddie, which went something like, "Pack up your troubles in your old kid bag, and smile, smile, smile." A song or a poem or a story could bring peace of mind to her and to those around her when everything went wrong. She lived her religion in everyday life, more than she did in the church house. A beam of sunshine followed her into the darkest corners. Her family had disappointed her, her children had been snatched from her arms, fire threatened her very existence, her father and her mother were separated, and her twin sister was taken in the prime of life.

Teddie needed her steady countenance to stabilize his high and low moods, and yes, his low moods could drag bottom. But when he was on the streets of Fitzgerald he was Mr. Personality. Anna would quietly say, "You just want to be a big fish in a little puddle."

This new baby boy, Lenard, from the start gave promise of possessing the best qualities of both of his parents, a happy good child, quick to smile and learn childhood verses and songs. Anna played the well-worn piano that Teddie had bought second hand from Mr. Upshaw's music store on River Street. Why Lenard could sing along with his mother as she played songs both popular and religious. The neighborhood children loved to play games and were fascinated as Lenard told them stories. Grown people stopped to talk to Lenard on the sidewalk, for he never met a stranger. Teddie took him everywhere because the child seemed to have a wisdom about him that bordered on spiritualism, as if he was on a special mission in life. As each sunrise spread its glow, Lenard also spread a glow to those around him.

Anna enjoyed the lad, and dressed him in the best clothes she and Teddie could afford. In the summer, she and the boy boarded the trains and traveled to wherever Chase and Bob were living, be it Florida or New Jersey. Anna had a pass to ride the trains free, as Teddie had earned that privilege through his job as a stationmaster. He seldom went with the pair as his duties demanded his time.

Fitzgerald was a good place to live. The days of Shack Town, roaring bar rooms, painted women, lynchings and tent meetings had passed. Now its growing pains had subsided and Fitzgerald had become a fairly typical Georgia town.

Suddenly, the war clouds had gathered over the world, and Fitzgerald was no exception. The steamship *Lusitania* had been sunk by a German submarine, or U boat, sending her and many American lives to the bottom of the North Atlantic. Patriotism ran high. President Woodrow Wilson had to go back on his pledge to keep America neutral. With the explosion of one torpedo, America was plunged into the bloody European war. It would be the war to end all wars. Songs were written, "The Yanks were coming, the drums rum-tum-tuming," was one which was on everyone's lips. Uncle Sam needed able-bodied men. Yanks and Rebs alike crowded enlistment stations. Draft boards were established, even in Fitzgerald, and Teddie registered for the draft. He was exempt as he had a child and the railroads had been taken over by the United States government, because trains were vital to the war effort.

Yes, a new era was ushered in by the World War as it was named. Even Australia was sending troops to fight the Huns and destroy Kaiser Bill, as the German leader was called. Even those new-fangled flying machines called airplanes were introduced to warfare, as were trucks and tanks. Those monstrous steel-clad tractors, bristling with machine guns and crawling along on caterpillar tracks allowed them to penetrate any terrain. German submarines sank many defenseless ships and were the favorite offensive weapons of the German Navy. Battleships no longer ruled the seas, as they too went to the bottom.

Fitzgerald found itself situated on the main line of railroad traffic during the war, and many men were employed there as it was a terminal or crew changing point between Atlanta and the cities of Florida. It seemed as though the war had been a shot in the arm for Fitzgerald. Farms prospered as cotton was hot on the market; meat was scarce and lumber in great demand. Chemicals distilled from the pine tar sap were needed as was pine pulp for the manufacture of powder and dynamite.

Anna and Teddie prospered along with the town. Lenard was in school and stood at the top of his class. He was a leader in the church children's choir. He even sang solos far beyond his years. It seemed as though he strived to cram as much life as he could into his years. His Grandmother Chasity, or Chase as she was still known, saw his special qualities and wrote him letters and showed his pictures to everyone. Lenard's grandfather, afflicted as he was, gave him a pony, a small edition of the Welsh pony his great-grandmother loved so much, named Boo, long ago in Australia. Lenard galloped about the neighborhood on his pony in the little cowboy outfit he had found under his Christmas tree one happy Christmas morning. He was now eight years old and quite a little man. Perhaps Anna's friends thought she needed another child, but she seemed content with her life. What more could she expect from another child, who might cast a shadow on her ideal lifestyle? She would be tied down to working and cooking, housework that would only be humdrum, and she couldn't give Bible lessons and play the piano, or catch the train for some far off destination to visit childhood friends or relatives in the north or Florida. Yes, she was quite a gadabout. So the Newton baby bed was gathering dust in the attic of 320 West Central Avenue.

Could that be Anna and Lenard ticking along in a shiny Ford car? They went over to the Federal Street neighborhood to visit Milli Knight, her girlhood friend who had somehow seemed to replace her twin sister Olive. Anna, although she didn't approve of her father's untidy lifestyle, was attentive to his needs, even buying him tobacco for that same old pipe. He couldn't hear what she said, but she wrote him notes and Lenard knew how to communicate with him because the pony was a great go-between for them. Shep's clothes were worn and dirty, and Anna wanted him to make a better appearance. A gift of money was a disaster as he would only give it away to some person with a sad story.

One day, Anna went to the dry goods store uptown, and bought him new clothes, new shoes, and a new hat. Old Shep would cut quite a figure on his daily stroll to the fire station and his group of cronies, who gathered at a sunny spot on East River Street. Yes, she plunked down her money for the new outfit and Shep thanked her good nature as she drove away. Lenard waved his little hand. A few days later, Anna spotted her father, the stockman, trudging uptown in the same old stained, threadbare clothes and shoes he must have found in a garbage can. Her heart sank even lower when one of the other old men told her that Shepard had gone straight to the second hand store and sold his new outfit for a few dollars, and given the money to a young woman named Goldie, a street walker who was trying to raise her small son on handouts.

Yes, that was Shep. Perhaps that was why Chase had packed her bags and departed Fitzgerald. Anna, on the other hand, hated sorriness, and tried to set a good example to others. She also looked in on other old people. She still drove out to Clearance Sydney's estate to inquire of the now derelict old

"Lord." He still recognized her and Lenard.

Anna's hair was still red, and she styled it around her head. She was most attractive. She had a happy countenance, although her temper flared and her chin trembled if the occasion occurred as it sometimes did. Lenard didn't inherit his mother's crowning glory, the red hair. His hair was blond, he had Teddie's clean cut features, and he was a normal size. His good nature was even better than his mother's, and his wisdom was far beyond his few years.

Anna had no trouble mixing with wealthy people and had made close friends with a woman some years older than herself. This woman was from Oklahoma, and her husband was also a stockman or mule trader of great wealth by the name of Lee Perry. She was a large handsome woman with no children. Mrs. Perry had ridden the streets of Fitzgerald sidesaddle on a splendid saddle horse, often stopping at the Barrick house lot on Federal Street for Shep to trim the horses' hooves and repair their tack. Maude Perry took a special interest in young Anna and invited her and Olive to her fine home on Main Street for four o'clock tea. Anna had made recitations for the ladies and played the baby grand piano to the ladies' satisfaction. Maude couldn't play.

As the years went by this friendship only grew stronger. Anna was in demand to give Bible lessons and quote long poems, which she could deliver with no notes as her ability to memorize long volumes of verse seemed endless. Lee Perry died suddenly just as Olive Fairfield had from an infected appendix which burst. Yes, overnight Lee Perry lay a corpse in Mr. Littlefield's funeral parlor. Maude was left alone, if you don't count the millions of dollars her husband left behind. This tragedy only strengthened the bond between Anna and Maude Perry.

Automobiles had replaced horses on the streets and byways of Fitzgerald, but Maude never mastered the operation of these machines. She needed a chauffer for her Cadillac and Anna loved to drive a car, even if she had to have a cushion to see over the hood. Mrs. Perry, who had gained weight, and Anna, so small, made an odd couple as they motored through town on some mission of mercy or to collect a note long overdue on a pair of mules.

Death seemed to be a constant companion to Anna. Her childhood friend, the one with her when she was introduced to Teddie Newton at the railroad crossing years ago, Millie Knight, had been killed in an automobile accident. Once again Anna stood beside an open grave to see the earth swallow a loved one. The Grim Reaper seemed to hover over Anna and her mystic being. When her blue eyes stared into the distance never to shed a tear and her chin trembled a bit, voices unheard to others spoke to her. Had not the gypsy told of the ones born with the veil, or was that a bit of rubbish or hogwash? You have your choice, fellow traveler!

In the roaring twenties, as these post war years were labeled, America was on a binge. Let the good times roll. We had won the war. The boys were home, although many were buried in Flanders fields, where poppies grew, in Belgium. Anna and Teddie still saved part of the railroad paycheck he brought to Anna's hand, as she was the one who could make ends meet and even overlap. The house note had been met, funeral bills paid, and Teddie had even bought a cemetery lot. Although he had a brush with the city officials, he and two of his faithful black men had exhumed the two tiny caskets which held the remains of his dead babies, and re buried them in his own lot. He didn't even tell Anna of his activities, for she never darkened the gates of Evergreen Cemetery. It was just as though those other babies were only bad dreams. When she was informed by others of Teddie's covert activities, she fixed her stare as if she could see another open grave and a preacher standing above it with a prayer book in his hand, quoting the often repeated verse, "Dust to dust, ashes to ashes." Anna only said with a quick twitch of her chin, "I live among the living, not the dead. I look for red roses not white ones. Those souls have departed their frail bodies and now live on the other side of the river of life, which I myself will be rowed across by the boatman who never dies to join my babies and loved ones."

The summer of 1926 was a happy one for the little family. Teddie had prevailed on Anna to let him buy a new Ford automobile, a four-door Sedan, dark blue with roll up windows and a trunk behind to put picnic baskets and spare tires. The highway system had improved and good paved roads existed even to Jacksonville, Florida, where Teddie had a sister named Minnie O'Neal. Lenard had his birthday in June, and Anna decided to give him a party to celebrate the occasion. First she thought to wait until the next year when the boy would be ten years old, but that small voice which dwelled in the depths of her soul spoke to her, "Anna, my dear, I have told you many things to come. Now you have had this beautiful child for nine years, and he has brought you and Teddie much satisfaction and joy. He is only flesh and blood, only his soul doesn't belong to anyone but the great creator and the plans he has for everyone. Flesh is a fleeting thing, to be nourished and mature, only to return to dust. This child can live in your heart but the paths that he has trodden could be short. Give the child a party now!"

Anna had the party for Lenard and his friends, even the old widow woman who lived in a house across Central Avenue, Aunt Mammie Drew, came and brought him a book of poems. Most children would never have noticed a book of poems. They would have appreciated a baseball bat more. For some reason perhaps only Anna would have understood, he kept it in his knapsack and rode Boo, his pony, to a vacant lot and read and studied the verses until like Anna, he could recite them to the pony and a little rat terrier dog named Nut. He prized this book of verse, which was faded from the fifty years it had spent in Aunt Mammie's trunk there in her attic. Anna noticed this strange attraction the lad had for the little book, which was, to say the least, a little unusual for a child of nine years.

Teddie thought the sun rose and set on Lenard. He had even taken him to the bank to start him a savings account, as some day he had to have a formal education which he himself had missed. Lenard's teachers counseled with Anna. They thought he was without a doubt, a special child and were astounded at the esteem the other children held for him. At recess they gathered about him to laugh and talk. He in turn, loved their attention and love. Not only that, his grades were A and A+. The future held much promise for the fair-haired son of Teddie and Anna.

Perhaps now I should tell you a bit about old Shepard Barrick. He had never taken much interest in children, even his own, but he was under the spell of little Lenard, his grandson. About twice a week he trudged over to Anna's house nearly a mile and visit her and Lenard, but this didn't sit too well with Teddie, as he hoped Lenard would set his goals in life higher than Shep had. Lenard's simple love had melted the tough heart which had run down and mustered wild brumbies that roamed the Snowy Mountains of New South Wales, harpooned the mighty sperm whales of the South Pacific seas, felled the towering trees of the North Woods, tilled the soil of Pennsylvania, rode the first passenger trains to the uncharted Pine Barrens of south Georgia, fought the meanest men in town, tenderly doctored tired and abused horses, bet his hard earned cash on a race horse that he just liked, moved houses that everyone said never could be moved, and handed his last dollar to some bum less fortunate than himself. Yes, he led Lenard's pony away to his weed choked lot and the ashes of Anna's childhood home on Federal Street.

Chapter XXI

The Trip to Jacksonville

That summer, after Teddie had arranged for a free weekend, he, Anna and Lenard piled their things in the new Ford after dinner on a Friday afternoon in Fitzgerald to travel through the country. An automobile trip was planned to visit Minnie O'Neal in Jacksonville, Florida, one hundred long, bumpy miles on the Dixie Highway, still under construction. When they were ready to leave, Anna sat behind the wheel of their automobile. Her chin trembled a bit, and she thought she heard her own childhood friends calling her from the great beyond.

"Buck up, Tremble Chin, you can drive it as you could drive old Peggy, the blind horse, as she waded into a swollen creek on the way to school in settlement days."

Now she sat behind the wheel of a shiny new Ford automobile, very close to that same creek now flowing in concrete culverts beneath Central Avenue. This time it wasn't her childhood playmates and her twin sister Olive, it was proud Teddie, the lemonade salesman from Andersonville, and her precocious son Lenard playing with his toys. She could see the book of verse close by on the back seat of the car. Anna set the lever beside the wooden steering wheel, the "spark," then she set the other, the throttle, to "start" position as Teddie turned the crank handle on the front of the car. The little Ford car motor roared into action. Teddie climbed into the rider's seat beside her, and slammed the door shut. Anna glanced back to check on Lenard. For just one instant as her vision fell upon her child she thought she saw two little angels with all aglow halos about their heads that resembled her babies, Dorothy and Mayhew, who had been taken by an unseen hand long ago. The larger angel smiled at her, put his chubby little arm about Lenard's neck, and vanished before her eyes, the eyes which had been covered by a veil the night of her birth, a cold February night, thirty years ago. Was that veil a curse or a blessing? Only time can answer that question. Her mother, Chase, and surely Teddie would have only scoffed.

Anna loved a challenge, perhaps the only quality that she had inherited from old Shep, and that Dixie Highway certainly was a challenge. She drove the entire distance. Bridges were being constructed over creeks of black water rushing to the sea. Travelers had to ford these creeks at sandy shallow runs. At this spot, there were men with mules to tow cars to the other bank, as the engines would drown out in the water. Lenard cried once as his daddy rolled up his pants legs and held his shoes in his left hand, and with a stick in his right hand checked the depth of the rushing water. Anna waited for the team of mules to pull them to the far bank if the motor drowned out, for a fee of two dollars.

Teddie thought, "Next time I will go to Jacksonville on the train and leave that 'daredevil' wife of mine and my precious baby boy on the streets of Fitzgerald." After Teddie waded ashore to make sure there weren't any deep holes that would trap the car, he nodded his approval to the teamster with his patient mules. The old man on the far bank rolled a cigarette while waiting for the sign to pull the car across. Streets of water arose from the creek as Anna's sure hands held the steering wheel, and her feet released the clutch and positioned the foot pedal gears. Teddie's thoughts went back to the Sunday afternoon when he stood at the Fitzgerald airport holding Lenard's hand beside tiny Anna, her eyes following a daring pilot in a World War biplane called a "Jenny," doing loop de loop and slow rolls high over the town of Fitzgerald. These pilots were known as barn stormers, for what reason I will never know, and they flew those old crates from town to town, landing in fields and dirt roads. Anna was fascinated by their daring antics high in the sky and would not be content until she stood there beside the Jenny and the idling engine which was music to her ears.

She loved the city of Fitzgerald as she was actually a part of the story of the settlement. She longed to see the checkerboard streets, the St. Paul Hotel, the railroad shops, the cotton mill with its towering brick chimney, her old burned out home on Federal Street and her new house on Central Avenue. "But Anna, my dear," Teddie said, "the pilot wants five hard earned dollars to take passengers up and we need to pay the ice man, even the butcher bill, and besides you have a child to think of." All Teddie's admonitions fell on Anna's deaf ears, deaf as her father's.

All of a sudden Teddie fished in his pockets and produced a five dollar bill, which he placed in the open hand of the smiling pilot, or barn stormer. He in turn handed an aviator's leather cap to Anna, who leaned over to cram her red hair into its crown and snap the chinstrap around her trembling chin. She then pulled the isinglass goggles over her blue eyes. Her hair of waves and curls, which the cap failed to enclose, danced in the backwash of the spinning propeller.

The pilot hoisted her onto the lower wing surface of the Jenny. She climbed into the cockpit in front of the pilot's. He snapped her seat belt about her small body, and then he climbed into his cockpit. He advanced the throttle as the powerful engine roared into action and began to bump along the grass runway. The exhaust blew Teddie's Sunday hat, rolling it across the field as he clutched Lenard to his chest. Away they went. Anna waved as the Jenny gained speed and the tail lifted from the ground, soon to be followed by the aircraft, just clearing the chinaberry trees at the end of the runway. Soon the plane was but a speck in the blue sky above Fitzgerald. Down it plunged in a spin, only to level out and sweep a treetop growing over the barn of old Clearance Sydney's and the crowd on the ground.

Teddie's whole body trembled and Lenard cried for his mama, now climbing into a billowy cloud only to loop the loop and barrel roll several times. The more Anna screamed, the more the pilot maneuvered the plane. He really gave Anna her money's worth that Sunday afternoon. Finally the Jenny rolled to a stop. The pilot jumped down to the wing and unsnapped the seat belt that held Lenard's mother in her high flying seat. He pushed his goggles back and hollored, "Next!" The pilot then spoke to Teddie as he led Anna to him. "Quite a trooper you have there, fellow, and I want to present her with that aviator's cap she wears as a souvenir of her flight," he said. Anna shook her hair out and removed the cap which restrained it. She smiled her happiest smile and handed the cap to Lenard. She thanked the barn stormer and placed a blessing on him and his flying machine.

As Anna drove the Ford across the dark waters of Willacoochee Creek on the road to Jacksonville, she had the same sure smile on her happy face. Lenard had never seen the ocean and its sandy beach, nor his Aunt Minnie, for the Newtons seemed too busy on the railroad to keep family connections up to date. As a matter of fact, they were as devoted to trains and track, copying telegrams and train orders, as Shep Barrick was to his livestock. Minnie O'Neal, Teddie's sister, had left Andersonville long before Teddie was out of school. She was Agent Operator for the Plant System Railroad at Pearson, Georgia, deeper still in South Georgia. She would send a telegram to Sally Ann Newton, her widowed mother in Andersonville, to put Teddie on the train when school was out, and she would keep him at Pearson for the summer vacation.

Teddie was only a boy of around twelve years. Minnie was single and lived in a boarding house, where the boy could share her room and eat at the table where he drank his first iced tea. He took his bicycle with him on the train and earned his keep by delivering Western Union telegrams to sawmills and turpentine stills around Pearson. He also had to sweep the depot floor and the open platform every morning at daybreak, as hundreds of goats and cows roamed the woods by day and slept on the platform's wooden deck at night, safe from predators and weather.

The happy couple with the lad of nine years passed through Pearson, Georgia, Teddie pointing out places of interest to him. Lenard noticed the difference in Pearson and Fitzgerald, few brick buildings, sand rut streets, few automobiles. Houses and businesses were shabby, fenced in to keep the livestock out of the yards and gardens. There were pine board sidewalks, and to Lenard's glee he saw a razorback sow lying in a drainage ditch nursing a litter of piglets. He asked his mama why this town was so different from Fitzgerald. Anna answered that they needed a few Yankees to set a fire underneath them. Teddie just looked straight ahead down the newly paved road.

The new model Ford was an improvement over the "T" model she had learned to drive. Shep Barrick had never owned an automobile, and if he had he would have probably put "shaves" to it and hitched one of his horses to it. Anna was glad to be free of horses, as she often mentioned, "Mama and us kids often went without, as papa would buy horse feed first and groceries only if any money was left. I hated them and I don't care if I ever see another one. They only seemed intent on either biting or kicking you, or needed feeding!"

Teddie only laughed, "Come on, Anna dear, you seemed to like the buggy and the iron gray mare which trotted you and your sister Olive to Minnie Mill Pond on our first date."

"Mind your mouth, Teddie Newton. The boy is listening. I get tired of your cracker ways."

They passed through several more cracker towns and saw men in overalls and wide-brimmed black felt hats, driving plodding ox teams. These people of Georgia had been named crackers as they cracked their whips. Some even had plaited leather whips coiled over their shoulders to herd livestock and to protect themselves from the sows that would protect their pigs in a heartbeat.

Some colored people were fishing in the ditches along the highway. Lenard hoped he would see an alligator, but he only saw turtles and lily pads with their beautiful blossoms floating on the black water of the cypress swamps, or bays as they were called. The women wore calico bonnets to protect them from the hot sun, long skirts, and sturdy shoes. Yes, this was a different world than Fitzgerald, much more typical of Georgia of 1925, as time had kinda passed over it. These people were satisfied with their lifestyle and just let the rest of the world go by.

As I have mentioned before, this couple had set their cap for a better way of life. They were tired of laziness, old dirty overalls, bare feet, drunken weekends, pale and ragged barefoot children never sent to school, slaves to their parents' farms. Abraham Lincoln had overlooked freeing two generations of white children from slavery. There was no money to hire help. Fathers would brag about how many children they had; some had as many as twenty heads. They all had a job waiting for them. As soon as they could walk, there was cotton to chop, corn to pull, tobacco to crop and string, new ground to clear, firewood to cut, hogs to slop, and cows to milk. Do I have to tell you who was expected to do all this? Even twelve-year-old girl children could be seen plowing a mule, or doing a washing to hang on a rail fence.

Only progress would some day emancipate this army of southern farm children.

Waycross, Georgia, was named for the railroad tracks which seemed to radiate in all directions to all points of the compass, causing a town to spring up around the switch yards and shops that kept the three railroads going. The little new Ford crossed the Satilla and St. Mary's rivers on new bridges that replaced flat boat ferries. On the south bank of the black waters of the St. Mary's River, rising in the depths of the mysterious Okefenokee Swamp, home of who knows what, Florida welcomed the Newtons as they stopped at a roadside welcome station and bought a sack of oranges fresh from the trees that flourished in the subtropical climate of the Sunshine State.

Anna took Lenard for a walkabout at the station and lo and behold, there in a park surrounded by palm trees and behind a stick fence was a Seminole Indian camp, complete with their thatched huts or chickees. The small women folk, about Anna's size, in bright colored skirts, were busy pursuing their primitive way of life. Anna paid the twenty-five cents admission fee. Lenard was wide-eyed when there before him in a stagnant pool of water surrounded by a concrete wall, was a group of alligators sound asleep in the Florida sun. Some had their gaping mouths open to let the birds pick their fearsome teeth. A little farther along the oyster shell walkway was a snake pit. Lenard and Anna both enjoyed the sight of huge diamond back rattlesnakes and cottonmouth water moccasins coiled about logs and in pools of water.

Lenard was fascinated with the bear pen where two black bears were caged. They begged for bits of food and stood on their hind feet. What an experience for a town boy. He couldn't wait to tell his playmates back in civilized Fitzgerald. Anna herself had more adventures and love of nature than most women. Teddie only commented that he was from the country. He paid the man for the gas and was ready to go to the city of Jacksonville and its bright lights.

"Yes," Anna quipped, "you love to be a big fish in a little puddle." Teddie needed Anna's admonition to keep him in the middle of the road, as she often said. They, after another hour of travel on a better road, King's Way, as it was known, crossed the mighty St. Johns River and found themselves in downtown Jacksonville, a real city. Teddie got directions to George O'Neal's coal and ice yard. George was Teddie's brother-in-law, and had become quite wealthy selling coal for stoves and ice for home iceboxes. He and Minnie had no children. She no longer worked other than managing the rental property they owned. Teddie had often visited his sister, but he had gone alone on the train, an easy trip for him. This time Anna wanted to drive their new car, and hoped to show Lenard just what he had seen. She didn't say so, but she also had never seen these sights, and soon she hoped to take Lenard on the train to visit her mother and Robert in fabled Miami.

Minnie was expecting them and had a table set for them when they drove up. She was a great cook. Pies and cakes awaited her baby brother's arrival. Minnie had been somewhat reserved about the fact that Teddie had chosen a northern girl as a wife, and it kind of stuck in her southern craw, but she laughed and made them welcome. She even had a side trip planned in the big new Dodge touring car George had bought her. "We are going to the beach tomorrow," she said as she swept Lenard from his feet and gave him a big hug.

Minnie O'Neal loved to cook and George O'Neal loved to eat, as did Teddie Newton, and supper was served. Chocolate cake and coconut pie were on the sideboard. Only Anna and Lenard ate like birds. Teddie overate and had to take baking soda to settle his overloaded stomach. At the crack of dawn, a deep-toned whistle awoke the Newtons. It was Big Ben, the steam whistle of the Jacksonville power generating plant down by the St. Johns River. It blew every morning at 6:00 a.m. to awaken the city. Minnie was already in her kitchen, and the aroma of bacon and eggs floated upstairs. Teddie jumped up and went down the hall to the ample bathroom. As Anna helped Lenard into his clothes, she commented, "That Newton family, not one I have ever known, never lets daybreak catch them under the covers. I believe they were handed a pick and shovel at birth. They don't know the word 'lazy.'"

Lenard brushed his teeth, washed his face, and combed his flaxen hair as Anna slipped into a little cotton frock, brushed her hair and joined Teddie already down in the kitchen, laughing and talking to the sister old enough to be his mother. There was a little something that didn't set quite right between the two women. Minnie was loud and overbearing, Anna had mentioned to Teddie and Lenard, but good hearted, just that southern raising perhaps. Minnie had her opinion of Anna, as she obviously had quietly observed her ways, "Those Yanks are just a bit high handed and, in fact, no better than we are. Why in the name of heaven didn't they stay up north? We certainly don't need them down here to set us straight!"

George O'Neal called on the telephone and told Minnie to have Teddie meet him on the front sidewalk as he would pick them up to see the city wake up, and his ice wagons leave his ice plant to deliver ice to households all over the city. The mules that pulled them were George's pride and glory, and they were fine, well trained animals. Lenard wanted to go with his father and Uncle George.

Anna was much prettier than Minnie, who was approaching middle age. Her false teeth clicked when she talked just a little too loud. Her girth was twice Anna's. Her gray hair was thick and bobbed short as was the style. Anna looked like a doll in that prissy little dress, silk stockings knotted at her dimpled knees, high-heeled patent leather shoes, and hair that any woman would envy. Anna let her winning personality shine and the two women exchanged pleasant conversation, mostly about Lenard, Teddie's performance on his job, and promotions. Minnie told of her and Teddie's brother Charlie, as they had not heard a word from him or Lillie since they left Fitzgerald one dark night. Anna learned that the scamp had borrowed money from her, which he had never repaid. Lillie had sobered him up and he landed a job as a telegraph operator in Gainesville, Florida. He buckled down to work and had a better job than the one he had lost in Fitzgerald. Lillie seemed to know how to handle him, as the boy was capable and would work.

Minnie told Anna of the hard times their family had experienced after their father died, and their mother's early death. She also told of Sally Ann Newton's loving ways and how she and George had bought the headstone for her grave in Andersonville, with the inscription "Here lies Sally A. Newton, Beloved Mother, a Kind and Loving Woman and a Friend to All." And that she was. Minnie told Anna, who listened quietly, as she talked of Lenard and his sunny disposition and kindly ways, as he could play on the sidewalks with children he didn't even know.

Teddie bragged on the O'Neal plant. The mules were impressive as they leaned into their collars and went their ways into the city, but Teddie had his bait of plowing these mules' cousins and was tired of hopping over red clay clods on cold Georgia March days, him bare footed and trying to make one of the ornery critters behave, only being paid fifty cents a day because he was so small. He thought to himself, "I didn't come down here to 'review' mules!"

About nine o'clock his rich brother-in-law dropped him off to join Minnie and his beloved wife and baby, as he often called Lenard. Aunt Minnie backed her large Dodge touring car out of the garage behind the two-story gray stone house. Anna had a bag packed with beach clothes, swimsuits for the three of them, towels and beach robes. Neither of the three had ever seen the ocean or played on the broad sandy beach that Jacksonville was famous for, although they were over twenty miles from Neptune Beach.

Lenard's nose was pressed flat against the backseat window glass as he viewed the passing sights of the city along the mighty St. Johns River, the only river to flow due north in the USA. Fishermen in bobbing rowboats floated on the broad bosom of the dark waters. Minnie drove on. Buses loaded people at bus stops, traffic lights changed by unseen hands, traffic cops blew their whistles to get the attention of traffic, and tall buildings cast long shadows on the bustling streets. This was Teddie's world, business and commerce. Anna liked it, too, and Lenard was ecstatic. He had yet to see the Atlantic Ocean and its foamy waves, which crashed to the hard packed sand beach, and the thousands of vacationers like them, far from the humdrum of everyday life.

Minnie pulled into a filling station, and the uniformed attendant shouted,

"Fill her up!" Teddie, the big shot he tried to portray, answered, "Yes, and check the oil, tire pressure, and wipe the windshield off, and I will give you a tip."

Minnie beamed from behind the steering wheel.

Lenard wanted a cold drink, but Anna told him to wait until they arrived at the beach. She thought to herself, "Now, isn't that just like Teddie, always the 'big shot' he tried to portray. Now I will have to do without new curtains and have to trim Lenard's hair myself to balance the budget I have pinned to the kitchen door."

Away they sped. The attendant proudly admired the dime Teddie had tossed him.

Soon the Ferris wheel and huge roller coaster loomed against the sky and the horizon, which stretched endlessly to the east over the broad blue Atlantic Ocean as far as their eyes could see. There it was right before their eyes. Lenard jumped up and down on the spacious floor of the back seat until Anna had to tell him to sit down and behave. What would his Aunt Minnie think he was? A wild horse? They parked the car in the parking lot and strolled to the boardwalk. Anna had their beach bag, containing the three newly purchased swimsuits, even one for herself. Minnie declined as she never went into the surf. She only liked to sit on the benches along the boardwalk and watch the endless parade of vacationers and tourists who were Florida's bread and butter. The Newtons saw a huge sign reading "Bath House." Teddie paid the fare of twenty-five cents each, and each one was given a basket to store their street clothes and a ticket to claim them from the shelves behind the counter and the clerk.

Lenard was too grown to go with his mother into the ladies' side as he had done as a child in Fitzgerald and when they went on train trips. Anna slipped out of her street clothes in a stall along the wall of the bath house with its fresh water shower. The bathing suit was quite skimpy. It was a one-piece blue wool bathing suit, with an embroidered figure of a diving woman on the lower right side, and the word "Jantzen," a trademark indicating quality and style. Now Anna, small as she was, had just the figure that the designers had in mind when they designed the garment. Twenty years past, a policeman would have arrested her for public indecency, for exposing so much flesh, but the World War had changed many things and now bathing suits were no longer funeral attire. Anna had tried it on at home and was quite pleased that she had no stretch marks and her breasts were still well shaped, even after nursing her children, and her legs were smooth as she shaved them with Teddie's razor every week. She had sandals for her small feet and a rubber cap which snapped beneath the chin that would tremble if the occasion arose. The cap protected her hair from the salty wind and spray of the waves. Her beach robe of sky blue complemented her complexion and shielded her from the stares of ogling eyes of men, who only came to feast their eyes on bathing beauties' charms, with which Anna had been well blessed.

Teddie was as white as a ghost without his shirt and tie. He looked different without his glasses, and his hair was thinning. He was rather puny looking and his ribs showed beneath his skin. He had not had a proper diet as a child, as many poor southern children had suffered from a disease known as rickets, which caused bones to waste and grow askew. He was wiry, tough and strong and had survived. Lenard, like his mother, had a fine healthy body and spirit. What a fine young man he some day would be! The waves were high, the sun was intent, the seagulls whirled above and the sandpipers ran from tidal pool to pool. Seashells deposited by the waves that retreated with the outgoing tide intrigued the boy. He gathered them to take home to his playmates and show Miss McCall, his third grade teacher back in Fitzgerald, far away. He had picked up these seashells and sand dollars while the tide was out. Minnie had gone to a bingo parlor to pass the time. Anna and Teddie, with Lenard between them, joined hands and waded out to meet the incoming tide and the larger waves. Lenard laughed as he leaped over the breakers. The sun turned the bathers red, and Anna insisted they had to go to the bath house and rinse the salt water off themselves and dress as she didn't want to sun burn.

The romp in the surf had whetted their appetites. Back in their street clothes, they walked the boardwalk hand in hand again. Teddie stopped at a saltwater taffy stand and they shared a bag of the chewy candy. Then Teddie and Lenard rode the Ferris wheel while Anna waited, as she wanted Lenard to have the experience of seeing far out to sea and the ships that were passing. Then they sat on a bench and before too long Minnie appeared on the boardwalk smiling broadly as she had won a small pot. Don't think for a minute that Minnie had left her kitchen without a lunch. She had planned to continue their tour to Mayport, where a park existed for tourists to see the ships pass on their way to the open Atlantic Ocean as they left Jacksonville harbor on the St. Johns River. Anna thought how far she and Teddie had come since they had eloped to marry and the heartaches they had shared. These trips had somehow made it easier for her to face life and its tribulations.

Minnie dominated the conversation. Teddie and Lenard ate fried chicken and chocolate cake, washed down with ice cold Coca-Cola. Anna picked at a piece of chicken and wondered how these southern people could cram so much food. The sun was sinking as the big touring car came to rest in its garage behind the gray stone house.

They didn't need to be rocked to sleep that night in the upstairs guest room. Teddie and the boy's bodies were red from the sun, but the soda paste that Anna plastered them with soon took the fire out of their skin.

Before daybreak, Teddie heard George O'Neal crank his old truck an hour before dawn. He had been raised to rise easily. His mother was an industrious woman and his father was usually away for the week on rail gangs. Teddie's chore as a boy in Andersonville was to retrieve the all important milk cow and her calf from Mr. "Candy" Johnson's pasture next to the railroad house, which the Central of Georgia provided for its track workers. The hardships of boyhood had instilled a lifestyle thta had brought him to the station in life he now enjoyed, and his ambition was to give his son an even better opportunity. Anna also shared his ambition as her life had not exactly been a bed of roses. She had endured a broken home and her family was family scattered to the four winds and the graveyard. She was not as vocal as Teddie was about winning the victor's crown in life, but her heart was in the race. She attached herself to successful people without losing the common touch, and I must say she had a knack for winning friends and influencing people in all walks of life. But Minnie was a hard nut to crack.

She dressed herself and Lenard for the homeward trip in the little blue Ford. Perhaps this trip would crack Minnie's shell and they could meet on level ground, as their hostess had tried to give the young family an unforgettable trip to the seaside. Soon Anna and sleepy-eyed Lenard joined Teddie and Minnie, already sitting in the large kitchen with a plough hand's breakfast on the table. Minnie had already confided to Teddie that Anna had quite a charming manner about her and knew when to keep quiet, but still she had a northern background and it was impossible to change a Yank into a Rebel! Goodbyes were said and necks hugged. Anna had some reservations about Minnie referring to her as darling. How syrupy could southerners get?

Over the St. Johns drawbridge to the west bank of the broad river the little Ford and its cargo of happy vacationers sped, just as Big Ben boomed its wake up call to the awakening city by the mighty river. To the town of Calahan, Florida, and its sulfur water, which smelled like rotten eggs, they drove. Lenard held his small nose as they passed the open water trough where a teamster watered his mules. Lenard told his mama that he felt sorry for the poor animals, let alone the children who had no choice but to drink that water or collect rain water.

They drove across the St. Mary's River Bridge. The floor boards of the bridge rattled when Teddie put the new car through its paces. Back in Georgia, he slowed down for Folkston, the first town across the state line. Teddie had a heavy foot on the gas pedal, and the telegraph poles zipped by like a fence post would have if they had been in a buggy. Anna and Lenard amused themselves by reading the "Burma Shave" signs placed at intervals to deliver witty verses of wisdom to travelers. The lad asked his mother why there were so many little signs nailed to roadside trees proclaiming "The end of the world," "Be ready" and "Jesus is coming." Anna tried to explain the ominous message to her son. She then grew silent, a pall of dark thoughts crowding her mind. Her explanation of the stark warning was that his bedtime prayer, "Now I lay me down to sleep," that he said over folded hands would take care of that warning. Next she had to explain the huge words printed on dilapidated tin barns, "See Rock City." He wondered what and where was Rock City, and if they would see it. Anna could handle that question better than the last, telling him, "No, not today, maybe on another trip."

Anna hoped Teddie would read the speed limit signs of thirty-five miles per hour going into Waycross, the railroad city. Teddie stopped at the train station and entered the telegraph room as he well knew the man at the key, which was clattering away with a Prince Albert tin can stuck behind it to effect a sounding board. Greetings were exchanged with the operator. Teddie asked permission to call Fitzgerald, seventy-two miles north of Waycross. He then sat down at the desk and his fingers moved with expert movements upon the handle of the clicking instrument that was his and his wife and "baby's" bread and butter. He tapped out a message which went on humming wires alongside the tracks hung on cedar poles along the right of way that led to Fitzgerald and his office. After a short pause, the key with the tin can clattered a message of return in Morse Code, a short message Teddie understood and didn't copy on the typewriter as was the usual custom. "All is well in Fitzgerald," he repeated in a relieved voice.

He arose and joined Anna and the boy, who were stretching their legs a bit on the paved sidewalk of the station. Anna wanted to drive the rest of the way home, and she usually got her way. Driving cars was a talent of hers. She never missed the horses she was raised with as her papa had given her an overdose of horseflesh. She loved to hear a gasoline engine hum and obey her every command, instantly and powerfully.

Soon they forded Willacoochee Creek beyond Pearson, Georgia, where the bridge was under construction. Next they crossed the Alapaha River on a rickety old wooden bridge. Anna's thoughts went back in time to the little engine pulling the one boxcar loaded with happy young couples, with Homer Fairfield at the throttle and Olive holding Lenard. Why had she been taken so young? Where were Homer and their children? Why didn't he ever write her? Several questions came to her mind as she glanced at the now abandoned swimming pool and pavilion which once rang with happy laughter and songs, and now was silent as a graveyard. Why such dark thoughts? She never called the names of her babies who had been taken in the night. Even Lenard didn't know their names. That wall she built between her and the grim reaper had no windows.

Snap out of it. Anna, Teddie and Lenard don't need a sad countenance. They need a smile to cheer them on.

Chapter XXII

The Tragedy

The streets of Fitzgerald were crowded as usual. That town had a wide awake profile, very different from the sleepy hamlets they had passed through on the long weekend. School would soon commence, and school clothes needed to be purchased for Lenard, who would enter the third grade. He was different from most boys who dreaded vacation time to end. He could hardly wait for the bell to ring, when he would get his new books. Teddie's paycheck would soon be in Anna's hands, and she could buy her boy a new wardrobe as he was growing like a weed.

She had a long letter in her mail box from her mother, Chase. Chase and Robert were struggling to make a living in Miami, Florida. The post war boom had burst and building had come to a screeching halt. Things were rough but they could tough it out. Chase never asked of Shep or the old home place that had burned. It seemed that she too, as Anna, could build strong walls between heartaches and disappointment. In fact, Chase had never been the same since the day they buried her father at Evergreen Cemetery. Anna was the only exception. Even though they couldn't live under the same roof, their hearts were bound by a common bond never to be broken, no matter what tragedy struck either of their lives.

Lenard gave most of his seashell collection to his neighborhood playmates and told them of the beach and the sights he had seen. He even quoted one of the Burma Shave slogans that he had remembered, "Twinkle, twinkle one-eyed car, we all wonder where you are." They all laughed and played the live long day as the school bell would soon ring, and they would have to work on their lessons.

Teddie didn't let his shirt tail touch his behind as he juned about his beloved railroad business at Fitzgerald. Anna was tired and rested from the trip. She seemed full of emotion. She was happy that Lenard was having a happy carefree life and didn't have to worry where the next meal would come from, or listen to nightly family problems. She also remembered the admonition, "Not to love anything or anyone too much, or it would be snatched away."

She tried to overcome a sense of oncoming doom by going to her piano and playing some joyful songs, but she found herself playing and singing, "I looked over Jordan and what did I see, a band of angels coming for to carry me home." She "banged" her clenched fist down on the piano keys and cried, tears streaking her face. "Good Lord," she prayed, "give me strength to bear whatever the future holds for me. Only you have been my Rock of Ages from the night I was rescued from the chamber pot. Will I, the weakest member of the Barricks, somehow be the only survivor? Please, don't take Lenard from me, please, oh Lord."

She dried her tears and prepared Teddie and her boy a midday snack of sandwiches and iced tea, the only beverage that Teddie craved other than a Coca-Cola, if he had a nickel.

Times were good, people were at work, and lines formed at the bank. People were actually saving money. Teddie and Anna had nearly a thousand dollars tucked away in Mr. Oldcomer's bank, and their bills were up to date. Anna wrote a letter every week accompanied by a neatly folded dollar bill to her mother, now living in Jersey with Bob, as he had found work there. Each time, Lenard ran to the post office, bought a three-cent stamp, and after licking the back side, he stuck it to the envelope addressed to Chase Barrick, Camden, NJ. He stood on his tiptoes to drop it into the slot marked "outgoing mail."

Just as regularly, Alvin Black worked Central Avenue from his pony drawn mail van. The neighborhood children loved the brown and white pony named Billy, which whinnied when he smelled Lenard's pony Boo. They sometimes gave Billy a carrot. The postman handed Lenard a letter from his grandmother, addressed to Anna Newton. He would run to give the letter to his mother, and if the news wasn't too bad she in turn would read it to the thoughtful lad.

School started early in September. The school which Lenard had to attend was quite a distance, and he couldn't ride his pony. So Anna took him in the car every morning as traffic had increased so much. He was excited about being in the third grade and meeting his new teacher, Miss McInnis. Lenard usually took a lunch to school as there was no school lunchroom. The children were free to go home to eat, but that day Anna told Lenard she would pick him up at lunch, as she had a ham cooked and would bake a lemon pie. It was Teddie's favorite dessert, and he wanted especially that day to see and visit with his son. Anna set the table for three, checked her stove, and took her lemon pie from the new electric refrigerator Teddie had bought for her. She climbed into the Ford and it cranked right up, as it had a starter powered by a storage battery. She backed out into Central Avenue, hoping she hadn't forgotten anything because she had a strange feeling that something was wrong, bad wrong. She thought to herself, "Why can't I just be like normal people, carefree and trusting. No, I have to eternally be peering into the future. Why me, Lord?"

She blew the raspy horn in front of the railroad station, which was but a hop and skip from the new brick schoolhouse, where Lenard would hear the bell ring for lunch period by the principal Miss Jones. Anna put the car in gear as Teddie slammed the door closed and greeted her, "Let's go. I can't wait to see my baby." Anna didn't take her eyes from the street as she reminded him that Lenard was "their son," not "his baby."

Anna was a good driver, alert, careful, and quick to see danger, which lurked at every turn. She stopped at Federal Street, looked both ways and soon pulled up before the schoolyard just as the students poured from the double doors that were swung wide open. "There he comes," Teddie said, "hasn't he grown?"

Lenard waved and ran to open the door to the back seat. He had his papers to show his dad and mother. He was a loving child and from behind he hugged both their necks. The happy trio soon parked in the driveway at their bungalow on Central. Lenard ran to the small lot and stall where Boo waited for Lenard's voice. He always hugged the pony's neck and talked softly to him. After the usual greeting he turned back for some reason, and said loud enough for Anna to hear, "Goodbye Boo, you are a good pony and take care of yourself, because I love you!" She had never heard him say that before, but children are apt to say most anything, you know. "Come on in and eat Lenard," Anna said, "as we have but an hour to be together."

It was a happy lunch period, and the lemon pie was the highlight. Teddie and Lenard ate most of it. Lenard seemed to bubble over as they loaded into the car, Anna again at the wheel. Teddie hopped out at the station, turned and spoke to his son, "Study hard, boy, and I will see you when I can."

Time had slipped up on Anna. She hoped the take in bell hadn't been rung by Miss Jones, as Lenard was never tardy. The bell had rung, and the children were forming a double line, one for the girls, the other the boys. Lenard would have to run.

Anna had parked on the offside of the street as there was no space next to the campus. As the boy hopped from the parked car Anna noticed that his hair was mussed and she always wanted him neat and fixed. She called him back to primp him a bit. Lenard turned to answer his mother just as a gas truck sped by the school. Lenard dashed into the truck's path. There was a sickening thud and a screech of brakes.   Anna screamed, "Lenard, oh Lenard."

The truck's front wheel had passed over the boy's head, and he lay beneath the truck. The driver slumped over the steering wheel, frozen in shock. Anna leaped from the Ford, drug her son's crumpled, lifeless body from beneath the tanker truck, clutched what was left of him to her bosom, and took off running to the railroad station, some two blocks distance. The horrified onlookers could not wrench his lifeless little body from Anna, as she ran with superhuman strength to meet Teddie now running to meet her. She was shouting, "Oh, Teddie, they have killed Lenard!" She fell in a bloody heap at Teddie's feet. A crowd of men had followed and soon had the child's body away from the couple. Only then did the reality of the situation settle upon Anna and Teddie: once more they were only a couple.

Anna was taken to the hospital semiconscious. Teddie had to be held by his friends until the police arrived. Anna was kept overnight in the hospital, Teddie by her side. He was bitter, very bitter. She was in a trance, seemingly in another world, and said nothing. Old Shep came to the Central Avenue house, which was so still and quiet, as Teddie had vowed to never enter it again. He had a cot in the warehouse of the station. He would live there. Shep seemed to come back from his dream world and led the pony Boo away to his lot. Then he walked back across town to the hospital to see his daughter lying so still in the high hospital bed. He held a small bouquet of flowers he had picked from the rose bushes in the city park. Anna spoke to her father and seemed to come back to this world.

"Where is Teddie?" she asked. "He needs me." She arose and dressed with the help of Maude Perry, her closest friend. She thanked Dr. Dare and was driven to the station where Teddie was. She didn't embrace him, she only took his hand and said, "Let's go home. We have nowhere else to go. Lenard is in heaven with our other children. I know he was here, but for a while we must go on with our lives."

That was the last time anyone ever heard her call the boy's name. Teddie respected Maude Perry and began to behave himself. He had many friends who gave him their devoted support. Even the railroad gave Teddie a leave of absence with pay. Mr. Littlefield, the undertaker, counseled with him, as did his devoted preacher, Brother Pafford. People differ in their reactions to tragedy and the grief that follows it. There is no greater grief than the loss of your own flesh and blood. Death can come instantly as it had in Lenard's case. Perhaps shock dulls the initial crush of pain and heartache. Lenard knew no pain. The pain stayed on this earth to stab the hearts of his parents. Teddie felt anger, a confused anger directed toward the driver of the truck which should have gone some route other than by a crowded schoolyard, and yes, I hate to say it, at Anna for not looking out for him, and lastly, God himself, for taking three of his children before they were twelve years old. It would be a while before he could deal with these bitter feelings. He was a good man, and time would heal these wounds to his heart.

Anna had spent some of the initial inner hysteria in her super human strength to rescue Lenard and deliver his broken body to his father. If the truth were known, perhaps Anna was the strongest emotionally. She could hide behind the protective inner wall she had built around herself and be reasonably content until the storms of life passed over and the sunshine would chase the gloom away. The sedative shot Dr. Dare gave her had dulled the horror of the accident. She slept now with Maude Perry at her side. Teddie tried to speak with her but she was far away in her dream world.

Teddie vented his emotions another way. Being the man of action he was, he called his faithful black men and soon gathered every stitch of Lenard's clothes, his beloved books, even his baby pictures and all the pictures he was in. The pony was gone, thank heaven. He couldn't find Lenard's dog.

The colored men went about their grim task and when everything that reminded him of his beloved son lay in a pile in the back yard, he told the men to stand back. He doused the pile with kerosene and stuck a match, which soon sent flames dancing into the night air as they consumed the earthly belongings of Lenard Newton, following the boy into the night sky. When the smoke had cleared, Teddie spoke some bitter words, sunk to his knees, and remained there for some time. The neighbors and friends stood at a distance only to protect him from himself.

The patient black men, three I think they were, removed their hats and hummed an age old spiritual, "Roll Jordan Roll." One of them stepped up to the bent figure and kneeled beside him. It was Doc Laseter,, the one who had stuck by his boss man through many hard troubled times on the railroad. He spoke softly, "Time to go, Mr. Newton. Tomorrow is another day. Us all loved de little boy. Our hearts are sad and tired. You know that boy be blessed with special good spirits. The child belonged to de Lord in heaven. He only loaned him to you for nine years, and you and the missus enjoyed his bright light. Now de Lord needs him about his throne."

With those words said, the two men, one black the other white, arose and Teddie became more rational. "Doc, will you and the other boys take me to the station office to my cot? Build a fire in the stove, cook me a breakfast as only you can. Stay by my side. I need all you men to help me recover."

When day broke Teddie in his white shirt and gray suit, black bow tie and hat pushed back on his head was in his office, his hand on the telegraph key tapping out a message, "O.S. Fitzgerald, cancel leave of absence, I am on duty, request permission to attend the funeral of my son tomorrow, Chief Clerk and office force will protect all movements." With that matter tended to, Teddie had taken the first step of many to come to somehow mend his broken heart, which had regained some of the rhythm that had faltered and longed to go with Lenard.

The Newtons, the lot of them, were railroad men to their core, duty came first, whether it be laying rail, stoking a locomotive, or sending a message on humming wires. Low boiler water, foggy nights, and tragedy were the everyday of life on the rails.

Maude Perry took Anna to her home that tragic night, and her housekeeper Laura, a colored lady, sat by her bedside until the sun peeped through the bedroom window curtains. "You just rest, Miss Anna. I will bring you some coffee and breakfast if'n you feel like eating. Mrs. Perry will speak to you when you be ready, us be nearby."

Anna's first thought was "I must get up or Lenard will be late for school." Then in a flash it all came rushing into her awakening mind, his still warm body clutched to hers for the last time here on this green earth. What about Teddie? "I hope he has done nothing rash as he is so quick to react."

Suddenly a vision came to her, for once even her chin was steady. The vision was of an angel, a small angel. She cried out, "Lenard, oh my baby, you look so calm and happy." The vision spoke, "Now don't you grieve, Mama. Don't you worry. My heavenly father did take my soul to keep, and I now dwell in his house to await you and my earthly father to join me and the others I am getting acquainted with this morning. Please don't grieve for me as I will always live in your heart."

With that, Anna found an inner strength she didn't know she possessed. She walked to the mirror on the wall and looked at herself, all a mess, and spoke to herself, "Someday I will have another little boy, just you wait and see. He won't be Lenard, as he is gone home, but a different boy. I can almost see him now." She tossed her hair into place and bathed herself as she didn't want her friend to see her in weakness and knew that Teddie would need her strong and collected. She would never to her dying day speak the name Lenard. Her lips were sealed to that name, buried beneath her shielding wall. Her head was held high. It was as though the spirit of Bridgett O'Leary Barrick had entered her small frame, the grandmother she never knew, as she sat in her cart pulled by her Welsh pony Boo on the cobbled streets of Swanpool, the day she became acquainted with Captain Frederick Barrick.

Strength seemed to come to both the bereaved parents from their friends and relatives, Dr Dare and even the spirit world. Maud Perry met with the undertaker as Lenard's body lay in state in a closed coffin that Mrs. Perry had arranged. The parlor of the funeral chapel was overflowing with people, of all walks of life and ages. All Fitzgerald was grieving and had come to pay their respects before the small casket, which sat before a bank of flowers. A telegram had been sent to Chase Barrick in far away New Jersey.

Some of the neighbors and the firemen from the fire station who loved old Shep Barrick, had come and told him of the accident or rather wrote him a note. He only cleared his throat and groaned as though a dagger had pierced his tough old heart. He was tended by his daughter-in-law, Daniel's wife Ada. She shaved him and told him to be ready as he was to attend the funeral, and she and Dan would accompany him to the cemetery as the old man had no church affiliations and now needed help. Dan, who was always in the background, was good at heart but never climbed the social ladder and lived much as Shep had, from hand to mouth. The pony Boo, Lenard's pony, would be put in the string of ponies Dan used to move houses with and kept from

Teddie's sight.

The funeral was held in the big new Methodist Church where Teddie and Anna were so active. The church was filled to overflowing as if all Fitzgerald had taken the day off to mourn. School was dismissed. After all, Anna had been one of the first babies born in Fitzgerald. All the northern families were in attendance, not to mention the southern families that had loved Anna and Teddie since day one. The family section of two front rows held only Maude Perry, Teddie and Anna, her brother, his wife, and their adopted son, and the fire chief assisting Shepard Barrick, perhaps his first attendance at church. Teddie looked as though his face was chiseled from granite, his expression gone. Anna without a tear had hidden behind her wall. Her staring eyes looked as if she saw something in a land far away. Only old Shepard was weeping. That child who lay in the closed casket had melted even his closed heart, which was so tender inside. The eulogies were short, the songs were sung, and many tears were shed.

Mercifully the service was short. The pallbearers took their places about the casket. They were the railroad men who worked with Teddie and neighbors. The long black hearse led by a policeman on a motorcycle threaded its way to Evergreen Cemetery to pass once more through the wrought iron gates swung wide to an open grave and banks of flowers. There, standing with bowed heads and hats in their hands, were the colored men of the railroad, softly humming their spirituals. Teddie spied Doc Laseter and told him to stand by his chair beside the grave, he, Lewis Bell, and Alzie Kennedy, just in case he needed them. He knew how the boy had loved them.

A closing prayer was said by Brother Pafford. The crowd began to mill about. Close friends passed before the parents of the dead boy who stood to receive them. Maude Perry was next to Anna as she needed support. Her father and brother were with her, but strangely Teddie stood alone as he went through the motions of receiving the sympathies of the crowd. Mr. Littlefield lowered the casket into the open grave and ushered the family away. Teddie would not leave and told the black men to stay. He ignored Anna as Maude led her to her waiting Cadillac. Laura held the door to the back seat open, the driver waiting.

Shep put his arm around Teddie, embraced him without a word, and he and Daniel melted into the crowd. Teddie and Mr. Littlefield had a conference. Reluctantly the undertaker called the gravediggers, who stood some distance away, to bring their shovels to the open grave. As they neared the gravesite Teddie and his men took their tools and as the grave diggers moved the bank of flowers to the side, shovels bit into the loose red clay bank where the flowers had been. Teddie, always good with a pick and shovel, cast the first and last shovel full of earth into the grave. Within minutes he and the strong men had put the boy under six feet of fresh dug clay, leaving a well-molded bank over the grave. Now there were three mounds of earth. One larger than the other two. Teddie refused to have slabs and headstones mounted on the graves. He only said he could not bear to see his children's names chiseled in marble. No one tried to persuade him different as he was a strong-willed young man. Anna let him have his peculiar ways and stayed for a few days as the guest of Maude Perry, saying only, "Let Teddie find himself. He will come for me when his grief has found some peace. Work is his best remedy. I know him better than anyone."

The afternoon passenger train from the north ground to a screeching stop at Fitzgerald. Teddie watched as the conductor dropped down the stepstools. He saw him help a stooped slip of a crippled woman to the platform. As the porter set her wel-worn suitcase beside her, Teddie stepped out to greet her. Yes, it was Chase Barrick, who had traveled six hundred miles to be by the side of her daughter, the tiny baby she had nursed to young womanhood, the brave one, whose only hint of fear was for her chin to tremble and for the others to tease her and nickname her Tremble Chin, the one who had turned out to become the bravest one of them all.

Chase hadn't bothered to send a telegram as she knew Anna, born with the veil, would know she was on her way. Teddie helped Chase into Willie Mahone's old Ford taxi and told him to take her to the St. Paul Hotel and sign her in a nice room. He, Teddie Newton, would be up that evening to register her and pay her bill, for as long as she wanted to stay. As he held the hand that Chase extended to him, a shaft of awakening light pierced the darkness that shrouded his aching heart. Yes, the curtain had begun to be drawn. He knew that Chase's heart was broken, as a special love existed between the dear departed boy and his grandmother, for he had grown to know her on the visits he and his mother made and through the letters he had mailed to her. Teddie spoke softly, "Blood is thicker than water."

When the day duties were over at the railroad station, he called to Doc Laseter, his right hand man as he called him. "Doc, go over to my house and put it in order. You know where the key is hidden. Sweep out, and if by chance you see anything that belonged to the boy, destroy it, as I want no reminders of him." Doc only nodded, as his heart was also broken. That little white boy had won those laborers' hearts, just as he had won the hearts of the finest ladies of the town of Fitzgerald. He had no class or color barrier as his heart was open to all.

Now, don't think for one moment that Chase Barrick wasn't a wise old woman. She had gone through many hardships and stood beside many open graves. She also admired her son-in-law's honest and hard working ways. She also knew his stubborn mind and his southern upbringing. Teddie, in turn, had often commented on Chase's intelligence and morals, although she wasn't a churchgoer as he was. He parked the little blue Ford under the magnolia trees that stood before the huge hotel which had furnished much needed work for unemployed carpenters and laborers, as building had slacked off after the initial boom of early Fitzgerald. A bellhop who sat on a stool beside the hotel's front door swung open the heavy door and smiled as he spoke, "Come right on in, Mr. Newton." Teddie handed him a dime and quickly said, "Sebeb, if you ever need a job, come right on down to my station. Your job is waiting."

Little did Teddie know that one day, many years in the future, Sebeb Walker would play a part in the scheme of his life. Anna would have felt the importance of those words, but Teddie was born without a veil and held no faith in destiny and fate, not to mention luck. He scoffed at the gypsy's crystal ball and predictions of the future. He rested his faith only in Jesus Christ and hard, honest work. He walked up to the beautiful heart pine reception desk and asked the clerk which room Mrs. Barrick had taken. As Teddie mounted the ornate stairs, his feet were almost as heavy as his heart. He raised his hand to knock on the door but paused a moment to speak the first prayer to his Lord and Savior since the terrible accident. Instantly, like a lightning bolt from heaven, he felt a power entered his soul, and a weak smile came across his ashen face.

As his knuckles knocked on the door, Chase's voice called, "Come in." Teddie turned the glass doorknob and walked into the room. Chase was sitting in an overstuffed easy chair and excused herself for not rising as her hip was bothering her. "Take a chair Teddie, and tell me what happened as I have not heard the details. The conductor on the train told me only what he had heard."

Teddie fixed his eyes on some distant object and slowly formed the words, "They have murdered Lenard."

Chase let the words sink in, then calmly said, "Tell me Teddie, who did this ghastly deed?"

"The Standard Oil Co, Mrs. Barrick.," Teddie said. "Their delivery truck, driven by a careless employee who should have known better than speed by a schoolyard and playing children. Anna herself shouldn't have let him out on the traffic side of the street." Silence settled over the hotel room. Teddie waited for her comment.

Chase drew a deep breath. She spoke in a crackling northern voice which showed no weakness. "Teddie Newton, why don't you come down off your high horse. I believe your Bible says, 'Be ye not a judge of people.' You seem to think you were the only one who loved the boy, and he certainly wouldn't want you, his father, to be bitter. Honor his memory and don't let me hear you say what you have said to me ever again, as long as either one of us lives."

Teddie, shocked by this stern command, gathered himself to leave, but before he could, she ordered him to sit down as she wasn't finished. "We are all in this sad event together, and I don't want you and Anna to end up as

Shep and I have. You need each other more than ever. You are different from my Shep. His mind has failed him and I gave up on him, but you are more intelligent than the stance you have taken. Bury your sorrows in the graveyard as I have. You and Anna have many good years before you; mine are spent, yours are only beginning."

Teddie thought gravely for what seemed an eternity with his head bowed. Suddenly his head rose, and he looked the wise old woman in the eye and said, "Thank you, Mrs. Barrick, my own mother would have probably told me the same thing as there has never been a divorce in the Newton family, and Anna has often said she believed in a fight to the finish." He had a different look in his eyes, and his step was lighter as he bid her farewell. Tomorrow he would have her and Anna moved back into the West Central house, and he would expect dinner to be on the table when he arrived home at twelve o'clock at noon, even if hell froze over."

Next morning Maude Perry answered the doorbell to see Willie Mahone standing with Doc Laseter, a smile on his black face. He spoke first. "Mr. Teddie sent me and this taxi cab over to fetch Miss Anna and her things back home, as he will be there for dinner today." Maude Perry wasn't up to taking orders from blacks, but she in her wisdom smiled, called her maid Laura, and instructed her to help Doc move Mrs. Newton, who had bathed and brushed her hair till it gleamed, back to her house on Central.

Anna forced a smile and began to gather her things. Maude Perry had heard that Anna's mother had arrived, but had not told her as Anna's rest was more important right then. She told Laura in a low voice to go with them and help fix dinner as she knew Anna's mother would be there. "Yes, Mrs. Perry, I knows what goes on. Us black folks have a grapevine. Sebeb Walker tapped on my door last night. Us don't need no telephone. Us know what pass among you white folks of Fitzgerald. I sho glad to know this grief be passin' cause they even pray in my church over at Mount Olive to give rest to the Newtons, and that there may be a new angel up in heaven."

A cloud of blue smoke left the exhaust of Mahone's taxi as the three left Maude Perry's home to cross town to the Central Avenue bungalow. Chase Barrick stood beside the front door, her arms outstretched. Anna fell into those arms, arms which had comforted her as a baby, arms which had cooked many meals, arms which had held the reins that led blind Peggy as she strode through Fitzgerald when it was but a shack town and the Civil War was fresh in the minds of the settlers. That old racehorse had depended on Chase to guide her to a safe haven. Now the streets were paved, and comfortable homes had replaced the rough shacks that once sheltered struggling homesteaders, who had staked their lives and savings on a fresh start at Fitzgerald. These same arms held Anna close, so close she could feel the strength of bygone years flow into her bereaved body, which needed holding.

Doc Laseter had the place in order, beds made, porch swept, grass trimmed and every trace of Lenard's short happy life gone. Even the pony stall was torn down. Boo was across town among the ponies that Daniel Barrick tended. Anna sank into a rocking chair and confided to her mother that she was now ready to pick up the pieces of her life, and look to the future as some power told her that the darkest hour was just before the dawn. This house she and Teddie had built would once again ring with happy laughter and the patter of little feet, which would brighten her and Teddie's days. Chase knew her daughter's strength of mind, as she had always lived in a world far removed from her other children. Was she indeed a psychic, and were the gypsies correct?" Where did she find her courage to scale the walls she couldn't climb, couldn't go under or around, in the Red Sea places of life?

For perhaps an hour the two women shared their hopes and dreams, feeling closer somehow. Had Lenard's sunny spirit entered their souls? Were they stepping in obedience to some unseen power? Was this tragedy somehow a plan or blueprint to a future that at the present was obscure? Only the passing days could answer these questions.

Laura, the cook hummed as she stirred the steaming pots on the stove, and cracked the oven door to see if the biscuits had risen. She had set the table for three, iced tea glass before Teddie's place at the head of the small table and hot tea cups before the ladies' places. After the white folks had finished, the dishes were washed and the kitchen floor mopped, Laura would take her food in a cloth-covered basket across town to her house and her people. Doc Laseter had gone back to the train station to report to Teddie, sitting at his desk, hard at work on a stack of way bills. Doc shuffled across the floor, removed his old hat, and cleared his throat to get the stationmaster's attention. As Teddie turned his eyes to meet the eyes of his faithful employee, Doc knew Teddie would treat him fairly, and he felt a sense of security in those gray eyes. All boss men were not as kind and thoughtful to a man of color as Mr. Newton had proved to be. "Yes sar, the house be shinin', no sign of Mr. Lenard. Laura she done had dinner started on de stove and it sho' be smellin' some kinda good. The lady folks be sittin' in da parlor in deep conversation, but da not be to cry. Me and Laura shed a tear or two for da boy, but dem womans, day be some kinna brave because dem Yankees, Mr. Newton."

Teddie thanked Doc and handed him a dollar bill, then bit his lip to keep from crying. He took his hat from the hat rack, squared his drooping shoulders, crossed the office floor down the rough wooden steps out to the Ford car, and drove away to the house on Central. How could he drive in the driveway and not hear Lenard's cheerful call, "Hello, Daddy!" But he did. Perhaps his prayers gave him the strength to hop out and leap to the porch as he always had. Anna met him not with a sad countenance and tears, but a slow smile and a straight chin.

"Where in the name of heaven have you been, my dear? Dinner will be cold and Laura will be having duck fits. She has about worn out those bedroom slippers of hers looking for you." Chase stood back and only smiled her approval. Teddie didn't go into any long apology or emotional outburst. A hard job lay before him and the Newtons never shirked duty. Hard jobs were their lot in life. Away we go! Let bygones be bygones. Once again, two against the world!

Chapter XXIII

1928

Two years had passed. Teddie had been born in 1891, so he was thirty-seven years old. Anna was now thirty-two, still petite and pretty, only a bit more mature. Teddie had some gray hair and thin spots at his temples. Although they seemed happy and gay, Lenard's memory was just as alive within them as the day he and his dad enjoyed the lemon pie before he left them. The only two things you must know are that the Standard Oil Company truck that ended Lenard's life, also ruined the life of the young man who was at the wheel that fateful day. He had left Fitzgerald to become a tramp and derelict. The claim department of the giant oil company had approached Teddie with a settlement, a check of ten thousand dollars, as their driver had been charged with reckless driving in a school zone, although Teddie had not pressed charges. He only said quietly to the company lawyer, "I won't accept blood money as my son was not for sale."

Teddie's lawyer, Colonel McArnold, called Teddie aside and counseled him to accept the check as the company wanted to clear their files, and the money would only help comfort his and Anna's minds. Teddie was a stubborn man and Colonel McArnold suggested that he should sign the check, endorse it, and he would forward it to a charity of their choice. Anna also shared Teddie's sentiment as they would only be reminded of the boy, after some thought approached the lawyers and endorsed the check, which would have put them on easy street, as few people in Fitzgerald had that much cash. They announced that the check both of them had endorsed would be sent to the orphans' home, the Methodist home in Macon, GA, as a memorial to the boy who so loved his playmates — but with one reservation. Neither his names nor theirs would ever appear in public. They wanted those dollars gone just as Lenard was, not blood money in their pockets.

With that issue settled, on the way home they felt Lenard's spirit with them. Anna never mentioned it to anyone, but she saw Lenard playing on the back seat once more, and her chin trembled until she had to cover it with her lace handkerchief to keep Teddie from seeing. They turned their backyard into a park. Flower beds were put in the vacant lots on either side of the house. Teddie and his workmen spent Saturdays building benches, and he worked late into the night to build a shelter over a stone fire pit, over which he placed a steel top. The car house was remodeled into a dining room that would seat fifty people on rough board benches.

Teddie went to Thomasville, and he and Doc brought back five hundred rose bushes, which he and his men planted in the back lot. He worked tirelessly on the project. His many friends gathered on weekends and many happy parties came to pass behind the house on Central. Never a curse word was heard, never was a drop of beer, wine or liquor seen, only a short prayer by a guest or preacher. Teddie loved to fry fish and feed the multitudes. Anna never cooked. In fact, these parties were the girls' night off, as Teddie and his men friends even washed the stacks of dirty dishes. Soon the yard of the Newtons was the show place of the neighborhood, and he was famous as a cook, and Anna as a hostess who could hold a crowd breathless as she gave her readings and stories, never with a note, always with her blue eyes looking far, far away, as if she was in another world, a peaceful, happy world.

Things were not that happy on the streets of Fitzgerald. Labor troubles surfaced on the railroad. Trains were running short, sawmills ceased to whine, the cotton mill had no orders for cloth, suddenly cotton was five cents a pound, people were unemployed, and workers struck on the railroads. Teddie came in to announce to Anna that his paychecks didn't come, and the company had gone into the hands of the receivers. He had only a voucher to get staple groceries from the Grab, an old coach turned into a commissary to help the workers get by until better times arrived. The Great Depression began to fall, not only on Fitzgerald, but on the whole country. Teddie heard rumors that the bank was closing, and he hurried to the cashier window and withdrew his savings of seven hundred dollars. The next morning the bank's doors were locked, and a sign announced that it was closed until further notice. Yes, by the skin of his teeth, his and Anna's savings had been saved. Others who lost theirs by procrastination felt hard at the ones who had withdrawn the money which supported the banks.

Teddie managed to keep his job as the telegraph wires had to be kept open, as was the train station. He had to work harder as his clerks, other than two, were cut off. Times only got worse. Teddie went three pay periods with no cash. Anna knew how to stretch a dollar, and as Teddie later confessed, "We got ahead." Prices were so low, why a dollar would buy what only last year would have cost five. A year passed. People were desperate. Teddie handed many of his workers a dollar bill that Anna never knew of, as he was not a greedy man, having come from poor working stock.

Anna surely had known the cupboard to be bare as her father Shep was a poor provider. The horses' needs came first, and his needs were small. The parties in the backyard continued through the hard times. Friends brought meal and lard. Teddie was good at borrowing from the Grab. Dressed fish at the Greek stand were only twelve cents a pound and help was free, only glad to get a square meal and a few laughs. Firewood was plentiful and good times were had in the Newtons' backyard. Even people who had been rich last year sat in a converted car house and listened to Anna's program and ate Teddie's fried fish and hush puppies, drinking hot coffee on cold Saturday nights from chipped cups from the dime store. Sparks rose from the open fire pit and the blacks waited for a plate of fried fish and hush puppies that Teddie handed to old Doc, who served his companions huddled around a fire. "Thank you, Mr. Teddie, us here if you need us!" Those seven hundred dollars and the ten thousand, Lenard's money at the orphanage, filled many empty bellies in the dark days of the depression.

Old Shep over on Federal Street didn't change his simple way of life. Anna wondered how he got by. He seemed to float with the tide of life. It seemed that was a way to survive in Australia, and as a boy he had learned well. Teddie buried himself in his duties of the railroad, which was struggling to survive, but refinanced itself and had begun to pay cash to its employees. Anna could run the house, and she did save one of the two paychecks he brought home monthly. Lenard's funeral bill was finally paid off.

Anna drove the little blue Ford and gas was only seventeen cents a gallon. She and Maude Perry drove the back roads of Musgrove County seeking out unfortunate people, delivering food baskets and taking sick children to Dr. Dare's office. In fact, people began to call the Ford car with Anna at the steering wheel, the Gospel Car. She often had the feeling that Lenard's spirit was right there on the back seat with a band of angels on recess from heaven. Maude Perry was a wonderful influence on Anna, calm, resourceful, strong and very wealthy. Anna was always the driver and Maude's oversized kid leather pocket book could solve almost any problem.

Teddie, on the other hand, never had an idle moment. If he was awake he was busy, never without his crew of workmen. The station yard became one of the show places of Fitzgerald. Not a sprig of grass was out of place. His yards were strung with electric wires and irrigation water pipes. His roses bloomed in profusion and dogwood trees, which he and the men had grubbed in the forest, looked like snow banks in the spring, interplanted with redbud trees. Palm trees greeted travelers as they detoured through Fitzgerald. Yes, Teddie had a green thumb and many willing hands, even old Otis Alford and his mule Beckey helped him out. Teddie was once asked why he pushed himself so hard. He never looked up from his digging and answered in a soft sad reply, "No one knows how many tears I have buried in this earth."

Teddie's family was gone with the winds, Anna's scattered with their families and work. Chase was in New Jersey with Bob. Shep had let a young woman I mentioned before, Goldie and her son, homeless and hungry, move in the little shotgun house on Federal Street. Anna didn't approve of the situation, but Shep had become old and could barely drag himself out on his little porch each day. He did not care to live with any of his family, his horses were gone, and he hung to life only by a thread.

Goldie was good to the old man. In fact, she seemed to improve his lot better than Anna could. Goldie was on his level and Anna always prodded him to do better. Goldie's boy chopped firewood and swept the yard. The woman cooked black-eyed peas and rice. Shep smoked his pipe and drank huge mugs of scalding hot tea. How they managed those twelve dollars and fifty cents a month to provide their needs, I can't explain, but many people did the same. Dan, his son, had little to share with his father, although he did bring him firewood. Goldie washed clothes for the neighbors. The boy didn't go to school, but he ran errands on a wobbly old bicycle. Times were hard, but people helped one another. Shep had many adventures between Australia and its River Darling, the south Pacific and the thrashing whales, which were harpooned and rendered into oil stored in barrels he built. Then to the life in America, riding the rails of the Northern Pacific railroad to Lake Superior, and the dark forests, where he helped saw down trees with cross-cut saws; the strip of a Yankee girl he married, the daughter of the camp cook; the beautiful team of Belgian horses he groomed and trained on the farm in Pennsylvania; the train ride to Georgia on the first railroads to penetrate the pine barren and brooding swamps. Though the group of settlers had disappointments and trials, they overcame them to build a fine city in just a few hectic years. He had witnessed it all, the rutted sandy trails, now paved highways, horses replaced by gasoline engines, trains that whisked a body to Atlanta in five hours, and celebrations in the center of Fitzgerald, the success story of the century. Yes, old Shep Barrick had a heart full of memories. Let him smoke his pipe and rock away his remaining years on that little front porch. Anna may drop by any minute. Her fussing and trembling chin will slide off his mind like water off a duck's back. If she didn't come, Goldie would have a bit of lunch. What more could an old worn out stockman, neither Yank nor Reb, a subject of the Queen, desire?

The summer of 1928 changed to autumn. The leaves fell to the ground, frost cloaked the shrubs, and cold winds from the north rippled the pond waters. Cold nights found people huddled around the fires in Teddie Newton's backyard camp house with the aroma of speckled trout frying in a huge steel fry pan, built by the blacksmith at the railroad shops. Anna and the other wives set the rough tables covered with brown paper from the railroad. Please, don't ask me how the people of Fitzgerald would have survived the Depression if the Atlanta Birmingham and Coast had not had its headquarters there. One of Anna's closest friends, Irene Ware, led her aside and commented, "Anna, I have been watching you lately and your little tummy is pouching a bit. Could you by chance be pregnant?"

Anna's eyes spoke first with a glint of happiness, "Yes, my dear. I was trying to keep it a secret from Teddie. I hope he can adjust his busy life to include another child, as this is my heart's desire to raise a boy, although Teddie has sworn to never love another baby. He has a strong will, but we are about to see."

Irene smiled and pledged her silence on the matter.

Spring came early that year, 1929 it was. The Depression had turned into a panic. Wall Street in far away New York had collapsed, soup lines formed, rich men of the twenties jumped to their deaths in the cities. Teddie now knew of Anna's condition as she had started wearing maternity clothes. Teddie pitched a fit. How could she do such a thing? It was her idea, not his. Now she could have this child but, it would be hers. He would provide for it, but she need not expect him to love it. While Teddie slept soundly most of the nights, Anna pulled the covers over her head, and enjoyed the movements of the life that stirred in her womb. Teddie could just bump thunder. He could scratch in his flowers all he wanted to. She would have the child, which she knew would be a boy, as the stars were in the proper position and it was too active to be a girl.

She wrote her mother of the coming event, early in June she hoped, before July brought its oppressive heat. Dr. Dare checked her often as they had developed a special relationship. The ladies gave Anna baby showers. They even gave her a baby crib to replace the one Teddie had burned that terrible night of the accident. Teddie had calmed down as he always accepted duty as all Newtons did. He spent much time at his station. He hired Doc Laseter to help around the house, as he was better than any woman to work in the house. Although Doc was in failing health and no longer good for heavy labor, he just about lived in Teddie's camp house, swept and washed and had dinner on the table when dinner time came. Why the bent old black man who himself needed a home became almost a member of the Newtons' family. Only on the weekends would he trudge to the East side, or black side, of Fitzgerald.

Anna was in her thirties and the birth wasn't easy. The baby boy was 8lbs and Anna's normal weight was 89lbs. Teddie was aware of her pain and held her hands during her labor. He was not far away all day that Saturday. Mellie Fitch and Dr. Dare in room 29 of the Hospital pulled the baby into the world. The baby boy refused to take his first breath of life. Anna, after checking its genitals to be sure it was a boy, turned her worries to the infant, who was holding its breath as if it didn't care to live in this troubled world. Anna's chin trembled. Quickly she shouted, "Mellie, get the ice from that water pitcher, grab a chunk of ice and rub it down his back!"

Dr. Dare held the boy by his tiny feet as Mellie Fitch gave his backside a vigorous massage with the ice. The baby's lungs filled with air, and it let out a yell that Teddie heard down the hall. The baby then breathed as he should. Anna smiled and her fist comment was, "He is too stubborn to breathe. And no doubt, he is a man child, just what I wanted!"

That first yell awoke something in Teddie's heart, although he didn't admit it right then. But he realized and was to say years later, "Love comes with the child."

This baby seemed strong and healthy, although Anna's milk didn't agree with him. Teddie went to old Jake Sedemeyer's store and bought a large earthen pitcher to mix a formula that Dr. Dare had recommended. Doc and Teddie kept house until Anna regained her strength and followed a diet to gain some weight. The baby was now doing fine, and had been named Paul Bryan Newton, as his father was a great admirer of the Apostle Paul in the Bible. Anna was never far from him and vowed to never let him feel that he was to be raised in the shadow of Lenard. She wanted him to have a normal happy childhood with no complexity.

Teddie had far more problems adjusting to parenthood than Anna did, as she was happy as a bird. Teddie still had some hang ups, and each time he started to compare Paul with Lenard, Anna shot him a quick glance that would button his lips.

After a few months, they got back to their normal social lives. The whole town of Fitzgerald was glad the couple again had another child in their lives. Fish were again being fried, and happy songs rang out of the camp house on cold nights.

One morning the next spring, as the roses bloomed, Anna heard the side yard gate open and a voice callrepeatedly, "Anna, Anna." She picked up little Paul from the pallet he lay on and went to the back door. Who do you think it was?

It was her old papa, holding a wilted bouquet of roses in his gnarled hand, his pipe in the other. He had walked from the Federal Street house over to see his new grandson he had been informed. Anna carried the boy to a bench and there under a crabapple tree Shep held the child, who explored the old man's wrinkled face and mustache with his small fingers. Anna took the small notebook from her father's shirt pocket and wrote a quick note, "Please don't mention Lenard's name, as I don't want him to hear the word." Shep's face changed expression as he read the note. He made several grunting sounds as he slowly read the words, and nodded his head. Anna for some unknown reason never invited him inside and only wrote him another note, as he was stone deaf. "Do you want me to call William Mahone to take you home in his taxi?"

They sat awhile under the crabapple tree and slowly he rose to trudge away. Anna's heart bled to see how bad he looked and how untidy he appeared, but she reasoned, "He will never change. It is his way of life and he seems happy in it. My mother gave up on him, and I won't waste my breath on the old stockman. I am glad he came, but I don't want my son to grow up to become another stockman."

All the childhood friends and schoolmates who had nicknamed Anna Tremble Chin, had mostly scattered to their own homes and vocations. Anna herself was now thirty-five, still thin but weighing almost one hundred pounds. Her hair was without any gray, but perhaps maturity and sorrow had brought a look of sureness and confidence to her face. Her chin seldom trembled. In fact, she could have looked at the devil straight in the eye. Only a few remembered her as Tremble Chin nowadays. Fitzgerald had forgotten many things from settlement days. Only two old Union Veterans were still alive, Mr. Burner and Mr. Hatfield. Only one Confederate, Mr. Bush, survived seventy odd years since they lay down their arms. The band no longer assembled to play "The Battle Hymn of the Republic" or "Dixie." The special train no longer ran to Andersonville on Memorial Day. It now honored the men who went to France to fight the Germans.

Many of the younger generation, such as Anna's Paul, shared a legacy of the south and the north, as southern boys had married girls from the original northern settlers and vice versa. The two bloods mixed well, seldom even to be mentioned. Whether you were Baptist or Methodist was much more important. Only the Methodist Church was divided in Fitzgerald. A congregation of dyed-in-the-wool citizens of northern extraction held forth over on south Lee Street, the Methodist Church North. They also buried the hatchet and marched in mass over to the beautiful new Methodist Church South, to become one congregation, henceforth known as the United Methodist Church, the church of Teddie and Anna. Would you believe that the church left vacant soon became the Jewish Synagogue? Yes, Fitzgerald seemed to be very tolerant of ethnic backgrounds.The families of the original Irish-German settlers clung to the Catholic Church, sitting right beside the Methodist sanctuary. The subjects of the English Queen, Clearance Sydney and Shep Barrick, seemed to be oblivious to churches, and both now were too far into their dotage to attend much of anything.

Anna's boy, Paul, as everybody on the sidewalks called him, accompanied his mother and Maude Perry on their rounds of the town and county, Anna at the wheel of the Gospel Car as the little Model A Ford was known. Maude, twice the size of Anna and her pocket book one hundred times larger, admired Anna's spirit and cheer, and the fact that she never tied herself down with house keeping. Teddie now ate on the streets and old Doc kept the yard and house tidy. Little Paul thought the backseat of the Ford was home.

Teddie became well known for his expertise on a bicycle around the streets of Fitzgerald, as he said, "Parking was no problem." Teddie still had only a passing relationship with his young son. He often cooked his and Anna's breakfast with the baby in his arms, as he always called him when the child was no longer a baby. As soon as he, the baby, could walk, Teddie wanted to take him for a walk up the sidewalk. They did fairly well together, until they reached the post office, two blocks distant. The post office sidewalk was surrounded by a metal looped wire fence, just the right height for a child to grab hold of the loops. "Anna's" son grabbed the fence and shook it with all his might. Teddie objected to this behavior and sought to discourage him from clinging to the fence. Paul continued to shake it with all his might. Teddie had never had discipline problems with Lenard. He finally had to carry the struggling lad by brute force back home to his mama. Anna rushed to the porch to see what all the ruckus was about.

Teddie, in his desperation, set the stubborn child down and angrily told Anna, "Here he is, you wanted him and you can have him, as I am washing my hands of him."

Anna laughed and told Teddie, "I love to see 'my son' rebel."

Teddie strode back to his office, but when the sun set he had cooled off and came home, as if nothing had happened. This incident was to set the stage for the rest of the father and son's relationship. The first words the child spoke, the first sentence he put together, was, "Let me do what I want to do."

Chapter XXIV

1935-41

The economy was still not much better. People had learned to survive. President Roosevelt in all his optimism had promised "a chicken in every pot." Young men joined the Civilian Conservation Corps (CCC), and the Works Progress Administration (WPA), a domestic army of young men who attacked much needed drainage problems, road building, national and state parks projects and anything that needed doing in a local community that was plagued by unpaid taxes. The New Deal had created jobs as America struggled on.

Anna and Teddie had to let the automobile go back, and the telephone was taken out. Teddie still somehow had his fish fries and the roses bloomed as if there were no Hoover Days. The sunshine and rain still came.

One day two young men with ladders and buckets of paint knocked on Anna's back door, and announced that they were to paint the house. Mr. Newton had promised to pay them two dollars cash and to feed them for their labor. That is how hard times were.

Many of the colored people were desperate. Once again they found themselves hunters and gatherers, much as they had been in darkest Africa. Opossums, rabbits, squirrels, even robins and doves were trapped and shot. Any of the above had to run for their lives or they would find themselves on the supper menu. Nearly everyone, even Teddie and Anna, had a milk cow, as the baby Paul would cry for "warm sweety." The German colonists did a brisk business in milk, eggs and chickens. Town folks placed empty quart glass milk bottles on their front step, each with a dime, ten cents, in it. Before daylight the clink of glass bottles could be heard. It would be the milkman who had left a full quart of fresh milk for breakfast.

Teddie ate up town most days, as a full meal cost only twenty-five cents, dessert included. Gardens flourished on every vacant lot around Fitzgerald. Children walked the path beside railroad tracks to pick up lumps of coal that had fallen from the steam engines. The firemen would even throw a few shovels of the black lumps out the side instead of into the fireboxes. People fished a lot at Minnie Mill Pond, they seined creeks, set traps and trot lines in the rivers. Bobwhite quail seemed to multiply as fast as they could be shot and trapped. Many of the delicious little birds were dressed and sold to some few people who could raise a little cash. The only fruit most kids ever saw was handed out at school recess some days by government relief workers. If kids didn't like some foods, they never mentioned it as it would only appear again on the supper table. Rural children, who rode to school on a bus, carried biscuits and ham, baked sweet potatoes and a jar of syrup. Well to do city pupils, with their light bread and pineapple sandwiches, would swap lunches with them.

Everyone seemed happy and people shared. Tramps had only to knock on a back door and offer to chop firewood for a plate of food. As far as I know, none of these homeless men were ever turned away empty handed. This scene was to continue for twelve years. People in big cities fared worse than the people of Fitzgerald and other small rural cities. Many independent people refused to accept government hand outs. They took pride in pointing at six or eight fine children and saying, "Ain't nare one of my youngens ever had a bite of Government food in their mouths." Pride showed through the dark clouds of the Depression!

Teddie and Anna held on to their little nest egg. Shep Barrick didn't change much as he was in a depression before the depression came. Anna no longer had a car, but Goldie's boy came to report on the old adventurer. A week didn't pass that Anna didn't write to her mother, now in Miami as times were better there than in the North. Into each letter she would tuck a dollar bill. One thing for sure, nearly everyone was in the same boat.

The picture show seemed to thrive. People would do without to pay show fare, adults twenty-five cents, kids nine cents. The theater was only a few blocks from the Central Avenue house, and twice a week, Anna and her boy would walk to the Grand Theater and spend a happy afternoon in the darkened building, sometimes to be joined by Teddie at 5:00 p.m.

One industry that was in no "depression" was the distilling of illegal liquor, corn liquor. It was traded freely for goods and services. Sheriffs made a living chasing these enterprising businessmen, commonly called bootleggers. Preachers made a living preaching long sermons to sleeping men, who had spent the night "tending a hidden liquor still" along some creek or beside a spring. To be in a position to buy seed and fertilizer to plant a crop next spring, and buy shoes for the baby, much hard liquor was drunk in Fitzgerald. Perhaps it was some liquid fortitude for men who performed super human feats to hold their jobs, which, if they couldn't hold them, a dozen other men were standing around waiting to take their places.

Perhaps this state of affairs was what brought the labor organizers out of the north to unionize the railroads, including the Atlanta Birmingham and Coast. Mobs of disgruntled railroad workers formed picket lines which stopped the loyal workers, mostly the transportation workers, conductors, engineers, firemen, and trainmen. Pick handles were swinging, heads bled, trains were delayed or tied up. As the strike worsened the company already on the verge of bankruptcy fought back. Strike breakers were hired, skilled fighters they were, professional toughs. The National Guard was called to restore order and protect property after the trestle was dynamited by strikers, and a passenger train plunged into a creek, killing an engineer loyal to the company. His black fireman jumped just in the nick of time. He was only bruised and cut. These were terrible days and worse nights. All Fitzgerald paid the price of the turmoil. Teddie and his work force were not directly involved in the strike, although the troops set up a machine gun on the roof of the station office, Teddie's second home.

Anna did not venture out on the streets. The blacks kept to themselves out of the melee. They knew what side their bread was buttered on. A labor union would probably better the lot of the white employees.

One night, a knock came on Teddie's back door. There in the dark, lantern in hand, stood the call boy, Willie C, a young black man. "Mr. Newton," he spoke quietly, "the switch engine is coupled to two carloads of mules that need feed and water pretty bad, and those strikers have Franklin Street crossing blocked and won't let the crew pass to the rest pens. What will we do?"

"Willie, you go get Alzie Kennedy, that new boy Sebeb Walker and you yourself, quietly go over to the pens and hide in the hay house as if you were sleeping there. I will be on over when I can get through."

For some reason he turned to Anna, standing behind him in her nightgown. "Awake Paul," he said. "Dress him to go with me as I want him to see how ugly desperate men can get. I myself do not fear them as most of them are my friends."

Within minutes, sleepy-eyed Paul watched his father light a flickering kerosene lantern. He hoisted the small boy to his shoulders and set out on foot, unarmed, for the Franklin Street crossing.

Paul clung to his dad's neck as Teddie strode into the mob gathered around a fire built in the middle of the crossing. The switch engine was sitting on the spot before the bonfire, coupled to two stock cars marked Atichson, Topeka and Santa Fe, gently rocking as the restless Missouri mules milled about with their nostrils flared as they smelled water. Teddie never missed a step as he passed through the opening left by strikers, who stepped aside. One bull of a man, pick handle in hand, grimly spoke, "Teddie, I hoped you wouldn't get involved in this scrap. you should have left the kid at home."

"No, Mr. Stone," Teddie announced, "this railroad is our home and I am here to feed and water these mules, and the boy always goes with me." His words calmed the men. Even old man Mills and his fireman climbed back on the hissing little switch engine. Without an answer to Teddie, the leader threw his pick handle aside and shouted, "Knock the fire, boys. These mules aren't in the strike. They are as innocent as this boy who sits on Teddie's shoulders."

Within minutes the crossing was cleared, the engineer blew "ahead," the fireman's shovel stoked the engines fires, and the mules soon were spotted before the unloading chutes. The waiting helpers had the water troughs overflowing, and the hay racks were loaded with number one Timothy hay. Teddie's helpers were happy, for he would give them a full day's pay for three hours of actual duty. President Roosevelt had a minimum wage law of thirty-six cents an hour for rail workers. No wonder Teddie had no trouble raising a work crew! Anna's boy had learned his first lesson there in the middle of the night in the middle of a railroad track at Franklin Street crossing, how to face trials and to stand up for yourself if you think you are right.

The strikers lost the strike, and their jobs were filled with scabs, as they were termed, who flocked into Fitzgerald to operate the trains. Many of the strikers just vanished.

Not long after things had returned to somewhat normal, Teddie's telegraph key tapped out a message advising all agents and stationmasters along the three hundred mile line that the president and chief executive officer, Col. Bugg, would have a special guest with him on his office car number 101, on the rear of the southbound evening train. The guest and his party would be extended every courtesy and welcome because the guest was none other than Franklin Delano Roosevelt, president of the USA.

Teddie had only five hours to spruce up the station. He called the mayor of Fitzgerald about the pending visit and speech the president would deliver. He called his black men to alert them, sending Alzie to pick two dozen of his prettiest roses, "Tell Anna and the boy to be ready at train time," Teddie said to Alzie. He got the line and obtained the names of the train crew, engineer, Ked Caushy; fireman, Frank Lincoln; conductor, Percy Drake; flagman, Lee Harper; baggage master, George Heffington. Depart Atlanta on time, arrive Fitzgerald station 3:50 p.m., see no failure." Within an hour, all Fitzgerald was on their toes. Anna had the roses arranged with the buds just opening. They were red radiance, Teddie's pride and joy, or rather his crutch.

When the train's whistle was heard a mile away, on the cat hop, the little high-wheeled engine, Number 79, recently bought from the Florida East Coast railroad after its overseas line to Key West was washed away in a hurricane, glided to a smooth stop at Fitzgerald Station. Half the population had gathered on the wide platform. Ashley Street was crowded, even chinaberry trees had been climbed to obtain good view.

President Roosevelt was popular with the masses of struggling people. Col. Bugg stood before a leather cushioned wicker chair next to another like it, placed on the rear vestibule of the ornate office or private car of the railroad president, the other reserved for the president of the United States of America. Teddie and Fitzgerald's mayor, Captain Jack Hayes, city councilmen, Chief of Police Gordon Henderson, and the yard foreman at Westwood yard, J.E. "Horse"Addison, awaited the president's arrival.

Who do you think was upon his father's shoulders but Anna's boy, little Paul. He clutched a bouquet of rosebuds, wrapped in green florist's tissue and nearly as large as he was, and his legs were locked under Teddie's armpits.

The rear door of the coach slowly opened and a broad-shouldered man appeared to stand for a moment as the crowd of blacks, whites, all walks of life, roared a welcome.. He leaned heavily on a walking cane as he moved to the waiting chair behind which stood his valet in a white uniform. He eased himself down as he waved heartily to the crowd. He sat very erect and flashed a bright smile of confidence as only he could in the face of personal trials, struck in the prime of his life with crippling infantile paralysis. He held his head high and received a key to the city from the mayor, then Teddie approached the vestibule where the dignitaries sat. He welcomed the president on behalf of the railroad as Anna's boy leaned high, small as he was, to hand a smiling Franklin Roosevelt the two dozen rosebuds from his father's garden at the Central Avenue house. The valet took the flowers from the president and with a bow held them high in a gesture of appreciation.

Between cheers, Roosevelt gave a short speech of great times to come, and how only fear itself was to be feared. Anna watched with interest as Teddie and her boy were in the limelight. Teddie was sharp as a tack. Somehow this child was different from Lenard as he had a mind of his own, and she was glad his chin didn't tremble. Deep in her inner self, some soft voice spoke, "This child is destiny's child,'" and a surge of happiness flooded her mind. She admired the way he thrust himself forward as he handed the roses to the president. Young as he was, he loved the fanfare and the crowd gathered at the train station.

Losing her automobile had been a blow to Anna's activities around town. She and Paul had to stay at home more, so she buried herself in her son and the lovely backyard that Teddie worked so hard in. Anna soon had Paul reading as he was nearly five years old. She was quick to see the difference between this child and the one she had lost. He didn't care much for poems or the Bible stories. No, he liked stories of pirates, "Robinson Crusoe," "The Adventures of Billy Whiskers," even "Ali Baba and the Forty Thieves." She read them to him over and over until he, with her help, could read quite well before he was school age. Teddie was puzzled that the lad leaned toward life's more adventurous side, but only shook his head in disbelief. Anna smiled as she knew, yes, well knew the Australian background and the voices that her Paul heard. She knew he would never sing in the choir at church, He would wear boots instead of shining slippers, but, she thought, "Please Lord, guide his footsteps in the paths of righteousness and deliver him from evil." She refused to let him grow up in Lenard's shadow, good as it was. She didn't want him to be anyone but himself.

The defiant spirit the boy had been blessed with almost caused him to be disowned. Anna was about her chores one morning in June. Paul was driving nails in a board with his dad's claw hammer, as he seemed fascinated with joining pieces of scrap lumber. A knock was heard at the back door. There stood the gentle giant, Alzie Kennedy, Teddie's right hand man. He said, "Miss Newton, Mr. Teddie sent me here to get the baby as his boss man will visit the station today, and he would like for him to meet little Paul."

Anna freshened up the boy, combed his tow head, told him to obey Alzie, and for heaven's sake, make his dad proud to have a fine boy with good manners. Now Paul loved Alzie as he spent many hours with the black man, who had a great talent for drawing. Why, Alzie could draw anything the boy's heart desired on the huge rolls of brown paper used to line boxcars. He even had Paul sketching animals and people. Teddie frowned at the pictures and discouraged Paul, telling him that artists were bums and he sure didn't care to be the father of one.

Teddie had a trying situation on his job. Fitzgerald was headquarters for the railroad, and officials of the road often dropped in to visit with him. Railroad officials were not famous for their kind words and gentle suggestions. In fact, they were rather spontaneous and their vocabulary almost matched a sailor's, with few exceptions. This boss, Mr. Huddleson from the Atlanta office, not being with the transportation department that had to deal with train crews, was a gentleman of the highest class and had helped Teddie in the past. In fact, they had come up together on the railroad and this was only a friendly visit. He had indicated that he would like to meet Teddie's new boy because he had known Lenard, always a model child.

At home, Teddie had let off a lot of steam to Anna at night about how he dreaded the visit of bosses and their tirades. Little Paul had listened to his father's hopes of what the future held for them, and what he would do and say if he didn't need a job so badly. Perhaps the boy had formed his own opinion of the men who threatened his dad and made him so unhappy, and a job meant nothing to his young mind.

The big moment came. Mr. Huddleson had arrived to greet his friend Teddie, who had called to Alzie to bring little Paul to meet the boss. That word "boss" somehow struck the lad wrong, bad wrong, and in his mind he became a pirate, sword in hand, as his imagination had no bounds. Mr. Huddleson became the ship he was to board, and he would certainly avenge his father and the work he had done for the railroad.

Old Shep's spirit must have arisen in the boy's mind as he grabbed the man's leg, clung to it and kicked with all his might. Teddie, unable to control him, called again for Alzie to remove the raging child from the office and take him home to his mother. Mr. Huddleson only smiled and assured Teddie that the boy had a future in the ring, a place Teddie abhorred. Everyone, even Anna, who only placed her arm around her son's shoulders and held him close, rather liked the incident as these officials had seldom had an adversary since the strike. Teddie was embarrassed and didn't hesitate to inform Anna that the boy was a Barrick, not a Newton. Anna shouldn't have laughed at this point, but she did.

"Serves you right, dear Teddie. Night after night the child has heard you low rate your superiors and he was only trying to protect you! So from now on, just button your lips as to what you would like to do to the boss. My boy, some day, will be a man of action and few words. Perhaps he is a Barrick, and if that bothers you, you can just go back to your little office and play little Jesus to your men and that smoky little railroad."

Teddie grabbed his hat from the sofa, slammed the door behind him, jumped on his bicycle and vanished into the night. After he cooled off, he came home, with the same hat in his hand, only to say, "You win again."

Chapter XXV

Trouble Again

School had taken in that September, and there was no Ford car to drive Paul to school. Teddie wanted Anna to walk the boy to school or he would have one of his men escort him, as traffic was heavy and the accident was still fresh in his mind. "No," Anna said, "I have shown him the route to take. He is alert, and I don't want him to feel protected. He must someday face the hazards of life. He has a little bicycle to ride on the sidewalk, and he is very serious and capable. I will send him and his lunch, as he needs to join the other children more than to be hauled back and forth."

She prayed for a guardian angel, perhaps Lenard, to watch over him. She watched him pedal away to school and he made it like a top, as he knew every inch of the route and the grownups along the way. He didn't know that these people whispered to each other, "Surely Anna Newton didn't send this boy to school on a bicycle, after what happened to the other one."

School was another thing to Paul. He was bored by the primary books, "Dick and Jane." He could already add and subtract, even divide numbers. Little did he or his teachers know that his school days would be short. Paul had become listless. Anna felt he was sick. He didn't eat well. She took his temperature, and sure enough it was over one hundred degrees. She called her faithful doctor, Dr. Dare, who came to their home as she had no way to take Paul to him other than Will Mahone's taxi and twenty-five cents was a lot of money to hand out. The doctor tapped on the Central Avenue house door with his black bag in his hand. Anna greeted him, taking his coat and hat. "I need you. My boy isn't right, and only this morning I discovered a knot on his neck that I don't like. Please help him. My whole life is in raising him."

Dr. Dare had a good bedside manner. Children liked him because he was kind and gentle. They felt he was their friend, not only their doctor to cram pills and caster oil down them or jab them with a dull needle. He took the boy's temperature and looked down his throat, examined the swollen neck with no comment. Paul had his favorite book beside his pillow and sick as he was, clutched it with one hand. "Robinson Crusoe" it was. Anna and the doctor stepped into the living room, and the good doctor was helped into his coat, as September had turned to October and a chill was in the air. Anna then handed him his hat and black bag.

The doctor was not quick to speak, and Anna only looked into his kindly eyes, prepared for the worst. Finally he spoke, "Anna, I hate to tell you, but the child has a chronic condition, and I am going to make him an appointment with Dr. Bershinsky, a top-flight baby doctor in Macon, as we must take no chances with that swollen gland in his neck. I will call Teddie when I return to the office."

After he drove away, Anna, heartsick, prepared herself to do battle with old enemies, fear and the grim reaper. She searched her mind for an answer that was slow to come. It was only a small voice that told her not to let her son see her worried and for her to keep a bright countenance, regardless of what the future held. She knew how brave the lad was, and he would not have to face life with a sad, worried, faithless mother. Together they would win this race and the victor's crown. She only hoped she could keep Teddie from doing something radical, as she understood him very well.

The trip to Macon would be a challenge for the couple and the listless child. There was direct train service to Macon. Teddie did not own an automobile and his job was most demanding. Dr. Dare always credited his patient's specialist as the ones in Macon wanted their fees up front and money didn't grow on trees, not in Fitzgerald. Anna quietly assured him that a way would be provided. Teddie's heart bled when he looked at the knot on the boy's neck. He realized that his worries were small compared to the young life that was at stake.

As word leaked out of the Newtons' problems their friends, the ones who had eaten many fish suppers in the back yard, rallied to their aid. Maude Perry opened that large purse of hers and handed Anna some folding money. Burl Richards, an engineer on the railroad, loaned Teddie his automobile and his wife to accompany the boy to Macon.

The morning of the doctor's appointment came, a freezing November morning. Teddie was at the wheel with Doc Laseter by his side in case trouble arose. Now Mrs. Richards, who had no children, was short and jolly, nearly as wide as she was tall. She held little Paul wrapped in his favorite Indian blanket on her lap. Anna had a lunch and the things her boy would need. Paul had been taught by his mother never to cry and to be brave. He was too sick and young to realize the true desperation of the ninety-mile trip over poor roads which were under construction. Teddie was a good driver, and soon Tootaville, Helton's Mill, and Clarksville were behind them. Big Indian Creek was swollen, and its waters spread over the bank. The new concrete bridge was not complete, and the old wooden one was on the verge of washing out. The highway flagman and Teddie had a quick conference. Teddie returned to the car and said to Doc, "The man will let us cross the bridge, but he wants the women and child to walk over and wait for me on the other side. You wrap the baby up real good and carry him. Help the ladies and don't set Paul down on the cold wet ground."

Teddie waited until his passengers stood on firm ground, then he rived the car's motor and mounted the board runners of the rickety old bridge, built to accommodate mules and wagons. Paul was quiet as Mrs. Richards sang "Polly Wolly Doodle" in her most cheerful voice. Teddie had a grim look of determination on his hollow face. Anna held the books her boy loved so much in case he asked for them. She also had the Case knife so dear to his heart, no Bible stories or things that Lenard had loved, as they had gone up in smoke on the dark night when Lenard lay in the funeral parlor. These thoughts haunted Teddie, but if you want my opinion, those memories were on the other side of the wall that Anna had built to insulate her from heartache. She only planned how she would cope with the problems at hand.

Deep down she felt that this child would survive. She herself had survived that night she was born in a slop jar in a shack on a sandy pioneer farm. Perhaps she drew her great courage from her grandfather, Yankee Captain Fred, the night he washed up on Kangaroo Island. Or perhaps from the beautiful Bridgett O'Leary, who took a chance on marrying the determined adventurer, who pushed his steamboat too far only to destroy it and himself on the Darling River, on Australia's far shore. These thoughts gave her courage as she waited to see if Teddie would make it.

As the little group on the far bank of Big Indian Creek took their places in the borrowed automobile, Anna knew this was a good omen, and it renewed her great courage. The only time Paul took any interest in the sights along the way was when they passed Clinchfield and its cement mine. He spoke, "Look, mama, at the steam shovels digging into a hillside, loading railroad gondolas with lime rock to be milled into cement and mortar." Again, when they stopped at a grade crossing to let a train pass, he was wide eyed.

Teddie recalled Mrs. Barrick's comment when the boy was born on that Saturday evening, six years past, "Saturday child shall work for his living." Silently, Teddie hoped that one wouldn't come true for the son who had been sent to him, for Teddie knew how hard labor could be and the demands that driving boss men could place on a workman. Why, for heaven's sake, hadn't Paul noticed a school or church, instead of the smutty old steamer engine? Watch the road, Macon and its traffic is just ahead. Doc couldn't drive a car or read road signs, and Anna was on the back seat.

When they arrived at the hospital Doc carried the bundled child. Mrs. Richards took a seat in the waiting room of the best children's doctor in Georgia. Teddie and Anna spoke to the receptionist sitting primly behind her desk. The report that Dr. Dare sent to Dr. Bershinsky was handed to the nurse. Anna read to Paul as Teddie paced the waiting room floor. Finally old Doc Laseter took him by the arm and spoke to him, "Please Mr. Teddie, sit down. You got a hard day ahead of you. Dat pacing ain't gonna hep dat boy. He'll be OK, just you wait and see. I don and said a special prayer fo de boy. Da good

Lord in heaven knows you and ole Miss don't be due no mo misery, Amen."

Teddie did sit down. Doc carrying the child and Anna at their side entered the clinic, where the doctor in his white coat stood beside his examination table and its bright lights. Doc gently laid his burden on the table and went out to wait in the hall. Teddie was tending to the business papers. For some reason, Anna immediately disliked the arrogant doctor. His bedside manners left something to be desired, and he was Jewish and very European, having studied in Vienna, Austria. He spent some time examining Paul and asking her questions. After a few minutes, he turned to her and left his nurse to tend to Paul.

The doctor led Anna to his office and told her that the gland in his neck was the symptoms of a syndrome of progressive nature, which eventually would lead to a chronic condition known as "water head." Little Paul's head would become enlarged and death would eventually follow. Anna never changed her expression, only coolly said, "Thank you, doctor. We won't take any more of your time."

Teddie paid the bill and called Doc to get the patient. Mrs. Richards had a questioning look on her face. Doc gathered Paul in his arms, Anna smiled at Teddie and said, "Let's go." The doctor came to the door to wish them well and said he would send a letter to Dr. Dare, and they could counsel with him in Fitzgerald.

Teddie had to turn the car's headlights on before they arrived home. Anna never told the others of the bad news. She pitched it on the other side of her wall, and all she said was, "Everything will be fine."

Teddie dropped his family at the home on Central Avenue, took the car to the filling station, filled it with gas and thanked Mrs. Richards for her kindness, then put the car in their garage, mounted his bicycle and pedaled to his office to report to the dispatcher that he was back on duty. Doc built a roaring fire in the fireplace, cooked Anna and the sick boy a hot supper and went to his quarters in the camp house. Teddie didn't seem to need rest. He was an iron man and worked late on his reports. Paul slept fitfully until Teddie came home around midnight, gaunt and hard looking in his overcoat. He sat beside the glowing coals talking to Anna in her nightclothes. "Tell me what the doctor said to you, Anna."

Anna spoke slowly, "It wasn't good. He pronounced him as a water head and mailed Dr. Dare a report."

Teddie told Anna that he would call Dr. Dare in the morning and tell him to stop by the home place when he made his rounds as she had to confer with him.

A knock on Anna's front door next morning brought her to her feet to run as she often did on her bare toes to greet Dr. Dare with his satchel in his hand. After a warm greeting, he spoke very directly to Anna of the phone call he had received from Dr. Bershinsky, stating that although Paul was very ill, he was past the age to show symptoms of water head and perhaps another specialist should be contacted. The doctor sat on the edge of Paul's bed and had a friendly chat with the boy, finding him somewhat better, somehow more alert, even telling Dr. Dare of his trip to Macon and the things he saw. Anna drew courage from Dr. Dare's words of hope.

Teddie came in to lunch saying Dr. Dare had called him at the office during the morning, and together they had agreed that the boy should have been taken to Atlanta, to Emory University and its medical school, being perhaps the best in the USA. Teddie had a close friend in Atlanta, a Fitzgerald boy who had risen from a railroad call boy to one of the top positions in the railroad general offices on Cain Street in Atlanta. Teddie had gotten on the wire as both men were telegraphers. The friend, Jimmie Addison by name, had a suggestion. He and his wife Emma Vee attended church with a very prominent doctor, as well as a professor at Emory Medical School. His name was Dr. James E. Paullin, also the personal physician of Franklin Roosevelt down at Warm Springs Foundation. Jimmie Addison assured Teddie that within two hours he would have a reply and to stay near his key. Sure enough, soon after he arrived back at his desk the Prince Albert can on the receiving key began to rattle its Morse Code message. "O.S. Fitzgerald," "O.S. Fitzgerald."

Teddie opened his key to answer the call.

"Appointment with Doctor J.E. Paullin, Medical Arts Building, 10:00 a.m., November 26, 1934, for Master Paul Newton. Emma Vee will meet train #102 at Union Station Atlanta on arrival Nov. 25th, signed off J.E. Addison."

Teddie sent Alzie to notify Anna of the appointment. Anna suddenly was filled with new hope. No hardships or sacrifices were too great for her to bear if only her boy could survive, as her life was rapidly passing and her childbearing years were nearing an end. She was thirty-seven years old. Anna's religion was deep, but different from that of most Christians. It was a thing that dwelled deep inside her heart. She needed no altar to offer a prayer or any shouting, as silently she asked her Lord and Savior to abide with her boy and see him to manhood. She then approached Paul and told him that they were going to ride the train to Atlanta, and if he felt like it, he could be her little man, as there would be just the two of them. Daddy would have to stay at the station to meet the trains.

Anna and her little man boarded the train at Fitzgerald Station. Teddie looked on the crew sheets to see which conductor would be on #104. Seeing the name George Talbot, engineer, and conductor Percy Drake, he knew Anna and Paul would be in good hands. George Talbot was one of the best engineers on the line. With that, he typed a message to conductor Drake, stating that his wife and boy would be on his train tonight, as the boy was very sick and had an appointment with the doctor. "Please keep an eye on them. Mrs. Addison will meet them in Atlanta," he wrote, typing his name at the end.

Doc Laseter had helped Anna pack her suitcase and bathe Paul, telling Paul stories of Uncle Remus, B'rer Rabbit and B'rer Fox. Doc loved the little white boy as if he were his own. His children were grown and gone north to work.

Paul, ill as he was, smiled at his mother and tried his best to assure her he could make a trip. He wished Doc could go with them, but he would have had to ride in the colored coach and couldn't have been much help to them. Anyhow, someone would have to keep the home fires burning.

Anna looked quite cute in her traveling attire. She smiled and chatted with the people in the waiting room, as she didn't want Paul to see her down, even though her heart was heavy and her chin trembled. She knew Captain Drake, the conductor, well and greeted him with her sunny smile on a cold night, headed for an even colder city and an uncertain diagnosis. Engineer Talbot, a handsome man, was dressed in his starched overalls with a red bandana neatly tucked in his blue collar and a tall cap with goggles set upon the visor. He came over and picked Paul up in his arms, and asked him if he was going to Atlanta. The fireman was Sebeb Walker, the young black boy who had been the bellhop at the St. Paul Hotel, whom Teddie had helped get a job on the railroad. He was now the fireman of choice on the passenger train Number 104.

The train sailed into the house track before the station platform, carrying several yellow refrigerated boxcars behind the engine. Teddie told Anna, "You will have a rough ride tonight with those reefers of perishable Florida fruits between the engine and the passenger coaches, but Talbot perhaps can put you in Atlanta only a few minutes late, and Sebeb will keep that steam gauge sitting right on two hundred pounds all night. Drake will make you comfortable, and there will be no creeks to ford or flat tires to change, as we experienced on the Macon trip."

After the passengers for Fitzgerald had unloaded, Captain Drake helped Anna aboard and lifted Paul up to his mother in the vestibule of the coach. Engines were changed as were the crews, which relieved engineer Tom McInnis and his black fireman, Westly McGowan. They exchanged greetings with Talbot and Walker as they mounted to the cab of the fresh engine Number 75. The car inspectors coupled the air hoses, but the steam line which heated the coaches could not be connected as the freight cars were not so equipped, leaving the passengers with only coal-fired stoves to stay warm. You must understand that those boxcars would bring in more revenue than the passengers who rode the train to Atlanta that cold dark winter night, beside the fact that the fruit they carried was needed up north and was revenue, which was the lifeblood of Fitzgerald, so complaints were few.

"All aboard," Captain Drake called, and signaled Talbot with a high ball signal of his lantern to leave Fitzgerald for the two hundred and five mile run to Atlanta. Anna waved goodbye to Teddie and Doc Laseter standing on the station platform. Engineer Talbot opened his throttle, released his brakes and the train crept ahead, first gently, then gathering speed. As the lights of Fitzgerald flashed by the coach windows, Anna breathed a sigh of relief. She felt confident that she and her boy could overcome this problem. At least, they were on the way to Atlanta and the finest doctors in the South.

Captain Drake turned a seat to form a double seat, facing each other, as the coach was not crowded. Anna had brought pillows and soon had made a bed for Paul so he could stretch out as she could also, and try to catch a few winks of sleep on the reeling coaches which often jerked as the slack played between the engine and cars. Anna knew that they were climbing Maulk Rise when the train came down to a crawl, the exhaust of the engine became more distant, and the sky flashed with an orange glow as Sebeb was shoveling more coal into the engine's firebox. It was an eighteen-mile grade or the fall line, at Manchester, two thirds of the way to the great city of Atlanta, separating South Georgia from North Georgia with its hills and pine mountains.

The train threaded its way through the maze of switchyards to Union Station in the heart of the city of Atlanta. Little Paul, sick as he was, sat upon the mohair seat of the railway coach as it came to rest in its berth at the station. Anna had been to the ladies lounge and freshened up a bit. She wanted to look nice when she stepped onto the platform. She smiled and thanked Conductor Drake as she handed him the overcoat he had spread over the sleeping lad during the night.

Emma Vee Addison was waiting at the gate's waiting room for Anna and her patient. A red capped porter pushed Paul in a wheelchair, as it was quite a walk from the tracks to the station waiting room. This was a big city, much different from Fitzgerald. Emma Vee embraced Anna and then, as she was much larger and stronger than her friend, helped with her things. The porter reached down and took the listless Paul into his strong arms, carried him to the parking lot at Union Station, and placed him in the automobile. Anna pressed several coins into the black man's hand.

Paul's eyes were open wide as he took in the sights of the city. The trolley cars that provided public transportation clattered along rails embedded in the paving, powered by overhead electric wires which popped and flashed as their contact shoes slid along the hot wires. The alarm bells clanged to clear the tracks. Paul even read the destination signs displayed on the front of the trolleys. New life seemed to enter the boy as he slowly spoke, "Capital Avenue, Marietta Street, Stone Mountain, River, Peachtree Street, Crittenden Homes, Bankhead, Ansley Park, Kennesaw, Barn." In fact, if it ran on rails,

Paul would smile and say, "Look, Mama," no matter how bad he felt. After all, what else could a mother expect of a child who had been raised beside the railroad track and spent so much time at the station depot, a world to itself!

As the two women stepped into the office of Dr. Paullin, Anna handed the telegram message that confirmed her son's appointment to see the doctor. A nurse in a starched white uniform opened a door and led them to an examination room, where they made themselves comfortable to await the arrival of the doctor. Anna felt a ray of hope enter her heart, which had brought her through so many trials and tribulations in the past. Emma Vee was paying her back for things she and Maude Perry had done for troubled people.

It seemed an eternity until Dr. Paullin opened the door of the examination room. He spoke to Anna in a kindly soft voice. He carefully felt the knot on the boy's neck, looked at the chart in his hand, noted his fever, looked in his mouth, then assured the young patient that he would soon be playing ball again. He carried him to the window and showed him the skyline of Atlanta, as they were ten stories above the sidewalk. The doctor showed him the blue haze of the distant Kennesaw Mountain at this amenable visit, only to break the ice and set the little fellow at ease, and to decide his future treatment. The doctor motioned for Anna to join him in the hallway, as the nurse dressed the boy.

"Mrs. Newton, I cannot make a complete diagnosis until he has undergone surgery to biopsy that swollen neck gland, which is located in such a critical area. I will have a room reserved for your son in Piedmont Hospital and a room for you across the street, on Capital Avenue, at a boarding house that caters to the families of hospital patients. I will write a letter to Dr. Dare to inform him of my findings and treatments, and he in turn will inform your husband. Good day, and don't you worry, as I will provide you transportation to the hospital. I want the boy kept quiet and warm."

Anna thanked Emma Vee, as she and the patient were put on the service elevator. Within thirty minutes, they were being settled in a hospital room. Although Anna was weary from the all-night trip on the train, she drew some inner strength and read to Paul until he fell into a fitful sleep. Anna hated to leave him alone in a strange place, but this was a children's ward, and a kindly nurse assured her that she would stay close to him until morning. Anna was met by a Mrs. Martin, owner-operator of the boarding house across from Piedmont Hospital, where her sick child lay asleep tucked beneath the covers with his book entitled "The Adventures of Billy Whiskers in Panama."

The medicine that the nurse gave him controlled his fever, and he slept well that night. Anna tossed and turned all night, not only in concern for her fourth child, but also for Teddie and how they could pay the doctor bills and the hospital. She prayed. She even felt Lenard's spirit near her during the long night. She fell asleep about daybreak, and slept a deep sleep until Mrs. Martin brought her a tray with coffee and breakfast, not to mention some kind words.

As Anna crossed the street and climbed the steps to the hospital lobby, she saw many people like herself there to comfort their loved ones. This reinforced her will, perhaps an answer to her prayers. She never again felt alone as her heart went out to others in the same boat she was in. Paul was in a room with several other children who were not in critical condition. He seemed quite bright and was glad to see his mother. He complained that the nurse talked like a Yankee, and that he had liked the train ride to Atlanta and those little trolley cars on the streets of Atlanta much more than any ball game that the doctor had mentioned. Why, Anna wondered, had he not mentioned missing school, church, the choir at church or missing his nightly prayers with her as Lenard would have.

A quiet voice, the one which had always spoken to her, even as a child when her chin trembled, startled her back to reality as it spoke. "Anna, you asked me for another boy child. I now have Lenard here with me in heaven. I gave you this baby, a boy as you asked, but I saw fit to give you a totally different boy, who will never be the same as Lenard, but I will abide with him and I will never take him from you. He will never be like the one I took from you."

A smile came on Anna's face. Never again would she question her Lord, for he had spoken to her. The future, whatever it held, was now clear to her. Peace settled about her and doubt had been vanquished to some dark recess of her mind. A surgeon had been sent to examine Paul and his swollen neck, a Dr. McCrea, a dashing young man gifted with a scalpel, who wore a leather jacket, rode a roaring Harley motorcycle around the streets of Atlanta and harassed the young nurses. He and Paul struck it off at the first glance, and he assured the boy that soon he would be fine and he would take him to ride on his bike. Anna noticed that the young doctor picked up Paul's books of adventure stories, not a sign of a Bible story. Perhaps he realized that they somehow were brothers underneath the skin.

The biopsy brought bad news. The gland showed cancer cells developing in it, perhaps pre-cancer cells, but Dr. McCrea had removed the entire gland as Dr. Paullin had advised. Now the boy had to go under X-ray treatment each day for a month to make sure that the malignant cells were all destroyed. This radiation treatment was in its infancy in 1935, and the side effects and results were still not fully understood. Anna took new hope and consented to try the treatment the following day. Paul was rolled to the specially equipped X-ray room. There he was placed on a table beneath a huge machine with an extension that could be adjusted to focus a beam of strange light to any part of the body of a patient. He was covered by a heavy rubber sheet and surrounded by a wall of lead bricks. The only opening was a window that allowed the strange ghostly beam to shine for a few seconds on the afflicted area of the patient's body. Paul never showed any fear of the treatment, which seemed to him as just another adventure. Anna spent time consoling other frantic parents.

A month passed with the X-ray beam aimed at the scar on Paul's neck, where the diseased gland had made some improvement. He smiled some, read in his books, even drew pictures of animals and trains. His mother did most of the praying. One morning, Dr. Paullin came by his room, and asked if he was about ready to go home to Fitzgerald. "Oh, yes! I will get to ride the train," he answered.

Anna spoke with the doctor in the hall, and it was decided, provided his fever was near normal, he could in fact go home the next day. The next morning, despite the cheerful front the child exhibited, his fever was a hundred and one degrees, and the nurse announced to Anna that the doctor thought he should stay another few days. His fever indicated some unseen infection or inflammation. Paul was very disappointed and threw a fit, fighting at the orderly as he took him back to his hospital room. Anna, being accustomed to disappointments, called her friend Emma Vee, telling her of the change in plans and asked for her husband to wire Teddie that she and the boy would not be on the night train when it pulled into Fitzgerald.

The next morning Teddie walked unannounced into the hospital room where Anna and Paul were having a school session, as each day she held class in reading, writing, and arithmetic. Teddie had ridden the train all night. He was unshaven and covered with soot from the smoke of the train. He stood there in the doorway in an overcoat as the weather was bitter cold in Atlanta. Paul was taken aback at how haggard his dad appeared, standing there with Anna. He was reading his letters from his Grandmother Chase and a special packet of letters with no stamps on them, all addressed to Paul Newton, Atlanta, GA, Piedmont Hospital. It seemed that Miss Barfield, Paul's first grade teacher, had each of his classmates to write him a letter to express how much they missed him and hoped he would soon be able to come back to school, as they missed him.

The rest of the day was a happy reunion of the little family far from home in a hospital full of sick people. Teddie paid Mrs. Martin across Capital Avenue for Anna's room and board, and handed Anna a five dollar bill to spend. After a tearful goodbye, Teddie caught the trolley car and rattled away to the Union Station to catch the night train, Number 103, to Fitzgerald, and all points south, to terminate at Brunswick, Georgia, on the shores of the Atlantic Ocean.

Two more weeks passed before Dr. Paullin dismissed Paul. He still ran that constant fever, a hundred and one degrees. He was frail and weak, but could walk and was seemingly adjusted to his elevated body temperature. His condition was well known among the men of the railroad. In fact, his condition was talked of all over Fitzgerald, even as the tragic death of Lenard had not been forgotten. Surely the Newtons wouldn't loose their fourth child!

Teddie answered his telegraph key, which clattered the news, letter by letter, word by word, "Dismissed hospital this a.m., meet train Number 103 Fitzgerald, tomorrow a.m." Teddie was elated. Perhaps this life or death struggle had awakened a love for the boy, who had been overshadowed by the loss of Teddie's beloved Lenard. He sent for Doc Laseter to come to the station, as Doc had been keeping house during Anna's absence. As Teddie read the message to the old colored man, whose head was now white as snow, a tear rolled down his wrinkled black face to be wiped away on his faded shirtsleeve. He stood a little straighter and assured his boss man that the fireplace would have a roaring fire in it, the baby's bed would be warm and he would have hot coffee for ole Miss, as he referred to Anna.

All night long, and as the first streak of dawn lit the dark sky above the sleeping town of Fitzgerald, George Talbot shut the throttle back and reached a gloved hand for the brass handle of engine Number 87 that set the air brakes on the coaches in which Anna and Paul had ridden from Atlanta. Sparks fell from the steel wheels of the coaches as the brake shoes drug the speeding train to a halt before the station platform to discharge the weary passengers. Teddie and Doc stood in the chill of the dawn on the well-lit platform of the station, Teddie's station. Doc pointed to the step of the coach and ssaid, "Dar he is, him able to walk on his own foots."

Teddie and Anna didn't embrace or kiss, as Teddie did not like public displays of affection. Conductor Drake bid them a fond farewell and Teddie thanked him for his services on the train. George Talbot had no children, but paused on his way to the station to say hello to Paul, as he had taken quite an interest in the lad and so had his fireman Sebeb Walker, who was well acquainted with the Newtons. The former bellhop never forgot that Teddie had helped him get the job he now held on the road, which paid perhaps four times what day labor would draw.

Teddie swung the frail boy upon his shoulders as he always had. Doc got Anna's suitcase, and they walked the block to 320 W. Central. Home at last, Anna spoke of how she had to stick up to have that lot in a good location.

Doc was as good as his word. The house was ready for the patient and his mother. A long recovery was in store for Paul, and Anna devoted every waking hour of her time to following Dr. Paullin's orders to keep him quiet and in the fresh air and sunshine, not to let him exert himself and to try to feed him a good diet, as his appetite was poor. Spring came with a gentle breeze and rain showers. Tree buds swelled, flowers bloomed, and mocking birds sang. Anna was a good nurse, also a good teacher. Paul's classroom was his sand box beneath the gnarled old crab apple tree in the back yard. The fish fries resumed on Saturday nights, and the camp house rang with songs of church. Life had returned almost to normal. Paul's fever still lingered, but as the months passed it lessened, until one day in the summer it read normal. Paul met with his teacher at the school house and had taken a promotion test, which he had no trouble passing as he was perhaps on a third grade level, especially in reading. He was seldom seen without some kind of reading material, even if it was funny comic papers or adventure stories by Zane Grey. His mother helped him with some words, but perhaps this was all the education he would ever need, as he seemed to be self-taught, even to tying knots in every piece of rope he could find.

Teddie began to take a lot of interest in his son as he stayed at his daddy's station a lot and seemed fascinated with the trains, especially the steam engines that sat around the house track. These engines served the station by providing a clear main line for passing traffic on the rails, which seemed to serve every industry and warehouse in Fitzgerald. Despite the Depression, it was the business hub of the area. The historic background of the early beginnings of the town had faded somewhat. This new generation's bloodlines were diluted between Yank and Rebel. That was history now, as everyone struggled to put meat and bread on the table. Paul could now ride his bicycle and go to school to become an "A" student in history, geography and art, reflecting his best effort.

Chapter XXVI

The New Car

Teddie was a sucker for any automobile salesman, and Anna knew this. Even though she also loved a car, she was thrifty, or as some people described her, she was "tight." Life gave her no choice but to be thrifty. Her father lost every penny he ever earned, and some said he squandered his family's inheritance or it was buried somewhere up north. If he had money, it never seemed to show up, and he soon let money, hard-earned money, slip through his work-worn fingers. He still sat on his little front porch and smoked his pipe, stone deaf, perhaps one of the few remaining settlers of Fitzgerald. His life long friend, Clearance Sydney, had long since been placed in his mausoleum in his pasture.

Getting back to Teddie and the auto salesman, one summer day at noon, Teddie announced that Mr. Williams, the Chevrolet dealer, had called him in off the street and made him an offer that he couldn't turn down. It seemed that car sales had dropped to nearly nothing, and he had a stockroom, in fact, a warehouse, full of unsold automobiles. Knowing Teddie's good name to pay off debts, he had told him to take the little woman, as he called Anna, over to that warehouse to meet W.C. Henton, his head salesman, and let her pick out a new car. There would be no down payment, no set monthly payment, and no interest, only Teddie's good word, and he could pay what and when he could. The car cost six hundred fifty dollars. Anna agreed that the offer couldn't be beat.

Dr. Paullin had billed Teddie one thousand dollars as his fee for services to Paul in Atlanta, but had kindly offered to halve that amount as he knew times were tough and Teddie, only a salary man, was not wealthy. They, mostly by Teddie's hard work and Anna's thrift, settled Paul's hospital and doctor bills. Paul now seemed quite well. The house on Central Avenue had been brick veneered and another bedroom added. Perhaps they could now afford a new car, and hopefully a telephone on a private line. "Yes," she said. "Paul and I will walk to your office at 5:00 p.m., and we will meet Mr. Henton at the warehouse. I want to pick the color and style I want."

Mr. Henton opened the warehouse door to admit the evening sun into the dusty interior of the warehouse, and the line of new cars waiting for an owner. Mr. Henton had to take his handkerchief out to wipe a spot on the light blue two-door standard model, clean enough for Anna to be sure the color suited her. Paul jumped in and sat behind the steering wheel. He was now tall and slim, very slim, and he could see over the dashboard. Why, he was taller than his mother now.

Mr. Henton told them that it would be serviced, polished, filled with a tank full of gas and parked in the driveway of 320 W. Central tomorrow noon, all on Teddie's good word and handshake. Just as Mr. Henton had promised, the blue car was sitting in the driveway the next day. Teddie rode his bicycle home for lunch. After a quick bite the three happy people piled into their new car, with Anna at the wheel. She had some trouble learning how to shift the gears. With that accomplished she backed into the street and away they went around the drives of Fitzgerald, where once she had held the reins to old blind Peggy, hitched to the shay loaded with gleeful school children who called her Tremble Chin when danger approached.

Teddie solemnly announced before he mounted his bicycle to return to work, "Anna, I want you and Paul to enjoy this car, go places, and have fun. I will tell Jim Clever at the Gulf Station to credit you with a tank of gas a week. We have seen enough sorrow and trouble, now try to forget the past. Live today always hopeful for a better tomorrow."

Anna was only too glad to hear Teddie speak those words. He was a good man, and somehow they had weathered insecurity, family disappointments, divorce, upbringing prejudice, fire, tragedy, depression, strikes, demanding railroad officials, and hard work. All these things had only matured Teddie and Anna.

Paul was doing well. Anna never doubted for a minute that he would get well. He was quick to learn the things all boys have to learn. A bicycle took him places, roller skates gave him much needed exercise and fresh air, then a B.B. rifle was followed by a twenty-two caliber rifle that he treasured. George Talbot, the locomotive engineer who had taken an interest in the boy since the train trip to see the doctor in Atlanta, coached Paul in the skills of marksmanship and the finer art of fishing, accepting only his best effort. Talbot himself was a perfectionist at whatever he did.

Anna watched Paul's development with great amusement. She had hoped and prayed that above all things he would have a strong individual will of his own. The good Lord in heaven had certainly answered her prayers. He and Teddie were as different as day is from night. His father finally accepted the fact that this boy would never walk in the footprints of Lenard, fine as he was. No, Teddie had no idea he would ever have a son who would be an outdoorsman, not a choir singer.

Paul often came home after dark with a string of fish that drug the ground or a game bag heavy with game, or caught up on a locomotive to throw a few scoops of coal in its firebox. He rode a bicycle backwards, sitting on the handle bars, swam the Ocmulgee River, played hooky from school to trim bamboo fishing poles by the hundreds, or to see the fishermen peddle fish on the black side of town, not to mention rabbits, raccoons, and opossums, or have a pen of hound dogs. He got up in the middle of the night to meet a group of men older than Teddie himself to go fox hunting.

Why didn't he ever mention going to the University? Why would he climb out the window at Sunday school to ride that infernal bicycle to Minnie Mill Pond? Why did he build a pen beside Teddie's beautiful rose garden to house a female gray fox and seven pups he had caught in a hollow stump? Paul wasn't twelve years old when he built a boat right in Teddie's camp kitchen, where old Doc Laseter had stayed before he died. What possessed this boy? Perhaps the spirit of his great-grandfather, Captain Yankee Fred Barrick, or Limon O'Leary, the squatter. Surely not Bridgett O'Leary, although his hair fell in waves as hers did.

Teddie, my boy, perhaps you opened Pandora's box when you gave that old one-legged crossing watchman a dollar bill to introduce you to that little bundle of charm with the flowing red hair, named Anna Barrick, daughter of the old stockman and the free-thinking daughter of the Yankee calvary man. Consider all these factors Teddie, my boy, for you yourself have wondered what characters by the name of Newton may have roamed the green paddocks of Ireland or danced in the pubs with the ladies as they quaffed food and Irish whisky. Perhaps the lad, Paul by name, is only marching to a drummer you can't hear.

Anna reflected for a moment, knowing that life is like an upward journey where a young person climbs a hill and risks making foolish judgments before one can see the true values of life lying beyond the summit, beyond "Fools Hill." Anna, the one born with the veil upon her eyes, only smiled and hoped her son didn't carry things too far, and some fair day he would be over "Fools Hill."

Chapter XXVII

1941- Pearl Harbor

Sunday morning, daybreak December 7, 1941. Remember this date for nothing will ever be the same after it. Oh, the sun will rise in the east and set in the west; spring will follow winter, babies will be born, but a chapter in world history has been closed.

Anna had heard Paul arise, slip into his clothes and leave the porch where he slept on a cot. It was still dark, but he was twelve going on thirteen, and very mature for his age. She never questioned where he was going on that bicycle. Teddie was snoring in another room, and she was left alone with her thoughts. Suddenly she sat upright in her bed. That feeling she often had came over her mind, but not for Paul or Teddie. It was as if a black curtain was being drawn before a stage. Could it be the end of the world? As she drew the covers about her, that small voice spoke to her, "Anna, great changes are coming to pass, you and yours are safe."

Her father, Shep Barrick, had died only a month before. His time had come to go. She didn't grieve much, as he would be better off than wandering the streets of Fitzgerald. He was buried with only a handful of neighbors and old friends attending the funeral at Evergreen Cemetery. All his riches were in Australia. His horses were gone, as was his wife. Only Goldie, his housekeeper, and her boy now grown, stood by. Anna had sent Chase, her mother, a telegram but received no answer. The county buried the old stockman in an unmarked grave on a lonely hill called Potters Field.

Paul had ridden his bike ten miles to Bowen's Mill on that beautiful December morning. The weather was cool enough that the snakes and turtles slept in their hollows. He should have been at Sunday school, as his father would surely be, but he had baited twenty-five set hooks the evening before and hoped to have a mess of bass, catfish, and jacks. He only hoped that big old alligator was hibernating and hadn't robbed his limb lines.

This was the millpond where the first steam trains had crossed a long trestle which his grandfather Newton had worked on in 1896, when the typhoid fever had struck the work camp, claiming his life so quickly.

The wind had risen with the sun and had kicked up ripples on the channel through the lily pads that choked the shallows scattered with ancient cypress trees draped with gray Spanish moss. As Paul reached for a line tied to a low limb of one of these cypress trees hoping to find a fish that had been hooked, he heard a man shout from the railroad trestle, "Paul, come quickly, I have some kind of bad news."

Paul paddled the homemade boat closer to the figure on the trestle. The older man, Bowen Shepard, the owner of the mill, told the boy, "The Japanese have bombed Pearl Harbor, sinking many of the US fleet of warships and killing many sailors and soldiers." Paul had never heard of Pearl Harbor and asked his friend where it was. Bowen, himself a navy veteran, told him: "Honolulu, Hawaii." Paul would never forget that message, as he wondered what or where he would land.

As he cleaned his catch of fish beside the free-flowing well, his mind tried to accept that their way of life was threatened, and he would become cannon fodder, as he had heard the old folks say. He pedaled that old bicycle hard with the sack of dressed fish in a gunny sack in his basket mounted on the bike's handlebars back home.

Dr. Paullin had been correct, the X-rays, fresh air, and sunlight had worked wonders, not to mention the care and love his mother Anna had poured on him, the bills that Teddie had paid for him, and the blue Chevrolet that they had enjoyed so much. Was war to bring an end to all these happy scenes? Only time would tell. He longed to sit down and talk to his mother, for she had the most level head he knew of, and he could ask her any questions without the fear of a lecture, which his dad was sure to give him, a lecture of woeful consequences to fall on a young man who didn't follow the straight and narrow. Often he wondered why when he did well at something, his father would brag, "Good work son, you take it from my bothers," or when he was in a mess Teddie would frown and say, "I might have known you would turn out just like your mother's brothers and her father."

Paul only shrugged and kicked the ground. His mom would say, "Try harder next time. You can do it. Don't come to me with an 'I can't' attitude."

War came to Fitzgerald. People crowded around crackling radios to listen to speeches by President Roosevelt. Anna predicted a long hard war. The Civil War had been talked about so much that Anna felt as if she had been there. The First World War was still very real to her, although none of her family or Teddie had been in uniform, and it was over in two years. She read a lot and her radio was beside her bed. The war clouds that were on the horizon were ominous.

Hitler and his powerful German army had already rolled over most of Europe, and England was an embattled island. Japan occupied most of Asia and the South Pacific Islands. America's army was small. Planes and ships were old and obsolete.

She told Paul of her fears. Teddie only stayed on duty at the station more, as troop trains and ammunition trains loaded with military supplies rumbled through Fitzgerald. Anna and Paul didn't see any great change. Gas, meat, sugar, tires, and shoes were rationed. New cars and trucks were not manufactured. Teddie rode his bicycle on the job and gave Anna the gas ration. Anna visited Maude Perry more often as she had a telephone and car now.

Paul could drive the car now and had a driving license by the time he reached fifteen years. He drove for Mrs. Perry and even got a summer job driving a truck for a farm supply store, as nearly all the able-bodied young men were gone to war. Boys only a year or so older than him joined the Navy or Marines with their parents' consent.

Paul did very well in high school, although he never took much interest in sports such as football, baseball or track. He seemed more interested in adding to his quite sizeable savings account at the bank. He sold fish, cut fishing poles, and during the summer he always had a job as the war effort had created many job opportunities and money began to flow once more. Teddie had saved to send Paul to college. Anna knew her boy would never leave Fitzgerald to become a lawyer, doctor or schoolteacher, let alone a preacher. She knew, from the times they had ridden the trains, that his true interest was the trains he had seen since he was a baby. They had a grip on the boy that would burn brightly all his life. Her only doubt was whether he had the strength to meet the demands that those jobs would put on him. She knew that his childhood sickness had drained him of strength, and she told him so, but she well knew his rebellious spirit and rather liked it. Teddie had long ago washed his hands of counseling with the headstrong boy.

The years began to take their toll on Anna. Her frail body was feeling the pain of arthritis, her hair, her crowning glory, was cut short and graying. She still loved to go with Paul to fish in the creeks and lakes. They had spent many happy hours together. She had truly enjoyed the eighteen years she had devoted to raising him. Never once did she call Lenard's name or go to his grave.

Paul himself realized this and never asked her about him. It was as if he had never existed. Teddie weakened a few times, but never before Anna. On one occasion, as Teddie and Paul sat at the table eating lemon pie that had been served to them by Anna, Paul noticed tears running down his father's face, as he quietly sobbed. Knowing that the boy was aware of the tears, he said to his son, "This was the last thing that Lenard and I ate before he was taken." Anna never heard the words he spoke, and Paul was never to hear his parents speak Lenard's name again. In Evergreen Cemetery, not a single headstone with a name upon it appeared, only three grass-covered mounds of earth to mark the graves of three children, so precious.

Anna had only one brother, the last of the Barrick family living in Fitzgerald who was still moving houses around town. He and his wife Letta had only an adopted son, Joe, but he did not bear the Barrick name. Chase,

Anna's mother, still lived with Bob, her oldest son, who found work as a mason in Miami, Florida. His two daughters were gone with their families. Anna still stayed in touch with her mother, as the weekly letters continued to go and come.

Anna again was seen about town in that new blue Chevrolet, driving Maude Perry on their missions of mercy. Paul did well in high school, always busy with his many projects, and Teddie worked steadily on the job at the station. The war was far away, and at times the tide of battle seemed to favor the Axis Powers. Ships were torpedoed just off Georgia's coast. Blackouts and mock air raids were practiced even in Fitzgerald. The luxuries of life in America were available only on the black market. Women began to take outside jobs in industry. Old men ran the railroad, farmers were exempt from the draft and worked hard to feed and clothe first an army, then the civilians. Anyone who could hear thunder or see lighting could find a job.

Teddie had Paul a job working with his crew at the railroad station when he was sixteen years old, during the summer vacation, but required him to return to school in September. Many boys quit school, joined the fighting forces, or simply went to work. American and British forces had seen victory in the battle for North Africa. Many prisoners were captured, and would you believe five hundred fine-built German prisoners of war were sent to Fitzgerald to labor on farms by day and camp by night at the local ballpark in tents. They sang songs and did calisthenics under the lights of the ballpark. Paul and his buddies crawled under the fence at night and traded items with the Germans. Soon all the students at high school were wearing caps of the defeated "Afrika Corps, Hitler's pride in better days.

The Allied Forces gained control of the sky over Europe. Allied bombers pounded German cities relentlessly. The Japanese were showing signs of weakening, but fought to the last man on a dozen South Pacific Islands, only to retreat slowly back to their homeland, as their navy was devastated in the battle of Midway and the Coral Sea. Still the war drug on in Europe. D-Day came, the day Allied troops landed in Normandy, France, to begin what would turn out to be one of the bloodiest battles in the annals of modern warfare.

America had truly rolled up its sleeves and its industrial might, and brave troops crushed the Axis Powers. Germany surrendered to the Russians in the east and to the Allied forces in the west. Victory in the Europe or V.E. Day was celebrated. The Japanese fought on in the Pacific, until the decision to drop a totally new type of explosive, the atomic bomb, two of which were dropped on Japanese cities, one on Nagasaki, the other on Hiroshima, leveling these major cities. A few days later the Japanese, too, surrendered. The victory in Japan was known as V.J. Day.

The five-year war was over. America would never return to its pre-war days of depression. Women had joined the work force. New model automobiles were much more luxurious than the pre-war puddle jumpers, and super highways were being built. Five years of war effort had to be made up on the home front. Shiploads of mustered out soldiers who had left home as boys returned as men. They lay down their arms and took up tools and plowed fields. Tractors replaced mules on the farms. Steam engines, some still in service since the First World War, were retired, replaced by diesel electric locomotives. No more coal to shovel into fireboxes, no more smoke to breathe, and no more melodious steam whistles to herald some midnight local train as it clattered through the piney woods. Banks loaned money to build new neighborhoods in cities and towns. Even Fitzgerald saw a building boom. Change was in the air.

Teddie was still stationmaster, and Anna was in demand to give Bible lessons. She now had time to give to her social life. Paul, tall and skinny, had decided to bloom where he was planted, and continued to live at the Central Avenue home. He had graduated from high school and declined his father's offer to send him away to college to become a professional man, a doctor perhaps, in some far off city. Teddie should have known, as Anna had tried to tell him, that the boy's heart was on the railroad, not in some high rise hospital or office building far removed from the rivers and swamps of South Georgia. You might know, there he was, the boy who wasn't expected to survive, standing in the gangway of a smutty old relic of a remaining steam engine, stoking the firebox of Engine #75, the very engine that had taken him as a sick child to Atlanta.

Paul was happy on his job around the old engines of the Atlanta Birmingham and Coat railroad, which was slow to replace its old locomotives. Anna never failed to stand on the corner to wave to him as he passed through town on his run. Teddie did the same as the trains passed his station. Things were on the up and up. The war had seemingly accomplished what no politician could for the economy.

A major rail line had purchased the Atlanta Birmingham and Coast, routing more trains between Florida and the northern states, with the original route through Fitzgerald being the most direct route north. Paul was making perhaps more money than his father.

Anna flitted around town in the Chevrolet car while both her men were gone about their duties on the railroad. Teddie was disappointed that Paul seemed to care little for church services and even less for higher education. To add injury to insult, he had purchased ten acres of land near town with his own money, built a stock pen on it, and filled it with cattle. He spent only a few hours sleeping at the home place on Central. Anna would take his calls for trips on the trains. She encouraged him in his endeavors. Teddie only hoped he wouldn't become a stockman as his grandfather had been. "Heaven forbid!" The boy certainly had some of Shepard Barrick's qualities, but so far they seemed to be his better ones.

On one occasion, the day he finished high school I believe it was, Teddie asked the lanky lad to take a walk down the railroad track with him. Paul in his overalls, and Teddie in his white collar and tie, strolled down the track deep in conversation. His father was doing most of the talking as he thought it was high time he set the boy straight on a few items of great importance. "Son," he started, "your room and bed are still at our home. If you are tired and sleepy you are welcome to lie down to sleep. Your mother sets a table every day. If you are hungry, stop in and you are very welcome to eat with us, but don't you ever ask me for a thin dime!"

Paul said only one word, "Thanks." The young man read his father's mind. The fact that he hadn't taken the route his father had selected for him would, his father feared, probably lead to something similar to the state of poverty that his grandfather had died in. However, Paul had also inherited many of Teddie's qualities, a willingness to work hard and a sense of responsibility, along with his mother's likeable personality, her love of stories and poems, not to mention his hair, which curled much as hers did. Teddie took the money he had saved for Paul's education and invested it in real estate and over the years multiplied the unused college fund many times.

Chapter XXVIII

Busy Days

Anna missed her son. She knew the idyllic days they spent together were gone forever:; going fishing, the trips she drove him to the woods to shoot his rifle, the swimming parties at Blue Springs when her car would be loaded with Paul's playmates, the times they had gone to St. Simons Island to spend Thanksgiving holidays at Maude Perry's cottage, the times she drove him to Minnie Mill Pond to deliver hundreds of carefully trimmed fishing poles, and the times she had agreed to let him play hooky from school if he would kill and clean enough robins for her to make a robin pie.

They had some sad times also, like the day Paul took aim at a mockingbird that sat on a limb of the old crabapple tree, which shaded the now gone sandbox where he had regained his health years before. Anna saw Paul from the back door and spoke to him in a low voice, "Don't shoot that mockingbird. The night before you were born it was so hot and you kicked me so hard. I don't think I would have survived the night if a mocking bird hadn't sung so sweetly."

The devil spoke to the defiant boy, "Pull the trigger. What do dumb old moms know about guns and hunting?" The rifle reported, the bullet flew straight to the bird's heart, the song ceased and it fluttered to the ground, squawking, never to sing again.

Anna cried, her eyes looked to the heavens and she spoke, "Oh Lord, what have I brought onto this earth?"

But the good times far outshone the bad. In fact, if she could, she would change him very little. After all, he had lived, and his chin didn't tremble!

The next threat on the horizon was another war brewing in the Far East, in Korea I believe the papers reported. Where in the name of heaven was Korea? Paul was drafted for military duty. He was single and well past eighteen years old. How could his mother stand to see him leave for war? Somehow, she felt that he would be spared. She didn't want four graves in that cemetery lot that she and Teddie had bought so many years ago, a place she refused to visit. Her prayers were answered. Paul was deferred because his job on the railroad was deemed essential to the war effort. Troop trains rumbled through Fitzgerald once more.

Train men worked on their rest. Cattle prices were good. Houses were rented or sold as fast as they could be built. Teddie prospered as did Paul.

Teddie's dire predictions for his son's course in life hadn't come true. In fact, the two, father and son, seemed to compete with each other, different as they were. Teddie even compared his son with some of his own brothers.

Time flew. Anna, knowing that her son was nearing thirty, hoped he would find a good girl and get married, but marriage didn't seem to be in Paul's plans. Most of his friends, the ones he went to school with, had left Fitzgerald to seek their fortune afar. Fitzgerald, thriving as it was, offered only limited opportunities for young people who wanted a different lifestyle from what their parents had lived. Girls as well as boys sougnt professions and positions that only the cities could offer. Farming, railroading, and cotton mill jobs held little attraction for educated young people, as hard labor, all-weather, all-hour jobs, which paid only an existence level of pay, could never pay for the things of the modern world, such as fine homes, luxurious automobiles, and college tuition for the children. Shovels and pick handles just didn't seem to fit their hands anymore. If a tool wasn't a power tool or if it didn't have a steering wheel, they avoided it as the devil did holy water. For a hundred years or more the hard labor of the fields, forest, and construction had fallen on the backs of mules, horses, black people, and Irish immigrants. But the steam engine had perhaps performed the hardest labor.

I am here to tell you that era had passed into history. Those young people who had seen the world and its many wonders during the war years would never again be content with the things that contented their parents. Anna and Teddie had reached a living level of moderate comfort which contented them. Not having brothers or sisters to crowd the nest, so to speak, Paul had shared this lifestyle of his parents. He shared their contentment, so why rock the boat? His parents' terrible experiences trying to have a family only reinforced the negative approach that he himself felt at starting a family, which would only tie him down to a regular grind in Fitzgerald. No, he wanted to fly through the night on a train pulled by a shrieking steam locomotive, fired by a man in overalls, goggles over his eyes and shovel in hand. Each run was a thrilling adventure. He wanted to line up at his father's station and hear his name called by his father as he handed out the bi-weekly paychecks, which often exceeded five hundred dollars.

Teddie and Anna were concerned about the dangers inherent to the job, as they had known of many train wrecks and scalded engine men. They had actually seen men run over by the train and ground to jelly beneath the steel wheels that blindly followed the locomotive. These things only held a fascination for a young adventurous man, who had so many forefathers who loved the challenges of life. Their blood flowed in Paul's veins. Lady Luck had surely been on his side so far. Could he ever be content to live in a fine home, ride in a shining car, sit by a fireside surrounded by electronic wonders? Seems he had rather be calling a herd of "piney woods" cows, counting his calves, or riding on the cab of a battered bobtail pulpwood truck with a crew of black wood cutters, as the overloaded truck lurched onto the wood yard scales.

Paul cut quite a figure as he stepped from the scale shack with the signs over the door reading "Office," check in his hands. Things had slowed down on the railroad. Diesel electric engines had retired the ancient coal burners as well as many men of the rails, as there were no more double headers that required six men to operate them. Two men could handle the same tonnage and never shed a drop of sweat. Sometimes trains would have over one hundred cars. Passenger trains ran with only a few passengers. Only the US Mail and express passages, along with government regulations, kept them on the rails for a while longer, but soon they too fell to the cutting torches of the rip track or junk piles.

Paul himself had seen the best days of the historic railroad. He stayed on the last lines, the branch lines which hauled fat pine stumps to the mill at Brunswick, working beside his friend of many years, the black fireman Sebeb Walker, the fireman on the passenger train that had carried him and his mother to Atlanta to see Dr. Paullin twenty years ago, before the war. One white, the other black, they labored side by side all night long, seven days a week until the line was abandoned and the last of the steamers fell to the torch of the scrap men in the Waycross scrap yard. No longer did the crack passenger trains bring tourists to Florida. The trains, one by one, were erased from the schedule boards. Never to be heard again were The South Wind, The Seminole, The City of Miami, The Royal Palm, The Dixie Land, The Flagler, The Orange Blossom, The Silver Meteor and The Dixie Flyer.

Even the little two-car train with one coach for white shop workers, the other for black workers, which transported two widow women, Mrs. Jay and Mrs. Reid, to their work at the Westwood shop offices no longer ran for the shops which kept the steam engines running were no longer needed. Now most of the men were dead and buried. So were the brave engineers who took such pride in bringing their trains in on time. Father Time had claimed them all. People traveled by airplanes, private automobiles, and eighteen-wheel trucks, which claimed much of the freight traffic.

Paul found himself on the cut off board more and more. He and old Sebeb never would fit on those new locomotives with their roll up windows and air conditioned cabs. The whistles were electric horns that blazed ear-splitting warnings. A new class of trainmen, who had to go to school to learn railroading, now manned the trains. Sebeb and Paul had a bellyful of railroading. Sebeb started picking up pecans, and Paul got interested in his cattle and pine woods, which he had purchased with his own hard-earned railroad money over Teddie's objections.

Anna watched her boy with a look of satisfaction, never trying to change him, only thankful that he had lived, that and that alone. She had been a good mother and her job was finished. Teddie, who loved the limelight, so to speak, certainly wished the young man no bad luck, as he loved him dearly, but stood by his predictions that he would end up on his father's doorstep with an open empty hand. Paul, like his father, was sober, didn't smoke or lay around the juke joints. He would be on his rural property at work or hunting, perhaps taking his mother fishing at his boyhood haunts.

If Anna had a weakness, it was fishing. The woman would arise at daybreak to sit beside her son in a battered old Ford car that the boy had cut down to a flatbed truck to haul hay and his hound dogs on. In the mornings that he took his mother, fishing poles were tied to the side bodies. Through Fitzgerald they went to the riverbank with high expectations of a fine mess of fish. Anna wore skirts until they arrived at the waterhole Paul had selected. Anna had two brown paper sacks, one with a plain lunch, the other with her overalls and a scarf to tie her red hair with, which now had threads of silver among the waves and curls on her forehead. Paul left his mother a can of worms, a jug of drinking water, and several of the bamboo poles, his trademark, carefully set where she would certainly catch the big one she dreamed of.

One day they were at Mariana Lake, in the self-same spot on the Alapaha River where Teddie had taken Anna when they were courting to have picnics and swim in the lake. Only now the place was deserted and gone back to nature. Some while later, Paul, who had been exploring down river, heard his mother call him to come quickly. He tore up the path along the river to find his mother sitting back in the bushes with her chin trembling. "Are you snakebit, Mama? What is all the hollering?"

She only said, "I caught the biggest fish I have ever caught."

"Where is it?" Paul asked. "Did it flounce back into the water?"

"No, Paul, can't you see? I am sitting on it." Sure enough, there was a very large fish tail extending from under her overalls. Paul laughed and put her stringer through the fish's gills and told Anna to stand up. I do believe that she was happier than if Paul had graduated from Emory Medical College in Atlanta, Georgia. But they were only beneath the spreading live oaks on the Alapaha River bank, near a rotting tram road trestle, which the little engine passed over long, long ago one Sunday afternoon, with only one boxcar from the Atlanta Birmingham and Coast railroad borrowed by Teddie Newton, her true love, and a laughing crowd of their young friends from the settlement of Fitzgerald.

Fishing trips were not the only outings on which Paul took his mother. Why, that boy even took her on his runs on the railroad when he stood for a passenger run. He took her to Brunswick when he ran on that line as it lay over in that town. They had a room in a workman's boarding house. She ate at the table with the men of the train crew, and Anna loved the new faces and conversation of the boarders, all of them away from home. Some of the older men knew of her tragic luck with her other children, but never mentioned it, not even among themselves. Paul was often referred to by the older men as Anna's boy, as he was a carbon copy of her, only taller, with abundant blond hair with the same waves and curls she had, no doubt inherited from the spirited Bridget O'Leary, who rode her Welsh Pony on the cobbled streets of Swanpool, New South Wales, on the other side of the world, before this mother and son were even thought of. Perhaps they were only a gleam in the eyes of the Yankee River Captain as he spoke to Bridgett aboard Boo.

Surely by now this pair was sleeping beneath the sod beside another river in that faraway land down under. All through this saga we have believed in spirits, fairies, wee people, even witches and fortunetellers. Surely Anna's grandfather, who was blown to flinders by the leaking old boiler aboard his steamboat, had marked Paul in his fascination with steam engines, not to mention his love of animals from his grandfather, the stockman Shep Barrick. By the same token, Anna was only stepping in obedience to the drummer that her grandmother Bridgett marched to when she married the adventuresome captain.

Nowadays, educated people refer to spirits as genetic makeup. I still think I saw spirits from the past hovering about this present day pair, mother and son, as they pursued their adventures while Teddie tended to business, both, his own and the railroad's. Don't get me wrong, Teddie took his pleasure in the simple fact that his wife and son, the son she prayed for, were well and happy, although they hadn't followed the course he had chosen.

Chapter XXIX

A New Face

As the curtain opens on the final act of this saga, a beautiful face was among the well-known actors, a young woman named Gladys. She would take her place with the Newtons:. Paul had selected a wife! Cupid, that ageless elf, had scored a direct hit on Paul's heart. He fell under the spell of the love god's potion and even bought a diamond ring as a token of his honorable intentions.

Gladys not only possessed a beautiful face set on a level head, but to Teddie's delight, she was educated and a graduate of college, Teachers School, and she herself was now a teacher in a school house located in a nearby village by the name of Waterloo. Paul had not only been smitten by her beauty, but by her indifference to his approach, which most girls fell for. He soon realized this was no ordinary date. In fact, she wasn't even his date! She was his best friend's date. The two boys were double dating when Cupid let his arrow fly. Perhaps he received an overdose of the love potion. However, it was Paul who couldn't sleep that night, and the next day he had trouble on his run. He nearly let his fire die in the old locomotive, as the fire seemed to be in his heart, and it burned brightly all the way to Thomasville, the end of the run. Paul tried to explain to the engineer that the coal was bad, but there was nothing wrong with the coal. The fireman was under the spell of Love.

Paul, cocksure of himself as he was, was soon to find that this fair lass was not to be swept off her feet by a line of blarney or a few trinkets. She would never go out with a guy who drove about in a cut down Ford twenty years old, or who had a week's growth of stubble beard, wearing work clothes that smelled of pin grease or perhaps even of the stockpen. He would have to clean up his act if he was to get to first base, or appear on the good Gladys' hit parade.

Gladys had a teaching certificate that she had earned by hard work and her ever-optimistic outlook. She was doing fine without a brash young fellow so sure of himself. She barely gave him a second thought as she brushed her hair early the next morning, which was her Saturday off. She lived with her mother in a farmhouse some distance from Fitzgerald, on a lonely dirt road seldom traveled by outsiders.

Suddenly the peace and quiet was shattered by the slam of a car door, the door of a strong old jalopyr that the yard dogs barked at while the chickens ran under the porch.

Gladys laid her hairbrush down, slipped into her kimono, tied the sash about her waist, and called to her mother in the kitchen, "I'll get it." She wondered who for the love of Pete would knock on her door so early. She parted the lace window curtain a bit to see a lanky young man, still in his railroad work clothes, eyes deep set in his head from the lack of sleep as he had worked all night on a switch engine out at Westwood yard. Gladys opened the door and stepped onto the porch where he stood. The dogs ceased their barking now, only holding their heads high and growling deep in their throats when they caught the strange scents of the fellow. She shaded her eyes from the rising sun so bright. Little did she realize that her life was about to change, very slowly but surely.

This forward young man who stood before her was not the first fellow who had been struck by her charms. In fact, she could have selected most any young blade who cavorted on campus at the college she had attended. She had been in no hurry to betroth herself to any man because her career was her primary concern. However, she pretty well knew why he had come quite a distance to see her so early. He looked so tired, but he had the same gleam in his bright blue eyes as he had the evening before.

"Could we be seated in your porch swing, Gladys, as I have but a few minutes to visit?" Paul said, removing his cap and wiping his face with his red bandana. He answered her question about what brought him to her door with a smile and the words, "I had more important things than sleep to tend to."

"Oh?" Gladys answered.

Paul informed her that he was leaving on a run to Atlanta that evening and would return the day after tomorrow, and perhaps she would enjoy a movie with him on his return to Fitzgerald.

Gladys knew little of the railroad as her background and her people had long been cotton farmers. She had heard the train's whistle as it blew for the road crossing a mile away, Coons Crossing as it was known. She smiled enough to show her perfect teeth and answered, "Why not?" for she had no serious sweetheart.

After Paul had climbed into his wreck of a vehicle, dropped the nail into a hole which kept the door closed, cranked his engine, and sped away, peace and quiet returned to the well-swept yard. The dogs slept, the chickens once more scratched for a living. Gladys sat back in the swing, her mind in a swirl after the whirlwind visit of the enamored young man. Her date only last night, a longtime friend of hers whom she trusted, had told her of Paul and his personality, his mom and dad who had no bad habits, and his burning ambition and thrifty ways. They had quietly agreed with a laugh, "Not to judge a book by its cover."

Anna noticed a change in her son. She heard him singing in the shower, and searching for his Sunday shoes. Suddenly he had sold a pen of calves and a hundred and six acres of pasture near "Coons Crossing," and ordered himself a brand-new 1955 Buick automobile. Perhaps she should check his temperature, as he was acting strange lately and he hadn't taken her fishing. Anna was hard to fool. She said nothing to him or his father. Time would tell, and it did.

The day he drove up in his new car and parked it in the side yard, Anna was sitting on the bench beneath the old crabapple tree, the one that Paul had played under when he was sick twenty-one years ago. She slid the pan of peas she was shelling closer to her side, making room for him to sit down beside her. "Now, how do you propose to pay for a fine car like that? And who may I ask will be sitting up under your arm?"

Paul laughed, "Which question do you want me to answer first? The car is paid for. Second answer: you and Teddie have been good to me, let me live here. You have packed me many lunches, and stood on the corner to wave to me on the engines. I have driven our little '39 Chevrolet since I could just see over the dashboard. Don't you think it's about time I bought myself a car, Mother dear? Hold onto that pan of peas you have shelled, and save me those hulls for my mama cows to eat. That x-ray vision you possess can probably see that big diamond ring in its box hidden in the glove compartment locked so tight."

These words must have hit Anna squarely in her chin for it started to tremble. She found her voice and shot a volley of words back at her son. "The woman who marries you has my sympathies."

Paul retorted, "And as for the bit you mentioned of the girl I would have tucked under my arm, forget it. I tried that and she removed my arm and informed me that if that was all I had on my mind, to take her home to her mother. That is when I went diamond ring shopping."

"Have you told Teddie yet?" Anna inquired. "When he sees that new car, his shirt tail won't touch his fanny until he buys one. You know him."

Teddie did drop in for lunch and came in the house after examining the long green Buick. "Whose car is that, Anna?" he asked.

"My son has lost his mind! He thinks he is in love, as I have already heard over the telephone, with a young schoolteacher who lives out in the Coons Crossing area, and he is blowing his money on cars and rings. He is almost acting as your boy!"

Teddie kind of liked the idea. He had always wanted a daughter, and she had graduated from college, and was a schoolteacher! Anna told her husband not to slam the screen door when he left, as she had ordered Paul to bed. The call boy would be knocking on the door giving him a call to fire a watermelon extra, a turn to Omega, Georgia, to return to Fitzgerald around midnight.

Teddie wondered how she knew what the call would be. Her only reply was, "A little bird told me."

It wasn't a bird that told her of the news, it was the telephone. She had a pillow on it so it only jingled a time or two before she grabbed it for she wanted Paul to rest. The party that called her told of an accident that Paul's intended had been involved in. A car had pulled into her path as she was returning to her home. No one had been killed, but Gladys's mother and niece were injured and at the hospital. Anna took Paul's call to work at 5:00 p.m., I believe. She slipped into the darkened bedroom where Paul lay asleep. She sat down on the side of his bed, and as he stirred she quietly told him of the accident.

"The girl named Gladys that you had failed to mention to me had a wreck this afternoon. I thought you would like to know as she is at the hospital."

Paul said nothing, as he leaped from the bed and into his overalls, splashing some water in his face and running a comb through his mop of hair, which fell in waves as his mother's and Bridgett O'Leary's had. He had but a little time as his engine would be set out on the round house track and would need a fireman to stoke its fires. Those watermelons were ripe. They were packed in ventilator cars and should arrive in Atlanta tomorrow morning.

Paul burst into the hospital to find Gladys limping up the hall to meet him. She told him she was all right, only her leg hurt some. She was concerned for her mother's condition, as the older lady was quite banged up. Paul could see his love was hurt more than she admitted. He promised her he would return tomorrow, if not sooner.

Paul rolled through Fitzgerald on the Extra South 2719. Teddie stood beside the track at the station to hand Paul a note with only one word: "Congratulations!" The squat little steam engine, the 2719, had low driving wheels, but those wheels could pull hell off its hinges if the fireman could keep the steam gauge on two hundred pounds of pressure. The extra train had no boxcars for Omega, only a caboose trailed along. Paul worried about Gladys and her problems, but the thirty-two cars of watermelons that the 2719 struggled with didn't give Paul or the little puffer belly engine any rest. Past midnight the whistle of the 2719 blew its station blow a mile from Fitzgerald.

Anna heard the whistle blow and was relieved that Paul would soon drive into the yard in that new car. Why, pray tell, hadn't he talked with her first? But hadn't he always had his own mind? All she could do was pray. This wasn't the first hurdle he had cleared. Anna didn't have to wonder what went on, as she somehow knew the score.

Paul, smutty as he was, parked the new Buick in the hospital parking lot before daylight. Paying no heed to the sign, "Visitation 9 to 11," he rushed down the hall to meet Gladys. She limped heavily on a swollen leg. Paul could see she was in pain and hadn't been out of her clothes all night, as she had tried to sleep a little on the waiting room couch. She was very concerned about her mother's condition. Paul, being somewhat of a stockman himself, knew that swelling could indicate a broken bone. The nurse who Paul sought help from, a close friend of his, agreed that Dr. Dare needed to reexamine the knee. Sure enough, Gladys had sustained a fracture of the knee and within an hour her lower leg was in a cast.

This turn of events perhaps cemented the relationship between the two young people. Paul, not being one to tarry, lived up to his mother's admonitions: "Fools rush in where angels fear to tread." I am proud to say that this time the young man with such a diverse, shall we say, background, did the smartest thing he had ever done. He followed his own admonition, which was, "Strike while the iron is hot." Only he struck while the diamond was brilliant.

It is beyond me to explain to you why or where he had that ring box and its contents hidden in those sweat-stained overalls, but out he popped it and raised the lid. There, before Gladys' sleepy eyes, was a solitary stone which any girl would have been proud to wear, much less refuse. All this happened so fast, just in her most trying moment. Before she could speak the young fireman, so sure of himself, announced, "I have selected the girl I intend to spend the rest of my life with, as I will soon be standing before the Justice of the Peace, Bill Smith, with a license of marriage in my hand, and the girl of my dreams on my arm."

Gladys, her mind in a spin, knew he liked several girls, so she spoke next, "And just who, may I ask, is the lucky woman?"

Never batting an eye, the intent fellow ended her wonderment. "You, darling, are the lucky woman."

If Gladys hadn't had a broken leg she probably would have run far and fast. Take the word of an old storyteller. That slip of a boy trying so hard to hold down a man's job was badly in need of a bath, a good night's sleep and holy cow, why didn't he shave off those silly sideburns? Who did he think he was, Clark Gable? Many of his friends were well mannered, had no stock pen or cattle and employed no black woodcutters stripped to the waist, with bulging muscles that glistened with their honest sweat beneath the Georgia sun, who loaded pine pulpwood on railroad flat cars from battered old bobtail trucks. Paul had not learned to ballroom dance at the country club, but at a dime-a-dance dance hall, with ladies from life's other side. Some of his friends had been football heroes who carried the ball over the goal line while our candidate for marriage had stood knee deep in trimmings as he trimmed bamboo fishing poles for which he got ten cents a piece or planted pine seedlings on land he had bought and cut over. He had never belonged to any organization, not even the Boy Scouts of America. Never an Eagle Scout was he, but he could build a fire under any situation with only one match, and there's no telling how many old ladies he had helped across a busy street crossing.

But who was he, pray tell, to think he could set sail on the stormy sea of matrimony? Anna herself had commented, "I feel sorry for the woman who marries him."

Teddie's only comment was, "He is a little wild and can't see the forest for the trees. I only hope he doesn't land in one of those striped suits with leg irons hammered on his poor legs, to eat bread and water, as some of his buddies will, without a doubt, hear those jailhouse doors slam shut." Come on Teddie, didn't you only yesterday down at Mr. Oldcomer's bank ask to see the balance on your son's savings account, only to raise those black eyebrows of yours when you saw those five figures?

Anna, oh Anna, why doesn't that boy of yours come home? You have called the train dispatcher you know so well, Red Spibey, who once played under that old crabapple tree beside the back door with Lenard. You lost him to heaven, now you have lost Paul to a pretty face you have never seen. Paul, Red informed Anna, was on a work train to Ideal, Georgia, he believed it was, not to return for a few days.

Even though her powers to see the future were great, that telephone could be a great help to her. The small voice that dwelled deep inside Anna now spoke, "Anna, you have raised the boy against all odds. He is grown now, your duties are fulfilled. The happy days that you spent with him teaching him to talk and walk, to face problems and disappointments, the ways of nature, even to drive nails, to read and write, and to excel at whatever he undertook are over now. Didn't you push him out in deep water and say, 'Sink or swim'? Remember the day you dressed him, combed his hair, just as you had done Lenard. Only this time you had taught him to be his own little man. Can't you remember how you gave him a shove on that little bicycle as he wobbled away to attend his first day of school across town? No one knows how, when he was out of sight, you ran back in the house and cried your eyes out. The vision of Lenard's broken body that you clutched so close to your breast reoccurred to you. You grew no roses to bury your tears. You had many tears but no one saw them, for you buried them in a sick little boy, your little boy. Now, you knew the day would come when he again would wobble off. Only this time in a new green Buick he bought with cash, the fruits of his own labor. Come on, Anna. He can't be tied to your apron strings forever. I have answered your prayers. This is a fine girl. She embodies every wonderful quality you and Teddie so admired in Lenard. You mortals can never be satisfied. She will bring you no grief and perhaps be Paul's balance wheel, as you yourself have been to Teddie."

Gladys herself had to do a bit of soul searching before she would wear that diamond ring he had thrust upon her. She lacked a session of summer school credits to complete her degree. Her mother was somewhat dependent on her. She had a new car to pay for and now the accident. Paul was definitely not Prince Charming. Was he a diamond in the rough or a lump of coal polished to shine a few days? She decided to let him prove himself if possible.

When Paul returned to Fitzgerald, exhausted from his tour of duty, he only took his shoes off, slipped out of his overalls, and lay upon the cot that he had put on the screen porch of the Central Avenue house so he could go and come without disturbing his parents. He never came or went that Anna didn't know. Teddie had long since ceased to keep up with the rounder. Paul slept the sleep of the dead for perhaps five hours.

Anna was still in her room reading a book when she heard the shower valve open and the water flow. Above the water's spray she heard her son's voice singing with more vigor than ability one of his favorite songs, "My Wild Irish Rose." She breathed a sigh of relief to know that he was all right and happy. Soon after she heard the water turn off he came bouncing into her room with only a towel about him. He was shaved, hair still dripping, and was dressed in the overalls he had stomped out, in an attempt to launder them. He bathed as she had taught him to save soap and water.

She was quite proud of him. She even gave him a bit of a compliment as she rarely did, "You look almost human. You are grown now, twenty-seven this coming June and I must say, you appear just a mite better than I ever thought you would. Are you about ready to tell me of your romantic adventures, or must my friends call me on the phone and tell me of your escapades as they have so faithfully done in the past? You always show me your new cows, even that Brahma bull that probably will trample you into the dust. You are worse than my papa, always poking around some old livestock of his, which never went to sleep hungry as his own children often did! I will fix supper for her one evening if you ever come to roost long enough."

Paul felt playful and stepped closer to his mother's bed, pulled the covers over her head and tumbled her about her bed. "You are always trying to be a fortune teller. Why don't you get yourself a striped tent and a crystal ball, a long skirt of many colors, and a turban with a brooch in front. You might even pick up a little change, enough to pay the light bill you are always grumbling about. If I can get that headstrong heifer Gladys to either say yes or no or even maybe, you will be the first to know. Don't tell Teddie or he will only try to take her away from me."

Anna scrambled to cover herself with her covers only to let a magazine that she had hidden beneath them slide to the floor. Paul grabbed the shiny publication and held it up to the light and laughed, "What am I going to do with you? Perhaps I will place you at a waterhole where no fish live or tell Teddie. This isn't the *Upper Room* magazine you pretended to be reading when I came in. It is my latest copy of *Playboy* that you found in my room."

With that, Anna threw it with all her strength at her son. Her aim was poor. The young man was fast as he scrambled to retie the towel that had fallen to the floor during the melee. Anna's face reddened and her chin trembled once more. All she replied was, "I am only glad to know I have not raised a homosexual. I had rather you rob the bank than be a fairy!"

The back screen slammed and the green Buick roared into action. Paul drove to the county schoolhouse, the one in which Gladys was teaching her first grade pupils. She was on crutches, her knee and lower leg in a plaster cast. She seemed to be able to live with any situation that was thrust upon her, even now with the question of the diamond ring which was not on her finger but hidden in her purse. Paul wondered if she had any idea of how many fishing poles he had trimmed to pay for that ring. Although Gladys was crippled, she agreed to go out to eat at an Italian restaurant a short drive from Fitzgerald, one very popular with young couples called Gargano's.

Paul met Gladys' mother that evening. She was not young, being a bit older than Anna, and was the mother of eight children, Gladys being the baby. While he sat on the porch, Paul sensed that all her life the woman had heard stories of railroad men and their reputation for having a wife on both ends of the run. Gladys had barely remembered her own father, as death had claimed him when she was only five years old. Her mother under these circumstances, no doubt, had been very protective of her. Gladys came out on the porch smiling her best smile, assuring her mother, who still had a bandage on her forehead from the wreck, that she would be fine and would return early.

The new car rode great. The dinner was scrumptious, even Paul's manners and conduct were impeccable for a change. Three generations ago, in faraway Swanpool, if it still existed, at the junction of the Murry and the Darling River, these same acts of courtship had been played out. Only this time the stage was set not on a river bank in New South Wales, Australia, but beside the tracks of the Atlanta Birmingham and Coast railroad, about as far south as a body can go in Georgia, USA. The great-grandson of a river steamboat captain was trying to impress a decent girl of great beauty, trying to convince her that his intentions were, to say the least, decent.

Again a woman demanded proof of a man's intentions. The Yankee Captain had cleaned up his act and rebuilt his steamer as a home for Bridgett O'Leary, who asked the captain on her father's porch, "Do you have a home to take me to?" Chase Cooper had wanted something better than a logger's tent in the North Woods. Anna had demanded Teddie buy those expensive lots in the settlement of Fitzgerald. Now Gladys implored of Paul the same question that his great-grandmother Bridgett had, simply a shelter over their heads to call their own. This seemed more important to the women of this family or family to be, than the size of the diamond a man would slip on their fingers!

Paul and Gladys that evening at Gargano's became better acquainted. Paul soon realized his intended did not wear her heart on her shoulder. He also understood that his frolics at the dance halls and honky-tonks were a thing of the past, and this courtship would be no whirlwind affair. Gladys had worked hard for the position she had secured for herself, and she wasn't about to blow it now on some pinhead train hand. She did agree to wear the ring of engagement for one year. Paul assured his love that during that time he would build a house in a good neighborhood and furnish it, debt free.

Chapter XXX

The Wedding & the Honeymoon

Gladys, at school's closing, attended summer classes at college, while Paul rallied his woodcutters about him. When he was not out on his run, he and his men were sawing down pine trees in his forest, he himself on one end of a gator-tail cross-cut saw. Teddie and Anna watched with interest the progress of the two young people. Teddie was quite proud of Anna's son. "He hasn't asked me for any help," Teddie stated. "He seems to be good as his word, just like my brother Grady."

Anna only said, "I hope his strength holds out." They were riding in their little Chevrolet car, and kept going a bit farther. Anna told Teddie, "It is only fair that we help them a bit. I know Paul very well, he has a talent at building, and this is a good time for him to develop his skills. You and I know the uncertainties of the railroad, and he may need a trade in the future."

"Yes, you are correct Anna," Teddie said. "These good times won't go on forever. I have a vacant lot in a new subdivision on the edge of town. Tomorrow I will come out here and offer it to him, free and clear, a deed to be his upon the completion of a house upon it."

"You don't trust anyone, not even our son, do you, Teddie?"

The very next day Teddie drove to the forest that Paul had bought. The black workers greeted him as he got out of the little car. He had each of them each a cold drink and a candy bar. He asked if Paul was around as he surveyed the huge stack of logs they were piling. They pointed across a creek, Otter Creek, and said, "He bees ober dar wid Henry Bell, ah sawin' wa wid dat ole gator-tail saw of hissen. Lawd God, dat son o' yours sho' do bin bit by da lovebug. He wanna cut down ebby pine tree him got."

"Where are you boys taking all those logs?" Teddie asked.

"Mr. Jim Taylor's truck com her fo dem," they answered.

Teddie never liked to stop a workman from his task. He blew his car horn, and soon Paul, followed by a small black man with a saw over his shoulder, was walking a foot log over the creek and on up the hill to meet Teddie. Paul was always glad to see his father, ever since he ran as a small boy up the sidewalk on Central to meet him when the day's work was over. The father, a small man now sixty-odd years old, with thin gray hair, dressed in his collar and tie, and shoes shined, faced his only son, soon to be twenty seven years old, dressed in overalls, no shirt, a bottle of kerosene in his hip pocket, and barefooted as most of his men were. He smelled of sweat, pine pitch, and the kerosene that kept his saw clean. White patches of salt encrusted his overalls where his sweat had evaporated. He had a stubble growth of blond beard on his chin, blue eyes set deep beneath high cheekbones.

Teddie wondered how this could be the same delicate child he had raised. He remembered the night when he rode that midnight local train to Atlanta to visit him and Anna at Piedmont Hospital out on Capital Avenue, twenty-two years ago. Anna's devotion to the boy, along with sunshine and fresh air, not to mention his prayers, had cured him,. The man before him could have stepped out of the Australian Outback. His blond hair, which was so abundant, "waved" much as that of Bridgett O'Leary had, but to be sure, his devotion to duty had come from the Newtons.

Teddie spread his handkerchief on a log, a Coca-Cola bottle in hand, and invited Anna's son to sit down as he had a business proposition to offer him.

Paul laughed as he sat down. He knew only too well that his father's generosity always had a hitch to protect himself. "I'm listening, what's the deal?" Paul said.

"It's about that vacant lot, the one on the corner of First Street and Central Avenue that I recently bought from Cowboy Smith with some of the college money that you refused. Why don't you build your honeymoon house on it? Your mother and I have discussed the matter, and we think well of the young school teacher who is wearing your ring, and we want to give the lot to you and her as a wedding present. I will make a deed to you, fee simple, when the house is completed and the wedding is spoken."

Paul smiled and shook his father's hand. "It's a deal. You are the best old man a fellow ever had, but still, I see I will have to prove up, as I might revert back to the Barrick side of our family, and you would then hold the deed to the lot and the house on it. I would never let you, my mother, or Gladys down. When I was fourteen, I believe, you put me to work with that old carpenter, Mr. Hall, during the summer. Your intentions were good. You hoped I would learn a lesson that hot summer and disdain the hard labor of a carpenter and finish school and become a professional man. Good try, but I loved the construction work. I loved to see a pile of lumber become a nice house that would be home to some family. So thanks, but no thanks to a professional life in some far away city, I am happy with these laborers here in the fresh air and sunlight. Bill Hall is too old to work, but you will see him at the building site helping me to lay out each day's work. My work on the road is slack at present. Mr. Jim Taylor will swap me logs for lumber at the sawmill, and I have the cash on hand to pay my workmen. I only hope to make you and Anna proud of me and Gladys!"

Things were not that easy for Paul or, for that matter, Gladys. Thieves loaded his logs at night. The neighbors around the building site circulated a petition to the city fathers to halt the building in progress. They doubted Paul's abilities as a builder, and besides, he had no license or experience. This was a nice neighborhood, not shack town. Paul stood his ground with the city officials, even to the point that he took his Winchester shotgun to the worksite. The city attorney, lawyer McArnold, sided with Paul as he was not contracting, only building on his own lot, or his father's, with his own material and day labor. The neighbors went home, and the house went up.

Gladys stayed at school that summer, her leg in a cast. She hobbled about and drove her car somehow. Paul helped her every way he could. He even read her required literature and made her book reports between stations on his run to Thomasville. He slept little and got a lot accomplished.

Anna wondered how her son could hold together through it all. Her telephone rang quite often to report Paul's activities, the controversy over the unorthodox methods of construction, no papers, only a building permit nailed to a tree. Anna's friends felt she should know that her son was on shaky ground. She only smiled and watched in great amusement.

Anna had been raised on the wrong side of the track, as the social structure of a southern town, even friendly Fitzgerald famous for its tolerant atmosphere, was divided by a mainline railroad track. She gloried in Paul's spunk. His great-grandfather Limon O'Leary had not let his neighbors push him off his claim a hundred years ago in Australia. His great-grandfather Yankee Fred, you remember, was blown to flinders before he would let another steamboat pass him, long ago on the Murry River. Shep Barrick, Paul's grandfather, was beat to a pulp in a boxing ring by a punk kid. All he had to do was to remain down for the count, but he kept getting up before the bell rang. Anna somehow believed all his forefathers' ghosts were standing behind this son of hers. She even doubted if Lenard, fine as he was, would have had the adventuresome spirit of defiance that Paul always displayed in the face of adversity. She had never seen his chin tremble as hers had.

He took Gladys on the train, one of the last passenger through trains that ran to Atlanta. She selected a cherry dining room table and chairs at the finest store in town. Paul had to stand up to the conductor as Gladys had no ticket and he didn't know her. Paul only told him he would not go if she stayed. He laughed and made her welcome to his train.

Anna selected a new white eyelet dress for the wedding in June. Teddie sent his best suit to the pressing club and shined his shoes in preparation for the ceremony.

Gladys planned her own wedding. She wanted a nice wedding, one she could be proud of. A dear friend of Anna's, Althea Landers, volunteered to have the rehearsal supper at her home. Her daughter, Paul's classmate, baked and decorated the wedding cake. The church at Waterloo was reserved for

June 9, 1956, soon after school closed for the summer vacation. Gladys selected her attendants, and Paul asked his friend, the one who he had double-dated with the night he met Gladys, to be his best man.

The Saturday afternoon in June was beautiful, as was the wedding. Teddie and Anna looked good. Paul wore a blue suit and a tie he had bought at a hole in the wall Hong Kong tailor shop, on Cain Street, Atlanta, Georgia. If my memory serves me correctly, Yankee Captain Fred, Paul's great-grandfather, was dressed by a Chinese cook-valet aboard the *Victoria* for his wedding to the beautiful Bridgett O'Leary, the groom's great-grandmother of long ago. Could perhaps her ghost be among the guests who crowded the little white church house at Waterloo? Then I saw not her spirit, but the curly, once-red hair which still fell in waves on the head of Bridgett's grand-daughter, Anna Newton. Even Paul's hair, close cropped, managed a curl on top of his bare head. The green Buick automobile, decorated as it was, bore the newlyweds to the house of Gladys' older sister near the church for the wedding reception. Paul had planned a nice honeymoon. The couple spent their first night at the "Half-Moon" motel, at Lake Park, Georgia, very close to the Florida State line.

Florida had always seemed to have a mystic attraction to this young generation of Barricks. Paul Newton piled the newlyweds' suitcase into the green 1955 Buick automobile, and they hit the asphalt road which would lead them to Miami, with only one overnight stop at Silver Springs. Paul was no stranger to the attractions that awaited the couple, as Anna had taken him many times to Miami on the train. Gladys had never been to South Florida, she being more interested in seeing her brother Clifford, the one she loved so much, as he and his family had moved to Miami to find work. She couldn't have cared less about the waterways and springs or the name of the railroad tracks and where they led to or the cargos they hauled north.

Paul had to stop and wave all kinds of hand signals to the train crews who blew the whistle and waved back. She wondered where she fit into this giant family, or perhaps brotherhood, of men, all dressed in overalls, bedecked with gold watch chains, red bandannas tucked into their shirt collars, tall cloth caps neatly creased and clamped upon their heads with goggles over their eyes to protect them from the smoke and cinders that belched forth with each exhaust of the black, greasy locomotive. They all looked alike to her, only big ones and small ones. As a girl, she had only been acquainted with her relatives and a few neighbors. She silently wondered what she had married, much as Anna had wondered what she had brought onto this earth.

Gladys looked great in her blue going away outfit. Paul was very proud of her when they stopped in Gainesville to acquaint her with his uncle Charlie Newton, the only relative he knew on the Newton side of his family. Gladys smiled her winning smile, which displayed the perfect white teeth that had so impressed Paul when he first met her. She seemed to take in all the many sights Paul pointed out to her. The Spanish Florida cattle, the stock of the same cattle that the old admiral Christopher Columbus had brought across the broad Atlantic Ocean from Andalusia, Spain, four hundred years ago on creaky sailing boats. These cattle had adapted to Florida's swamps and forests, and now were wading around in the vast marsh named Paine's Prairie. They seemed to thrive on the lily pads and reeds that choked the marsh. Old Shep Barrick would have been proud of his grandson when he pointed out the bony old mama cows with the spreading horns.

His bride had fallen asleep with the monotony of the countryside and Paul's never-ending descriptions of the flora and fauna of the semitropical landscape. They stopped for gas at a small town, Micanopy, which had several dilapidated storefronts that had been turned into antique stores, loaded with vintage furniture and select items from the past. Paul's bride came awake and made a tour of each store, admiring the many dust-covered treasures that somehow had survived many generations of settlers. He was chomping at the bit to push on to Silver Springs and the Seaboard railroad tracks at Ocala, where they might even see the Orange Blossom Special or, with luck, The Silver Meteor, as it brought another load of Yankee tourists to the land of flowers and sun. Perhaps they could even see the fountain of youth that Hernando De Soto had searched for in vain so long ago.

The next morning at Silver Springs Paul sat on the curb beside the road drinking chocolate milk, munching on a doughnut, and watching the sun peek through the palm thickets to herald his third day of matrimony. Gladys was sound asleep in their motel room. Paul wondered if all young women needed that much sleep, when there was such a wide wonderful world to explore. The bride finally emerged from the room looking like a doll in her shorts and top, with only one eye open. Paul watched her eat a full breakfast washed down with plenty of coffee. He had not been raised to eat breakfast as farm people did. Yes, some adjustments would have to be made if this couple was to live happily beneath one roof forever.

Paul purchased the tickets for two and they lined up for the ride on the glass-bottomed boat that would float over the world famous Silver Springs which brought forth millions of gallons of crystal clear water from the bowels of the limestone caverns that were the backbone of Florida. This boat loaded only newlyweds. I believe the line had a sign reading in bold letters, "Honeymoon Special." Among the dreamy-eyed couples, several cuddled up close, holding hands in their own dream worlds.

Paul had a good supply of bread to feed the fish that flocked around the boat as it drifted over the springs. Gladys enjoyed seeing the fish, but she would rather have been standing on the bank. It seemed boats were not her thing. They soon hit the road for Miami.

Now, mind you, Paul wanted his bride to have a jam-up honeymoon, away from prying eyes. Neither one had flown on a commercial airliner. Paul was excited about the flight over the ocean, to Nassau, principal city of the Bahamas Islands, their ultimate destination. Gladys' brother, Clifford, and his wife Ruth, along with their nine children, welcomed the honeymooners to their small home. It was a happy reunion for Gladys for she became acquainted with her nephews and nieces, whom she had never seen. Paul liked Clifford. They were much alike. He, too, was a workaholic and avid hunter and fisherman. In fact, a hound dog was tied at Clifford's steps and an airboat parked in the driveway. Fish were frying in the back yard. The children mobbed their Aunt Gladys, showing her their school papers. Paul, being an only child, was a bit taken aback by the clamor of family life, but they seemed to accept him, and it was a happy scene.

The next day Clifford took Paul and Gladys to the international airport. There they boarded the plane that would fly them to the Bahamas for their true honeymoon. Paul called the names of all the out islands as the plane winged its way to Nassau; the first was Bimini, then Andros and Spanish Wells. Paul knew them all, as he had collected foreign stamps during his long recuperation at Anna's knee, many years ago. The plane slowed, its wing flaps went down, the propellers were feathered, and the wheels lowered soon to touch the asphalt runway at Nassau airport. The sleek silver airliner of the Pan-American fleet taxied to the terminal, which was much smaller than the one in Miami, and landing steps were rolled out. Our honeymooners removed their seatbelts, gathered their things, moved to the exit door, and flowed with the crowd of vacationers and several obvious honeymooners holding hands. Gladys held only to the step rail for support as she was not one to display her affection in public.

Paul studied the people and landscape, only to wonder who was driving the Vintage Packard limousine parked nearby. As the passengers greeted friends and claimed their luggage, Paul and his bride of four days were approached by a black man in a snappy uniform of navy blue and a visored cap upon his head with the words "Royal Victoria Hotel" spelled out in small gold letters.

"Mr. and Mrs. Paul Newton?" he politely asked.

Paul was rather taken aback but rallied to the occasion. He felt right at home, seven hundred miles away from Fitzgerald, Georgia. Black people had always been close to him, good, sincere, respectable black people, only trying to make a living in a white man's world. Now the tables were turned. Nassau, without a doubt, was a black man's world, and he was the guest for a few days.

Gladys' eyes opened wide in wonderment as a tall serious man carried their luggage to that vintage Packard, opened the back door, and ushered her and the man she had pinned her future on into the spacious rear compartment of the limousine. Paul hadn't realized that the package tour of the Bahamas he had purchased from Cook Travel Agency in Atlanta had included this service.

The long black car raised white dust as it sped along the winding one-lane road, paved with crushed coral rock and leading to the town of Providence, capital of the Bahamas Islands. The clapboard shacks roofed with rusty corrugated tin, which lined the airport road to town, were home to many people who were dependent on the tourists who came to enjoy the balmy climate and crystal clear waters of the harbor which teemed with sailboats, yachts and cruise ships. The homes, although dilapidated, nestled among a riot of tropical flowers, which seemed to receive more care than the buildings with the shuttered windows swung open to admit the morning sun and the sea breeze.

Small children chased one another and waved to passing traffic. They wore little or nothing as the nearby Gulf Stream warmed the north winds. Jack Frost was unknown on these shores. Women, black as ebony and feet bare as yard dogs, dressed in colorful skirts beneath white blouses. They seemed in no hurry as they ambled down the road with handwoven straw baskets loaded with bundles of sticks to fire their cook stoves, the morning's laundry, or tropical fruits, mangoes, pineapple, bananas, guavas, lemons, and oranges. These native children seemed to be the most abundant product!

People probably spent more time outside their minim houses than they did inside them. The chauffeur seemed to delight in blowing the Packard's horn to clear the road. Paul asked the driver why they seemed so happy to share the road. His answer was, "My people are very rich in tradition, flowers, babies, fruit and music. They are very, very poor in money and the goods of this world. You see, bossman, they are working for the Yankee dollar and hope you Yankees are well supplied with them!"

Paul flushed a bit at being called a Yankee but remained silent. The rearview mirror must have sent a message to the driver as he quickly amended his last statement with, "You folks speak as if you were from South Carolina."

Paul quietly answered, "How would Georgia do?"

"Oh, just fine, bossman."

The able-bodied young men, and there were some fine specimens, were far from here as daybreak found most of them at hard labor. Large groups of them worked in gangs, building roads or high-rise hotels for tourists, mining salt on the tidal flats, or maybe fishing or diving for sponges. Large farms on the out islands, Abaco and Andros, employed many laborers. During the 1920s rum running to the Florida coast during the experiment with prohibition that the United States had tried, had lined the pockets of many British Bahamians. Great Britain administered the government. The governor and judges were black men of letters, probably educated in England. Yes, the influence was a mixture of African cultures and British pomp.

The clerk at the desk of the Royal Victoria Hotel spoke softly with a warm greeting, "Welcome to Nassau, Mr. and Mrs. Newton, we were expecting you." The young couple was pleased with their spacious room, which boasted a balcony that overlooked the waterfront, the crystal clear bay, and beyond the Paradise Beach. Paul felt more at home in the side streets and waterfront than he did in the hotel's grand ballroom with a crowd of tourists from the United States engrossed in pulling the handles of the slot machines that lined the walls. He had failed to read the small print of the package tour concerning the meals, which were "on your own." The couple dressed for dinner that evening, Paul in his marriage suit, white shirt and tie. Gladys wore her formal, floor-length gown with a large purple orchid from her bridal bouquet pinned at her waist. There would be dancing after diner in the elegant ballroom that adjoined the dining room. As the couple descended the curved mahogany staircase, Paul felt a flush of pride as his bride was perhaps the fairest of all the guests who had assembled in the lobby of the elegant old Victoria Hotel, which had seen many, many such entourages.

The headwaiter opened the French doors and drew the curtains of the dining room, his waiting staff at his elbow bowing to the diners with menu in hand. Gladys flashed her best smile. Paul ran his finger around his collar in an effort to relieve his neck of the collar and tie, which he reluctantly wore. They were really in high cotton. Gladys was about to learn a thing or two about her new husband, things that would resurface many times over the years to come.

She had already suspected this dark side of Paul. The tie he had to wear to gain entrance to the dining room seemed to be choking him and soon was in his jacket pocket. He didn't even notice the food items on the menu. His finger went down the column that quoted the prices in Yankee dollars. She realized that this elegant dinner would stick in his craw as he had already turned pale, as white as those coral roads that had taken them from the airport to the Royal Victoria Hotel. The cheapskate, her bridegroom, announced that he wasn't hungry; perhaps something in the drinking water had taken his appetite. The wine list was Greek to him. He strained up and told the waiter he wanted only a chocolate milkshake and a cheese sandwich. Gladys would have loved to sip a glass of vintage wine from a long-stemmed glass and dine on lobster bisque, or perhaps filet mignon. No, maybe pheasant under a glass cover. She did order conch salad, the house special, which cost five dollars.

The music that trickled from the ballroom seemed to bring the color back to Paul's face and the tie back to his collar. He did leave the black man who had waited on them a generous tip, as he placed his hard-earned dollars in the folder that contained his ticket or bill.

Dancing would follow. They both loved music, and Paul tried to live up to his nickname of Twinkle Toes. Gladys only commented, "You know, my love, you aren't Fred Astaire or Gene Kelly."

Her partner laughed, and the band played on and on.

It was well past midnight when the dancers left the ballroom. The elevator man was sound asleep in his straight chair before the elevator. Paul didn't awaken him as he liked the staircase. He grabbed Gladys's hand and drug the poor tired girl up the stairs to their spacious room with the twelve-foot ceiling. Its creaking ceiling fans gently stirred the sweet smelling tropical night air. Gladys had enjoyed the evening and was preparing for bed when Paul excused himself only to soon return to their splendid room with two flat tin cans of sardines and a box of soda crackers. He had purchased them from a Chinese man who had a hole in the wall hand-out stand down on the waterfront that never closed. Our bride and groom soon had their first marital friction, would that be the proper term, as they were in such a proper surrounding? Gladys put her foot down and Paul had to eat his sardines on the balcony.

Meanwhile, back at Fitzgerald, Anna tossed and turned in her bed as she knew that her son had a lot of the ways of her father, the old Australian stockman Shep Barrick. Genetic makeup is hard to overcome. She only hoped that her son had a balance of qualities as there were good traits on both sides of his family. Teddie still was strong and on the job at the station, tough as a lightered pine knot. He never spoke of being tired or feeling bad. What he lacked in size, he made up in pure old stamina. He tended to his and Paul's business endeavors with much aplomb. Move on, old stationmaster, you have many miles left in you. Now, Anna, stop your chin from trembling. Haven't you taught Paul to be self-reliant and to face the trials that life may confront him with? You, yourself, know that the Barrick lineage has overcome untold hardships and trials, both in Australia and America. Your new daughter-in-law has a calm steady way that you yourself have admired and accepted. You know that Paul will return to sit beside you and relate every detail of his adventures like he always has since he pedaled away on his little bicycle to start school in the first grade. Where is that stiff upper lip you always required your son to have? Don't let him see your chin tremble. All your childhood friends, who called you "Tremble Chin," are mostly gone on to the other side of that beautiful river of life you have sung about even in your sleep! How did it go, way in the dead of the long winter nights? "Shall we gather at the river, that beautiful, beautiful river, gather with the saints at the river that flows by the throne of God." Anna's clear high voice would awake Paul, and cause goosebumps to travel from the nape of his neck down his back and legs. Teddie would comfort the lad as he softly spoke, "Be quite, don't wake your mother. She is singing in her sleep, grieving for our children and her sister who are buried out in the cemetery. She never mentions this grief that dwells deep in her heart. Only now in the still of the midnight hours does her subconscious mind let these memories come to the surface and vent themselves always in that same song. Go back to sleep, son, and never mention it to her! Please!"

The sun that rose in Fitzgerald also rose in Providence, Nassau. Gladys awoke to find Paul long gone because he had slipped out of the huge bed at the Royal Victoria Hotel at the crack of dawn and gone heaven knows where. She knew he wasn't drunk because he never drank. He wasn't gambling for he only gambled on the price of cattle. He was probably down at some construction site among the black laborers or at the fish market to see the fish that the native fishermen had landed during the night at sea in their bobbing skiffs with the lanterns hung on the bow. She also knew the native dance halls and bars were not open this early or he would be in one, not to drink rum or beer, but to tell stories to the seamen or dance with the bar girls, black or white, maybe even in-betweens. She smiled at these thoughts of hers, as he had tried to show her his better side. He had spent a lot on her, built a nice house on a gift lot, and the diamond she was wearing hadn't been found in a box of cracker jacks. The alley cat fled from the balcony where it had been licking the empty sardine can that Paul had left lying there from his midnight dinner. Paul was the man of her dreams, even though he was following the footsteps of that old now departed grandfather of his, Shep Barrick. Only time will tell you, me lady.

Tours were arranged by the travel agency that morning. The group of tourists visited the local straw market. Paul stuck out like a sore thumb in the diverse group, which included aging widows on their last go round, old maid school teachers on vacation from their classrooms, middle-aged dropouts from the school of romance hoping for a fling, and last but not least, several honeymooners, who gazed with starry eyes at each other. Gladys selected a straw handbag with the word "Nassau" woven into the sides. She also selected a wide-brimmed hat that a native woman placed upon her head. Paul was proud of his bride; she cut quite a picture in the straw hat that framed her beautiful dark hair. Her smile would have melted a heart of stone frozen in a block of ice.

Paul, on the other hand, seemed out of place. Where were his shorts with a colorful shirt printed with flowers, his camera on a strap over his shoulder, his Jesus sandals on his feet? Why in tarnation was he wearing those scuffed old boots? Anna had packed him a suitcase of nice things to wear on the trip, pajamas, socks, even a T-shirt with "Fitzgerald" printed on it. That suitcase was up in that fancy room back at the hotel, barely touched. Oh well, how would a stockman dressed as a dandy Yankee tourist or a moonstruck bridegroom appear? You might dig up Shep Barrick and ask him.

The tour guide led the group of sightseers to the end of the municipal pier to witness the local Bahamian boys dive for coins, which the pilgrims threw into the deep, crystal clear waters of the bay. Paul was fascinated with the myriads of colorful reef fish that abounded around the pilgrims of the pier. The native boys dived for the coins that fluttered slowly into the deep water, which was clear as gin. When a young diver asked Paul to throw a quarter into the water, Paul refused. The little young man, water dripping from his ebony body, said "Come on, bossman, throw a dime and I will dive for it."

Paul, with all eyes turned to him, drawled, "I have a better idea." He shed his unbuttoned chambray shirt, kicked off his boots, rolled his kaki pants legs to his knees and said, "You throw a dime in the bay, and I will dive for it." The tourists laughed and the native diver refused to throw his dime into the bay.

Next on the tour was lunch at Papa Johnnie's Café and bar. The café was decorated in good taste. Fishnets were nailed to the walls, and a mounted sailfish glowed down from over the bar, his great dorsal fin permanently erect. Large brass cookpots, which sat over a charcoal grill, contained a seafood gumbo consisting of native vegetables, squid, octopus, red snapper or whatever the nets had brought up from the briny deep the night before. The pineapple pie looked very good.

Paul again turned pale. Have, pray tell, you ever seen a red-faced man go white as a ghost? He might have looked better if his chin had trembled a bit. It seemed he had glanced at the price list beside the exotic dishes the menu offered. Man alive, a bite of lunch would have cost twenty-five dollars, which sounded like no fun! Paul again faked stomachache and excused himself.

Gladys knew him quite well by now and felt he would suddenly recover his health if the price was reasonable. Gladys followed her man down the sidewalk down to the waterfront. Soon they came to a dock where sailboats, traders they were, from many of the West Indies, were moored. The tropical sun bore down upon the dark-skinned men and women as they bartered and traded for the cargos which lay in the holds of these schooner boats. They were loaded with charcoal, dried fish, coconuts, goats, chickens, peanuts, straw and bamboo baskets, rice, beans, and twist tobacco. This native market was exactly what Paul wanted to see. He was one of the few white men there, and it reminded him of East River Street on a Saturday night back in Fitzgerald, the town noted for its friendship and cooperation between the Yankees and Rebels.

A sailor on a boat from Haiti loaded with peanuts took quite a shine to Paul and his bride. After a friendly conversation, the well-muscled sailor stated that the reason he was so strong was the fact that he ate many peanuts. Was it the spirit of Shep Barrick or even perhaps Yankee Fred Barrick's spirit that entered Paul's body, there on the dock amid the bobbing boats? Call it what you may, but Gladys almost dropped her straw bag when Paul stepped to the bow of the vessel and challenged the Haitian to armwrestle him, the prize to be a basket of peanuts. Paul had stripped his shirt off, and he didn't look too bad, suntanned to dark brown, his full head of curly blond hair a bit like his great grandmother's. A crowd had gathered on the dock. Paul had shoveled many scoops of coal into steam locomotives, and pulled his end of a cross-cut saw. Anna had kept him in the fresh air and sunshine as a weak sick child, never losing faith that her boy would survive.

The young men, one black, one white, shook hands and sat at a table in straight chairs facing each other, tense as a banjo string. At a signal they joined right hands and began to exert pressure. Their arms rocked back and forth. Smiles were on the men's faces. Paul felt the pressure of his opponent bearing down on him. Paul set his feet squarely on the deck and managed to keep his arm from being pressed to the table, but his face turned red and sweat beaded on his forehead. The sailor was trying to drain Paul's strength, little by little, in order to plunge his arm backward to pin it to the table and win the dollar bill that Paul had wagered. The sun bore down on the men. Cheers went up when it looked as though Paul was tiring. Suddenly, the black man's feet, bare as they were, slipped on the deck and his butt left the chair bottom, which disqualified him and the nod went to the old stockman's grandson. The crowd roared their approval. The bucket of peanuts was handed to Paul, who pocketed a handful and tossed the rest of the nuts back into the ship's hold.

A drink vendor was called and the dollar bill was spent for cold lemonade. Gladys was relieved that Paul was OK and had held his ground, but why did he always want to compete? This wasn't the only question she had about him as he walked away.

Along the way was a shed roofed with palm thatch, inside which was a rickety table that would seat a dozen people. No tablecloth, only a tin Coca-Cola sign for a top. "Mary's kitchen" the hand-lettered sign announced. Paul relaxed. Gladys only smiled again, as the stew did smell good. Mary had heard of the contest at the peanut boat and rose to welcome the couple. Mary was a huge black woman, perhaps forty years old. Her ample figure was clothed in a colorful Mother Hubbard dress that could have doubled as a circus tent.

Paul spoke first. "Do you good folks serve white folks in this café?"

Mary beamed her best smile, "If your money is green, sit down. That little woman you are leadin' around needs some of Mary's stew to put some meat on her po' bones." Mary seemed to be proud to be a black woman, with no desire to live in a white man's world and its many social problems, as her world was simple and carefree. Mary shouted at some young boys, who called themselves musicians, to stop beating on those empty dishpans and oil cans and "Sot' a table outside fo dis couple o 'white trash' to be my guests."

Two glasses of cool clear water with a slice of lemon hung on the rims were set on the table. Soon Mary returned to set two bowls hand-carved from teak wood filled to the brim with steaming seafood gumbo dipped from the cooking pot that sat on a spider over the glowing hardwood charcoal. Paul had eaten his gumbo before Gladys got started good and sopped his bowl clean with a piece of hoecake. Dessert was another piece of bread, spread with guava jelly. Paul settled his bill with Mary. The gumbo was twenty-five cents a bowl, the drink and bread ten cents, a dollar bill was left on the table as a tip. This meal was well within Paul's price range.

The old Victoria Hotel was quite a step back into British colonial rule. Impeccable taste had been used in its décor. No air conditioning was needed as the high ceilings and shuttered windows admitted the gentle sea breeze that had coursed all the way from Africa. The Prince of Wales or even the Queen Mother would have felt right at home within its aging walls.

Gladys told Paul that she enjoyed the trip and that he was a great tour leader, much better than the guy from the agency. Paul only laughed and said he was working for peanuts, and he gave most of them back.

The next morning their luggage and souvenirs were loaded in the ancient Packard limo along with several other people who had been on a holiday on Nassau. The airplane gained speed on the runway and gently lifted into the air, engines roaring goodbye to the Bahamas. Altitude was gained as the silver bird slowly circled the bay at Providence town. The ocean reflected the sun, causing the sea water to turn many shades of blue according to the water's depth. Soon, puffy white clouds were passing by the small round windows of the plane. A westward course was set, and far below Paul told Gladys he saw Bimini and its coral reefs fade behind them. Miami and the east coast of Florida would soon appear as a haze far in the west.

Chapter XXXI

Back to Fitzgerald

As the green Buick neared Fitzgerald, Paul remembered the words of one of Anna's poems she had recited to him as a boy under the crabapple tree, so long ago. The words welled in his memory: "It's a rare world, a fair world, its many paths to tread." This was the first path that he and Gladys had trod together. He was pleased that Gladys had not held a tight reign on him for she knew that he was unlikely to change very much. She would only be, as Anna had been, Paul's balance wheel, to say to him, "Haven't you had about enough of that?"

Life in Fitzgerald stayed about the same. The trains still rumbled across the street crossings. Teddie and Anna had aged a bit, she the most, and her frail body was failing her. Anxiety, sorrow and disappointment had taken their toll. Seventy winters had begun to frost her hair gray; aches and pains wracked her small body. Her hands had begun to tremble as her chin once had. The bed, books, and memories became her world. Teddie still sat behind his desk at the railroad station, ten years beyond retirement age. He managed his own business and did the household chores after office hours.

Anna's mother Chase, as she liked to be called, was over ninety years old. She lived with a granddaughter she had raised. That fall would be Chase's last visit to Fitzgerald. A reunion had been planned by several of Anna's nieces and their families. Chase's eyes had grown dim, but her mind was bright as a penny. Memories of the settlement days of Fitzgerald seemed like only yesterday. Only a handful of the original settlers had lived to see the dream of a city built by people who had once been enemies, living and building in harmony. This would be the last time Anna would gather with her mother, younger brother and nieces and nephews. The bells for Chase Barrick tolled soon after this reunion.

Chase's body was returned to Fitzgerald for burial in the family cemetery lot, near her mother and father and one daughter, Olive Fairfield, and near but not beside the old Australian stockman, Shep Barrick, all now sleeping beneath the sod of Evergreen Cemetery. Teddie had long since buried his brothers and sisters. His mother and father were buried in Andersonville in a county churchyard. He perhaps had some nephews and nieces whom he knew only by name. The Newtons, dedicated to work and duty as they were, never took time off for reunions.

On occasion, when Paul and Gladys stopped by the Central Avenue home place, Anna called them to the porch on the side of the house where she spent many evenings in a large rocking chair. By her side she had the old antique gold box, the one she had found on her front steps forty-five years ago. Anna had always felt that her father had left it on her steps, as he often left little things for her and Teddie. Shep would only shake his head and nod negatively when she questioned him about its origin. She even questioned her mother, only to get a puzzled look.

The box had a small key inside and the lid had a heart shaped mirror on the inside, so you saw yourself when you raised the lid. The only thing it contained was a cuff from a dress sleeve with four pearl buttons still attached to the yellowed satin material. The letters Ltd. told that the box was of British origin. The date was engraved on the bottom, the date around which Bridgett O'Leary married Frederick Barrick. Had it come from Australia? Was it a keepsake of Anna's grandmother, from so long ago?

Anna told Paul and Gladys that some time ago she had a dream about this mysterious box that had rested on her mantel board for so long. In this dream her grandmother's spirit had visited her subconscious mind and had told her that the buttons were cut from her wedding gown and placed in the gold box because they were an omen from the spirit world. The omen was that she, Anna, who was not yet born, would some day in far away America, bear four children of which the first three would join her in the spirit world. Only the forth and last child would survive to manhood, and some day he would stand beside her grave at Swanpool, New South Wales, Australia, and that her spirit would lead him there, if he took the gold box with him, as that box was where her spirit dwelt. Anna had never seen her grandmother but she, born with the veil, felt that she knew her and could communicate with her spirit. Paul felt goose bumps at the nape of his neck as his mother handed the gold box to him. Anna then told Paul and Gladys that her life was about spent, and that she was glad to get these things off her mind.

Gladys spoke in her calm soft voice. She said that she would see to it, that the box would rest on their mantel until the spirit spoke to Paul, and that the buttons would be undisturbed. Teddie, on the other hand, believed in only one spirit, the Holy Ghost, and in his savior, Jesus Christ. He didn't believe in luck, saying that a person made their own luck in this life.

Just as his father had warned him, the railroad let Paul down. Many men were laid off the jobs that wars had created. Trains were consolidated. Steam locomotives were cut up for scrap iron. Passenger trains were a thing of the past. Paul found himself laid off, unemployed. Gladys went back to teaching school that fall. She loved her new house and decorated it with her handicrafts. Paul worked on his land, planted pine trees, and traded cattle. He bought several lots below the one Teddie had given to them. Upon one of these lots he started building another house, alone, but for one helper, one of his father's most faithful black men.

Paul had really opened a bucket of snakes. The neighbors doubted his ability to build a house nice enough to complement the neighborhood. Lumber and bricks were piled about the lot, batter boards were set, foundations dug. Not once was a professional tradesman seen about the job. Teddie drove up in his little car with a worried look on his face, got out, and approached Anna's son. When he spoke there was a note of objection in his voice, "What do you intend to do, build a house all by yourself? You and Henry Bell don't know beans about building a nice house. You are only going to ruin a lot of good building material, and have to hire someone to straighten a big mess out."

Paul never stopped digging, letting the dirt fly. "Whatever I ruin is mine, I have a permit and everyone who possesses one will give me advice."

Teddie put his hands on his hips after pushing his hat back on his head and said, "You are like the Barrick men. No one can tell you anything. You are just a smart ass." After saying his bit, Teddie got back in the little Chevy, slammed the door shut and drove away in a huff.

Paul and Henry worked long and hard. The house turned out well. One evening, six months later, Teddie and Anna drove up in the same little car. They parked out front, got out, walked in, and Teddie spoke first, "You sure fooled me. You are like my brother Grady. He could build anything."

Anna quietly said, "I knew all the time he could. A little bird told me he could, and in my dreams I saw this very house."

Her son kept on till he had built several more around the neighborhood. By the way, he never returned to the railroad, as it was no longer the operation he had known and loved so much. Although the trains and the men of his boyhood were gone forever, they still lived in his memory.

Teddie's railroad station was being demolished. Passenger trains no longer stopped at Fitzgerald. Only mile long freight trains rolled quietly on roller bearing wheels; blaring electric horns heralded their approach. Twenty years had seen much change, not only on the railroad but around Fitzgerald. The St. Paul Hotel, the pride of the settlement, and even its giant magnolia trees, were gone. A modern supermarket occupied the lots at the corner of Lee St. and Central Avenue. Horses and mules no longer clopped their way down the brick streets. Automobiles now sped over the streets. Sparrows no longer tore horse dropping apart to retrieve the grains of yellow corn.

But change isn't always a bad thing. Teddie and Paul had prospered. Their rental houses were in demand. The paper industry had moved to the Georgia coast, creating a market for the second growth pine forest. The pine plantations that Paul had planted became valuable. Gladys matured into one of the most respected educators in Fitzgerald. Anna was the one who struggled to exist for her health was failing. Teddie seemed to shed the passing years as a duck sheds water from its back. After his station was gone he was dealt a telling blow.

One day Paul found his father sitting on the back steps of the home place on Central Avenue, his chin resting in his gnarled hands. The two men, father and son, took a walk up the sidewalk towards the business district of Fitzgerald and its bustling traffic, as they had done for so many years. "I have come home, son, to take care of your mother, as she needs me as she had never needed me before. She is worn out in body and soul. I have not gained great riches or fame, but I have enough of this world's goods to see you, and I, and Gladys through to the great beyond. I do have a good name, and no unpaid debts. I am proud of you and the fine woman you have married. Never have you asked me for a dime. You have surprised me with your abilities, although they weren't the ones I had planned for you. I spent sixty years on a railroad job, and I have had a belly full of railroading. As a baby I arrived to a mother lying in a railroad section house. I arrived cold, wet, naked and hungry, and I may just leave this old world in the same condition."

"Not if I can draw a breath, old timer," Paul said as he put his strong arm around his dad's stooped shoulders.

Teddie did his best to make Anna's last days comfortable, but the day came when he, Paul, or Gladys could no longer take care of her. She was moved from the bedroom she loved so much to a nursing home on the edge of Fitzgerald. The Lord was kind to her; she never realized where she was. Age had claimed Teddie's ability to drive a car as he was eighty years old, so he pedaled his old bicycle. The business duties fell to Paul and Gladys, who had lost her mother to old age some years before.

Paul found the fact that Anna was difficult to communicate with hard to accept. The only gift that remained with her was her power to see the unseen. She stared at the ceiling and slowly told her son exactly what he had been doing that day and what lay before him tomorrow.

One spring day, Gladys came to where Paul was laying bricks. "Get yourself to the nursing home if you want to see your mother alive," she said. "I had a telephone call just now and I have your dad in the car. Come on as you are. She is low."

When Paul arrived in the darkened room, he joined Gladys and Teddie beside Anna's deathbed, where she lay still struggling for each shallow breath she drew. The doctor came into the room and spoke softly, "She is going. I have done all I could."

Paul took Anna's hand in his, the hand that had nursed him to health and guided him to manhood; the hand that had waved to him as he passed through Fitzgerald on his beloved steam engines; the hand that had mended his worn clothes. Her hands now had ceased to tremble. She opened her eyes, which were once covered by a veil seventy-six years ago. Anna fixed her eyes on Paul. She didn't call his name, but a look of great satisfaction flooded her tired face. A faint smile spread through the wrinkles as she spoke, "You are mine, not your father's." She struggled for one last breath, then was gone to join her three babies so long gone to the other shore.

Paul felt as though a part of him had left with her. Somehow he thought he should have gone with her, just as they had gone together on so many trips. Then there was the feeling that part of Anna's soul had entered his body to dwell within him. Her blue eyes remained open. He laid her lifeless hand beside her, and noted the small diamond ring on her finger, the one she had won in an essay contest on the radio. Teddie assured Paul that he was his boy also, that Anna didn't known what she had said. Paul knew what she meant and was pleased that she had claimed him, as he was so much like her and the Barricks.

Gladys led both silent men out of the room. A nurse called Paul aside and handed him a glass half full of a clear liquid and told him to drink it. Within a minute he was steady as a rock, and could have looked down the throat of a cannon and given the command of fire.

Gladys helped Teddie select a coffin and burial gown that night. Paul was sullen and silent. He barely knew who was present or what they said. His brain seemed numb. It would take time, as no tears came to his cheeks. Could it be that a part of him had died with Anna? At the funeral he felt that a bit of anger enter him. Why were all of these people crowding about her as she lay so still and silent in the coffin surrounded with flowers that she never really liked? She was his. He only wished all those mourners would go away. He could have dug her grave, and yes, he would have loved to place her in it, to grab a shovel and cover her remains with the red clay that was beneath the fake green grass carpet that covered the cemetery's sod, beneath which she would rest until Gabriel blew his trumpet. As the crowd dissembled, Paul stood there wishing he had his shovel in his hand. Teddie and Gladys led him away by the arm. He never said a word.

Daybreak found Paul sitting on the concrete coping that enclosed the Newtons' cemetery lot. Tremble Chin was gone. Many times she had said, "Stop the world and let me off." Paul felt much better with the new day. He felt she was at rest at last with the babies who had been snatched from her, not to mention the satisfaction she had in knowing that she raised her boy child.

Teddie, Paul, and Gladys started a new era of togetherness that lasted for ten happy years. Paul hunted, fished and gardened, supplying the table with game and fish, not to mention enough vegetables to feed an army. Teddie's railroad pension paid the bills at the home place on Central, and he still had some left over. Gladys was at the height of her career, surrounded by children.

Teddie still liked to fry fish and cook birds for Paul and himself. On Sundays he still went to church. Then he insisted that the three of them, his family as he liked to call them, go out to a café for Sunday dinner on him. The family went on trips, and good times were had by all.

After lunch each day, Teddie dressed in work clothes and took long rides on his trusty bicycle. He seemed tireless. People on the street told Paul that they had seen his father on his wheel ten miles from Fitzgerald. Paul followed Teddie one afternoon and was not surprised to see him turn through the wrought iron gates of Evergreen Cemetery to visit the grave of Anna and their babies. He never mentioned the railroad, only that he was glad to be free for once in his life.

These happy days came to a screeching halt one sunny day in May. Teddie fell on the sidewalk and struck his head on the granite curbstone. He survived the fall, but he had suffered a fractured skull. This injury robbed him of his faculties. Never again would he be the same Teddie. Paul devoted his time to caring for his father, who now was only a shell of himself. Time drug on. Paul was spread thin tending to the daily business and caring for his father. The home place on Central Avenue became an assisted living facility, with one patient and one nurse, Paul. Teddie's energy still burned brightly, only his body and mind were devastated. Gladys helped as she could. Paul spent nights with Teddie at the home place while Gladys kept the home fires burning at the new home, which she and Paul had recently built on the edge of Fitzgerald.

Early one morning, before the sun had risen, Gladys leaped from her bed to answer the phone which was ringing off the hook. As she pressed the receiver to her ear, she heard Paul's voice, soft and low, "Teddie crossed the river last night. Only his tired old body is here. He is gone."

Gladys and Teddie had shared a special relationship, he the father she never knew, she the daughter he had lost. Teddie Newton was laid to rest at the feet of Anna, who had been laid to rest ten years earlier. Paul felt relief knowing that his father would join his beloved Anna and the babies, whose short lives they had shared. Paul knew his father had spent his nearly ninety years striving to do the best he could, under circumstances in which lesser men would have thrown up their hands and laid their burdens down.

The only thing Paul didn't do to honor his father's wishes was to place a simple headstone at his mother's grave, and one to match at the fresh grave of his father, with just their names, date of birth, and date of death chiseled in cold hard stone. Yes, their lives had been full of long journeys that had begun in the piney woods of South Georgia, and excursion trains to Andersonville on Decoration Day, where Anna saw for the first time the young man at the lemonade stand, who later on gave the best dollar he had ever spent to the crossing watchman to introduce him the a sixteen year old Yankee girl, or was she Australian, to a cracker lad who had no job and was living from hand to mouth? They had had many discouragements and many happy times, but Paul and Gladys had a sense of satisfaction as Anna, Teddie and their children were finally at rest, a well-earned rest.

Perhaps my story should end at this point, but you would not know the rest of it if I ended it here. The curtain is not completely drawn. True, the old guards of Fitzgerald were gone forever, as the next few years took the rest of the faces that once dominated the streets and sidewalks of the settlement and Musgrove County. The grim reaper had taken his toll, although the city itself has escaped his scythe. The town had prospered with its industry, good leadership, and location. The climate had born fruit, perhaps even greater success than the original settlers had envisioned, the ones who came from the north by wagon, horseback, and river steamer. And never forget the Georgia and Florida railroad which found its way on tracks laid by sweating, hard-working, hard-drinking, happy-go-lucky Irish rail gangs.

Much credit for the success of Fitzgerald, the farms and forests that surrounded it, and the industries which processed the raw materials that were the life blood of this thriving community, must be given to the citizens of the black community, only a generation or two away from slavery. True, tolerance was shown by both, the Yanks and the Rebs, by both factions, which did in fact put their shoulders to the wheel of progress and success. Hot heads were cooled; stubborn hands laid their swords down and beat them into plowshares, with few exceptions. They had found that the acid of hate could only be neutralized by tolerance and understanding. This acid was greatly diluted by intermarriage and time, much time, which was filled by hard labor and dreams of children yet unborn.

The year two thousand was ushered in to find Paul Newton and only a handful of the visionary settlers' descendants still living in Benedict. How could Paul be seventy years old? Anna's thrift and Teddie's hard work had made his life better than theirs had been. Although he rose early, he still strived to find what he would like to be when he grew up. His goal in life had eluded him and his time was running out. He had only two things that bothered him. Each time he passed before the mantel where the gold box sat, the mystery box it was, he had a feeling that before he crossed the river of life he had to take it to Australia, on the other side of the world.

The other unsettled question in his heart was why had Anna glared and yes, allowed her chin to tremble when her father Shep Barrick came to visit her at the Central Avenue home she and Teddie had built. Paul himself had questioned old timers about what misdeed Shep had been guilty of. Anna, as her mother Chase, would never speak a disparaging word against a family member. The worst Paul ever heard was that old Shep was a poor manager of the fruits of his labors, kinder to his horse stock than he was to his children, and had a knack for associating with people far below his level. He had no religious affiliation and never darkened a church door. Why had the county paid his funeral expenses? And why no member of the family stepped forth to place a headstone at his unmarked grave? Come on, Paul, some questions have no answer, and the more you stir a bad stew the more it stinks. Let bygones be bygones.

Chapter XXXII

Let the Curtain Fall

Gladys could see that Paul would never be satisfied until he trod the banks of the Murry and Darling rivers, which were the arteries of commerce in the early colony days of New South Wales, Australia, to search for his roots. Why didn't he just go to Tennessee and search for the Newtons' or Appleton's relatives? Was it that their lives were plain and simple? No mysteries or spirits, just a struggle to put bread and meat on the table.

One day, Paul came in to find his bags packed and sitting on the back steps beside the gnarled old crabapple tree, under which he and Anna had spent so many days in his youth. Yes, the same tree that the pesky old mockingbird had sat upon, only to come squawking down to its death at the hands of a rebellious young sharpshooter. Gladys now stood in that same back door, as Anna had, and again Paul heard the voice of a woman he loved telling him what to do. Would he listen this time? Had seventy years softened his heart?

This woman told him to catch the next jet airplane to Australia, however long it took, and wander to his heart's content, to go on a walkabout as his ancestors had called it. "I am well able to mind the business and keep what is left of the home fires burning," Gladys told him. "My only request is that you take that haunted gold box with you, as you think it can lead you to your great-grandmother's graveside on one of those rivers in that Godforsaken Outback, which seems to call to you so clearly."

The next day Paul was on the phone connected with a travel agency in Atlanta to book passage on a flight to Sydney, Australia, and a ticket for one on the Indian & Pacific Railroad to the town of Menindee, near the Darling River. Paul studied his maps of Australia on the Qantas Jet with the image of the kangaroo on the side and streaked through the blue skies over the South Pacific Ocean leaving a long white vapor trail from east to west. During the twelve-hour flight Paul wondered how his Barrick forefathers had mustered the patience and fortitude to travel these vast oceans in frail ships powered only by the whims of the wind. Paul's mind could hardly grasp the reality that he was experiencing. Why hadn't he gone on this walkabout fifty years ago? He realized his age was limiting his strength, although the experiences through the years had mellowed his outlook on life, not to mention his

patience. To amuse himself, he studied his fellow travelers. Some wore
business suits, crisp white shirts and ties, briefcases open and pouring over
important papers.

Then there were the stout young men wearing shorts and shirts with
many pockets open at the collar, obviously Aussies. They used words that
were strange to Paul's ears, like "mate," "bloke," and the "bloody weather."
They were a friendly lot, and came to life each time the shapely hostess
passed down the narrow aisle. Where had they been? Wherever it was they
seemed to have enjoyed themselves.

Paul wondered when it would be night again, as the sun was rising again
in the east. Far below, when the clouds opened enough, he could see islands
and atolls, studding the seemingly endless expanse of the blue Pacific Ocean.
He asked the stewardess if the long low coastline below was Australia. No, it
was Borneo. Another three hours were left before they could possibly see the
coast to Queensland, on the north coast of the island continent of Australia.
The billowing dark clouds obscured the tropical coast of Queensland as the
rainy season was about.

One of the Aussies informed him that Sydney would still be quite a hop.
Paul studied his map again. He realized that he had to expand his mind to
accommodate the great distances that these happy-go-lucky blokes referred to
as hops.

Sydney Harbor is, without a doubt, one of the world's most beautiful
natural wonders, a sight that held Paul in awe, never to be forgotten by the
aging traveler, whether he lived another day or reached a hundred. Sailboats
dotted the smooth blue water of the harbor. The plane passed over the modern
concrete balusters of the world famous Opera House that dominated the
skyline. Paul also saw the long famous wrought iron bridge with its two
oblong spans, which from a distance gave the appearance of a woman's
brassiere, hence the nickname, "Brassiere Bridge."

The jumbo jet lost altitude and speed as it passed over the endless
suburbs of the modern metropolis. The tandem wheels of the great silver bird,
which was about to come to roost at the end of the long runway, gave a jolt as
they touched terra firma to end the long journey from California, non stop.
The powerful jet engines roared and vibrated as they were reversed to slow
the still speeding airship as it neared the terminal flying the flag of the
commonwealth nation of Australia. The passengers unsnapped their seat belts
when the steps were rolled to the exit door which the crew was opening. Paul
felt as though he was setting foot on ancestral ground, and just a bit singular
as it was. As far as he knew, he was the only Barrick descendant to return to
this mysterious land which had nurtured his ancestors well over a century ago.
It was the site of their romances, their dreams, the work and hardships,
fortunes won, fortunes lost, laughter and tears.

The tourists from around the world who passed through the gate of that modern air terminal were here on a pleasure trip to see the sights, strange animals, birds, and reptiles of the interior view. They were here to enjoy the stark scenery and the lush forest of the coastal Blue Mountains, to taste the ethnic foods of the upscale cafes or enjoy the world class beaches and watch the huge waves that thundered on the white sand, affording some of the world's best surfing. Some were snorkeling and skin diving to view the wonders of the Great Barrier Reef, which stretched for a thousand miles north along the Gold Coast. Others were ready to ride the trans Australia railroad, the Indian & Pacific by name, to the city of Perth, possibly the most isolated modern metropolis city in the world, thousand of miles west of Sydney, through some of the most desolate and sun-baked land on this earth.

Alice Springs is a town in the heart of the Outback. Tourists travel many miles to admire this natural wonder and to stand in awe at the foot of the Ayers Rock, standing as a sentinel on a plane, which seems to stretch endlessly to a horizon that dances in the heat waves that the sun reflects.

Only Paul was on a mission to an area on the western slopes of these Blue Mountains which nurtured the Darling River with its clear cold water, which was the life blood of the fertile pastures and vineyards of New South Wales. Not only did this beautiful river revive a thirsty land, but it had provided a route of transportation for the settlers, who now reaped the harvest that fed hungry mouths of stalwart men and their families and flocks.

Paul was glad that it was a train on which he would be riding the day of his arrival at the town of Menindee, a name that he had gleaned from some old records which one of his cousins had recovered years ago. He glanced up at the luggage carrier that cradled the duffle bag containing the few items of clothing, toilet kit, and, last but not least, the gold box, which had spent over a hundred years patiently waiting to return whatever unseen contents it had held for so long. Would it, as Paul was so confident, lead him to the graves of his own flesh and blood which had lived and loved in this verdant river valley?

This scenery unfolded before his very eyes with each turn of the steel wheels of the railroad coach as they sang a shrill song upon the rails, which had been laid by Irish and Chinese track gangs so many years ago. Could it possibly be a hundred and thirty-five or a hundred and forty years ago that the Captain Barrick had by chance, met Bridgett O'Leary on the cobblestone streets of Swanpool, only an hour's drive along the river?

Menindee was larger than Paul had expected it to be, more like a city than a town. Fellow travelers on the train had spoken of the heat that the area was famous for, but heat was a way of life for Paul, as South Georgia shared the same reputation. He claimed his meager luggage, or should I say, duffle bag. A pair of boots and baggy kaki pants, topped with a short-sleeved cotton print shirt and no hat — this would be his attire as soon as he could locate a room to rest his weary bones.

As luck would have it, Menindee was a division headquarters for the railroad and was a terminal for the train crew. These young men would overnight here, only to return on the eastbound train the next day, much as Paul had done forty years ago when he worked on the Atlanta Birmingham and Coast back home. Rail workers are brothers under the skin. Vast oceans or trackless deserts fail to dilute their personality. Their conversation will always turn to their last trip or the one they stood for the following day; the more grueling or challenging, the more they enjoyed it. The pleasant trips were never mentioned, those tough ones were never forgotten and were retold forever it seemed. Well, be that as it may. Paul had wasted no time acquainting himself with the engineman and the conductor as they stood on the station platform beside their train back in Sydney. Those men, the Aussies, were very friendly and outgoing. They inquired early, "Where in the bloody USA are you from? Most of the Yanks don't speak as you do."

"That might be because I ain't no 'Yank,' as you say. I am a Reb from the deep south, and I would appreciate it very much if you would remember that, and I won't refer to you fellows as 'limies.' You might just appreciate the two facts that I cut my eyeteeth on a coal scoop aboard a steam engine in the 1940s and '50's, before you mates were born. The other fact is that my dear departed great-grandmother, God rest her soul, is surely buried heaven knows where in the valley of the Darling River. I am here to stand beside her grave and settle a few questions that have never been answered now for two generations."

These trainmen took this stranger right under their wings, even telling him to come up to the engine at the first stop and ride with them, so they could point out things of interest. It turned out to be a long slow drag up the Coastal Mountains, which were called the Blue Mountains. The towns they passed weren't much different from those of theUSA, only with a bit more of British flavor. The next day before old Paul reached his destination the crews had changed, although the first crew had supplied Paul with a note of introduction to the relief crew who shook his hand and extended every courtesy to the now weary traveler.

As the long passenger train neared Menindee Station house, an attendant, a young lady no less, smiled and handed him a note from one of his newfound friends of the railroad. It contained the address of an elderly lady who rented her front room to laying-over train hands. She was a bit of a historian and would welcome a gentleman guest at a fraction of the cost of a tourist hotel or pub, as the locals referred to such an establishment. Could it be possible that such luck could occur to a stranger ten thousand miles from home? Paul thought of the old country music songs popular during the Depression days, when hobos were common: "Sitting by the water tank, a thousand miles from home." He sang the sad words as he lifted his duffle from the luggage rack.

The train crew had even radioed ahead that a mate would need a taxi to haul him to Mrs. Arnett's rest house, to rest his weary hide. The hack or taxi driver was slouched on a waiting room bench, a jaunty cap sat askew on his tousled head of hair. He wore no shirt, only his undershirt over which a stout pair of suspenders supported his baggy britches that gave the appearance of having been slept in. It was hot and the driver was dressed for the situation. Things were already falling into place, as the hack put Paul in mind of his long departed grandfather, Shep Barrick.

Why in the name of the saints had the British decided to drive on the left side of the road and place the steering wheel on the right side of a vehicle? As the hack stowed Paul's duffle in the rear of the battered old hack Paul handed him the note bearing the address of Mrs. Arnett's home, the only person he had to trust in Menindee.

"I knew where to take you, mate, as the stationmaster informed me of your walkabout and place of abode. We knew you were coming. The old lady is probably sitting on the porch already. She is a good old dame but she will bend your ear."

Sure as guns iron, the man was correct. There Mrs. Arnett sat on her veranda rocking away. As Paul paid the cabbie and tipped him well, the man carried his duffle to the porch steps, tipped his soiled cap to the lady of the house, and sped away before she could buttonhole him. Paul introduced himself to the spry lady of perhaps sixty years. She invited her guest to come in out of the heat as it was frightful. Paul was all smiles when he expressed his good fortune in finding a home away from home.

The house was built for a hot climate, with high ceilings, shuttered windows, and transoms over the bedroom door to let the hot air escape to the vent fan in the attic.

Unnoticed by the weary traveler, an old aborigine man was trimming the lawn before the house. His keen ears heard every word that was spoken between his boss lady and her new tenant as he sat on the porch and spoke of his mission along the river, which had witnessed the lives and loves of his forefathers and the women who had borne the children who had scattered to the ends of the earth.

Paul slept through the heat of the day as the long trip had exhausted him. He was getting over the hill age wise. That evening he freshened himself up a bit and strolled down to a pub his land lady had recommended to him. The crowd turned to stare at him when he walked in and took a seat at the bar. They were a neighborhood crowd and a stranger stood out like a sore thumb. He was handed a beer, introduced around the room, and welcomed warmly. The beef stew was good and the music was lively.

As Paul walked back to his room he looked up at the night sky which was aglow with a million stars, strange constellations that he had never seen before. He did recognize the Southern Cross which had guided ancient mariners through the South Pacific from time immemorial.

Morning came to Menindee, the same as it did in Georgia. Strange birds hopped about the yard. The eggs and bacon smelled the same as those at home. Mrs. Arnett handed him a cup of strong hot tea to sip on.

The old man who had been working in the yard the day before squatted on the steps sharpening his tools. He was a strange looking fellow. His hair was kind of yellow and he had broad bare feet with thick calluses, feet that had never known the feel of shoes. He spoke to Paul in a dialect strange to his ears. It was English, Pidgin English. The words came slowly, just a dabble, "I know where the town of Swanpool is, up the river some ways away. My people lived in the lands about that town and on the O'Leary station lands long before the English came. Many stories have I heard about the campfires of my clan. There is a stockman hereabout who will be going upriver to the very one you spoke of to the lady I work for."

He reached into the well-worn sack he carried his belongings in, brought forth a stone about the size of a marble, and handed it to the stranger. "The stockman often takes me up there to help him load sheep and cattle, and this stone will be all you will need to open his door."

Paul lingered at the breakfast table to talk to Mrs. Arnett, who seemed in no hurry to clear the breakfast dishes. After a bit of chatting she mentioned that she had noticed her yard man had taken an interest in him and even handed him an object. "You must have given him a special impression as he rarely speaks to anyone, much less a stranger."

"He told me of a stockman who is familiar with the area I am interested in, the land of my forefathers."

The woman, herself a long time resident of this river town, told Paul she was well acquainted with the stockman, a mister Sanford, Tom Sanford. He and his family were among the first settlers along the river, having dealt in stock for generations. They seemed to have a special link with the strange aborigines. She made a call, and a taxi cab soon pulled up to the rooming house and honked its horn. Paul told the driver to take him to the stock pens of Tom Sanford.

The cab came to a stop in front of a large wooden barn that stood beside perhaps two acres of stock pens. A small office across the street had a sign reading "Sanford's Pens, Ltd." Paul liked the aroma and bellowing of the penned animals, even the flies made him feel at home. The office door was open, and a radio was blaring over the roar of an electric fan, which stirred the air of the office. A young woman sat at a desk behind a low division fence with a gate that swung both ways. She motioned to him to sit on a bench, as she was expecting a call to come in on the radio. He sat down and waited. The radio crackled and a voice blared, "Come in, me dear, tell me of the orders of the day, over."

She pressed the button and answered the voice, "None today, come home, over, out. My father," she said with a smile. "And what might you be up to this hot day?"

As Paul spoke, he saw a quizzical look come on her wholesome face, "Now where pray tell have the winds of fortune blown you in from, old timer? Never have I heard the Queen's English butchered as you speak it. I love it."

"I am American," Paul said, "from the USA, of Australian extraction as two generations before me moved to a state named Georgia, in the deep south of the country. I am a descendant of a steamboat captain on the Murry and Darling Rivers by the name of Barrick, who married an O'Leary woman, the daughter of a large land owner near a settlement named Swanpool."

The girl laughed a good-natured laugh and said, "You Americans are always looking for your ancestors. We Aussies are trying to forget ours. You do know this land was at the beginning a penal colony. the King of England decided to clear the streets and prisons of London town of bums and criminals! Aye, there are many skeletons in our closets. My dear old dad will return in an hour. I am his daughter, Kate, a chip off the old block, so to speak. Make yourself comfortable for a bit as he likes to talk of the past."

Paul drifted out the open door and walked down the alley ways of the stock pens to view the cattle. They were of British bloodlines, Hereford, Shorthorn, Essex, Angus, mostly cross breeds. The heat and the flies cut his survey of the stock short. There was a large eucalyptus tree that afforded a very inviting shade and a well-worn bench beneath the tree. A group of ringers (stockmen) had gathered there because their chores were done. Huddled together was a group of native or aborigine ringers awaiting the arrival of the cattle truck of Mr. Sanford, as they hoped to get a lift back to the distant station in the Outback, which they called home. The men stared at Paul Newton, who felt he was being computerized.

These natives of Australia had extra perceptive abilities which Europeans had lost through the centuries of so-called civilization. They knew nothing of DNA cataloging, but their extra perceptive abilities were awesome. One glance and you were identified. They lived in a spirit world that they understood far better than any white man with a PhD would. Why, for instance, could they swim beside saltwater crocodiles and know at a glance that the big reptiles had fed recently and were not hungry? How did they know the exact spot to dig a hole in dry sand when the rains had not fallen for a year, cover it with a special leaf, and lay beside it, only to find the hole full of fresh water the next morning? Their numbers had been decimated by the European diseases that white settlers had brought in, not to mention the fact that they had been slaughtered by the thousands by white explorers and settlers. Even against these odds, not to mention alcohol and a climate most humans would have found, to say the least, unbearable, they were living partly in the modern world, the other part in the Stone Age.

Little did Paul Newton dream that word of his coming was preceded by an unspoken or unseen power, but it was. That small stone he carried in his pocket had a powerful spell placed upon it that heralded his identity and mission. A giant tractor-trailer rig swung into the parking area of Sanford's stockyard. As the air brakes were set, the exhaust blew a cloud of red dust into the hot dry air, which seemed to hang so heavily over the area. A long, tall, gaunt-faced man slid to the ground from the driver's seat, which needed reupholstering as a shiny wire spring was showing. This man was Tom Sanford, descendant of a long line of Australian stockmen. How destiny had brought these two men together must remain a mystery, but all through this drama haven't spirits and destiny played a leading role? The characters have only been pawns, shall we say.

Back to the real world of adventure and exploration. Tom Sanford strolled over to the shade of the tree, knocked the dust of the road from his pants with his wide-brimmed hat, and extended his hand to shake Paul's hand. "You must be the Yank who is searching for his roots. Welcome to the land of your forefathers, old chap!" Kate had told him on the radio that he had a visitor. Paul was rather taken aback by the friendly outspoken manner of the Aussies, which was, in fact, much like his own. When Paul asked him if he knew of the town of Swanpool, Tom Sanford related that he did in fact know the area. The town had dwindled over the years as river traffic had gone to the railroads, and a drought of long duration had wreaked havoc to the vineyards and grazing land that once were so productive. The area had never recovered to the bloom that once existed. Mr. Sanford told Paul that if he would wait a day or two, he was scheduled to make a turn to Broken Hill, and in fact, he would like a rider for a bit of company. That was music to Paul's ears. He needed to rest, then a ride, and a guide. Kate insisted that Paul spend the time at their home on the outskirts of Menindee.

Back at the home of Mrs. Arnett, Paul paid his bill and thanked her for her hospitality.

That night in the home of Tom Sanford, the two men talked late. Paul related his family history as he knew it. Tom listened with great interest. His grandfather had told him of the O'Leary lands and enterprises at Swanpool. In fact, he had a vague recollection of a Barrick woman who had held her family together and prospered greatly until her death. The great drought had dealt the clan a double whammy.

Mr. Sanford said, "The Italian vendors held on. The Monsorretti name exists thereabout till this day, but the Barricks and O'Learys are gone. The graveyard claimed all of the old timers. The offspring are gone to the four winds. Much like you, yourself, they have found themselves far from Swanpool."

Paul went to his duffle and brought forth the tarnished gold box, the only possession he had of his great-grandmother's, unless the cuff with the four pearl buttons counted. The small smooth stone which the old native, the yard man back at Menindee, had given him as an object of introduction to Tom Sanford was unnecessary. The two men had, at a glance, shared a common bond. Paul had even forgotten the stone, which now on the dim light of late evening had taken on an eerie glow as soft as a moonbeam. Could it be that a long departed spirit dwelled beneath the stone's smooth hand worn surface? Or was it simply its phosphoric content?

The men fell silent.

"Who gave you that bloody stone, mate?" Tom finally blurted. "That is a rough sapphire that those fellows pick up on their walkabouts."

Paul answered, "An old aborigine who worked at the home I overnighted in, where I got off the train in your hometown."

Tom's eyes shot up to meet Paul's. "This stone is worth some money, as they often bring them to me to buy. They never give them away. You must have awakened some long dormant vision that those older generation blokes harbor within their complicated minds. They are not on the same wavelength that we white people are on. They sit long periods just staring into the distance. They refer to it as dream time. It is impossible to disturb them, as they are no longer on this planet. During those dream times, they seem to become a tree or stone, inanimate, I think you might say. This stone is a much more powerful indicator to the grave of your kin than any directions I might give you. You are in possession of an omen. Both this stone and the ruddy box and its contents are perhaps the compass that will direct you to pay dirt."

When Tom Sanford finished, he rose to climb to the sleeper bunk on his rig. "Don't plunder about in the night as the tiger snakes come out from under the rocks in the cool of the evening. Better men than you have gone mad staring at the stars that twinkle in the heavens above. Sleep well, old Yank, or you may join your kin quicker than you plan."

The pub on the corner of the crossroad was open. Paul had a bowl of stew and a steaming mug of tea, and soon retired to the guest room at the home of his newfound friends. He had wild dreams through the night, dreams of Gladys on the other side of the world and of abandoned graveyards claimed back by the bush years ago.

The morning arrived all at once as nothing was there but a flat plain as far as the eye could see, nothing to break the rising sun's first rays. Paul splashed some water on his face, pulled on his pants, and grabbed the duffle bag containing his meager belongings.

There across the road a band of aborigines awaited his appearance. The elder of the group arose from where he squatted. His skin was a different shade, much lighter than the other members of the mob. A smile came to his ageless face. The few teeth he had left had worn to the gum line long ago. His reddish hair and hazel blue eyes bespoke the mixed blood lineage. His clothes were tattered. Shoes would have been an extra burden as his feet were like leather. How would one judge the age of a rock? Likewise, how would one judge the age of an aborigine?

"We knew you were coming," said the elder." We welcome you to our reservation. Little do you realiz,e we are kinsmen under the skin. May we be your humble servants?"

Paul was so taken aback his mouth dropped open, but no sound came forth. There was a huge gum tree nearby, at the foot of which a spring bubbled forth a small stream of water. Paul and the group of aborigines gathered about the pool of water there as the sun began to bear down..

The old fellow patiently explained, "Once many, many years ago, before the great drought, there was a Yankee Captain who had a steamer, called the *Victoria*, later renamed the *Bridgett O'Leary*. If my memory serves me right, as I was but a child around my father's campfire, I heard the story from my elders of this steamer, one of the first on the Murry and Darling rivers. The Captain's name was Frederick Barrick, himself a Yank, as you are. Under his gruff old outside beat a kind heart, kind enough to adopt a half-breed boy who was stranded between two very different worlds. The captain adopted this boy and raised him as a son. As time passed the captain married a very beautiful Irish woman, a daughter of the area's greatest landowner, who owned livestock and a vast station. This man was kind to my people. After a few years, the steamer exploded and killed your great-grandfather. My great-grandfather, the half-breed, lost only the lower part of his leg. He answered to the name of Sinbad.

"Many, many wet seasons followed by many, many dry seasons passed. The spirits prospered your mother's grandmother. Sinbad's body was claimed by my people, and buried at a sacred burial spot in the Outback. My dreams have told me there is a very old metal box in your possession which contains four pearl buttons on the cuff from the wedding gown of your mother's grandmother, Bridgett O'Leary. She, herself put her blessing on that box and gave it to her youngest son, the one who was your grandfather, Shep Barrick, who left Australia as a young man, for far away America . . .or did the spirits of the dream world misinform your humble servant?"

Paul finally found his voice. "Your spirits have likewise visited my dreams, as spirits are not confined by great distances as we mortals are. They have no doubt led me to your reservation, which once was my forefathers' home. Also, I do have the metal box that has disturbed my dreams enough to bring me to where I stand today. You are correct as to the contents of this box, only there is a small stone therein, a stone given to me by one of your people upon my arrival in Australia."

Paul opened the duffle bag and withdrew the box, which no longer was dull and dented; it had taken on a luster. The lid popped open on its own to reveal the buttons, four in a row. The satin material looked new, even the pearls appeared polished. The stone the old man had given him even moved a bit, seeming alive. The natives smiled as the head man closed the lid. He drew a powder, a potion that he mixed in a gourd of fresh dipped spring water. He himself drank deeply of the liquid that had begun to bubble and sparkle. The gourd was handed to the white traveler, and at a command, he also drank deeply until the bottom of the gourd shown.

Both men soon fell into a deep sleep. When they awoke, they were beside a grave which time had nearly obliterated. Suddenly, a cold breeze surrounded them and an eerie glow enveloped the two figures. The two men rubbed their eyes as a woman's misty form arose from the moss-covered slab with a broken headstone leaning against another one, with the dim, chiseled words Bridgett O'Leary Barrick. The beautiful vision of a young woman with flowing red hair stepped forward to claim the shiny box. She smiled as she opened the lid, withdrew the cuff with the four buttons, and placed it on her own gown. She then plucked one of the pearl buttons off the cuff now attached to her gown. She removed the stone and gave it to the old aborigine.

A voice, sweet and low, spoke to Paul, "Why do you think your mother Anna, my granddaughter, was born with a veil over her eyes to see into the unknown? I chose her to return my box. The three buttons represent her three babies who now live with me in Paradise. One day you will bring me the pearl I just gave you and until that day, rest well. Your mission on this earth is accomplished." With these words, she vanished.

The men fell into another deep sleep. Again they awoke, arose and found they were standing beside the spring under the towering green baobab tree. Perhaps it was only a narcotic dream, only the gold box was gone and a pearl button was in Paul Newton's hand. His chin trembled just a bit.

www.ingramcontent.com/pod-product-compliance
Lightning Source LLC
LaVergne TN
LVHW011218080426
835509LV00005B/190